	DATE DUE		

TEN MINUTES FROM
NORMAL

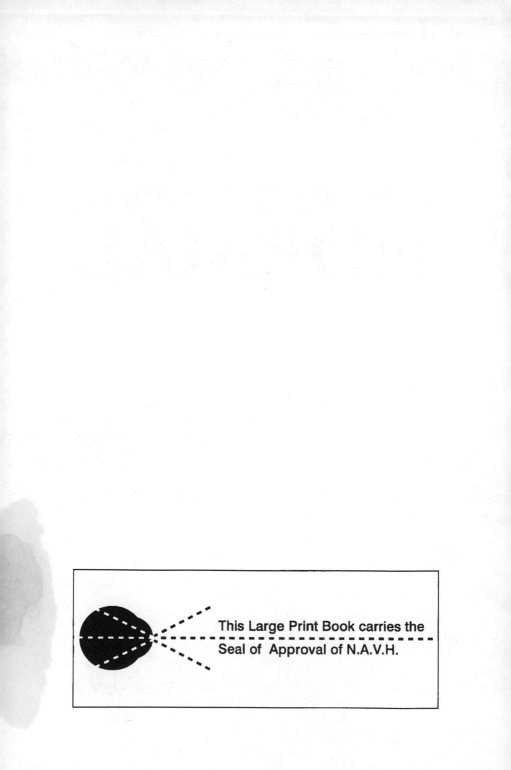

This Large Print Book carries the
Seal of Approval of N.A.V.H.

TEN MINUTES FROM
NORMAL

Karen Hughes

Thorndike Press • Waterville, Maine

Copyright © Karen Hughes, 2004

Published in 2004 by arrangement with Viking Penguin, a member of Penguin Group (USA) Inc.

Thorndike Press® Large Print Americana.

The tree indicium is a trademark of Thorndike Press.

The text of this Large Print edition is unabridged.
Other aspects of the book may vary from the original edition.

Set in 16 pt. Plantin by Al Chase.

Printed in the United States on permanent paper.

Library of Congress Cataloging-in-Publication Data

Hughes, Karen, 1957–
   Ten minutes from Normal / Karen Hughes.
     p. cm.
    ISBN 0-7862-6713-5 (lg. print : hc : alk. paper)
    1. Hughes, Karen, 1957–   2. Presidents — United States
— Staff — Biography.   3. Women lawyers — United States
— Biography.   4. Political consultants — United States —
Biography.   5. Bush, George W. (George Walker), 1946– —
Friends and associates.   6. United States — Politics and
government — 2001–   7. United States — Politics and
government — 1993–2001.   8. Presidents — United States
— Election — 2000.   9. Large type books.   I. Title.
E840.8.H835A3 2004b
973.931′092—dc22
  [B]   2004049827

To Mom and Dad, for the foundation.
And to Jerry, for building up with love.

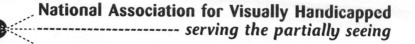

As the Founder/CEO of NAVH, the only national health agency solely devoted to those who, although not totally blind, have an eye disease which could lead to serious visual impairment, I am pleased to recognize Thorndike Press★ as one of the leading publishers in the large print field.

Founded in 1954 in San Francisco to prepare large print textbooks for partially seeing children, NAVH became the pioneer and standard setting agency in the preparation of large type.

Today, those publishers who meet our standards carry the prestigious "Seal of Approval" indicating high quality large print. We are delighted that Thorndike Press is one of the publishers whose titles meet these standards. We are also pleased to recognize the significant contribution Thorndike Press is making in this important and growing field.

Lorraine H. Marchi, L.H.D.
Founder/CEO
NAVH

★ Thorndike Press encompasses the following imprints: Thorndike, Wheeler, Walker and Large Print Press.

CONTENTS

ACKNOWLEDGMENTS

First and foremost, I thank President George W. Bush and First Lady Laura Bush for giving me the opportunity and privilege of working for them. Without that experience, there would not be a book.

I thank the Penguin Group (USA), especially President Susan Petersen Kennedy and my editor, Vice President Pamela Dorman, who had the vision to see what this book could be long before I started putting words on paper. Their commitment and support were vital at every step, and Pam's editorial ideas, suggestions and questions guided the book from start to finish. I thank my two partners in the daily work of producing the manuscript. Pat Mulcahy's editorial expertise and judgment were instrumental in shaping a book from a collection of scattered stories and experiences, and her great humor made the project a lot more fun. Kate Disston dropped everything and moved to Texas for six months as my research assistant, and her insights, editorial suggestions

9

and organizational skills were invaluable. Kasey Pipes did a wonderful job of checking facts and my recollections and I thank him for his careful attention and fast work. My assistant, Kim Black, was crucial at every stage of the process. She offered insight and opinions, checked facts, tracked down missing information and did anything else that needed to be done, always maintaining her calm even when I asked her for the nine millionth time to double-check something. My attorney, Bob Barnett, has helped me navigate life after the White House with fabulous advice, friendship and encouragement, and he has offered valuable input on the book. I also thank Don and Ellen Walker, Dara Gruen, Leila Brahimi and the staff of the Harry Walker Agency, whose wonderful professionalism, attention to detail and friendship have made my new career in speaking and writing so enjoyable.

I thank my friends and family for their careful review of and suggestions to the manuscript. My husband's comments were few but important, and he encouraged me during the entire endeavor. I thank my son, Robert, for his invaluable contributions, which made the book much more interesting, and my daughter, Leigh, and granddaughter, Lauren, for their support and encouragement throughout. My sister, Beverly Byrd, has a future in editing if she ever leaves health care because she found mistakes no one else did. My friends Steve and Janice Margolin, Margaret Tutwiler, Mary Matalin, Doug Fletcher, Fred Meyer and Bob and Juliee Bliss also helped save me from myself, asking, "Are you sure you really want to say it this way?" when of course I didn't. My parents, Pat and Hal Parfitt, and friends Jill Angelo, Gordon Johndroe and Nicolle Devenish also read parts of the manuscript and offered help and encouragement along the way, as did the members of my Bible study — Bev Moore, Shelly Aunspaugh, Debbie Hair and Christi Engemoen. Many friends shared recollections: Lee Elsesser, Bob Mann, Israel Hernandez, Frank Perkins, Fawn Escalante, Linda Edwards, Vance McMahan, Mark McKinnon, Dan Bartlett, Andy Card, Condi Rice, Karl Rove, Andi Ball, Brian Montgomery, Jim Wilkinson and Logan Walters. Peter Wehner shared wise insights and many ideas during my time at the White House and continues to do so. I thank Steve Scully of C-SPAN for providing tapes of its primary coverage.

I thank the team at Viking Penguin for its excellent work and strong support for this project: President Clare Ferraro, publicity director Carolyn Coleburn and senior publicist Yen Cheong, art director Paul Buckley, design director Jaye Zimet, marketing director Nancy Sheppard, director of advertising and promotion Julie Shiroishi, the subsidiary rights team of Leigh Butler, Hal Fessenden and Cypria Dionese, the sales force led by Dick Heffernan, managing editor Tricia Conley, Susan Johnson, the terrific copy editor, and Rakia Clark for keeping us all on track! I thank Jamie Wolf for his thorough legal review and for being so pleasant to work with.

Finally, I thank all my colleagues at the White House, those who served on the senior staff with me and those whose work was not as high profile but was every bit as important, especially my assistants: Jill Angelo, Krista Ritacco, Christina Roberts and Kate Disston. I thank Nannette Everson for her wise counsel on ethics law as I prepared to leave the White House, and ever since. I thank Dr. Richard Tubb, Cindy Wright and Robin Schultze and everyone in the medical unit for taking such good care of us; Ferdie Garcia and Melanie Campbell for always being so gracious and helpful; Ashley Estes and Blake Gottesman in the president's office, who are so organized and efficient and helped me in thousands of ways; Carl Truscott and Eddie Marinzel and all the men and women of the Secret Service protective detail, as well as the uniformed personnel who are always so helpful at the White House gates; Tina Stein, Reggie Dickson, Mike Neville, Wanda Joell and John Otto and all the crew of Air Force One for making travel so efficient and pleasant, the staff at the White House mess; the Marine guards and military aides; and all the White House and residence personnel — those who were here long before any of our team arrived and will still be serving long after we are gone — thank you for helping me and for your dedicated service to our country.

The stories, quotes and conversations recounted in this book are based on my recollections, personal notes and journals, public statements and documents and, in some cases, review of published media reports. No classified material was used to produce this book. As required by my national security clearance, the manuscript was reviewed by the staff of the National Security Council and the U.S. Secret Service to make certain that I did not inadvertently reveal any information that could jeopardize America's national security.

INTRODUCTION

The rhythmic rocking of the train felt unnatural, slow and lethargic, a marked contrast to the hyperactivity of the just-finished Republican National Convention. A convention is a riot of balloons, speeches, people and parties. But suddenly, the noise had stopped: someone had slammed on the brakes and we were on a slow roll across the Midwest, seeing only the occasional cow. The convention had been a great success, the moment we had all been working toward, when we nominated my boss as the Republican candidate for president of the United States of America: a culmination, a celebration — yet like so many big events in a presidential campaign, oddly unsatisfying.

The planning and organizing that had led to that moment had been years in the making. The past several months had been devoted almost entirely to building toward the convention, writing the speech, organizing the themes, planning every scripted moment of national television coverage. But then, before we were able to truly savor or absorb it all, it was over, and we were back on the trail, or in this case, the train track, always on to the next thing.

A presidential campaign is relentless. You win a straw poll, or a primary, or a debate, or the daily news headline, and wake up to people already talking and asking about the next one. You win in Iowa, lose in New Hampshire, and get back on track in South Carolina, only to lose in Michigan three days later and wonder yet again, "Are we missing something?" But you're on a plane to California, where there's a debate coming up, then flying cross-country for next week's critical primary in Virginia. Once you start, the only way to stop is to lose — and that, of course, is not the way you want to get off this train.

The reporters on board were all restless. Through long stretches of rural Pennsylvania and across Ohio, their cell phones hadn't worked much of the time.

"Al Gore could have dropped out of the race and we wouldn't even know it," one complained to me.

"We should be so lucky," I countered.

The biggest excitement came when a woman mooned the train, causing a great stir and endless speculation about what, ex-

16

actly, she was trying to say with her show.

By the second day, the sleepy routine had begun to feel a little more natural: long hours of rocking along the track, punctuated by brief rallies in small towns and waves off the back to small groups of people who gathered at crossings, bringing their children to witness a little piece of American political history. We were approaching a town in Illinois when the conductor came over the loudspeaker and proudly announced: "Ladies and gentlemen, we are ten minutes from Normal; ten minutes from Normal."

"If I ever write a book, that's the title," I told my colleagues in the staff car. "Ten minutes from normal is *exactly* how I feel about this whole bizarre experience."

I've always considered myself a very normal person who had led, at least until recently, a very normal life, with a normal family and normal friends, except, of course, I have a boss and friend who became the president. And though this is often thrilling and even sometimes still surprising, it is most definitely not normal.

At times, it still feels surreal when I'm standing backstage or out in the crowd and the band plays "Hail to the Chief." I don't hear the music that often because the president is a humble person, and tries to balance the grandeur and stature of the office with his desire not to inflate his own sense of self-importance. So when the trumpets sound, it's a special occasion when he walks on stage, and I am amazed: that is the president of the United States, and I know him, and he knows me.

I know his wife and daughters; he knows my husband and son. We have had dinners together; I've even cooked some of them, and so has he. I know how he takes his coffee. He knows that I am tall — not big — because we have had that conversation. Women who are five foot ten and a half and wear size 12 shoes do not like to be called big. We prefer the statelier *tall*. My friend Condi Rice says it's like sweating. Ladies do not sweat, especially if you grew up, as she did, in Birmingham, Alabama. Southern women only perspire. "Tall people in back," the president says to me during the group photograph at last year's senior staff Christmas dinner, winking to show he got it, he remembers.

I have a very normal family: a teenage son who thinks that I am totally annoying, especially when I ask intrusive questions like "How was your day?" or even try to talk to him when he gets in the car after school, be-

18

cause he's "tired." (Tired of talking? I wonder. How is that possible, since he doesn't?) I have a husband who puts up with us all and only occasionally gets irritated when I ask him for the third time in a day whether he loves me, then refuse to be satisfied when he tells me yes, but it's hard.

"It's not that hard," I protest.

"Not *too* hard," he replies, agreeably, which of course is not the answer I want to hear.

I have a grown daughter, Leigh, who is a licensed vocational nurse. For the sake of complete accuracy, I should say Leigh is my stepdaughter — but my husband had custody of her, and we met when she was seven, and married when she was nine. She lived with us and I nursed her through chicken pox; besides, creating categories of children in a family always struck me as wrong, so I call her my daughter. And we have a daring and darling eight-year-old granddaughter, Lauren, who has inherited a strong will and streak of independence from all sides of our family.

We have an orange-and-white cat, Griffey, the only cat our family has ever had that actually comes when he is called. He would be an almost perfect pet, which my husband defines as not requiring much in the way of service, except for a terrible habit of getting sick only on the carpet instead of the tile floor, even if the tile floor is closer and he has to go to another room in midcough to find some soft, lovely, hard-to-clean carpet on which to deposit his most recent hairball.

I also live with an exuberant golden retriever, Breeze, a rambunctious, bouncy and eager dog that never has learned to keep all four feet on the ground or her tongue in and nose out of unwelcome places. She's quite lovable, if a bit enthusiastic. That's what I think, at least.

My husband and the dog have a strained relationship. Part of it dates to the time I let the dog spend the night in the house because it was cold outside in Washington. The first night, she was perfect, but the second night she chewed up a ballpoint pen, leaving a trail of blue ink all over the light beige carpet. But the tensions between my husband and my dog are deeper than that; Jerry didn't want the dog in the first place. He only relented after I appealed to his sense of fairness: "Every child should have a dog. Leigh had a dog; it's not right not to get one for Robert."

"Robert won't take care of it," my husband had sighed, but finally acquiesced.

Jerry ended up taking care of the last dog, Leigh's dog, a ditzy cocker spaniel named Fritzi, who was sweet but kind of stupid. While I was fond of her, I never really bonded in the way that you bond with a real dog, a large and intelligent one.

"Your dog gets in the cat litter, how intelligent is that?" Jerry asks. Notice the pronoun. Not "our" dog, as in the family pet, but "your" dog, as in all mine. Jerry used to laugh when the media described me as a control freak or the person who "controlled" the White House message. "Anyone who thinks she's in control ought to come and meet our animals," he would say.

Writing about the pets is oddly personal, and I realize that this story will involve the people close to me more than I initially understood, or wanted. "I'm going to have to write about you in my book," I inform my husband, in between commercials for *ER*, one of the few shows we watch on television.

"I didn't agree to that," he protests, ever the lawyer.

"You agreed I should write this book," I answer. "I can't write a book about my life without writing about our family: it wouldn't be true, it wouldn't be honest," I counter.

Jerry looks unconvinced. "This is supposed to be a book about your political life, your life at the White House," he says.

"No, remember, it's a book about a lot of things, how a normal person like me ended up working at the White House, what it was like. It's not a typical political gossip book," I sputter. "This book is about life and family and faith — important things — and I can't write about what is important without writing about you and Robert and Leigh and our family."

"You can mention us, but keep it brief," he replies.

CHAPTER 1

Tug-of-War

I still remember the moment I first said it out loud. My husband and I were standing at the sink in the kitchen of the beautiful house that wasn't ours, talking as we cleaned up the dinner dishes.

"Maybe we should just move back home this summer," I said, and the look of relief that immediately crossed his face confirmed what I had suspected, what my husband still denies, but that all our friends believe — that he deeply missed Texas and was ready to go home.

"Why do you say that?" he asked, cautiously, much more cautiously than in the usual after-dinner, after-eighteen-years-of-marriage conversation. This was uncharted territory, and only I could venture there first.

"Robert's unhappy; I'm not even relevant in his life anymore. He misses his friends; we miss Leigh and Lauren and all our friends. Everyone said it would take a year to adjust, but it's been more than a year,

23

and I don't see signs that we're making any progress," I said, the months of frustration and worry about my family spilling out into the open yet again. "Robert doesn't go out or have fun or have friends over or do anything except sit downstairs and watch TV and study. He's never even had a single kid come to our house except for the ones we invited with their parents," I said, my voice getting louder as I recited the litany that had played too many times in my head. The subject of our greatest concern, my teenage son, was away on a school baseball trip, so my husband and I didn't have to worry about his overhearing.

"I go to work when you all are asleep and I come home long after Robert's home from school and he's downstairs studying and he doesn't even want to talk to me. He never asks me to do anything for him anymore because he knows I probably can't. And if he did, I would probably be too tired, as I was last week when he wanted to make brownies. Too tired to make brownies — what does that say about our life?"

"We've been talking about reevaluating after next year, after tenth grade," my husband replied calmly. He had been saying this every time I raised concerns, which was becoming more and more frequent: It was

24

his holding pattern, a quick way to quell the questions.

It reminded me of another pat answer, years before, which had also proved wrong — this one not from my husband, but from my boss. Back in 1997, when reporters had first started asking Governor Bush whether he would run for president, he had put them off with a quick, "I'll talk about that when I announce my campaign for reelection."

Something about the timing was wrong, and it had nagged at me. I walked into the governor's office early one morning after it had finally hit me: "If you wait until your re-election announcement to answer whether you might run for president, all the news coverage will focus on that," I said. "Don't you want to start your reelection campaign by talking about what you still want to accomplish as governor, not by refusing to rule out that you might run for president? That will be the lead of every story, and what you want to do for Texas will get lost in speculation about the presidency."

"You're right," he said, nodding thoughtfully. "So what's the alternative?" Governor Bush asked. "I don't know whether I'm going to run for president or not, and I'm not going to be one of these politicians who says he won't run and then changes his mind later when it's convenient. As long as it's a possibility, Texans need to know that and take it into account when they vote."

"Then we need to find a way for you to say that before you announce your reelection campaign," I responded, which led to our scheduling a news conference in late October 1997 to deal with what I called the P question. "P question" was the inscription I had written in black Sharpie marker on the thin but growing green file I carried in my car to keep anything related to a possible presidential campaign separated from my official work at the state capitol. If only separating the P question from the rest of my life had been so easy!

The mere existence of the question was already changing our lives, a fact underscored by the scene at the governor's mansion that fall morning. A huge crowd of reporters, including some national ones who didn't usually cover much state news in Texas, waited in the garden, and satellite television trucks lined the streets surrounding the stately white house. Governor Bush stepped up to a small podium and delivered the statement we had worked on: "I hope Texans have come to know that I'm a straightforward person, and I want to deal

26

with the question in as straight a way as I know how. I have not made a decision to run or not to run for President. I do not know, and I cannot possibly know at this time whether I would ever run for President . . . I can promise I will always do what is best for Texas . . ."

"You mean you called a news conference to say he might or might not run?" Mike Holmes, the bureau chief for the Associated Press and thus the dean of the Texas Capitol press corps, asked me incredulously.

"That's right; he thinks people deserve to know before he asks for their votes to reelect him," I replied.

Mike walked off, shaking his head. What was the news here? He might or might not run? We all *know* that, Mike's body language seemed to say disapprovingly.

Yet from our perspective, it was news, news that underscored our view that our boss was different. Politicians from both parties had previously promised home-state voters they would not seek the presidency, and then changed their minds later. Governor Bill Clinton had done so in Arkansas; so had Governor Pete Wilson in California. By choosing a different course, Governor Bush was doing a rare thing in politics: letting people know something that might not serve his own best interests. Our staff in the Texas governor's office had seen him do it many times: when he spoke out against California's proposition 187 and said Texas would educate children whether their parents were here legally or not; when he took on a massive tax restructuring that one of our savviest friends described as politically suicidal but otherwise exactly the right thing to do; when he commuted the death penalty to a life prison sentence for a despicable murderer who had killed many women but probably had not killed the one for which he had been sentenced to death. It was one of the things I most admired about Governor Bush, one of the things that had earned the trust and loyalty of all of us on his senior staff: he was too astute to ignore the political risks of any situation, but they didn't govern him. He listened to all the arguments and opinions, but the final compass was his own conviction.

In the case of a possible presidential campaign, the risk was not great. Most Texans are proud when their fellow Texans seek national office. But Governor Bush's refusal to rule out seeking the presidency could cost him votes in his reelection, reducing his margin of victory and the appearance of strong home-state support. And it would hand his opponents an easy issue. We could all imagine the television commercials: "He's asking you to hire him," the announcer would intone, "but he won't even promise he'll finish the job."

And as we expected, the chairman of the Democratic Party immediately criticized him: "The people of Texas deserve to know whether Governor Bush will be a full-time Governor," he said. Some of the cynics thought Governor Bush had already decided to run for president, and was therefore misleading Texans by not acknowledging that fact, but I knew better. This son of a president had seen firsthand how seeking the presidency would change his life, especially if he won. He was thinking it through, calculating its impact on the rest of his life. Many times, I thought he just might decide the cost was too high, though it had nothing to do with money.

"I'll never again be able to just walk into Wal-Mart and buy fishing lures," he said to me once, a telling little picture of the normal, often unappreciated things our nation's presidents give up when they succeed at their ambition. Mostly, though, Governor Bush was worried about the impact a presidential race would have on his family,

29

especially his teenage daughters, who were in high school and would have his presidency hanging over their college years if he won. He knew the scrutiny he and his brothers and sister had endured during the years his father was president, and remembered the pain of watching his father criticized in the glare of the harshest spotlight in the world. "I was forty and it was hard," he said one day, thinking out loud as he did often during the next year, debating with himself. "I can't imagine what it would be like to be in college with your dad as president."

I understood how torn he felt. My own feelings were mixed, and partly selfish. I thought George Bush would be a wonderful president — I also thought he was too decent a person to wish the presidency on him. National politics seemed cutthroat, meaner, more venal and self-serving than politics at the state level, even in the rough and tumble of Texas. "The process doesn't seem very Christian," I said to him once, worried about entering an environment whose values were so different from mine.

"The process isn't Christian, but it's important for Christians to be involved in the process," he retorted, making it clear he had thought about this, too, and concluded it was important for people to get involved in the political process to serve their community or country. But the cost of the presidency, in the loss of any private life, in the strain on your family, in the punishing criticism that would inevitably come, seemed to me so high that many times, I secretly hoped he would decide not to run.

Yet my reluctance was born not just of my concern for him and his family. I was worried about my own family, and myself. I liked my life in Texas. Throughout his years as governor, I had been able to balance my roles at the office and at home. I had an interesting, challenging job, yet I took my son to school most mornings and made it home for dinner most nights. We lived in a community where we knew other families, coached youth sports and had great friends we enjoyed. Jerry loved the courses he was taking at the Presbyterian seminary; I swam laps at a neighborhood pool and taught Sunday school at church. My nice routines would be upended, and how could I possibly be a good wife and mother to Robert while traveling the country on something as intense as a presidential campaign?

"You love him more than anything, don't you?" George W. Bush had asked me on that day in the fall of 1993, as he looked at Robert's picture on the credenza behind my desk at the state headquarters of the Republican Party of Texas where I was the executive director. George W. Bush had come to my office to file the formal papers to become a Republican candidate for governor of Texas. I knew quite a bit about him, but didn't really know him then. We had met a few times at Republican events, and I had worked with him briefly at the state convention several years before, but I had seen him primarily on television and in the newspaper promoting Texas Rangers baseball and the team's new ballpark.

"I do," I said, meaning that I love my son more than anything, somewhat taken aback by the sudden intimacy of the question from a relative stranger. Most people would have said something far more generic: "Is that your son? How old is he? What a good-looking boy." Not George Bush. He went straight to the heart.

"He's more important than anything else in this world," he said.

"He is," I said, nodding, feeling strangely tongue-tied, wondering if this man could read my mind or whether he was talking about his own children as much as mine.

My longtime boss, the party chairman, invited everyone to sit for a few minutes, and we talked about the campaign ahead. George W. Bush felt the way to beat then-governor Ann Richards was by articulating their profound differences on issues and philosophy.

"I will treat her with respect," he said, "but on issues from schools to welfare to juvenile crime, she is stuck in a status quo that isn't working. Too many kids are trapped in schools where they aren't learning; we're sending juveniles the wrong signal by giving them a slap on the wrist when they commit serious crimes; we're creating a culture of dependency with welfare, but she hasn't said a thing about it even though some national Democrats are beginning to admit the need for reform. The way to win is to talk about the issues, not about her," he said.

I couldn't have agreed more. For the previous two years at the Republican Party, I had been trying to build a case with the media that although Ann Richards was personally popular, her philosophy and policies were ineffective and out of step with the views of most Texans.

I had joined George W. Bush's campaign for governor later that year, and had stayed with him for all six years in the Texas governor's office, some of the best years of my life and career. But my satisfying routines changed abruptly during the presidential campaign and at the White House. I was away from home most of the time; when I was there, I was often worn out from the incredible intensity, long hours and grueling travel. Despite the privilege and challenge of serving the president and my country, my once-vague unease about how busy I would be, and how my family might react to being uprooted from Texas, had now become a piercing, daily anguish. My colleague Mary Matalin and I talked about it almost every day, the agonizing tug-of-war between career and family. I felt trapped between what was best for my family and what was best for my boss, who now had the most difficult and demanding job in the world.

The Sunday before I first broached the possibility of moving home with my husband, our minister at National Presbyterian Church, Craig Barnes, had preached a sermon on freedom: "Our goals are good, but in the reckless pursuit of them we don't see how many people we hurt along the way. Some of us just wanted to climb up the ladder at work, but our families paid for our success with hurt." I didn't think I had recklessly pushed my way up the ladder, but I had found myself on a pretty high rung, and I knew it had put my family in a difficult place. I had been praying for guidance, and now Craig Barnes seemed to offer it: "We keep asking God to tell us His will," he said. "Should I turn left or right in life? Take this job or that job? Stay single or marry? Move or stay put? I wonder if sometimes when the risen Christ hears those prayers He doesn't shrug His shoulders and say, 'You know, we have the big stuff taken care of now. You are forgiven and freed. So take responsibility for your freedom, make a choice, and surprise Me.' " Maybe I didn't need to be in a place where I felt trapped between my responsibilities to my job and my family, the sermon reminded me. I didn't have to feel guilty, or obligated. I was free to make a different choice.

After months of accepting my husband's reassurance that we would reassess after next year, after Robert finished tenth grade, I questioned the logic that waiting another year would somehow change our circumstances. "If we stay here for another whole school year, we will have been gone for two and a half years. Robert will be totally disconnected from his life in Texas. His friends will have changed and moved on. He won't really know anybody anymore, so he'll have a hard time fitting in back there, and I don't see much prospect of things getting better here. Maybe we should just move home this summer."

Surprise, and relief, competed for space on my husband's face. "What about the president? Can you really leave the White House this soon?" Jerry asked skeptically.

"A lot of people do," I said, my words far more certain than my emotions. Mary Matalin remembers that I had been shocked when months before in the White House gym she had first talked about leaving her job. "You mean you don't have to stay all four years?" I had asked her that day.

"I'm not going to; most people don't," she had said.

Our chief of staff, Andy Card, reinforced that observation — and caused unfounded speculation that he was perhaps leaving — when he said the same thing in an interview at about the same time.

"Remember that interview Andy Card did?" I reminded my husband. "He said the average time people serve at the White House is eighteen months. If we leave this summer, I will have been there eighteen months."

"That wasn't senior people, though, was it?" Jerry asked.

"I don't know; I think it was an average — everybody," I replied. "And Mary said she had never planned to stay the whole time."

The words, and questions, started coming faster then, my willingness to talk about walking away from my job the can opener that released the pent-up pressure into the air with a sudden rush. Was it really possible? How would the president react? Who could do my job? How could I leave while we were in the midst of a war? I reminded my husband that the president himself had said we were going to be at war against terror for the foreseeable future, throughout his presidency and probably for the next several administrations. "By that time, Robert will be gone, graduated from college, living on his own, and I will have missed his last years at home because I spent most of my time at the office."

"What about Margaret's house?" We had rented the house we were living in from my friend Margaret Tutwiler when she had moved to Morocco to serve as our ambassador there. How could we leave her stuck without a tenant when she was thousands of miles away?

Jerry, always objective, even argued the positive. "Another year at this school and Robert will have the foundation to go to any college he wants to," he said, referring to St. Albans, the top Episcopal all-boys school our son had chosen to attend in Washington. "I would really like him to have another year of these academics, and then he would have a foundation for life," he said. Jerry is a former school board member who worries that the public schools too often direct more effort toward creating an inflated sense of self-esteem than they do requiring genuine academic achievement from their students.

"But at the price of being happy?" I asked. "Robert is a good student; he'll succeed anywhere. His school in Texas was pretty good. We both went to public schools; we didn't go to Ivy League colleges. Remember what you always say: you went to Texas; I went to SMU; and we've done all right in life. We know he isn't happy, and I don't think another year will make it any better. Maybe we should just move home this summer," I said, becoming more and more convinced each time I said it out loud.

I was, of course, the only one who could really make the decision to leave. We had moved to Washington because of me, or more accurately, because my boss had been elected president of the United States. As my son had so plaintively put it on one of the rare occasions when he expressed his unhappiness in words: "I don't like it here; Dad doesn't like it here; even the *dog* doesn't like it here . . . and it's all because of you."

We had talked about it in advance, of course. After the nightmare of the Florida recount, after it was finally, painstakingly clear that George W. Bush was going to become the president, Jerry, Robert and I had had a family discussion and agreed to move to Washington. But the conversation had been perfunctory. We had all realized long before that if the campaign was successful, our life would change dramatically, and I would have to go to Washington. After traveling around the country with him for two years, after being an instrumental part of his team, I couldn't just wish the president well and send him off with a "So long; it's been fun. Good luck." I could have left my family in Texas and commuted, but I didn't think I could stand seeing them only every other weekend.

Jerry had been unequivocal: commuting was not an option. "We've been apart enough during the campaign," he said, "we're all going." Robert was cautious. I knew he didn't want to leave his friends, but he didn't really protest the move. It was exciting for a teenager to know the man who was about to become the president, and Robert had become a part of the team, too, after traveling all fall on the campaign airplane with us. He loved President and Mrs. Bush; we all did. Our friend had been elected to the hardest job in the world, and we could not conceive that our family would not do everything possible to support him.

It was hard to think about my family in a totally separate context from President and Mrs. Bush. I could trace much of our family's life and my son's growth through pictures of various special occasions with them. There's Robert, only five years old, a shy smile on his face, in front of the spring flowers at the governor's mansion after the annual Capitol 10,000 run/walk. There's Robert and a friend dressed up for Halloween — Robert in a baseball uniform, his friend Kemper wearing a President Clinton mask his mother had thought was a great joke — sitting on the front porch with Governor Bush. There's Robert with Jenna and Barbara Bush in front of the lighthouse on Matagorda Island, during the trip we took with the Bush family to encourage Texas families to visit Texas parks. Robert's changing height is measured in the annual family pictures in front of the Christmas tree in the living room of the governor's mansion. And the thoughtful invitations continued when we moved to Washington, as President and Mrs. Bush included their staff and cabinet members and all our families in so many special occasions. Robert, Jerry and I had been to private movie screenings at the White House. We had had Thanksgiving dinner with President and Mrs. Bush and Karl, Darby and Andrew Rove and Condi Rice at Camp David. We had flown to Texas after Christmas and for Easter weekend on Air Force One with President and Mrs. Bush. Yet after being so closely intertwined for so long, after fifteen months in Washington, the best interests of my family and my boss were clearly colliding.

I could no longer drive Robert to school in the mornings, as I had enjoyed doing for years, because I would miss the senior staff meeting at the White House. Jerry had to do almost all of the grocery shopping, a fate from which I had rescued him years before. When Jerry and I first met, the chore he hated most was going to the grocery store at the end of a long day, after picking up Leigh from day care. I actually enjoy shopping, but I was so busy in Washington that I only made it to the grocery store about three times. Once, I had been interrupted by a conference call. I couldn't help but wonder what my fellow shoppers would think if they knew the woman squeezing tomatoes in the produce section was on the phone with Colin Powell and Don Rumsfeld and Condi Rice, helping them prepare for the Sunday talk shows.

My work at the White House was challenging, fascinating. I was exploring a whole new world. Working for state government in Texas, I had dealt with education and criminal justice and health care and the environment, a wide range of domestic issues. But the only foreign policy we dealt with was Mexico — and Oklahoma, I used to joke. Thanks to Condi Rice, who had included me on the U.S. delegations for our foreign trips, I was meeting foreign leaders, visiting their countries, learning the nuances of American foreign policy. I had watched in Slovenia as the president of the United States met the president of Russia for the first time. I had walked on the Great Wall of China, stood at the DMZ in South Korea, and visited the palace of Their Majesties, Empress Michiko and Emperor Akihito, the 125th in an unbroken line of rulers of Japan. I had watched from inside the Kremlin as President Bush and President Putin signed an agreement dramatically reducing nuclear weapons. I had met the pope at his summer residence and had lunch with the queen at Buckingham Palace. I had worked on historic speeches about some of the most complex issues of our time, from the moral ramifications of stem cell research to advancing peace in the Middle East.

And the attacks of September 11 had given me a vast new communications challenge. Before that day, I was primarily concerned with communicating the president's policies to the American people. Now I was in charge of helping the president communicate during a global war against a diffuse and dramatically different enemy to people both at home and across the globe, many of whom clearly didn't seem to like us very much. We dispatched members of my staff to Islamabad and London to set up new information centers. I was increasingly convinced that our country would never win the war against terror as long as little boys and girls across the world grew up hating America. And the plight of the women and little girls of Afghanistan had touched me. I wanted to do everything I could to help them regain the dignity and the opportunities that had been stolen from them during the years of the Taliban. Yet as important as

I thought the work ahead was to our country and our future, I also found myself longing to pick my son up from school, to make sure I was there when he needed me, which I was learning was even harder with a teenager than it had been with a toddler. I found myself longing to be rested enough to want to go out to dinner with my husband or get together with friends.

I didn't make a decision the night Jerry and I first talked about moving home; I agonized for weeks. And when I finally made up my mind, I realized the seeds had been planted long before, by parents who had taught me that faith and family matter most in life. Once again, as I had when I had left reporting for my first political campaign almost twenty years earlier, I found myself yearning for a life that was a little more normal.

CHAPTER 2

"Karen, Don't Sing"

My mother says I could hardly wait to be born. I moved constantly while she was pregnant, flipping, wiggling and kicking. I was so active that she couldn't sleep. And I grew up the same way, an energetic, talkative, inquisitive little girl whose family was always on the move.

Once while my dad was in Vietnam, and we were living in my mother's hometown in Kentucky, my aunt Frankie picked me up from school. After a few minutes, she pulled the car over to the side of the road and turned to the backseat: "Karen, honey, you have got to stop asking so many questions. You're making me so nervous, I can't drive." In school, I was always the one enthusiastically waving my hand, eager for the teacher to call on me, certain I knew the answer. And if I didn't understand, or wanted to know more, or thought of something else, my hand thrashed through the air to ask about it. My mother went up to the school office to complain once when I was in ninth grade, because the substitute teacher had told me that I asked too many questions. Mom was really annoyed. She thought I was supposed to ask questions, and the teachers were supposed to answer them.

My sister never really liked to move; I looked forward to it. I learned early to enjoy meeting new people and seeing different places. I had been born across the ocean, in Paris, where my dad was stationed in the army. I arrived at the American Hospital there at 6:55 p.m. on December 27, 1956, a little late for Christmas. By virtue of being born in Paris to American parents, I had dual citizenship, French and American. When I was eleven, my parents had a ceremony where I renounced any ties to France and was given an American certificate of citizenship. It's ironic that I wound up working at the White House, because my parents always taught me I could be anything I wanted to be — except, Mom said, the president. Mom always believed that the Constitution prohibits American citizens who were born in a foreign country from serving as president. My lawyer husband thinks that's wrong, and says I should consult a constitutional lawyer. He'd like to see it contested, though he wouldn't wish the job on me.

I grew up with two certainties: I could not be president, but I could be anything else I wanted to be, provided I put my mind to the task and worked hard at it. That's a breathtaking assumption when you think about it — so quintessentially American. I want all the other children who grow up in our country to have it, too: the certainty that enormous opportunities are available to you if you seek them and work hard to achieve them, no matter what neighborhood you come from or who your parents are.

We were a fairly typical mid-1950s American family, much like Ward and June Cleaver's on *Leave It to Beaver*. While Dad served in the army, Mom made it her career to stay home, support Dad and rear my sister and me. She always ironed Dad's uniforms by hand because she did it better than the laundry, and she gave great dinner parties and worked on volunteer projects in the community. Mom always said she earned a salary as an army wife; the army just didn't pay it.

We hopscotched around the globe as I grew up, moving to a new house, a new city, sometimes even a new country every couple of years. I don't remember anything about my first two and a half years, when we lived in Paris during the Suez Canal oil crisis. Our apartment was always cold, my parents say, and I still like a house that way, especially at night so I can sleep under a thick down comforter.

My parents took me with them as they traveled throughout Europe as young newlyweds, taking advantage of the opportunity to see the Alps in Switzerland, the fjords in Norway, the canals in Venice, the great art and antiquities in Rome. It must have been an amazing experience, especially for my mother, Patricia Rose Scully, who had grown up in Kentucky, one of ten children in a rambunctious Irish Catholic family whose world was shattered when her father died suddenly of a massive heart attack when she was eleven. My grandmother struggled to make ends meet, and when Mom graduated from high school, there was no money for college. She moved to Alexandria, Virginia, to live with one of her brothers and his wife and to work as a secretary for the army. She was a striking woman: five foot eight with wavy black hair, deep blue eyes, and a tiny waist. Dad saw her at Fort Belvoir one day, and after weeks of stopping by her desk, he finally asked her to dinner, a month in advance. They went to a fancy restaurant, and he ordered chateaubriand, which Mom had never had before.

The handsome young army lieutenant colonel, Harold Robert Parfitt, had broad shoulders, blue eyes and dimples and had already fought in two wars. His senior year at West Point, where his classmates christened him One-Hop Hal because he didn't participate in the dances, was cut short because of World War II. Dad was sent to England and put in charge of a platoon that landed on D-Day in Normandy, where he was wounded by artillery fire as he made his way across the beach toward Point du Hoc. The other injuries around him were so much more serious, and he was so intent on reaching the bluffs that were his goal, that he didn't seek medical attention until they had secured the area the next day. When he did, the medics sent him back to England for surgery, but to this day his thumb still doesn't function properly. A month later, he rejoined his unit and marched across France, the Netherlands and Germany. Later, he was stationed in Japan, and fought in Korea and Vietnam.

As a boy, my father had never been more than a couple of hundred miles from his hometown of Coaldale, Pennsylvania, where my grandfather was a coal miner. Grandpa had been adopted by the Parfitt family after his mother died during childbirth, shortly after she'd arrived in this country with a group of immigrants from Wales. He attended school through the fourth grade, then had to go to work as a coal miner; and he wanted nothing more in life than for his boys to get a good education so they wouldn't have to work in the mines. He and my grandmother sacrificed a great deal to send both their sons to college. My uncle earned a teaching degree and later retired as the superintendent of schools in West Hempstead, on Long Island. Dad went for a year to a costly prep school to prepare him to succeed at West Point. After Dad excelled on several examinations, a family friend alerted the local congressman about the smart and serious young man who wanted to go to the military academy. Despite not having any political clout or connections, Dad was selected on merit.

When Dad's orders took them to Paris on their first assignment as a married couple, Mom showed early signs of the pluck and resilience required of an army wife. Immediately after arriving in France, Dad was sent to Turkey for three weeks. On her own, knowing no one in the city, Mom decided she would spend her time learning to drive. She signed up for lessons, and laughs to this day about driving a strange car through the dizzying traffic circles of the City of Light, with the instructor giving directions in French; she understood nothing beyond his frantic body language.

She cooked her first Thanksgiving dinner in an apartment kitchen for our neighbors and a group of Dad's bachelor friends, and they spent Christmases and special occasions with American, British and Canadian neighbors who lived in their building. My parents tell me that when we returned to the United States two and a half years later, my grandmother burst into tears when the toddler she was greeting spoke to her in French, not English.

We moved to St. Louis, Missouri, where I was two when my sister, Beverly, was born. "I'm holding her very carefully," I assured my mother, who was taking a quick bath and had thought Beverly was safe in her crib. Instead, my mother looked on in horror as her two-year-old carried her days'-old baby across the hard tile floor of the bathroom. The baby had been crying, so I did what seemed the right and responsible thing and went to get her, and brought her to my mother.

St. Louis is where my dad started a family tradition we would never allow him to abandon. Once while Mom was out shopping and he was babysitting, he made a lemon meringue pie to show how well he could handle it all. We pronounced it his specialty, and he still makes one occasionally — along with my grandmother's old-fashioned, yeast-rising raisin bread — although when Mom is gone, Dad has trouble fixing himself anything besides cereal for dinner.

A few years later we moved to Kingston, Ontario, where Dad attended the Canadian National Defence College and I went to kindergarten. My sister and I both have vivid memories of persuading our parents to drive the family car across a frozen Lake Erie, an experience both thrilling and terrifying as we nervously imagined cracking the thick surface of the ice — despite the long line of cars successfully crossing the lake in front of us — and falling through to the freezing waters lurking just below.

After a year in Canada, we moved to Jacksonville, Florida, where I went through the first two years of elementary school. That's where I was on the first day in my lifetime that we all remember exactly where we were — the day President John F. Kennedy was assassinated. The school sent us home early, without saying why. I lived right down the street, so I walked to my house. Because it was early, my mother wasn't home; and that was frightening, because my mother was always there when I got home from school. She had taught me what to do just in case, so I had a key; but I had never had to use it before.

After letting myself in, and turning on the television, I found out that the president had been assassinated. In my duty-honor-country-bound house, the president of the United States was a larger-than-life figure; I couldn't imagine someone killing him. I remember crying, and wondering why all this was happening, and worrying about my mother; and that's how she found me when she and my sister got home.

Like other Americans, my parents were stunned, angry and terribly sad that someone would dare to shoot the leader of the Free World. They were more conservative than John Kennedy was and didn't agree with many of his policies, but he was the president; they had been taught, and in turn taught me, to respect both the office and the individual holding it. Kennedy's assassination was a confirmation of my parents' growing concern that our country and its citizens were shedding, like an old dried-out skin, a formerly shared code of conduct and moral authority. This feeling intensified in the tumultuous years of protests and assassinations that followed.

Two other moments stand out from our three years in Florida: the first was a hurricane my mother and sister and I weathered hovering in a dark hall in our house while Dad was stuck at the office. I remember my always-prepared mother entertaining us with games and cards played by flashlight while the wind howled outside, downing electric lines and flooding streets. We knew the storm was severe because my mother was worried about the cat and even let him in the house. We always had animals when we were growing up, but it was a big sacrifice for my mother and they usually had to stay outside because she was afraid of them.

The second memory was a snub. After Florida's public schools lost their accreditation, my parents decided to send me to private school for third grade. This was my first exposure to cliques, and no doubt shaped my lifelong aversion to people who think they are better than anyone else. By the unspoken code of the third grade, a little girl named Peggy decided with whom all the other little girls would play; she also decided that none of them would play with me.

I remember Peggy had blond hair, and she wore a little gold heart locket around her neck. She was pretty, and everyone looked up to her, but I also thought she was stuck-up and mean. I couldn't understand why the other girls would give her so much power and dominion over them. A few told me they wanted to play with me, but they couldn't risk making Peggy mad.

So my best and only friend in third grade was an aspiring scientist named Howard, who was incredibly smart, and always working on some kind of experiment. We rode the bus home from school together, and went afterward to my house or his, where we played outside or worked on Howard's latest project in his tree house.

The place that really defined my childhood, though, was not Florida but Panama, where our family moved the summer after third grade. Shortly after our arrival, my parents sent Beverly and me to a church camp, thinking it would introduce us to the place and help us adjust. It worked for me: I loved the beach and the horses, and fell in love with the exotic, tropical new environment. Frightened by the unfamiliar setting, my sister hated it.

My embrace of our new home and my sister's despair about it were stark reminders that my parents had two very different daughters. I was an extrovert and athlete, a swimmer and a good student who could talk loudly and openly with anyone; Beverly was introverted, a musician who sang beautifully and talked little, especially with people she didn't know very well. She struggled in her early years at school while I succeeded easily. She starred in musicals, while my game efforts to join in singing "The Bear Went Over the Mountain" on car trips usually resulted in choruses of "Karen, don't sing."

My parents were careful never to choose between us, and to honor our gifts equally, encouraging each of us to do our best always, and to compare ourselves only with ourselves, not others. Beverly recalls coming home upset one day after getting her first and only D on a report card, and having my mother ask: "Beverly, did you do your best? If you did, that's all anyone can ask. If you didn't, you need to work harder next time."

I learned the limits of my abilities in the swimming pool, where I struggled to keep up with more gifted swimmers who sometimes didn't work as hard in practice but could always beat me in the meets. I had more heart and drive than talent. By swimming endlessly up and down until I was so tired I could barely heave my body out of the pool, I could improve my time, though never quite enough. During elementary school, I dreamed of going to the Olympics; by high school, I realized that if I did, it would only be as a spectator.

My mother always thought it was surprising that I kept swimming, because it was one of the few areas where I did not succeed easily. Sometimes even I didn't understand why: I remember arriving for early morning swim practices and watching the steam rise off the heated pool into the cold air; I had to will myself into the water.

Swimming taught me the joy of doing something for its own sake. To this day, I love the way my body feels in the water, long and effortless as I reach out as far as I can stretch over one arm, then shift my hips and pull that arm through the water as I swivel out over the opposite arm, then repeat the shift again and again. Swimming is a rhythmic sport that encourages the mind to wander and explore. I've always done some of my best thinking in the pool. And swimming taught me the satisfaction of working both on my own and as part of a team. You compete against your own times, always pushing yourself to go faster toward your personal best; yet because points from individual events contribute to the team total, you root for your teammates and swim with them in relays. Both lessons served me well years later when I went to work on political campaigns, which are about not only the candidate but also the little old ladies who stuff envelopes, and the young people who volunteer because they want to make a difference, and the families of staff — and the sacrifices they all make to support the individual whose name is on the ballot.

Other childhood lessons stayed with me, too. I learned message discipline early. I talked so much, my sister couldn't get a word in edgewise. So my parents began putting an alarm clock on the dinner table to limit the amount of time I could speak. They set it for five minutes, and when it rang, it was my sister's turn to talk. I couldn't say anything else until Beverly had finished her five minutes. I had so much to say in my allotted time that I had to organize my thoughts and conserve my words as much as possible. The early training would prove invaluable years later in television and politics, when I had not five minutes, but frequently only twenty or thirty seconds to concisely state my point of view.

My parents also worked hard in my early life to teach me to control my temper, and to be more patient. In one of the longest and most instructive episodes of my childhood, my father made me wait for an entire month to find out whether I could get a horse. I was ten years old and loved horses; or at least I loved what I thought I knew about them. I had practically memorized *The Horsemasters*, *Bonfire*, *Black Beauty* and *The Black Stallion*. I had never really thought about owning a horse before, but in the Panama Canal Zone, many of the girls I knew had them. They talked about sleepovers at the stables and weekends at horse shows, and I began to long for a horse of my own. I drove my parents crazy asking if I could have one.

One night Dad sat me down. "Your mother and I are going to think about whether or not you can have a horse. We're going to think about it for a month. I don't want you to ask about it — not even once. If you do, the answer will have to be no. And at the end of the month you can ask, and we'll let you know our decision."

All month I thought I would burst, trying to contain both the question and all my hopes of owning and riding my own horse. I counted the days. At the end of the month my father came home and I could wait no longer. Even though he was in the bathroom with the door closed, I knocked, and said through the door, "Dad, it's been a month. Can I have a horse?"

"No, honey," my father replied quietly.

I left the room heartbroken. I was sobbing in my bedroom when my father came in: "Karen, we're going to get you a horse. Your mother and I agreed that we would get you one if you didn't lose your temper when I told you no."

Several weeks later, we drove out into the Panamanian countryside to the home of a friend of my father's who had horses for sale, and I picked out a beautiful palomino pony. I named him Bonfire, after the horse in one of my favorite Walter Farley books. For the next three years I would spend long hours at the stables and at horse shows, riding and grooming and caring for my horse.

When I wasn't at the stables, I was at the pool, or in the mango tree, reading books. Beverly used to complain that when my parents went out to dinner, I brought a book to the table and wouldn't talk to her. When my parents found out, they made a new rule: no reading at the table. Beverly spent her time playing with her dolls and her girlfriends, and singing. My parents had both great love and clear expectations for us. We were taught to make our beds every morning, clean our rooms every week, address our elders as sir and ma'am and go to church on Sunday. We were both expected to go to college; it was never questioned. My mother felt strongly about it because she had not been able to go, my father because his parents had sacrificed so much to send him.

As children of the Depression, my parents both subscribed to the "waste not, want not" school. They took great care of all their possessions, squeezing the maximum possible use out of every item, and if they wanted something, they saved until they had enough money to buy it. They never owned a charge card until after they retired; then they used it only for convenience, and paid the full balance every month. They even paid cash for their cars; only the house payments were made over time. My dad taught Beverly and me how to balance our checkbooks, and how to do our own taxes. We were expected to be responsible, and we were taught the skills to be so.

Most important, they stressed giving 100 percent to everything we did. "Anything worth doing is worth doing right" was my father's mantra, and he applied it to every chore, from mowing the lawn, which he did every Saturday, to home repairs, which sometimes took a while, given his perfectionism. I remember one Christmas morning when we had awakened early, eager to open our gifts. Dad disappeared for what seemed like forever: he had been cleaning the floor in the room where our surprise gift, a puppy, had gone to the bathroom during the night. Anything worth doing was worth doing right — and right then and there, Christmas morning or not.

Years later, after I had graduated from college, we were staying at my aunt and uncle's house on Long Island, and I was preparing a Thanksgiving basket for a friend. Turning around, I realized that my father was on his hands and knees on the floor behind me, picking up tiny pieces of straw wherever I'd dropped one. We laughed for ten minutes; it never would have occurred to my dad to wait until I had finished before picking up. We added pieces of tinsel to the Christmas tree one at a time too, and the Christmas wrapping paper went straight into the garbage bag while each present was still being opened. I have never been as neat as my parents are: my husband says you could eat off their garage floor; whereas you usually have to move some clutter to eat on my dining room table. He claims to have cured me of various Parfitt perfectionisms over the years; for instance, I have learned that when company unexpectedly arrives, turning down the lights or lighting candles in a room is almost as good as dusting.

Because of my father's career as a military officer, my parents never felt that it was appropriate to get involved in politics: we never had yard signs or bumper stickers. My mother volunteered at the hospital as a Red Cross worker, but never did any political work. We did often talk about current events, especially at the dinner table, and we grew up with a sense that news and world affairs were important. My most vivid impression of politics from those early years came from our Panamanian maid, Celsa, a young woman who spoke no English, and had little formal education. Celsa and her boyfriend started attending political meetings at night, after she left our house, because they were so excited about a presidential candidate named Arnulfo Arias. Her enthusiasm made a strong impression; she believed in his populist cause and was absolutely convinced he would make life better for her and the people of Panama.

In Panama, my father served as lieutenant

governor and, later, as governor of the Canal Zone, the American territory that stretched for several miles on either side of the Panama Canal. Dad's job required my parents to spend a lot of time at parties with military families, community leaders and personnel from the many foreign embassies in Panama City. Occasionally, we were invited to go with them. I remember visiting the Chinese embassy and being fascinated by the exotic art and food. We became friends with the American ambassador and his wife, and once at a dinner party, I managed to communicate with an Italian girl who spoke no English by stumbling through Spanish words that were similar to their Italian counterparts. When my parents had parties at our home, I always wanted to meet all the guests. My mother allowed me to attend for half an hour and mingle before they sat down to dinner and I had to go to bed. I loved talking with the adults; they came from different, fascinating places, and I always felt I learned something from everyone I talked with. I feel the same way today when I give a speech at a convention or university or trade association meeting; I always learn something new about the people or the work they do.

My dad hated the saying "good enough

for government work" because he thought it conveyed a cavalier attitude, an indifference to quality that he found deeply offensive, particularly toward work that served the people of our country. And he was a humble man. We had only one car during most of my junior high and high school years, and Dad frequently took the bus to work so Mom would have the car to take us places. Many of our friends had no idea of his rank of general; whenever people asked him what he did, he would say simply, "I serve in the army."

One of the most significant memories of my childhood is of sending my dad off to Vietnam. I had heard the reports on television about American soldiers dying in this war, so I knew how dangerous it was. I was twelve, old enough to realize that Dad could be killed. When he got his orders to go, I remember that he and Mom seemed very subdued, and they didn't say much about it to Beverly and me. Mom decided we should live in Kentucky while Dad was gone because her mother and several sisters and brothers still lived there. My sister and I flew ahead to Lexington and stayed with my aunt Edna while we started school, and Mom and Dad joined us after they had packed up the house in Panama. The

Sunday before Dad left for Vietnam, I cried through the entire service at church. Nanny, my grandmother, drove with us to Cincinnati to put Dad on the plane. I remember the long walk to the gate, and the even longer walk back to the car. My dad was my hero: strong, calm, always in charge in his own quiet way. I was worried I would never see him again. For years, I couldn't see anyone in a uniform at the airport without crying.

As she had done so many times before, Mom kept us together. We had dinner every night in the apartment, Mom, Beverly and me, and Mom tried to make it the same as dinners had always been, asking each of us about our day at school and talking about current events. But she was worried, too, and she couldn't always hide it. We would catch her staring at the sugar bowl, and she wouldn't respond to our questions, and we knew she was far away from us, thinking about Dad. Ever since, my family's phrase for "lost in thought" has been "staring at the sugar bowl," being physically present without really being there.

Mother's work had always been her family, and I attribute much of the joy I find in life to her example. Her love of holidays was contagious: our house was always decorated for Christmas, with gumdrop trees and beautiful lights and special ornaments collected from all over the world, and our family spent hours trudging through Christmas tree lots to find exactly the right, perfectly shaped tree. We carved pumpkins for Halloween, and had Easter egg hunts to which we invited children from an orphanage. Dad always hid the eggs, including a big golden one that he would fill with a great treasure: a five-dollar bill. One year he hid it so well that no one found it; it was unearthed a year or so later by the Panamanian gardener while he was cutting weeds with a machete.

I've always considered our frequent moves to be mostly blessings; they taught me an openness to new things and new people. The army was an equal opportunity employer; we knew no divisions of race, and my parents taught us that all people are precious in God's sight. After living in Europe, Canada and Central America, I was accustomed to people who spoke different languages, had different skin colors and practiced different faiths; I learned to respect people's different beliefs and cultures. I remember being shocked when we moved to Dallas and people were organizing marches to protest busing as I began high school; I had gone to school in Panama with children whose skin was black and brown and white, and it hadn't seemed to make any difference.

Living in Panama and being exposed to conditions poorer and more primitive than those in much of America gave my sister and me an appreciation for things many of our peers took for granted. I also learned in a very concrete way the value of freedom. I remember how frightening it was in the interior of Panama, on the way to the beach, when our cars had to go through a checkpoint manned by armed personnel from La Guardia, Panama's version of a national guard. They brandished machine guns as they stopped and inspected our cars, demanding identification and intimidating us. And I remember attending dinners in Panama where all the women sat in the kitchen while the men ate in the dining room. Once, we visited the home of a distant relative of the then-president of Panama, and the president himself stopped by. The men stood outside and shot birds, and I remember watching them aim their rifles and fire, then seeing the birds fall from the sky, blood staining their feathers. I was horrified when someone boasted the fresh game would be in the soup. The women all ate in the kitchen, including the hostess, but respecting American custom, our hosts insisted that my mother eat with my father and the men in the dining room. My mother later told me she was very uncomfortable. So was I, since I realized my parents would want me to be polite and I had to force myself to choke down the soup, knowing the birds I had watched die were in it.

Our family was very close, and our many moves were just a fact of life, part of Dad's job. It never would have occurred to me to question them, but I am envious when I meet people who have lifelong friends. My husband still keeps up with friends he's known since his early years of elementary school; I wouldn't know how to begin finding anyone who went to first or second grade with me. Whenever I moved to a new city as a kid, I would write to my friends in the place we'd just left, but only for a while. It was hard to keep up; young kids move on and make new friends wherever they go.

When Dad came back from Vietnam, he was sent to Dallas. It was the first time I had ever been to Texas and the first time I remember being disconcerted by one of our family's moves. I was in the middle of eighth grade, the same age my son would later be when we moved to Washington, and although we were all enormously happy to have Dad back from the war and our family together again, I remember it was hard to make new friends in middle school. I felt out of place, and different. Of course, with age and perspective, I've realized everyone feels out of place, and different, at that point in life. I also had to give up the horse I had kept on a vacant lot behind our apartment complex in Kentucky. The cost of boarding it at a stable in Dallas probably would have equaled a month's rent!

I wouldn't have wanted to be my mother during those teenage years. I was difficult, strong willed and defiant. I remember screaming that I hated her, usually because she wouldn't let me do whatever I wanted to do at the time. My calmer, quieter sister would retreat to her room, trying to avoid our fights. I never yelled at my dad. He wasn't home as much, and he was quieter; he would not have tolerated it. And I didn't yell at my mother when he was around; he would not have tolerated that, either. I think parents and children of the same sex have more in common than we want to admit, and it makes the teenage assertion of independence harder on the mother of daughters, or the father of sons. Our son can make my husband madder, faster, than anyone else I know; our daughter could drive me crazy and talk her dad into almost anything. I remember being especially infuriated by my own mother's refusal to buy me a pocketbook by the designer Etienne Aigner. The Aigner purses were all the rage when I was in junior high school. They were made of rich, wine-colored leather with a little gold A-shaped emblem, and I desperately wanted one, but my mother thought they were ridiculously expensive.

"Everyone at school has one except me," I told her. "Everyone doesn't have one, because you don't," she replied, making me even madder, but no doubt giving me a lesson about remaining independent from the crowd and not becoming addicted to brands. I still remember the jolt a few years ago when it hit me: I am now several years older than my mother was when I decided she was hopelessly old-fashioned, and I don't feel old or out of touch at all.

In junior high and high school I wasn't the most popular student, or the smartest or The Most Likely to Succeed. I had my foot in several high school groups: the brainy bunch in my honors classes, the fringe-popular aspiring cheerleader crowd through drill team, and the zany, free-spirited set on the swim team. I had friends in all of them, and didn't belong completely to any of them. I even had two best friends, fellow swimmer Kathy Sweeney and drill team member Diane Kerr, who went to church and worked at McDonald's with me.

My parents were shocked when I got the job. They had always taught me to work and be responsible, and I can't imagine I didn't mention it, but they say I didn't. My mother recalls that I asked to borrow the car the same afternoon I got my driver's license, and when I came home, I announced I had a job at McDonald's. Several days a week in the early evenings after swim practice and on Saturdays, I worked behind the counter. McDonald's had a great training program and I learned the value of precision: the fastest way to make french fries, the most efficient way to fill an order. I was reliable and conscientious, so I remember being taken aback when the aggressive young manager asked me why I couldn't be more like my friend Diane. She always wore nice makeup, he explained, and had her hair done and looked "cute," whereas I showed up after swimming practice with no makeup, my hair stringy and a little green tinged from all those hours in the chlorinated water. I didn't think much of the boss after that; I knew I looked presentable if not as "cute" as Diane, so my only concession was to add a little lipstick. I still don't like to wear makeup, and I've never been one to have my nails and toes polished at the same time. If I do, they're inevitably chipped.

I faced other challenges, too. The coach of the swim team and the sponsor of the drill team didn't like my participating in both sports, and complained whenever I missed one because of the other. It didn't happen often, and my mother thought it was ridiculous because she felt kids should be encouraged to participate in anything they were interested in. Our house rule was that when practice and a meet or performance conflicted, I would go to the event and miss the practice.

The summer before my final year in high school my dad was reassigned to Fort Belvoir in Virginia. To keep from disrupting my senior year, my parents allowed me to stay in Dallas and move in with our next-door neighbors, Margaret and Johnny Pearson, whom I had come to know well after babysitting for their two young daughters, Melinda and Meredith. In retrospect, I realize that it must have been a huge sacrifice for my parents to miss my final year at home before college, but the experience gave me an early start on independence. I spent a lot of time with the family of my friend Kathy, becoming the "eighth" Sweeney in their boisterous household. My sister had to move because she was younger, just starting ninth grade. She missed me and her friends in Dallas, had trouble adapting to life on a military base and was very unhappy. She never adjusted, and the next year, when I went to college, my parents allowed Beverly to return to Dallas to board at The Hockaday School, another tremendous sacrifice on their part. I'm sure my parents' concern for our happiness during our high school years would later make me more conscious of my son's unhappiness in Washington.

The other tie that bound my early years was faith. I grew up going to different churches; whenever we moved, my parents would visit nearby Protestant churches and choose whichever one they liked best. When we moved to Texas, my eighth grade English teacher invited me to First Presbyterian in downtown Dallas and my family ended up joining the church. Years later, after Jerry and I were married there and our son was baptized there, I realized the power of that simple invitation.

My Sunday school class was taught by a

friend's parents, a wonderful couple named Gil and Billie Thomas. I learned a great deal about the Bible from them, and in a high school group called Young Life, where a young seminary student led our study of several books of the New Testament. I enjoyed the many friends I met from all over the city at Sunday school and Fellowship of Christian Athletes meetings, and during trips to Young Life camp in Colorado, where we sang Christian songs around the campfire.

Most of our high school group sat in the balcony at church, and we occasionally skipped out during long sermons to go to a nearby hotel to buy a soda or candy bar. But I had also felt the first stirrings in my soul, a yearning to be part of something I realized was bigger and more important than my individual life. Some people can recount a singular moment when they became a Christian; I experienced a more gradual process of realizing that God's love is personal, meant for each of us, and that He offers forgiveness for our shortcomings and a way back to Him for all who choose to accept it. Faith for me is a foundation, a set of beliefs upon which my life is grounded and from which all decisions can be based.

One of my favorite books of the Bible is

Malachi, in the Old Testament. My husband says I like it because it is so argumentative. The prophet Malachi describes God chastising the religious leaders of Israel for what I call a garage-sale mentality, giving God only the leftovers of their time, sacrifice and respect. " 'Try presenting that to your governor; will he be pleased with you or show you favour?' says the Lord of Hosts." That verse reminds me how much more deference we often give to our earthly leaders than we do to our Creator. But the reason I most love Malachi is its promise: " 'Return to me, and I will return to you,' says the Lord." I cling to that hope because far too often I forget about God in the midst of my daily life.

Another of my favorite verses is in the Gospel of Luke: "I know my sheep and my sheep know me. No one can snatch them from my hand." I take great comfort in that promise because I've always been a stubborn sheep. Throughout my life, my strong will has butted heads with my faith.

Nowhere was this better illustrated than in my youthful suspicions about heaven. Dare I say this out loud? I'm sure I was wrong. I know I didn't think it through, and I've long since changed my mind. Forgive me. But as a young girl, I was tormented by a nagging, fleeting thought — fleeting because it was so terrible that I banished it as soon as it entered my mind — the thought that I was not entirely sure I wanted to go to heaven.

I knew it probably beat the alternative. But I didn't like the choice. Hell was hot and horrible; heaven was peaceful and angelic. I wasn't sure which sounded worse. What did loud people do in a quiet place like heaven? Was there really room among the angels for a competitive swimmer? And most annoying, heaven seemed to be full of singing. To quote the Grinch: "Oh, the horrible, awful singing. If there's one thing I can't stand, it's the singing." I love music, but I can't carry a tune. I can't even hum, so why bother spending time in a place where singing seemed to be one of the most important extracurricular activities?

My family believed in God, tried to live good lives on earth and aspired to heaven. And when you're worried about heaven, that's a problem. I'll be honest: I wasn't sure I wanted to visit heaven, much less spend an eternity there.

This troubling thought, a stark reminder that I might not be normal, nagged at me throughout much of my childhood and adolescence. Then I just quit thinking about heaven at all. With the ease of the young, for whom death seems incomprehensible, I merely ignored it.

Eventually life caught up with my attempt at ignorant bliss. And that's the rest of this story: how a willful, somewhat rebellious, always curious little girl who incessantly asked questions one day wound up asking them at the White House.

CHAPTER 3

Learning My Trade

He handed out the addresses on little slips of notebook paper, passing them to us one at a time, a sly smile on his face as he anticipated the reactions of his mostly young, mostly sheltered students. Bob Mann thought that one of his jobs as chairman of Southern Methodist University's journalism department was to introduce the young people who ventured into his reporting class to a wider world, a world beyond the safety of the manicured red brick campus and their own middle- to upper-class backgrounds. The slips each had a number and a street name, nothing more. The assignment was to visit that address and write about whatever you found there.

Mine was on Elm Street, just east of downtown Dallas, not a good part of town. My boyfriend at the time insisted on going with me because he had read that several murders had occurred near there. We left campus late one afternoon and drove south on Central Expressway toward downtown's glittering glass skyscrapers, briefly entering

79

their shadows, then escaping them as we traveled east on Elm. With each passing block, the buildings got smaller and shabbier, the peeling paint and faded signs finally giving way to a dilapidated collection of shacks surrounded by old tires and auto parts, punctuated occasionally by abandoned lots.

Then we saw it: a tacky, flashing neon sign announced the IT'LL DO CLUB, a seedy-looking place I never would have entered had I not been assigned to go there. Inside it was gritty and smoky, with country western music scratching out from a jukebox whose speakers needed repair. Everything looked old and tired, especially the women who stopped in after work at a nearby factory hoping to meet up with a truck driver who would take them away from everyday life, at least for a while. They probably weren't all that much older than I was, maybe ten years or so, but the decade between twenty and thirty had left them looking worn and defeated. The men talked too loud, leaned too close and leered. It was sad and depressing, and I wanted nothing more than to leave as soon as I could. I talked to a few people, enough to get some quotes and complete the assignment, but even as I wrote the story, I knew it wasn't very good. The realization was sharp and sudden: I didn't have any insight into these women's lives or experiences; I couldn't identify with what I had seen. And that feeling was reinforced in class a few days later when Bob asked one of my fellow students, an older woman who had been out in the working world before deciding to return to school, to read her paper aloud. She had also visited the It'll Do Club, but she had understood and been able to articulate the lives of the women in a way that I had not. I might have traveled the world more than some of my fellow students, and I might have been an honors student, but I realized I had a whole lot to learn.

I had signed up for the journalism class on a whim because I liked to write, and thought it would be different from the standard English department literature and poetry offerings that were filling most of my second-year schedule. I certainly hadn't started college wanting or expecting to become a journalist. My parents, my mother especially, qualified for membership in that silent majority of Americans who, along with Spiro Agnew, didn't think much of the "nattering nabobs of negativism," as the former vice president had called the national news media. My mother was the most outspoken, but Dad never disagreed when she outlined a vast chasm between what they had experienced, especially when Dad was in Vietnam and the Panama Canal Zone, and what the media had reported about events they had witnessed. So although they always told me I could be or do anything I was willing to work at, it never occurred to them or to me that I would consider becoming a reporter. It's odd in hindsight because two of my most persistent personality traits, arguing and asking questions, seemed a natural fit for journalism.

I was so argumentative, and always so insistent that my point of view was right, that my mother was convinced I would become a lawyer. She could picture me standing before a jury, full of logic and certitude, an impassioned advocate for my client. When I arrived at SMU in the fall of 1974, I wasn't sure what I wanted to do, but on all the entrance exams and college applications, I had described law school as my goal; it seemed more likely than anything else. Always in a hurry, I had decided to attend SMU primarily because of a new three-year degree program it offered honors students, which allowed me to skip my freshman year and delve immediately into more diverse and challenging classes: Laurence Perrine's English Poetry; Joe Tyson's Philosophy of Religion; later, David Dillon's Renaissance Literature. I avoided math and science; during high school I had to suppress the urge to gag during our dissection of a fetal pig and feign interest as we whipped up weird potions in chemistry.

I was a reader and a writer. All my tests involved long essays in blue books, and I liked it that way. I studied poetry and art history and religion and thought big thoughts and explored them in papers. My professors were creative and fun; we compared dramatic monologues in literature to those in popular movies, and attended a Renaissance banquet at David Dillon's house. He draped a yellow scarf around my neck as I arrived, only later telling us that it was the Renaissance equivalent of a scarlet letter. He chose me to wear it, he later told me, because he knew I was outgoing and confident enough to laugh about it.

I had signed up for Bob Mann's journalism course without knowing exactly what to expect; I found it engaged me in a way no other subject had. We met three times a week for a regular hour-long class, then one afternoon a week for a special three-hour lab. He closed the door at the exact minute class was to begin, and if you missed it, you got a zero for the day. Journalists had to learn to meet deadlines. And journalists had to evaluate events and people and write about them, fast and accurately. We would sit in front of big old-fashioned Underwood typewriters and pound out copy: what happened, when, where, to whom; why was it important, and how was it relevant? We had weekly pop quizzes on current events. As college students, we had been in the habit of ignoring the wider world; Bob broke us of that habit. News mattered; it affected people's lives. We needed to pay attention.

Every assignment was a new challenge: get it right, explain the context, offer unique insight or understanding, paint a picture, use words that conveyed exactly what you meant. Later, Professor David McHam would underscore the importance of choosing the right word in his editing class. I can still hear him today: "*Hopefully* is not a proper use of the word *hope;* I don't care what the modern dictionary says. You would never say, '*Wishfully,* have a Merry Christmas.' '*Not only* must be followed by *but also,*'" David drilled into our brains. "Always, not just sometimes. *None* is a singular noun because it is a condensed version of *no one* and thus requires a singular verb, even though it sounds funny to say 'None is.' "

Thus began my lifelong preoccupation with choosing just the right word. Years later, at the White House, a sentence I had suggested in one of the president's speeches to acknowledge the fact that many Americans had "legitimate" questions about the situation in Iraq was changed during a process known as staffing. Presidential speeches are sent to all members of the senior staff for suggestions and approval, and this one came back with the word *legitimate* gone, replaced with the more ordinary and overused *important*. I argued, and ultimately prevailed: "*Legitimate* is the right word. This sentence lets the president of the United States acknowledge people's right to ask those questions in a way that calling them important does not." In the next day's newspapers, it was one of the most widely quoted lines in the speech.

The summer between my second and third years of college, a group of professors took eighteen students to New York City to observe the Democratic National Convention. We stayed in a seedy old hotel right in the middle of Manhattan, and walked everywhere, to delegation meetings, parties

85

and gatherings of delegates interested in a specific cause or issue. Tickets were hard to come by; I remember attending only one convention session, and not a particularly important one either. It didn't matter because the fascinating thing was not the pomp and ceremony at the podium, but the people. Each (one is implied, so the verb that follows is singular) of them was passionate, convinced that his or her candidate or cause was important, even noble. I was captivated by the energy and electricity all around us, not only in the city, which I had visited a few times before, but also among the delegates and activists who had gathered for this once-every-four-year rite of American democracy. I never saw the Democratic nominee, Jimmy Carter, except on television, but I went to a breakfast meeting where Senator Frank Church spoke, and I remember being impressed by his command of the room. He hadn't won the nomination, but he hadn't lost his passion and commitment.

Getting off the elevator in New York one day, our SMU class ran into a television news director from KXAS-TV in Dallas/ Fort Worth, Lee Elsesser. Bob Mann explained that the journalism school was trying to offer students more practical experience, and mentioned that he wanted to hire a broadcast professional to teach a course in radio-television news writing that fall. Lee was interested, and so was I; I signed up for the course that fall. The first night, Lee asked us to write a paper telling him about our backgrounds and why we had chosen the class. Years later, when I worked at the Texas governor's office, Lee sent me a framed copy of my paper, which he had saved for all these years:

2 Sept 76
. . . This is my last year here, and I hope to go into broadcast journalism or news writing when I graduate in May. I was an English major during my first two years at SMU, but took a course in news reporting last semester and after attending the National Democratic Convention in New York this summer have decided I would [my professor crossed out the "I would" and replaced it with: "to"] double-major in journalism. I took this course because I am interested in learning everything I can about broadcast journalism, and because Bob Mann has encouraged me to take all the courses I can from people who

are directly involved in the business. I am excited about journalism and want to learn as much as I can from courses such as this one. I also have an interest in politics . . .

That fall, in Lee's class, I fell in love with a brand-new challenge: writing to pictures. During one of our early meetings, Lee had brought a tape of a documentary he had produced about the Rio Grande River, to show us an example of the art of writing for television. I was fascinated. The words — simple, few and direct — highlighted the beauty of the pictures; the pictures elaborated on the words. This was a fine art, and I would spend the next seven years of my life pursuing it.

That winter, I begged Lee to allow me to do an internship at Channel 5 during my final spring semester. I still tell young people who ask for advice that working as an intern is the best way to gain practical experience and decide if a certain profession is the right one for you. I plunged in, at first rewriting copy from the news wires for the noon news, eventually going out on stories, always watching and learning. I spent almost every waking moment that I was not in class at the newsroom, making the long drive from the SMU campus in Dallas to the studio in Fort Worth anytime I had a few extra hours. I spent all day Saturday and Sunday there; my church attendance had steadily declined since my first year of college, when I had gone to church fairly often, at least during the fall. But by the time my mother sent me a note congratulating me on being named to the honorary society Mortar Board, and had written: "Just remember to always live as the Lord guides you," I had pretty much forgotten. If anyone had asked, I would have said that I was a Christian, but I don't remember that it ever came up: God didn't seem to have a very prominent place in campus life. I went to church occasionally, always on Christmas and Easter; I read the Bible some; I said a prayer when I was lonely or needed something, but I wasn't investing anything in a relationship with God.

My spring in the newsroom was enlightening in other ways, however. I learned how to tear copy from the news wire machines and rewrite it for television, replacing words intended to be read by the eyes with words easily absorbed by the ears. I still talk to myself out loud as I write, making sure the words have a cadence that falls smoothly from the tongue. I learned that newsrooms are noisy, bustling places where each day is unpredictable. Each deadline successfully met only launches a countdown toward the next newsbreak, the morning news show, the noon news, or the five, the six and the ten.

I learned television largely from former newspaper reporters, veterans who knew how to develop sources and ask penetrating questions. Unlike the younger men and women who came later, who sometimes seemed to have been selected for their appearance, our anchors, Ward Andrews and Russ Bloxum, prided themselves on being newsmen, not news readers. Harold Taft, our weatherman, was an institution whose detailed reports were a nightly science class for viewers. Frank Perkins, Clint Bourland and Tom McDonald were newsmen first, television producers and editors second. And there were lots of women in the newsroom, including the gracious Bobbie Wygant, who had started years before as a secretary and now anchored the 5:00 p.m. news with Chip Moody and had her own arts and entertainment show. A woman anchored the noon news; we had women reporters and editors; and the station management included a woman as advertising director, so I never felt my gender made any difference. A newsroom is an all-hands-on-deck kind of place, and I was one of the hands.

And though I learned from everyone, most of all I learned the business from the cameramen, especially the ones known in those days as one-man bands. They could do everything to produce a complete news story — both photograph and report it — and they did so frequently. I would ride along, asking questions as I watched them work. One in particular, Bill Tippit, was a photographer who could talk to virtually anyone and find out more than any reporter I knew. Bill was the first person ever to trust the student intern from SMU to help report a story.

"Here," he said, thrusting a microphone at me, balancing the camera on his shoulder with his other hand, "interview that girl over there." A big concert was coming to town, and hundreds of fans were lining up outside Reunion Arena, prepared to sleep there overnight to be the first in line to get tickets the next morning.

"What should I ask her?" I said, not certain how to handle this unexpected opportunity.

"Just ask her why she's here," Bill said. "Ask her whatever you would want to know."

"Parfitt got a great interview," Bill said, as we walked back into the newsroom, giving me far more credit than was due for merely following his instructions. That night, the snippet from the woman about why in the world she would spend the night outside in the cold made it onto the news, the first of many Parfitt-Tippit collaborations.

One day in Fort Worth, while tagging along with a photographer to a hospital to cover a news event, I struck up a conversation with a nurse. She was worried about how legislation then being debated by the Texas legislature might affect her ability to do her job. I started researching the issue, and with the help of several photographers and editors, ultimately produced a five-part series on the Texas Nursing Practice Act, which set the legal boundaries for the nursing profession. It was obviously a hot issue in the medical community; when my bosses decided to air it, the station received hundreds of calls. In April, Channel 5 put me on the payroll to work nights and weekends. As my days in college came to an end, the news director wrote a letter to the journalism professor who was overseeing my internship:

May 5, 1977

Dear David:
After talking with you on the phone

the other day you know that if I were giving Karen Parfitt a grade for the work she has done here during her practicum, I would give her an "A."

Karen presented absolutely no problems. She arrived on time or earlier and frequently stayed longer than expected. She started the program by engaging in fairly rudimentary activities in the newsroom and by observing. But she quickly put that stage behind her. She began to take an active role in the pursuit of news stories.

Under supervision, she covered a news event and produced an extremely high quality report. As a result of that experience, she developed enough sources to produce a five-part series on the Texas Nursing Practice Act that was both newsworthy and interesting. The controversial subject drew a great deal of community interest.

As a result of the series and the professional quality of Karen's work, I put her on the staff here at KXAS-TV full-time. The job is only temporary and no one wishes more than I that it was permanent. In the past three weeks, Karen has been the most productive reporter on the news staff in terms of total stories. She is one of the most creative members of the staff in terms of story ideas. She is a leader on the staff when it comes to enthusiasm for hard work. I am sure there are long time professionals on the payroll here who are looking over their shoulders with a little apprehension.

At any rate, Karen Parfitt is an outstanding beginner in television news, and that has to put her, at least in my opinion, in the very highest rank among college students.

Sincerely,
Lee Elsesser
News Director
The Texas News

Somehow, in the weeks after he wrote that letter, Lee got approval for an additional reporting position and offered me a job in the station's Dallas bureau. I joked that they'd figured out that if I graduated and left, they wouldn't have had anyone to do stories on nights and weekends. My new job didn't pay much — $185 a week — but I knew it was a grand opportunity. Most aspiring television reporters had to prove themselves in small towns — Lubbock or Abilene or Wichita Falls — before they would be considered for a job in Austin or another midsize city, much less a top-ten market like Dallas/Fort Worth. The station manager, Blake Byrne, always said I was the first person he'd ever known who went directly from college into major-market television, and he was certain I would be the last. I had to skip the postgraduation trip to Europe that my parents and I had talked about for years because after my commencement on Saturday, I worked the 2:30 to 10:30 shift on Sunday night.

I started my career during a time of dramatic transition in television news, a transition marked at our station by the demise of the "meet." The meet was the once-daily, sometimes twice-daily car trip between the Dallas bureau, where I worked, and the main news headquarters and television studio in Fort Worth. One car would leave from Dallas with the film from that day's news events, and another car would leave Fort Worth at the same time. The two would "meet" halfway on the Dallas/Fort Worth turnpike, exchange the film, then return to their respective studios, delivering the film to Fort Worth for processing. As a newcomer to the team, making the meet was one of my regular assignments; by the end of my first year there, technology had made it largely a thing of the past. We had new Minicams, electronic cameras that used tape, not film. The tape could be transferred electronically, allowing us to report live from any location where the satellite dish on the top of our news van could beam to the satellite link on top of the downtown Dallas office building, which then transmitted the tape or live camera picture to the Fort Worth studio and through there, to homes across Dallas and Fort Worth. I worked nights, so I was often the reporter at the other end of those live pictures during the evening news, the "queen of the live shots," as some of my colleagues dubbed me. That was me, hair lashing my neck in the bitter wind, freezing as I stood out on the interstate with the streets icing over, warning everyone else to stay inside and off the roads. That was me, live from the Texas Capitol as the clock wound down toward midnight and legislators turned back the hands so they could finish their work by the constitutionally mandated midnight, or at least by midnight according to the clock in the house chamber, often two or three in the morning by a clock with any objective standard. That was me, live from the scene of the house fire that had killed several children, or the tornado that leveled a wide swath of Wichita Falls.

Tippit drove us to the tornado; I had just arrived home from the airport early one evening after covering the legislature in Austin when the station called to say a tornado had struck Wichita Falls, about three hours away, and Tippit was on his way to get me. He stopped and called me on his way to my apartment, asking if I had any food. Tippit was a large, heavy man who probably weighed close to 250. He was in his midforties, with graying hair and beard and a gruff voice that belied his soft heart. He chain-smoked, and whenever he wasn't smoking, he was eating or rubbing his hands with cream to control the psoriasis that covered them and forced him to wear gloves sometimes while filming. "Do you have any food we can take — candy bars, crackers? Bring it," he ordered. Later, when the granola bars and cereal and crackers I had collected were the bulk of what we ate for the next several days, I realized how wise he had been.

Almost twenty years later, when I was working in the Texas governor's office,

Tippit developed cancer. He battled it through several remissions, and I would periodically call or ask Governor Bush to call to encourage him. The last time I talked with him, he could barely whisper, but he got on the phone to say hello. He died the next day. I cried at my typewriter as I wrote a statement for the governor for his obituary: "Bill Tippit was a consummate newsman and a wonderful person. His camera chronicled the news of North Texas for more than 28 years, and he brought a unique insight and understanding of people to every story. He had a heart bigger than the bass he so loved to fish for . . . News conferences in Dallas won't be the same without him." I sent it off to Governor Bush for approval, knowing it was probably too long and flowery for someone he knew only from occasional meetings.

"I'm sorry about your friend," Governor Bush said when he called. "He was a good guy. The statement's fine."

I loved reporting. Every day was different and, most days, I learned something new. I interviewed Golda Meir about leadership, James Michener about writing, and George H. W. Bush about running for president. I had an eye for detail, and an instinct for the big picture; I could find a story virtually anywhere. One day when talking with some narcotics officers, I learned about several doctors they suspected were prescribing prescription pills rather than sound medical advice. I visited several of them, told them I wanted to lose a few pounds and walked out with prescriptions for amphetamines and narcotics. I turned it into a five-part series, "Doctors or Dealers?"

The state fair was a treasure trove of stories: the grandmother who'd made jellies for years and finally won the grand prize, the old carny who had more common sense than teeth, the kid whose 4-H project pig won the races, and the one whose prized pet came in last.

The skills I learned as a reporter I still use today when I walk into a room where people are doing or discussing something I know very little about. I learn as much as I can as fast as I can, figure out what is important and what is not, and then decide how to communicate it. I did it when explaining a story to viewers in Dallas/Fort Worth, and I did it when giving recommendations to the president of the United States.

Our Dallas bureau chief, Doug Adams, was a great boss, fair and thoughtful. My colleagues were a lot of fun; they all teased me about my powers of concentration.

Once when I was out on a story, photographer Cary Sims and engineer Don Kotrla rigged a small Chinese pull firecracker to the carriage of my typewriter, knowing that I would come in, charge to my desk and immediately begin typing. I did, and when I threw the carriage back, it exploded. Everyone was laughing, but determined not to let them get me, I kept typing.

Although I was good at the news-gathering parts of my job, I was theatrically challenged. As the business changed, and we got new bosses who brought in image consultants, I learned I needed to work on my voice, and that my clothes and makeup and hair could all be improved. I needed to have more personality, to smile more. I took it all so seriously when I was on live television, knowing millions of people might be watching, that I was more worried about what I was saying than how I looked. "Can old stone-face smile?" a viewer asked me in a letter. It would come up later, too, when people thought I was too certain, too intense, especially during the Florida recount. Asked by a reporter why I had an image of being controlling when most people who work for me had told him I am not, my deputy in the White House replied, "She could smile more on TV."

I don't mean to disparage the image aspect of the business. Television is, after all, a visual medium. The consultants and bosses care about appearances because the viewers do. I remember calling home from the Wichita Falls tornado and asking my mother about my reports from the largest disaster I had ever covered. "Your stories were great, but you didn't have your lipstick on," she said. My own mother! I have never liked wearing makeup, and my years in television made me dislike it even more: all that goop, which just wears off or smears or streaks and always has to be touched up or replaced. I do like clothes, and made a conscious effort to look more put together later in my career, especially when my boss began running for president.

But it's hard for me. "You're kind of a scruffy lady," my husband teases, and since he most often sees me in my favorite old T-shirt and a pair of shorts that have a hole in them — but only a small one, and I cannot bear to give them away because they are so soft and comfortable — he's probably right. The good part, at least for him, is that I can get dressed much faster than most women. Thirty minutes, and I'm showered, dried and ready for a baseball game or a black-tie event. Packing my suitcase takes a little longer, not because the packing itself is difficult, but because I spend a long time fretting about what, exactly, is appropriate to wear.

"You have such a glamorous job," my friends used to exclaim when they would run into me in the years after college when I was on television. But as anyone who does it knows, reporting the news is often very hard work. It sure didn't seem glamorous when we were running toward fires in hundred-degree heat, lugging tripods and heavy equipment, or when I was picking my way gingerly down a river bed in high heels in July on my way to report on a dead body someone had found in the river. Television is the ultimate what-have-you-done-for-me-lately business. You can produce the story of your life for the 10:00 p.m. news, but by 10:30, the producer is worried about the next story, the next day, the next newscast. "What have you got for me tomorrow, Parfitt bird?" Frank Perkins, the 10:00 p.m. producer, used to ask.

The producers' other mantra, the one thing they always wanted to know about every story, was "What does this mean for the average consumer, or homeowner, or taxpayer?" If you were covering a story about city hall, they wanted to know what it meant for the residents of the city. If you were covering a story about the school board, they asked what its policies meant in real, practical terms for the students. What about the teachers? What about the tax-payers? What did it mean for the average (you fill in the blank)? It became the question I always asked before my candidate would announce any proposal or any policy on any campaign, and I asked it a lot at meetings in the White House. When we were having trouble communicating the benefits of Governor Bush's proposed tax relief during the presidential campaign, I suggested inviting specific families to meet us at every stop, a concrete way to personalize how the American family would save.

I was reporting as decisions made at Dallas City Hall affected my garbage pickup and swimming pool and library hours, as decisions at the school administration building changed what children were taught in classrooms, as decisions at the Texas Capitol affected everything from the way that nurse in Fort Worth would do her job to the speed at which we could drive our cars. And the people who made these decisions were fascinating, too. I remember a state senator, an impassioned orator, sarcastically decrying a tough criminal justice proposal: "Maybe we should just give speeding the death penalty." I remember a young dairy farmer, Bruce Gibson, who ran for the legislature because decisions being made at the state capital were affecting his fellow farmers and their ability to earn a living. Relating the news to people's lives reminded me that political news is so human: sometimes tragic, sometimes poignant, sometimes inspiring, and almost always important.

I fell in love with two things during my years at Channel 5 — my husband and the political process, and politics came first.

I always insisted on covering political stories, and Sam Attlesey, a reporter at *The Dallas Morning News*, and I soon became the Dallas-Fort Worth area's regular political reporters. A candidate would announce his campaign, and Sam and I would be there. When Dick Armey, who later became the majority leader of the United States Congress, announced his first campaign for Congress, Sam and I were the only reporters who showed up. We frequently asked tough questions, but always tried to be respectful. I never thought my role was to argue with candidates, but to probe to better understand and explain them.

I remember being fascinated by the Texas

Capitol. Covering it was hard, and brought out all my competitive instincts. I wasn't assigned there full time. My station sent me only periodically, when something important was happening, so I felt I was always playing catch-up with my chief rival, a terrific reporter and wonderful person, Carole Kneeland of WFAA-TV, who was based in Austin, although her station was in Dallas. I was never able to cover the legislature the way she did and I wanted to because I didn't have the time to develop sources and an in-depth understanding of the legislative process.

The 1980 presidential campaign was a different story. We had two Texans running for president, John Connally and George H. W. Bush. I was assigned to cover George H. W. Bush, and I was determined to do it better than anyone else. I set out to know everything I could about the candidate, his policies, and the Texans who formed his team. I got to know Bill and Sally Mac-Kenzie, the Dallas-area chairmen of the campaign, and Ida Pappert, who always brought the spinach dip to campaign events, and Dorothy Golden, another dedicated volunteer. Through them, I learned that politics was a team sport: it revolved around the candidate, like the hub at the center of a wheel, but others fanned out from it, like Joci Strauss and the group of Texans who went to New Hampshire to walk door to door in the snow because they believed in George Bush and wanted him to be the next president.

The cameramen usually hated politics and politicians, and called them talking heads. That's cameraspeak for boring pictures — just head shots, with some politicians flapping their lips. Urged on by producer Elden Hale, who was determined to make political coverage more interesting, we worked hard to make our stories visual and creative.

Photographers Louis Zapata and Ronnie Ladd and I sat down at kitchen tables with farmers in Iowa, and followed them as they did their daily chores. We showed our viewers the candidates campaigning on frozen lakes in New Hampshire, among fishermen who built huts to keep warm and cut holes in the ice for their lines — such a novelty for our audience in Texas, where the air temperature rarely froze, much less the water. We interviewed workers at a shoe factory, an industry being slowly choked by foreign competition. Twenty years later, when I went back to New Hampshire with a different George Bush, I asked about the shoe factories, and learned they were all gone.

During the fall of 1979, I traveled with George H. W. Bush in a small plane just a couple of months before he shocked the political world by winning the Iowa caucuses. He had a young staff aide with him, and only three members of the media tagged along: a still photographer for one of the national news magazines, my photographer Louis and me. Twenty years later, when his son was running for president and I was helping run his campaign, we never had a single day like that. George W. Bush was the front-runner from the start, and the intense competition in the news business meant all the media had to cover him, including cable networks and Internet publications that had not even existed during his father's campaign. More than one hundred journalists traveled with us for our first campaign trip out of Texas, and even during slow times, we usually had at least ten or twelve journalists with us.

As the 1980 presidential campaign grew more intense, I witnessed an odd camaraderie develop between George H. W. Bush and the national reporters who now traveled with him everywhere. He called them the mournful pundits, teasing them because they were always prognosticating bad news. Once when he came out of an event, they greeted him wearing Groucho Marx masks with the big noses and funny eyebrows, and everyone had a big laugh. I remember being struck by how genuine and thoughtful Mr. Bush seemed. He and his press secretary, Pete Teeley, always made sure he stopped to talk with a local reporter, me, who was a long way from home and wasn't nearly as important to him as the national journalists who had far vaster audiences. I also remember the weekend he dropped out of the presidential race. It had become clear he could not win; Ronald Reagan had too many delegates. He and Barbara went home to Houston to decide their next step. It was hot, one of those stifling Texas weekends where the air feels likes a wet electric blanket on high. I remember imagining how awful it must be to have invested so much of your life, your energy, your time — to have given it your all, yet realize it had not been enough. And in the midst of that thought, out of the house walked George and Barbara Bush, bringing cold drinks to the reporters and photographers camped out on their lawn, concerned about us because it was so hot.

George Bush dropped out of the race that

Monday, and I next saw him at that summer's Republican National Convention, in Detroit. Lee Elsesser, our news director, and our camera crews and reporters were back in the hotel room that was serving as our convention office, exhausted after several long and intense days. We had been at the convention hall, but had returned for the night; the Texas Bush delegates had also come back to the hotel, dejected, feeling they had had little impact on their party's platform or convention. We ordered club sandwiches, one of the few edible things on the room service menu, and had the television on in the background. The convention had been rife with rumors, especially one that former president Gerald Ford was going to return to political life to serve as Ronald Reagan's vice president. But suddenly, we saw an NBC news exclusive report that Texan George Bush was Ronald Reagan's surprise choice to be his running mate. I leaped up and started issuing orders.

"Ronnie, go to the basement hotel entrance; that's where he'll come back in," I said to photographer Ronnie Ladd. "Tom, come with me," I said to cameraman Tom Loveless, "the Bush delegates are having a get-together in Jim Oberwetter's room."

The political wake of the Texas Bush delegates had turned into a great celebration, and we were the only Texas station to get the story, including an interview with George H. W. Bush at the basement hotel entrance the next morning.

I was in Houston the night he was elected vice president, reporting live from the hotel ballroom where his supporters had gathered to celebrate. The man I would work for years later, the candidate's oldest son, George W. Bush, was there that night too, but I didn't know him then. While we were waiting for the next vice president to enter the room and walk to the microphone, I summarized the long journey that had brought him to this moment of triumph. It was one of my favorite moments as a reporter: I had invested more than a year learning this story, getting to know the people and the policies, and I was able to bring it all together, live on television.

What my viewers did not know was that I had voted for George Bush, and for Ronald Reagan, who was on the ticket with him. And that's the way I looked at it. I had seen Ronald Reagan only from a distance. I couldn't pretend to know George Bush well, but I had interviewed him; I had spent quite a bit of time around him; and from my own firsthand experience, he seemed decent and honorable, just the kind of person I wanted to be helping to lead my country. I had tried not to let my admiration for him affect my reporting, and I was proud that when I left journalism several years later, many Democrats I had covered were surprised to learn that I considered myself a Republican. I had always tried above all to be fair, to help the public understand the candidate's views and positions, not my own.

Local television reporting was a competitive business, but also a civil one. I remember introducing Paula Zahn, now the host of her own show on CNN and then my new competitor in Dallas television, to people at Dallas City Hall because others had done the same for me. I wanted to beat my competition, but I wanted to do so fairly, because I had outperformed them, not because I knew who the city manager was and the new reporter didn't. Many of my fellow reporters became friends, along with people who worked in politics and public relations, and the lawyers and police officers whose news stories we covered. We shared difficult assignments and weird hours. My days off were Monday and Tuesday, and since I worked until after the 10:00 p.m. news and every weekend, my social life revolved around my job. Late at night, too wired to go home, we would gather at Joe Miller's on Lemmon Avenue, where everyone knew everyone else, and if you didn't, Joe would introduce you.

This is the reason my husband says we met at a bar. I say a friend introduced us. Both versions are true, if incomplete, a great example of how two eyewitness accounts can give completely different impressions.

"You just do that for shock value," I tell him. "It's true," he protests, "you're just worried about your mother's reaction, and she already knows because she's heard me say it."

Mom and I have never discussed it, but you can be sure she disapproves. I don't like to say we met in a bar, because it conjures up one of those bad movie pickup scenes where the girl walks into a bar, the guy walks up with a bad line, and they end up drinking too much and going home together. Joe Miller's was emphatically not that kind of place; in fact, Joe told me before he died that we were the only people he could think of who had ever met at his place and later married, and although it was all right in our case, he didn't especially want it to happen again.

Joe's was the local political hangout, a

truly smoke-filled room where journalists and lawyers and public officials and candidates gathered for camaraderie and conversation, all off the record, none able to be reported under the house rules unless it could be confirmed by ten the next morning. Joe enforced those rules, too. One St. Patrick's Day, some of my journalist friends and I decided to liven things up by doing the bunny hop into Joe's. Joe glared at us, but didn't say anything, at least not that night. The next time I came in, he sidled up next to me, "You wouldn't believe it. Some people came in here the other night and they looked a lot like you and Sam Attlesey. I knew it wasn't you because you would never act like that."

Single women felt safe at Joe's because Joe or his gregarious bartender, Louis Canelakes, or KayLee or Laura or the other women who worked there wouldn't let anyone hassle us. I was on television, so they were especially protective of me. One night I was scheduled to meet a friend, John Collins, to ride to Fort Worth for a dinner honoring one of my former journalism professors. John got stuck in court, and sent Jerry to get me instead. When Jerry arrived at Joe Miller's, the waitresses wouldn't tell him whether I was there; if he didn't know me, he didn't need to know, they thought. I wasn't there because I had to work late, too; Jerry still says I stood him up on our first date.

A week or so later, we were all at Joe's on a crowded Friday night and John introduced me to his friend, the lawyer he ran with at the health club at lunchtime every day.

"Here's the guy I sent over here to get you last week," he said, "my friend, Jerry." Jerry is tall, six feet, and in good shape. He had very dark hair at the time, before it began turning gray, and sharp features with soft, intelligent eyes, eyes that smiled and twinkled from behind long, doelike eyelashes. My husband is also completely comfortable with himself: he will never agree with you unless he really agrees with you, and he's not hesitant to let you know that he thinks you are dead wrong. We had a great conversation, and I remember laughing a lot. At some point, Jerry asked me to join him for dinner, but I was tired and had to work on my taxes. I know it sounds like an excuse, but my dad taught me to do my own taxes and to do them on time, and time was getting short. "It's been a long week; I think I'm just going to go home early," I told him.

"I could make some Campbell's soup," he replied, which struck me as something very different from what most guys would say. I'd never had a potential date offer to heat soup before. I wasn't persuaded, but I was intrigued.

A few days later, Jerry called and asked me to dinner. We met after I left work, after the ten o'clock news, at a restaurant called the San Francisco Rose. We went to listen to some music, but mainly we talked. Jerry is interested in almost everything and can talk to almost anyone; I always thought he would be great at running a bed-and-break-fast. He also has an edge, what he calls his mother's Irish sense of humor, a touch of a curmudgeonly streak that keeps things interesting. And he's a man of strong opinions; discussions with him are not for the fainthearted. Of course, you could say the same about me. We started seeing each other frequently. When President Reagan was shot and Channel 5 sent me to Washington in late March, my photographer and I checked in at our hotel and the clerk told me, "You have a message to call Jerry Hughes."

"Who is this guy?" Tom Loveless, my cameraman, teased. "Someone serious?"

"I've been dating him a little," I replied.

"I don't remember somebody you've been dating calling you on the road before," Tom pressed.

A few weeks later, I had Easter lunch with my family, and Jerry ate with Juliee and Bob Bliss, his law partner, but later that afternoon we went for a drive and then out to dinner. He wanted me to meet his seven-year-old daughter, Leigh, who was coming home from a weekend at her mother's. A self-possessed little girl with big blue eyes, freckles dotting her nose and shoulder-length blond hair came flouncing through the door to the living room, dropped her backpack and looked at me: "Are you and my daddy going out to dinner?" she demanded to know.

"We just got back," I replied.

"Then what are you still doing here?" she asked. She might as well have said, "This is our house and you don't belong."

Welcome to the complicated world of other people's children. "I wanted to meet you," I replied.

I've always thought I was fortunate to have met Leigh when she was seven, a delightful age when children enjoy adults and seek their attention. I had done some babysitting as a teenager, but I hadn't been around children much since then, although I had always liked them. I helped Leigh with her homework, put her hair up in rollers, played makeup with her and took her shopping. She had friends spend the night, and we would rent movies and play hide-and-seek. When she had the chicken pox, I helped take care of her. I bought her a pink bedspread for her bed, with ruffles and a canopy top. When I finally got off the night shift and started working the ten-to-six-thirty shift, the three of us started having dinner together most nights. I was accustomed to eating out, picking up fast food between stories; now we cooked at Jerry's house. I would go there after work so we could have dinner and help Leigh with her homework. Then Jerry and I would talk after Leigh went to bed. I went home just before or after the ten o'clock news. Once, when the pipes burst overnight at the duplex where I lived, I called Jerry and asked if I could come by to use Leigh's shower on my way to work later that morning. She left me a note: "Dear Karen, I heard what happened. Isn't that terrible. You can use my bath anytime. Love, Leigh."

I once asked my husband why he thought Leigh and I got along so well. "Because you're perfect," my husband replied, knowing that would annoy me, and meaning he didn't want to have this conversation.

"No, really, was there anything about how we got along that struck you?"

"Well, you always had a good feel for Leigh," my husband says.

"Leigh was an affectionate little girl, and I like kids and I'm pretty affectionate myself," I mused out loud.

"I wouldn't go that far," my husband replied, "You're kind of prickly, if you ask me."

We acted like a family long before we actually were one. I tried to do a lot of the grocery shopping because Jerry hated to go to the grocery store, a hangover from his early days of single parenting, when he would leave work, rush to pick up Leigh at day care, then have to stop to get groceries while they were both tired and hungry and cranky. Jerry was accustomed to the responsibility of parenting; he had separated from his former wife when Leigh was four, and had won custody of her during their subsequent divorce trial. I had never had to accommodate a child in my life, but Leigh was a part of dating Jerry, and most of the time, I considered it a blessing, not a burden. Leigh went to her mother's every other weekend, so Jerry and I could go out then, but otherwise we got together at his house. I tend to be a homebody who would rather cook a nice dinner with friends than go to a party, but if we wanted to go to a party, we got a babysitter or took Leigh with us. She was an easy child, friendly and vivacious. When we ate out at a restaurant, she always went to check out the bathroom, but it was really an excuse to visit with people at other tables on the way there and back. She loved to color and play Pac-Man, so she was easily entertained for a few quarters at the video machine.

By that fall of 1981, Jerry and I were going everywhere together. We hosted a Texas-OU party at his house, and some of his friends who were visiting from out of town stayed with me. We had a Christmas party together at my place. A number of young women had joined the staff at Channel 5, Jane Boone and Kevyn Burger and a photographer named Julie Baldwin. We were all tall and aggressive, and we jokingly called ourselves the Amazon women. We all started dating the men who would become our husbands at about the same time, and we would get together for parties at each other's houses. I had fallen in love with Jerry and his sharp tongue, quick mind and great humor. I also loved the feeling of belonging that came with my relationship with Jerry and Leigh, and I began longing to make this

119

all permanent. I felt embraced by Jerry's big, bustling, welcoming family: his mom, who was still alive at the time, and his sisters and brother and their spouses, Nancy and Howard Bell, Ann and Dale Boyd, and Kay and Robert Hughes, and all their children and grandchildren. My own parents had modeled a happy marriage; I had always expected that I would one day get married and have a family. The only problem was that several of Jerry's friends had told me they weren't sure he would ever marry again. I knew he felt his first responsibility was to Leigh, and I thought maybe with a little more time . . .

A year and a half later, we took Leigh to Orlando to see Disney World during spring break. We visited one of my best friends, Kate McAlister, now Kupstas, the woman I had shared an apartment with early in my reporting days. We went to Sea World and fed the dolphins and saw Shamu; we watched the parade at Disney, and Leigh danced with the Chinese dragon at Epcot. We went to spring training, and Leigh swam in the ocean even though it was early March and much too cold for the grown-ups. It was a magical week, and the pictures of the three of us on that trip are still some of my favorites. One night, after a long and tiring day at

Epcot, Kate offered to keep Leigh and order pizza so that Jerry and I could go out to dinner together. I don't remember the exact words, but that night, he said something that for the first time indicated he might consider getting married. Some of that Disney magic had rubbed off on us.

By the time Jerry formally got around to asking me to marry him, almost everybody else already had. Our friends asked about it all the time. My friend Kate in Florida called to say she was getting married that fall; so were my friends at work, Jane and Julie. Were we next? everyone wanted to know. That summer, in one of her letters home from camp, Leigh enclosed a note for me: "Has Daddy asked you to marry him yet?" she asked.

One night in July, we stopped by Bob and Juliee Bliss's house for a glass of wine on our way out to dinner. Bob was Jerry's law partner, and he and Juliee are among our closest friends. After forty-five minutes or so, Jerry said we had to leave.

"Why don't you just stay for dinner? We'll put some chicken on the grill," Bob said.

"We can't," Jerry replied. "I have to take Karen to the San Francisco Rose (site of our first date) so I can ask her to marry me." That's the proposal I remember, although

121

I'm sure he said it again later.

I was at my mother's kitchen table, addressing our wedding invitations, when Channel 5 called about sending me to cover a hurricane blowing toward the Texas coast. We flew to Corpus Christi, then drove north, trying to get as close as possible to where the storm would hit. At times we thought the wind would blow us off the road; I filed a report by telephone from a roadside bar where a few brave souls had gathered to ride out the storm. Alicia hit Galveston, then moved inland to Houston. We worked our way there, and as we crossed the bridge toward Galveston Island, every other car I could see was headed in the opposite direction.

At that moment, it hit me: I was getting married. I was going to have a family. My contract was up the next spring. Maybe it was time for me to stop chasing hurricanes, and settle down to a more normal life. A reporter lives at the whim of news: a big fire, a tornado, an ice storm. I was also a little restless at work. After almost seven years at KXAS-TV, I was the senior reporter on the staff, and had covered almost every possible kind of story in Texas. The only way to move up in television news was to move on to a bigger market like New York, Chicago or Los Angeles, or to a network. I knew those jobs would be all consuming: I would have to travel anytime, anywhere. My life would be controlled not by me, but by unpredictable events in the world. And suddenly, I realized that I didn't want to live like that.

I came home from our honeymoon in Hawaii, put down my suitcases and became a working mother. Jerry and I had rented a new house in Richardson, a suburban school district in North Dallas, where we would be more likely to afford to buy a home. We had each been renting duplexes in the Park Cities, an exclusive, expensive part of Dallas, and Leigh had been going to Highland Park schools, but we couldn't afford to buy a house there, and we thought she and our family would fit in better in a suburban district with more working professional families like ours. In hindsight, the move was probably a mistake. Leigh went to Richardson schools from fourth through eighth grades, but she never really adjusted or felt comfortable there. She missed her old neighborhood and old friends, and when it came time for her to go to high school, we paid tuition to send her to the arts magnet high school, a Dallas public school with a program in dance.

That spring, in the midst of my contract negotiations at Channel 5, my friend Dottie De La Garza called me. Dottie was U.S. Senator John Tower's Texas press director, and I had always admired the way she did her job. She was straightforward and returned press calls promptly. She could answer a reporter's questions about her boss, or she could find the answer. In sharp contrast to some public relations professionals, who overwhelmed you with paper or drove you crazy with incessant phone calls, Dottie didn't send you something unless it was important. And she was very good at delivering her message.

I remember a news release she wrote about Senator Tower's upcoming visit to South Texas. Instead of merely announcing the trip, as most news releases would, Dottie made it relevant: "Senator John Tower will travel to Brownsville Saturday, bringing news of jobs and economic opportunity . . ." Dottie was also a working mother, the first person I knew who was really good at her job yet who often did it by phone from home, in between picking her children up from school. Dottie was calling to let me know that Senator Tower had been asked to cochair the Reagan-Bush 1984 campaign in Texas, along with a longtime Reagan volunteer named Martha Weisend. Would I have any interest in joining the campaign as their Texas press spokesman?

I don't think I would have had the courage to consider the leap from journalism to politics if I hadn't been married. Leaving television for a political campaign was an odd decision in many ways. It made no financial sense: I took a substantial pay cut. At the television station, I was negotiating a new contract that would take me from my salary of thirty-eight thousand dollars to more than fifty thousand dollars a year; at the Reagan-Bush campaign I would be paid half that, two thousand dollars a month. It didn't make family sense: I lived in Dallas and the campaign headquarters was in Austin, so I would have to commute. It wasn't a stable or long-term job: the position began on April 1 and ended in November, on Election Day. The campaign didn't offer benefits, or stock options, as my job at the television station did. I wouldn't vest in the retirement plan at the station until I had been there ten years, so I was walking away just three years short. But I was ready for a change. I was fascinated by politics; I had realized from covering it that the people who were elected and the decisions they made were important to people's lives.

Politics appealed to my competitive instincts; campaigns were exciting, captivating, a team sport. I wanted to know more, to learn it from the inside rather than watching it from the outside. The security of my marriage gave me the freedom to take a leap into the unknown, knowing it wasn't a free fall; I had a parachute at the end. Besides, I had spent seven years explaining what a difference politics made in people's lives; I wanted to be a part of making that difference. And I was sure that life on the other side of the camera would be more predictable, more manageable and businesslike. My venture into politics would be a six-month transition to a more normal life.

The *Fort Worth Star Telegram* called to ask about my decision, and I gave the reporter my first quote as a new public relations professional. It was terrible: "It has nothing to do with the station. I enjoyed working here very much. My contract was up in March, and I decided to look around for something else to do." Looking back, I realize I broke all my rules: I started with the negative: "It has nothing to do with the station," leaving everyone to wonder whether it really did. (All the people who have worked for me recently can't believe I ever said that; one of my most adamant mantras is to always lead with the positive.) And "look around for something else to do" sure doesn't sound very professional or profound. I had a lot to learn.

Tippit hosted my good-bye party at his house. My colleagues gave me a black and white television set for my apartment in Austin. And Tippit read the telegram he had arranged to have delivered from the vice president of the United States:

YOU'LL BE MISSED AT KXAS-TV; YOU'VE BEEN A HIT WITH US ALL. WE LOOK FORWARD TO YOUR JOINING OUR TEAM AS TEXAS STATE PRESS SECRETARY. WE'RE EXPECTING GREAT THINGS FROM YOU. HAVE A GOOD PARTY — AND WELCOME ABOARD.
SINCERELY, GEORGE BUSH

CHAPTER 4

Cried All Day

My new baby was fussy, inconsolable. He would not sleep or drink a bottle, or do anything but cry and shriek at the top of his lungs. I tried walking, rocking, singing, walking some more. By the early afternoon of April 24, 1987, I had called the doctor and rushed to his office: something was wrong with the precious new life that had been entrusted to me, and I could not make it better. "Babies sometimes cry," Dr. Prestidge offered as his only explanation, after he couldn't find anything specifically wrong. Robert and I returned home, where I walked and rocked, and he cried some more. When Jerry arrived home from work a little after five, I was hysterical. He took the baby and sent me to aerobics class.

I would later face consuming and chaotic times at the White House, long and trying days during the presidential campaign; but in terms of raw stress, a sense of total helplessness and hopelessness from someone who is accustomed to neither, nothing compares with the desperation of that long day. Sixteen years in the rearview mirror, it is almost, but not quite, amusing. I know I survived, and so did Robert, but I have never had a worse day in my life. It is memorialized on the baby calendar, amid the cheery stickers boasting of Robert's "first doctor's checkup" and "first smile," a three-word indictment of my maternal inabilities: "Cried all day."

We brought Robert home from the hospital in between an election day and the runoff; Fred Meyer was running for mayor of Dallas and I was his press secretary. On the original election night in April of 1987, Fred had come in a distant second. But because the leading candidate didn't get more than 50 percent of the vote, a runoff was scheduled for two weeks later, April 18, three days after my baby's due date. We worked frantically to close a big gap.

Fred's wife, Barbara, and some other friends had a baby shower for me at campaign headquarters because I was busy working. My favorite picture is one in which I'm standing in the doorway underneath two banners: one reads, IT'S A BOY, the other, IT'S A GIRL. My friends set up a mock election to vote for the baby's sex. In the picture, my huge stomach is obscured by the papers a colleague is thrusting toward me, getting my approval for a news release in the midst of the party.

I got up the next morning exhausted. I had been determined not to let my pregnancy interfere with my job, but for the first time, I just could not make myself go to the office; so I stayed home and puttered around the dining room, which we were converting into a nursery. Our house had only two bedrooms, ours and Leigh's, so we had moved the dining table into the den, and installed French doors to close off the room. Months earlier I had bought some cute sheets, with little blue teddy bears and colorful rainbows, and I washed them and put them in the new crib, which was already full of soft stuffed animals with two musical mobiles dangling overhead — rainbows and stars and suns dancing from their spokes.

Usually we ate dinner with friends on Sunday nights, most often at our house, but that night we were supposed to go to John Collins's house for barbecue. I just didn't feel up to it, so Jerry and Leigh went without me. Tired and grumpy that they'd gone off and left me, I walked over to my parents' house a couple of blocks away and visited with them, getting some advice from Dad about my almost-due income taxes, and then came home. When Jerry and Leigh got back from dinner around ten, Jerry poured himself a glass of wine, then looked at me, went back to the kitchen, and poured it out.

We went to bed, but I couldn't get comfortable. As I started to get up to go to the bathroom, my water broke. Jerry called the doctor, who told us to come to the hospital. But first, Jerry methodically took the sheets off the bed and carried them to the washing machine. I remember standing there, incredulous: "I thought we had to go to the hospital, not do the laundry."

I started having contractions and they hurt. I remember odd things about the next several hours at the hospital: how uncomfortable my dad looked when he came back into the room to see me, for one: I realized he was from a different era, when the women had the babies and the men didn't see them until afterward. I remember looking at Jerry and realizing there was no way he was going to lead the process we had learned in prenatal class, in which they teach the mother to focus on a spot on the wall while the husband encourages her to breathe through a contraction. I still laugh out loud when I think back to the first class: Jerry got confused, and thought he was the one who was supposed to focus on the spot.

After a few minutes of silence, I raised my head to figure out why Jerry wasn't talking to me, and saw him lost in space, gazing distantly yet intently at the spot on the wall.

The whole childbirth class was kind of a joke. Because Jerry had had a child before, I checked the box that said this was our second child, and ended up in a room full of mothers who said they were there because their experience of childbirth had been so awful the first time. Just what I needed to hear! It reminded me of a story Jerry loves to tell about our friends Juliee and Bob Bliss. When their daughter was born, the first thing Juliee said to Bob was "Get me a cigarette." After taking a deep drag, she added: "Don't ever let me forget how painful this was." Despite my husband's helpful reminder that early Native Americans used to get off their horses and have their babies by the side of the trail, my childbirth class had persuaded me that rather than trying to breathe and bear it, I would head straight for medication.

Like so many other things in my life, when my contractions started coming, they happened fast. My doctor almost waited too long to give me the epidural, and I'm not sure it fully worked, but the pain was not as intense as it had been, and suddenly the monitor started beeping, and the nurses rushed in and wheeled me down the hall. Robert was born just after eight o'clock on Monday morning, April 13, 1987.

"I have the shoulders; let's see (this part seemed to take forever) — it's a boy," the doctor proudly announced. I had said the politically correct thing: that I just wanted a healthy baby — but that wasn't entirely true. Deep down, I really wanted a little boy. We already had a daughter, I had grown up in a house with two girls, and I was overjoyed to have a son. My first glimpse of the baby was frightening; he looked bright purple, and I worried that something must be terribly wrong; but by the time the nurses cleaned him up a little, wrapped him in a blanket and brought him over and placed him on my chest, I thought he was adorable.

The nurses took Robert for a complete checkup and as soon as they moved me from the recovery room into my hospital room, Jerry took Leigh home to sleep and I called the campaign headquarters to check in with my candidate, Fred Meyer. He told me to worry about my baby, not his election, but the runoff was Saturday, and these last few days were critical. Fred was rushing around town, speaking to any groups and voters who would have him, and, frankly, there wasn't a lot I could do.

"He's just perfect," the pediatrician said when she came in to tell me about Robert's first checkup, a professional evaluation that confirmed my own judgment. I couldn't stop looking at him: the tiny little fingers, such detail in miniature; the soft skin, velvety smooth like the inside of a fresh coconut; the shock of dark hair; the mouth that was so little, yet could make such a big noise. The nurses kept trying to take him so I could sleep, but I wanted him in the room with me as much as possible. I have some favorite pictures from those first few days: there I was carefully giving Robert his first bottle, the look on my face more intense and focused than it would be even while working on a presidential speech; Leigh, beaming, her mouth full of braces, a dangly ring on almost every teenage finger, her arms encircling her new baby brother; Jerry, in the chair in the corner of the room, with Robert nestled in his left arm, looking utterly exhausted, as if he were the one who had the baby. He says he stayed up all night with me, but I know he nodded off a few times. You tend to notice things like that when you are awake and in pain and feeling a little resentful that your partner in this endeavor gets to sleep while you can't.

A now-faded Polaroid picture shows mother and new baby with a FRED MEYER FOR MAYOR T-shirt spread over us. Jerry took it and delivered it to my colleagues at campaign headquarters that first afternoon. Members of the campaign staff called me a few times for advice over the next couple days, and I felt the first pulls of the tug-of-war to come, responsibilities to my child anchoring one side, responsibilities to my job pulling at me from the other.

Fred's was one of a number of campaigns I had worked on since leaving journalism on my way toward a more "normal" life. My first, the Reagan-Bush 1984 campaign, had its state headquarters in Austin, so I had to commute while Jerry worked and Leigh went to school in Dallas. My friend Dottie, who had helped recruit me for the campaign, had worried about the effect of the distance on my seven-month-old marriage. Jerry and I talked about it and agreed that whatever happened, we would make sure to see each other at least every weekend.

The first few weeks, I flew home after work on Friday nights and then returned to Austin on the latest Sunday night flight. In between, I stayed in an extra bedroom at Jerry's niece's house in Austin. Lee Ann had a daughter and darling twin two-year-old boys. It was the first time I had been around very young children in a long time. I remember dressing to go to work with the twins sitting on the bathroom sink.

"What's that?" Zach would ask, reaching for my earring.

"Jake wants some," his twin would say, smacking his lips as he watched me apply my lipstick.

They were adorable, and being with their family kept me from being lonely, but it also made the separation hit harder the next week, when Jerry drove my car to Austin and helped me rent an apartment and some furniture. I dropped him off at the airport before he flew home to Dallas on Sunday night, then sat and cried in the almost-empty living room of my new apartment in Austin, my only company the ugly rented sofa and the television set that had been my farewell gift from Channel 5. What had I been thinking, leaving my new family, the husband and daughter I adored, my house and my friends and my familiar life for this zany adventure in politics? How could I have made Jerry do it all himself again: go to the grocery store, get Leigh to school, fix dinner, help with the homework? Was I being incredibly selfish?

At the office I was too busy to be lonely. Campaigns are constant motion, with reporters calling, volunteers coming and going, surrogate speakers arriving and leaving. In hindsight I realize that my first presidential campaign could not have been more different from my later travels with George W. Bush. I was at the bottom of the campaign structure, not the top, and for those of us in Austin, it was almost a campaign without a candidate. Not exactly, of course, but for us, Ronald Reagan was more a distant myth than a daily reality. We never even saw him except briefly at the convention and again later that fall, when we worked day and night for three days to get ready for a huge outdoor rally featuring both President Reagan and Vice President Bush. The rest of the time, we were doing what the national strategists told us to, organizing voter registration drives, assembling a grassroots campaign structure with volunteer chairmen in every Texas county, arranging and publicizing visits by administration officials and Republican activists.

The campaign gave me an early taste for the inevitable tension between those at the national headquarters who are in charge of the overall campaign and those in field offices who believe they know their own states better than anyone from Washington possibly could. Our cochairman, Martha Weisend from Dallas, an inscrutable white-haired woman in her fifties who had been Ronald Reagan's most active volunteer in Texas for years, was apoplectic when she learned the national team was sending Festus, from *Gunsmoke*, to the University of Texas campus to campaign for Ronald Reagan.

"Festus!" she huffed. "No one on this campus was even alive when *Gunsmoke* was popular," she complained. "They've never heard of Festus. Why in the world would people in Washington think college students in Austin would show up or be impressed by someone they don't even know?"

She was right — the turnout was lousy, and it was my first experience with the "national people," who don't always have the best feel for what's going on at the local level. (Or maybe they just couldn't find anyone else. When I became one of the people in charge of the national campaign, I learned that Hollywood wasn't exactly the best place to find supporters for Republican presidential candidates.)

Similarly, I remember Jim Lake, who oversaw all the communications at the national headquarters, periodically calling me to check in. He liked to hear directly from people in the states, he told me; he realized people in Washington sometimes got a skewed perspective of what was happening in the country at large.

I was the Texas press coordinator, in charge of getting as much Texas news coverage as possible for our in-state activities. I loved the work. Every day was different and our campaign manager, Linden Heck Kettlewell, nurtured a great sense of camaraderie and teamwork among our staff and volunteers. What we were doing was important; President Reagan was depending on us, and we could not let him down.

I was perhaps the only person in America besides Walter Mondale who honestly thought Ronald Reagan might not win reelection. I had never been in a campaign before, and I didn't know enough to be confident. I worked my heart out every day, spending long hours at the campaign headquarters, where every day began with a morning staff meeting. You were expected to be in your chair, ready to report on the activities of your division promptly at 8:00 a.m., or you would earn a disapproving frown from Linden, which no one wanted to have happen twice. The early mornings were hard for me, an abrupt change from my late-night reporting days. Linden was thoroughly professional, confident and in charge. She was a native Texan, but she had worked in politics in Washington and Nevada, for Senator Paul Laxalt, so she had much more experience than any of the rest of us. She was even taller than I am, almost six feet, and wore well-tailored suits and professional jewelry and makeup. She was savvy and tough, yet she also had a sense of humor and a wonderful laugh that I heard with much more frequency when we got together outside the office for dinner or shopping. Linden loved clothes and jewelry, and we would stop into Gem Jewelers or Scarborough's dress store downtown during lunch outings. She was in her midthirties and I was twenty-seven, a little older than many of the just-out-of-college campaign staffers, and we became good friends.

She respected my judgment about how stories would play in the media; she thought I had good political instincts; and she asked me to help edit the campaign plan she was writing for the state. I watched and listened and learned a great deal from her about politics and management. At night, when we were trying to get a big mailing out the door, Linden would sit in the midst of the volunteers, stuffing envelopes and sealing them. And you could find me and others on our staff there, too, because Linden's presence showed us that no job was too unimportant for everyone to pitch in and help.

The other constant daily presence was Martha Weisend, a lady who was gracious but never effusive; she had very high standards and most of the staff was afraid of her. She knew people all over the state and spent her time talking with them, learning what was really going on at the grassroots level. If you screwed up and a mailing didn't get out until late, you might as well fess up, because Martha would always find out when the letters arrived. She became a mentor, and a friend too, and taught us that the volunteers were the most important people in any campaign because we needed their help, and they had to want to show up every day.

Senator John Tower was our other chairman, and the Reaganites still mistrusted him because he had supported incumbent Republican president Gerald Ford in 1976. For a long time, that was the fault line in Texas Republican politics: Ford or Reagan in 1976. The Ford people were still mad at Reagan's supporters because they thought the Reagan challenge had weakened the incumbent president and cost the

Republicans the White House. The Reaganites thought the Ford people were suspect: go-along, get-along, status-quo establishment types who weren't true conservatives or they would have supported Ronald Reagan. Even eight years later, our presidential campaign organization was carefully balanced so as not to offend either camp: Tower was Ford, and Martha was Reagan.

I was neither, but I didn't tell anybody. As a nineteen-year-old SMU journalism student whose professors were excited about the Southern governor we had followed as he burst onto the national political scene, I cast my first vote for president for Jimmy Carter, the only time I have ever voted for anyone other than the Republican nominee for president. As President Bush would later say, when I was young and irresponsible, I sometimes acted young and irresponsible. I soon regretted my vote because I disagreed with most of President Carter's policies.

When Senator Tower visited the campaign headquarters every couple of weeks, we all worked hard to impress him. We tried to maximize publicity for his visits, since he was the highest ranking official we dealt with regularly. He was courtly and polite, a dapper man who despite being from a different generation, had a number of women working for him in high-level positions and treated us all equally and professionally. I would remember that years later when he was criticized during confirmation hearings after President Bush nominated him as secretary of defense. He was being vilified in the press as a womanizer, and I was frustrated that those in charge of his nomination wouldn't organize a news conference of the many women who had actually worked for him and thought highly of him. My friends Dottie and Linden and I all agreed he had been a good boss — fair, smart, and respectful. His wife at the time, the second Mrs. Tower, however, was volatile, and everyone had warned me to steer clear of her. I learned why when we arrived in Dallas for that summer's Republican National Convention.

I came in from Colorado, where Jerry and I had gone to take a few days off and attend the parents' day celebration at the summer camp Leigh attended outside Estes Park. Jerry and Leigh stayed and went on to visit Mount Rushmore, but I had to return to work for the Republican National Convention in Dallas, which the Texas delegation was hosting. We were staying at the

Fairmont Hotel, one of the most elegant in Dallas, but Mrs. Tower didn't like her room. She didn't like the second one either, and by the time she'd gone to the third and insisted that a couple of our staff members join her for lunch, we all just wanted to get out of her way. But she was adamant.

"What should I order you?" she asked me.

"Anything," I replied.

"Well, what?" she demanded.

"Anything, really, whatever you are having is fine."

"I can't order lunch unless you tell me what you want," she said.

"I'll have a ham and cheese," I replied, trying to come up with the easiest, most innocuous thing I could think of.

She studied the room service menu carefully. "You'll have ham," she announced. "The cheese costs extra." Somehow, I got through lunch, and left knowing that some people who gain power, even through proximity, abuse it and mistreat those around them. But over the course of a long career I have found that this is true far less frequently than the cynics would have you believe.

After the chaotic convention, which I spent mostly in the staff office at the hotel putting out news releases and publicizing the activities of the Texas delegation, the rest of the fall was a blur: long hours at work punctuated by brief visits with my family. With the election drawing closer, we worked Saturdays, and my time was so short that Jerry made most of the trips to Austin, taking in a Longhorn football game and bringing Leigh on weekends when she wasn't with her mother. I flew home for dinner with Jerry on September 10, the night of our first wedding anniversary, then returned to Austin early the next morning. President Reagan and Vice President Bush came to Austin for a huge outdoor rally, and none of us slept much for the three days before.

It's a big deal when the incumbent president comes to town, and the fact that the vice president would be in the same place at the same time, and that it was outdoors, drove the Secret Service crazy. For security, and to ward off the political threat that protesters would mar the occasion, we set up an elaborate operation to distribute more than thirty thousand tickets by mail and through our campaign headquarters, a form of screening designed to make it at least a little harder for some nut to gain access to the rally. After the long days of planning, the president and vice president were suddenly there, then gone, in less than an hour. I escorted a group of news photographers down to the front of the stage while President Reagan was speaking, and that was the closest I came to him, about twenty feet away. Afterward, I attended my first wheels-up party, which begins when the presidential plane leaves and the advance team and support workers celebrate their personal victory: getting the president and vice president in and out of town safely, producing both a big crowd and good television pictures. I was so exhausted I went home to my apartment after one drink and didn't even hear the phone ring when Jerry tried to call to tell me good night.

Suddenly, it was Election Day, and I had nothing to do. Election days are always the longest: the mail is all gone, media deadlines are all passed, and all the frantic activity just stops. Somewhere, in phone banks, a combination of paid telemarketers and volunteers are making phone calls, reminding regular Republican voters to get to the polls, but there is nothing for the campaign staff to do but speculate and worry. It's raining in Houston: that could lower turnout and hurt us. It's sunny in East Texas, so everyone's out fishing instead of voting. East Texas is Democrat country, but those are Reagan Democrats. We need them to vote before they fish. Of course, most of the information is completely unreliable, but it's all you have. After a few of these long nightmare days, I started an Election Day tradition: I go to the beauty shop and get my hair cut.

I was delighted when President Reagan won big, carrying forty-nine states; we packed up campaign headquarters, and I headed home. It was great to be back in Dallas with my family: I decorated the house for Christmas and picked Leigh up from school. We got a new cat and had a Christmas party for Jerry's office, then a New Year's party for our friends. I love to cook and went all out: a fancy dinner for the law firm, with grapefruit stuffed with crabmeat as the appetizer and filet mignon with béarnaise for the entrée. New Year's was more casual: we bought a ham and Jerry made his special chili. I made jalapeño cornbread, lots of dips, a black-eyed-pea appetizer, and Bloody Marys. (I know this because I always make lists of what I serve at parties.)

On January 2, 1985, I went to work at the federal offices of newly elected U.S. senator Phil Gramm, whose staff had noticed my work during the presidential campaign and asked me to serve as his press spokesman in Texas. I thought I had followed my own advice, the advice I now give young people who ask me how to balance career and family: make the ground rules clear going in. I had been up-front about my new family and my desire for a flexible schedule, and everyone had nodded and agreed. I guess I had envisioned working as my friend Dottie De La Garza had — getting the job done, but sometimes doing it from home. I quickly realized that the long office hours that seemed to be expected were at odds with my idea of a flexible schedule.

The first time I had to take my daughter to the doctor, one of my superiors (I won't name names to protect the guilty!) told me, "That's fine, just bring a note." A note! As if I were a schoolgirl who couldn't be trusted. I remember thinking, "If I need a note, maybe I don't need this job." The others in the office seemed to work all the time, late nights and weekends, and it didn't always seem particularly productive or necessary. Shortly thereafter, I learned I was pregnant (though I would later miscarry), and I knew with a new baby I would want even more flexibility, so after writing a nice resignation letter, I left after only two months in early March of 1985 to begin what I now view as my odd-job years.

A friend once clipped a newspaper cartoon for me that pictured someone standing at the side of a road with a sign: WILL CONSULT FOR FOOD. And that's pretty much what I did.

I wrote brochures for judicial candidates; and touted the zoo, and the arboretum, and the historic Old Red Courthouse in campaigns urging voters to approve the Dallas City and Dallas County bond elections. I worked first as a staff member and later as a consultant with Weekley, Gray and McKinney, the premier Republican political consulting firm in Dallas at a time when there were few such creatures. McKinney didn't exist; it was the name of the street where the office was located, but it made the partnership sound weightier. John Weekley was a handsome man in his early forties; I had gotten to know him during my reporting days as someone who was always good with an astute observation about the political process.

Enid Gray was a wise, insightful woman with great political instincts who had been a stay-at-home wife and mother for years, then joined the working world when she and her husband divorced. She had been instrumental in helping Fred Meyer — the businessman I would later work for during his campaign for mayor — engineer a Republican takeover of the Dallas County courthouse during his years as Dallas County Republican Party chairman. Enid and Fred and several other savvy local Republicans met every Saturday for lunch, and they invited me to join them.

Fred would come from the office, where he worked on Saturday mornings, Enid from the hairdresser, and I would come from home or aerobics class. They became my lifelong friends: Jim Oberwetter, Lee Jackson, Jeanne Johnson Phillips, Ed Kinkeade, Buck Wynne, Dick Smith, sometimes Phil Montgomery and Jim Richards. The participants have changed some over the years, but the tradition continues today, and if I'm ever in Dallas on Saturday, I try to join them.

We laughed and debated and strategized. We brought our most urgent problems to the Saturday lunch table: difficulty persuading voters it was all right to raise their taxes to fund arts projects; a candidate who was qualified but not charismatic; a message that wasn't resonating in the school board campaign. My political instincts were shaped and honed at those Saturday lunches as we plotted ways to win elections, at first for our local candidates in Dallas, and later, when Fred became the state Republican Party chairman, for Republicans across Texas.

I worked for some great business leaders during those years, too, including Norman Brinker, an inspiring leader who chaired the city bond campaign and Al Gonzalez, who went on to become an at-large Dallas City Council member. I learned a lot about management as they questioned our proposed tactics, budgets and expenditures. I advised a congressional candidate on press strategy and helped candidates prepare for debates, crystallize the issues, and deliver their messages in a way that would resonate with people. I wrote and even voiced several radio commercials for my friend Lee Jackson when he decided to run for county judge, and when we couldn't get a good picture of him, I took my camera to the park-and-ride lot that fall when I was pregnant, and snapped shots of him handing out brochures.

It was emphatically not, as journalist Paul Burka later wrote in an insightful *Texas Monthly* profile, "the fast track to the White House." Yet it taught me an appreciation for every aspect of campaigning: the volunteers who man the headquarters, the writers who develop the brochures and commercials, the demands on the candidates and their lives and families, the difficulty of putting together a schedule, and setting and sticking with a budget.

Most of my clients paid me; a few didn't, and it still annoys me. We didn't have a lot of money in those days. My husband had spent his savings and more on legal fees during his fight for his daughter's custody. He was a real estate lawyer, and Dallas was going through a real estate bust. Many of his clients had gone bankrupt, and Jerry and his longtime law partner eventually dissolved the firm and each went out on his own. We had put the money I had saved during my years at Channel 5 into our first house, a two-bedroom brick that was built around an open-air atrium and looked a little like a Chinese pagoda. I loved it. We had rented it for a year, and finally managed to finance it through the owner, who is still a friend. We loved living in our own house, in a real neighborhood. We were only a couple of blocks away from my parents, and we had the best neighbors in the world: a salt-of-the-earth, wonderful couple named Bob and Marie Cook, who spent every Saturday morning at garage sales and often came back with a toy for Robert.

When Robert was born, I knew I would have to go back to work, mainly for financial reasons, but in truth, I probably would have done some work anyway because it would have been hard for me to stay away. During Robert's early months, I scraped all the cabinets in the kitchen and repainted them, planted flowers, and spent his nap time engaged in frantic activity; but it wasn't enough. I enjoyed politics; I was good at it; and I liked the feeling that I was making a difference. I adored my baby, too, and I wanted it all: time to play and cuddle and love him, and time to advise candidates and earn a living.

I couldn't have done it without my parents, who volunteered to keep Robert a couple days a week while I worked. They also filled in for emergencies: some professional, some personal. When Robert was about three weeks old, I decided I had been so consumed with him that I had been neglecting my husband. My parents agreed to keep Robert overnight while Leigh spent the night with a friend and I "kidnapped" Jerry, taking him downtown to the Fairmont Hotel and out to eat dinner and listen to music. My parents also kept Robert that summer, when Jerry and I went to Colorado for our annual visit for parents' weekend at

Leigh's camp. I remember how much I missed him, and how shocked I was when we arrived back in Dallas. My parents met us at the gate, and Robert had grown so much in those five days that I barely recognized him.

I had an ongoing consulting arrangement with the Republican Party, but when they asked me to go to El Paso for an executive committee meeting one weekend in August, I didn't really want to leave my baby. Robert cried when I left, and I worried about him the whole weekend, even though he was with his dad and sister. The cat had been sick, and he died while I was gone.

I loved that cat. Fluffy curled up against the Fisher-Price baby monitor every night; he would move when the baby did, helping wake me up. I kept the monitor in my bedroom for more than a year, until my husband made me give it away.

Robert and I had bonded completely, and he cried almost every time I left him for almost four years. I'm sure my guilt about walking away, and my concern about whether anyone else would take care of him the way I did, had a lot to do with it. All I know is I love to teach the two- and three-year-olds in Sunday school, and I'm especially good with the little ones who cry when their mothers leave them. Robert loved me to hold him, and play with him and rock him; but there was one thing he didn't like. Once just after he had started talking, I was singing a lullaby, and Robert looked up at me: "Mommy," he said, "don't sing."

Robert was an industrious child. He "worked" at whatever we did, hammering boxes, helping his dad grill. One of my favorite memories is watching him follow Jerry up and down the lawn, with the Little Tikes lawnmower our neighbor Bob had bought him. He helped me water the flowers every morning, standing barefoot on his stubby little legs, directing the hose toward the begonias. One morning after Jerry had dropped Leigh off at school, he came home to find Robert's diaper and T-shirt flung across the front lawn, the hose still running. We had been watering flowers. Robert had suddenly started making little yelping noises; I looked down and realized his little legs and bottom were covered with ants. The only thing I could think to do was strip off his diaper and clothes and plunge him into the bathtub, before rushing him to the doctor for salve. Little raised bumps from the bites covered his legs, and I felt guilty for days for not watching him closely enough.

But we were to learn that accidents happen even when you are right there watching. One summer afternoon Jerry and I were sitting on the patio within two feet of Robert when he slipped on wet pavement and fell backward, hitting his head against the concrete. I rushed to him, and when he got up, he threw up; and we headed for the emergency room. Watching his tiny body slowly backed into that big CAT-scan tube was one of the worst moments of my life; Jerry thought I might need medical care before it was over. The doctors decided he might have a concussion, so we had to wake him up every thirty minutes all night. It was terrifying. Of course he didn't want to wake up, and he was so tired and groggy, I was convinced until morning that he might be brain-damaged.

By this time, Fred had been elected as the state Republican Party chairman and I did a great deal of his public relations and media work, so my phone rang all the time, with reporters, members of the Republican Party staff, or Fred himself on the line. I'm sure Robert hated it. We would be lying on the floor, pushing a ball back and forth, or sitting in the playhouse opening windows and doors; then the phone would ring, and suddenly he would lose my attention. One day he was sitting on the sink in my bathroom, brushing his teeth, when the phone rang and I ran to get it. I heard him calling me. I can't remember who was on the line, but it seemed important at the time. Robert kept calling, and I kept saying I was coming, until I heard a loud thud and a sudden cry. When I raced to the bathroom I found Robert on the floor, blood gushing from his nose. He had tried to climb down and fell.

I was scared to death, and furious with myself. At the pediatrician's office, the young doctor who was filling in that day first asked me what had happened, then started questioning Robert, who was only two. He wouldn't say a word, but I imagined he was eyeing me balefully, blaming me for what had happened.

I realized the doctor thought I might have hit him, which horrified me. Then I realized that, sadly, the doctor had to ask, because as any doctor or welfare worker will tell you, they see far too many cases of child abuse.

I can't understand how someone could hurt a child, but I did learn how difficult parenting can be: little children are demanding. They pull at you, try your patience, and wear you out. I remember many times watching my husband pull into the driveway, relieved that he was home to take

Robert and give me a break for a while. I have enormous admiration for parents who have to do it alone. I have never met a better match for my energy than my child, and I'm sure I was the same way for my parents — always questioning, arguing, challenging.

I learned that grandparents have wonderful reserves of patience. My father, an engineer, used to take Robert to construction sites, where they would watch for hours, fascinated, while Robert asked questions about the names and precise duties of all the machines. Years later, I went bird-watching during a nature tour of Texas with Governor Bush and his family. I was amazed as our guide, Victor Emmanuel, regaled us with facts and stories that made watching birds in a tree seem like enjoying a Broadway performance: "Look, the female is irate, look at her sticking her chest out, forcing her mate out of the nest, sending him on his way, and he's fighting back, letting her know he is not happy. Listen, that's a tree swallow and he senses an opportunity . . ."

In the same way, my father made a construction site come alive with stories about the machines and their missions. For a time, whenever I would ask Robert what he wanted to do, the answer was the same:

"Watch construction." But when I took him, I'm sure it was as unsatisfying for him as it was for me. Robert would ask me a question, and I would be thinking about something else. Robert learned early that his mother has an ability to concentrate and remove herself from any situation. My friend and longtime colleague Andi Ball once told me she had learned that even establishing eye contact didn't guarantee I was hearing what she was saying, and Robert and Jerry know the feeling well.

Robert adored his sister, and she was good with him, tickling, chasing, and playing hide-and-seek. She didn't like him to come into her room, which was fine with me, since it was so messy I considered it a health hazard, and she didn't like him to hang around when she had friends over, which was a little harder, because he wanted to be with the big kids. And their age difference meant that I frequently had to wake up Robert from his nap in order to pick up Leigh and her friends in the afternoon carpool.

The fall after Robert was born, I had joined Halcyon, a new public relations/public affairs firm in Dallas that had just been created by Dwight Smith and Jim Grant and several others, including my friend Enid Gray. They agreed to let me work part time, going to the office only two days a week and otherwise managing my work from home. I thought the support of an office, with in-house artists and computer experts and a secretarial staff to take phone messages, would make my work-at-home life easier.

It was a great group of talented people, and yet another learning opportunity, as I worked on media relations projects for some of the firm's corporate clients. When I had work to do and no one to keep Robert, I brought him to the office with me: Attila the Baby, Dwight christened him, because he could be loud and somewhat boisterous.

I had brought the Republican Party of Texas to the firm with me as my client, and with Fred as chairman, it was consuming more and more of my time. In 1990, Fred asked me to produce the Republican state convention, a ten-thousand-attendee event that was scheduled to take place in June at the Tarrant County Convention Center. It was the state version of the national extravaganza America watches on television every four years, except we have more delegates and alternates at the state convention. For six months, I stood in my driveway on my cell phone, talking about themes and lining up speakers and bands, discussing buses and fireworks and hotel and seating assignments, while Robert dug in the dirt with his favorite toys at that time, a big yellow bulldozer and dump truck. Andi Ball, the office manager at the state headquarters, handled most of the logistics while I focused on the program, but the two of us consulted about almost everything. Andi would fly into Dallas Love Field, and if the meetings weren't scheduled to last too long, I would bring Robert and drive the thirty-five or forty minutes to Fort Worth for meetings, then come back and drop Andi at the airport and head home.

Planning and overseeing the convention was one of the greatest challenges of my professional life. The level of detail was mind-boggling — planning how to house and move more than ten thousand people. Even providing coffee for morning caucus meetings attended by thousands of people is an expensive and complicated proposition. So is managing the themes and speakers and script of the convention to present a positive message for the Republican Party and satisfy the interests of as many of our candidates as possible.

Every guest and attendee at a convention believes he or she is a VIP, and most expect to be treated as such. Our volunteer chair, Billie Parker, was a flamboyant, outspoken, strong-willed Texas woman, determined to show off the best of her hometown, Fort Worth. At one very tense meeting, Billie announced we would be having a special fireworks display at the opening-night party; no matter what the fire department said, we would sneak it by them. I responded that we would comply with all the appropriate city and fire regulations or we wouldn't have a party. Everybody gulped; no one challenged Billie Parker, but I figured Fred paid me to do the right thing, not to get run over. In the end, the fire department approved a small display. The buses ran on time, the convention gave our candidates a grand send-off to the fall campaign, and I decided that in another life, I could be an events planner.

That fall, Fred talked to me about leaving Halcyon and working for him full time from my house. The Republican Party would install a computer and fax and phone lines, and I could spend more time with Robert, and devote all my professional energies to the Republican Party of Texas. It was yet another example of the innovative leadership of Fred Meyer: he got my full attention, and I was so grateful that I probably spent more time working for him from home than

I would have from an office. I spent hours on the phone with Fred or his administrative assistant, Judy Moran, and the Republican Party's office manager, Andi Ball; Fred didn't care where I was as long as he could find me.

Fred is a man of boundless energy and enthusiasm. A top-notch businessman who ran several major corporations, he called me every Sunday night for years because he wanted to get a head start on the week. By launching new projects and assigning duties to his key people on Sunday night, he stayed days ahead of his competitors, who showed up on Monday morning to begin looking through their in-boxes.

A tall, thin, wiry man, Fred is a disciplined runner and fierce competitor. For years he was a downhill skier, until he had to quit at sixty-three, because his knees wouldn't take it anymore. So he took up race-car driving, and drove ten or eleven amateur races a year on the professional racing circuit.

I learned to read a balance sheet from Fred, to develop a realistic budget, and to manage a large, complex organization. Fred knew every one of his employees by name, and he treated them all the same way — as crucial parts of the organization, from the personnel director to the woman making change in the cafeteria line.

Fred called the house all the time; even if Jerry or Robert answered the phone, I could hear his booming voice across the room, always cheerful, always taking time to talk with my husband and son. Once, when Jerry and I had to go out to a party, I asked Robert whom he would like to babysit for him.

"Fred," he replied. Fred loves that story and so do I, although I told Fred I didn't think I could afford him.

Under pressure from some in the Republican Party to establish a more visible and aggressive presence in Austin, where most of the state political news media was based, Fred asked me in the summer of 1991 whether I would consider moving to Austin the following year to run the state headquarters, and increase our presence as the voice of the opposition party. Jerry and I had been talking about moving to Austin anyway; he had even explored some jobs there. After Robert was born, Dallas had seemed too big, and cold. We wanted a smaller community with more of a family feeling, and Jerry had loved Austin when he'd grown up there.

Leigh had just finished high school, and moved out on her own. We tried to persuade her to go to college; she enrolled in some community college classes that fall, but I don't think she went much. Her last couple years of high school had been tumultuous. She chafed at our rules. After she got her driver's license, we insisted she call us when she got where she was going. She frequently forgot, and she was constantly losing her house key and waking us up when she came in late at night, sometimes long after her curfew. We would ground her; she would hate us, then be sorry; then the whole thing would start over again the next time she went out and forgot to call us when she got where she was going. Now she was living in an apartment, working in a restaurant. Robert was four, ready to start kindergarten the next year.

If we were going to make a move, this seemed like a good time. Jerry agreed that if I took this full-time job, he would work on his legal business from home so he could be there when Robert came home from school. First, though, I had to finish a job as media and advertising director for Steve Bartlett's campaign for mayor. Steve was a friend of everyone's in the lunch bunch; he was the longtime Republican congressman from North Dallas who had come home to run for mayor. Steve won, but the campaign was intense and grueling, and I told friends that I was retiring. I would work for the Republican Party, but there would be no more individual campaigns for me.

We moved to Austin between Christmas and New Year's. The packers came on my birthday. On the way out of town we stopped at the restaurant where Leigh was working. It was almost a disaster because the dog escaped from the car and was nearly run over in the parking lot. Leigh cried and promised to visit, and I said she could always move back home. Everybody laughed because we all knew that was the last thing she wanted to do. The move was probably hardest of all on my parents because they were accustomed to spending so much time with their grandson. But we felt the city, the job, the circumstances were all right for us, and as it turned out, we all fell in love with Austin.

"What exactly is it that you do?" the teacher asked me one day when I picked Robert up from his new preschool at Westlake Hills Presbyterian Church in Austin.

"I work for the Republican Party," I replied.

"That explains it," she said. She had been teaching a lesson on the Presidents' Day holiday and talking about George Washington, when Robert's hand started waving dramatically: "Mrs. Presock, Mrs. Presock," four-year-old Robert exclaimed. "The president is not George Washington. The president is George Bush."

I loved my years as executive director of the Texas Republican Party. For the first time, I moved out of a strictly public relations role and into management, overseeing millions of dollars and a vast statewide political operation. We ran schools to train our candidates on issues and media, conducted polls to develop themes and messages, conducted research on the Democrats, managed a massive voter database, operated a telemarketing operation to help fund it all, and led voter registration efforts and campaigns to support the Republican Party and all our candidates.

But throughout 1992, we were frustrated by the seeming unwillingness of the national party to listen to our concerns about the president's reelection. I wrote a lengthy memo to my boss, Fred Meyer, outlining a much more aggressive approach:

Currently, our program has major holes. We lack a clear, consistent message. We do not have a comprehensive earned media plan or an aggressive and proactive surrogate speakers program. County chairmen are calling to complain they lack information and materials . . . our mission is to run a campaign that functions primarily without our candidates yet is capable of maximizing the impact of their visits . . . special emphasis should be given to winning over the Reagan Democrats, the military/defense/veterans of Texas, Republican women in major metropolitan areas and younger voters, who may be swayed by the rhetoric and emotional appeal of the Democrats' baby boomer ticket . . .

Texas was President Bush's home state and he carried it, as expected. But after his national loss, my boss joined with several others to advocate reform of the Republican Party. In a letter sent to the entire Republican National Committee, Fred and his colleagues wrote:

The inside-the-beltway, non-elected Republicans have taken on all the characteristics of the Democrats. They believe all wisdom comes from inside the beltway. All those in the real world including Republican volunteers, workers, elected officials and voters are treated like mushrooms. The arrogance and disrespect displayed toward these Republicans by our own national organization is identical to that of long-term Democrat incumbent Congressmen who are accustomed to their perks and privileges and don't want anyone to change things. We've become too big and too bureaucratic . . . we need a better foundation, and that comes from the states up, not from Washington down . . .

The memo led to a series of sharp exchanges, with Fred later writing to the RNC chairman: "The Democrats' effort was strategically well-directed and well-coordinated. Yet we had no direct communication or input with our national party organization, and frankly, your RNC money was not well-spent here . . ." The effort made Fred something of a pariah, but I admired him for speaking out, and when a new national chairman was elected, he focused much more on working with the states. It was a lesson I would remember many times during our own presidential campaign: don't ignore the people at the grassroots who know their states best.

Throughout the rest of my tenure as executive director, my main attention was focused on the Texas state races. Communication was still my specialty, and I used a sharp tongue, a sense of humor and good relations with reporters to become a steady source of information for their stories. Pretty soon, whenever a statewide Democrat did something, the media would call me for a response. I had been criticizing Ann Richards for spending taxpayers' money on building a huge staff and bureaucracy in the governor's office, so when her staff gave her a parrot for her sixtieth birthday, I couldn't resist quipping, "I trust they taught it to say, 'Polly wants a bigger staff.' " When the Democratic lieutenant governor joked about the length of a state senator's skirts, I called him Archie Bunker Bob. And when Ann Richards couldn't make up her mind about whom to appoint to a vacancy in the United States Senate, and spent all of December and most of January interviewing and rejecting candidates, I called the eventual nominee the "holiday leftovers."

That remark was too personal, and not very Christian of me. I later regretted it, but a sharp tongue does deliver a clear message, and a Republican eventually won the Senate race. When the Democrats gathered for their state convention one year, I arranged for a massive billboard to greet them on the drive to the hall. On it was a quote from one of their candidates, back when he had run as an independent: THE DEMOCRATIC PARTY IS DEAD IN THIS STATE.

My most important mission, the one we felt would change the state most of all, was to help pave the way for our party to elect a Republican governor. Texas had had only one in the last century, Bill Clements, and Republicans held only two of seventeen statewide elected offices when I moved to Austin. The governor set the tone for the entire state, so Fred and I focused most of our attention and criticism on Ann Richards, leading a statewide campaign to defeat a school finance proposition she had supported. We developed and sent out massive mailings, and put together a statewide blitz of speakers and media events criticizing the Richards plan. The election was on the same day as the United States Senate race. We had a number of Republicans in the race — as a party organization, we couldn't choose a favorite — but we felt that mobilizing a big conservative coalition to defeat the Richards plan would help all the Republicans.

On election night, we exulted in two victories: Republican Kay Bailey Hutchison led all candidates and later went on to win the runoff for Senate, and we defeated Ann Richards's school finance proposition. Later I learned that that night had also been instrumental in George W. Bush's decision to run for governor the next year.

He had been attending the Kay Bailey Hutchison rally in Dallas when he saw Ann Richards on television, wringing her hands and saying she didn't know what to do about school finance. He thought: "I know what to do," he later told me, and seriously began to consider running for governor.

During my years at the state Republican Party, I also got to know and work with Karl Rove. Karl's direct-mail company handled the Republican Party's fund-raising mail, and he advised many of our statewide candidates. He was already viewed as the premier Republican consultant in the state, so I sought him out when I moved to Austin, and he and I began collaborating on ways to critique the Democrats. He was advising Kay Bailey Hutchison and invited me to her campaign meetings when she was finally the only Republican in the race; later, when she was unfairly indicted by the Democratic district attorney in Travis County, Ronnie

Earle, Karl and I worked together to fight back.

That was the first time in my career I remember feeling as if I were going to war every morning. The week after Kay had been elected as our new U.S. senator, investigators from the Travis County district attorney's office raided her office and later indicted her on what we all thought were trumped-up charges that she had engaged in politics from her state office. The words *indicted* and *senator* do not go well together; even being accused of a crime can often be fatal to a political career. Our research showed that the grand jury included nine people who had voted in Democratic primaries and no Republican primary voters. We felt it was a clear case of partisan political harassment, orchestrated in retaliation for the Democrats' loss in the Senate race.

Fred and I marched into battle. I have always said that the times when you want to hide under your desk are the times when it is most important to communicate, and we did with a vengeance, calling the prosecution a "witch hunt," and "vicious partisan politics orchestrated by a Democrat district attorney and a stacked Democrat grand jury." We started turning the heat up on other Democrats, too, especially Ann Richards and her thirteen political phone lines.

" 'Texas Governor Ann Richards and her staff apparently run a massive political operation by telephone from the state governor's office, using more private telephone lines in the taxpayer-funded state office than the entire Republican Party of Texas does from its state administrative offices,' Republican Party of Texas Chairman Fred Meyer said today . . ." one of our news releases read.

When it came out that other officeholders had made political calls on state lines, and that Richards's staff had destroyed some of the records of her phone calls, our criticisms dominated headlines across the state.

The February morning Kay was scheduled to go on trial in Fort Worth, I was at my office when Karl called: "They've dropped the charges," he exclaimed gleefully.

"I'm on my way to get you; we're flying to Fort Worth to meet with Kay," he said. We literally ran through the airport, making it to the Jetway just as they were about to close the door. The next day, for the first time in my life, my picture, or at least part of it, was on the front page of the newspaper, standing behind Kay Bailey Hutchison as she hugged a friend, huge smiles on her face and mine. Sometime thereafter, she sent me a handwritten note that I kept as a reminder

174

of one of my life's most intense public relations crises: "Dear Karen, You have done such an outstanding job for the Republican Party of Texas. I could never have made it through the last two years without your support and counsel. Thanks, Kay."

As we turned our attention toward the state elections of 1994, our hard work had paid off. Texas was changing, and we had an opportunity to elect a historic number of Republicans.

"We're not just running for office anymore," Fred said in a letter we sent to party activists that spring. "Republicans are ready to run Texas and when we do, we'll make it a safer place with better schools and productive jobs, a place where government supports, rather than undermines, our families and the values this country was built upon."

Despite Fred's tremendous successes, he faced an internal challenge. A lot of the new grassroots activists in our party were very conservative, and they thought Fred was too establishment, not one of them. It was hard for me to imagine that Fred Meyer, one of the most conservative people I knew, wasn't conservative enough, but we knew he would face a tough election contest. I thought he could win it, and so did he, but Fred de-

175

cided a bloody battle for chairman wouldn't be good for our candidates during that critical election year. He announced he would not seek reelection. Shortly thereafter, I announced that I would resign as well after the new chairman was elected, because I had seen the importance of a close working relationship between the chairman and the executive director.

The candidate whom Fred had supported to replace him was defeated, and it would be an understatement to say that the new chairman, a maverick activist from Dallas, didn't like any of us very much. Proving that politics can be very petty, the first thing he did as the new boss was to order me to fire Karl Rove. He couldn't fire me because I had already announced I was leaving. I had promised to stay for two weeks to ensure a smooth transition, but when I got to the office the following Monday, I learned my services were not needed in this new administration. Sometimes the problem with politics is it's just too political.

I had been attending weekly "George W. Bush for governor" meetings, organized by Karl, to give input on campaign themes and messages. After I announced I was leaving the Republican Party, campaign manager Joe Allbaugh called to say George W. Bush wanted me to join his campaign staff. I was torn. I had already participated in my last campaign, the difficult one for Dallas mayor. I knew that campaigns demand all your attention and thought, and I didn't want to be consumed. I had a seven-year-old son and a nice life. During the Republican Party years, I had been in charge of my own schedule, able to leave work to join Robert's class on field trips. I went to aerobics class at lunchtime, and was active in my new church teaching children's Sunday school. I knew a campaign would demand constant travel and I would be away from home many nights and weekends.

On the other hand, I had spent the last several years of my life helping to position our party to elect a governor. Surely I could give it six more months. That summer, I joined what most people thought was the long-shot campaign of George W. Bush for governor of Texas. You're going to be in a fish bowl, Fred had warned me when I had first moved to Austin to direct the state party, but neither he nor I could have imagined just how big the aquarium would prove to be.

CHAPTER 5

Campaign of Joy

Somewhere along the way, we started calling it "the campaign of joy." We were on a mission: George W. Bush was running for governor of Texas for all the right reasons, and against all the odds. Even his own mother had told him that he couldn't beat Ann Richards. The incumbent was popular, at one point posting the highest approval rating of any governor in the nation, and she had become a Democratic Party celebrity after the 1992 national convention where she famously derided then-President George H. W. Bush: "Poor George, he can't help it. He was born with a silver foot in his mouth." She directed the same air of condescension at George W., calling him "boy," and "young George" even though he was forty-eight years old; her supporters christened him "shrub."

The air of arrogant superiority Texas Democrats directed at George W. Bush would be echoed by the press and national Democrats later, when he ran for president, and each time it only made me more committed to his cause. I hadn't started the campaign expecting to like it; I knew how intense and draining it would be. Campaigns consume you, snatching every waking thought, forcing you awake in the middle of the night with unexpected ideas and wish-you-had-said retorts. But I could stand anything for the few months until Election Day, and then it would be time to find a nice, normal private sector job.

I didn't really know George W. Bush the first day I stepped onto his campaign airplane; my only experience working with him had been brief, a couple of days during the 1990 Republican state convention several years before. I had been in charge of producing the convention's overall message and script, and he was one of the temporary chairmen. I vividly remember my first impression: fast. George Bush talked fast, moved fast, decided fast. He was looking at a script that I had written and he was supposed to read the next day: "That's fine; this is too long. I'll cut it down. What time do you need me? See you then," he said, and he was gone. Only years later did I learn what a compliment his mostly minor changes were. Many a speechwriter has learned you do not just hand something to George W. Bush and expect him to read it. You had better be prepared to answer questions, crystallize the thoughts: "What exactly does this mean? This doesn't get to the point. Say it more directly."

Just before the convention was called to order that summer afternoon in the make-shift VIP room behind the stage, people crowded around to meet the owner of the Texas Rangers baseball team and eldest son of the president. He had an intense focus, a quick quip, an enveloping smile for each of them. I introduced him to my husband and son, who had stopped in to visit me. In the first of my family's many pictures with George W. Bush, he and Jerry look younger, and I am thinner. My hair was still brown with not even a hint of gray, and in my arms, Robert was just a toddler, aged three. Jerry had brought Robert to Fort Worth for the weekend knowing that would be the only way I would have a chance to see him. Because I was one of the convention planners, the Worthington Hotel had given us a grand suite that even had a piano. But as anyone who has spent time with an active three-year-old knows, even a piano doesn't make life easy cooped up in a hotel room.

My husband was committing his entire weekend so I could snatch a few minutes with my son. Jerry is the most unselfish person I know, and that's one of the things that made me so angry when incumbent Governor Ann Richards delivered what became known as her Prince Charming speech.

She was speaking to a gathering of teenagers called Texas Girls State, trying to urge the young women to become independent and take charge of their own lives, but her words were bitter, even hostile: "Prince Charming may be driving a Honda and telling you that you have no equal, but that won't do much good when you've got the kids and a mortgage and he has a beer gut and a wandering eye. Prince Charming, if he does ride up in a Honda, he's going to expect you to make the payments," she told them.

My appalled reaction was the first message I ever communicated for George W. Bush. I wasn't even on his staff yet, but someone from the campaign called and asked me to do some television interviews because they thought criticism from a woman would resonate more. It was terrible that a leader of our state would offer such a negative view of marriage and family, I said; our governor had failed to set a positive example for either our daughters or our sons. I also wrote a newspaper editorial just to blow off steam. I never tried to publish it because I didn't want my personal story to reflect on my new boss, but I've saved it for all these years. It sums up what I believe are some of the failures of a feminist movement that too often seeks to empower women at the expense of men:

Let me introduce Governor Richards and her bitter stereotypes to my Prince Charming:

When we met, he was a single parent working full time and struggling as all single parents do to juggle his responsibilities to his job and his young daughter. Far from a wandering eye or payments on a Honda, he was worried about getting to the after-school program on time and whether macaroni and cheese would be okay again for dinner.

He was awarded custody of his daughter after a trial in 1978, when she was just five, far too young to know that at that time, a Daddy winning custody of his children was a most unusual occurrence (by the way, Governor, he paid the legal bills for both sides). He battled plenty of stereotypes back then, once told haughtily by a pediatrician's receptionist that Saturday-morning appointments were reserved for working mothers. "I am a working mother," he calmly replied.

We've been married now for almost eleven years. His daughter, almost grown, still calls her dad almost every day, and he's known as the coach among our son's friends because of his volunteer work in soccer and baseball. When I made a career change ten years ago, leaving journalism for politics, he gladly helped support me while I took a substantial pay cut to join a presidential campaign. When our son was born, he again supported my desire to stay home and work only part time during his early years. Then, when our son was almost ready for kindergarten and I had a great career opportunity in Austin, we turned tables. My husband agreed to be the one who greeted the school bus every afternoon while pursuing his legal business, mostly located in Dallas, from our home in Austin.

An equal partnership sounds almost trite for what we together have allowed each other to accomplish, while ensuring that we gave our children the love and care to which they are entitled. That doesn't mean it's always easy — it's frequently not — or that we're not fortunate — because we are.

But we cannot allow a leader of our state — in this case Governor Ann Richards — to undermine what we do every day by letting her tar my husband and countless Texas men with her broad brush of bitterness and defeat. Sure, some of them may be less than perfect and some may be downright lousy people, but many, many more of them are good men, good husbands and good fathers.

The worst among us cannot be the standard we set for our children. We must not allow the governor to tell our daughters that our sons are all jerks who should not be trusted. We cannot allow her to tell our daughters to expect only philandering and financial irresponsibility from our sons. At all costs, don't allow our sons to hear or heed this tragic example of what our state's leaders intend for them. Don't allow the governor to tell us all that parenthood, rather than the most fulfilling experience in life, means you may get stuck with the kids.

Governor Richards, her public relations team and some columnists argue she was just giving young women an important lesson in self-responsibility. The intent may have been right, but the content was wrong, terribly wrong. Self-responsibility never begins with placing blame on other people or groups of people, in this case, according to the governor, all "those men" who want to leave you the kids and the bills.

Today's young women are not victims and they don't need the governor telling them they should expect to become victims of men, or anyone else. We should encourage our children, both young women and young men, to be independent, responsible, honorable individuals. We should also teach them to strive for the best rather than brace for the worst, to work for a life where they can have a happy family life and fulfilling career if they so choose. There are plenty of examples; it's tragic that someone in a position to tout them chooses to cast blame and suspicion rather than hope and opportunity.

So I was on a personal mission when I went to work for George W. Bush's campaign, committed to electing a governor who would set a better example for my own children. I even thought we had some chance of winning. As director of the Republican Party, I had often argued in the media that Ann Richards's personality was popular, not her policies; those comments and my critiques of Ann Richards's performance were what had brought me to the attention of the Bush campaign in the first place. I agreed with George W. Bush that Ann Richards was vulnerable on the issues, and he was focusing on them, from education to welfare to juvenile and civil justice laws. I knew that I liked George W. Bush's philosophy; what I didn't know yet was how much I would learn to like him.

My first few days at campaign headquarters convinced me that I had to get out on the road; the reporters were all calling me with questions about my new candidate, and I didn't know him well enough to answer them. So I got on the plane that July morning, clutching a large handful of pink message slips.

"What are those?" George W. Bush asked, pointing suspiciously at the thick stack.

"Press calls," I replied.

"Don't return them," he ordered, tersely.

My life as a press secretary passed before my eyes. Returning calls is the first rule of working with the media; it was the way I had established credibility at the Republican Party, the way I had been able to critique Ann Richards effectively. Reporters knew if they called me for a reaction to something the governor had said or done, I would always call them back before their deadlines with something quotable to say. It had taken years to build that credibility; now, my new boss was ordering me not to return calls. Maybe I had made a huge mistake.

"We have to return them," I insisted, appalled. "I always return every press call before I go home for the day."

"What are they asking about?" he wanted to know.

"Everything; it's all over the map," I said, beginning to read some of the message slips, containing queries ranging from details about his position on gambling to facts about his past business dealings.

"We have to have a focused message," he said. "Answering all those questions will get us off track."

"Well, then, we'll just have to figure out what to say," I replied. And figuring out what to say, how to respond to press questions, how to make news and stay on message is what we have been doing ever since.

It took a while, but I later realized he was testing me. He explores, prods, then carefully watches how someone reacts to his pointed questions, or orders with which they disagree. It's the way he evaluates how secure you are, how certain of your convictions. He wants to find out if you are willing to stand up to him, willing to argue for your point of view. I didn't know it, but I had passed my first test.

I also thought he was absolutely right about message discipline; it was one of my own mantras. The month before I went to work for his campaign, the campaign manager, Joe Allbaugh, had forwarded from the candidate a copy of a memo, prompted by his concerns that some of his campaign operatives were being too cute, playing a game rather than delivering a substantive message:

to campaign heads and honchos
this is a rare ranting by the candidate.

I am concerned about our message. We have established broad themes of change and the theme that texas needs a new generation of leadership

188

to effect the changes. The schools, criminal justice systems, and welfare are our beachheads. We should constantly aim every remark by candidate spokespersons and staff toward our strength.

We should never debate on their terms nor should we fall into their traps by playing got'cha with them. Take for example the stuff about whether I am experienced. We should say that look where we are with experience, schools stink, crime is up. We need new thinkers to solve the old problems that have gotten worse under ann.

Our message meetings should constantly review the necessary bridges to hammer our points. The temptation is to hit ann or some spokesman, which is ok so long as the ultimate objective is to score on the need for change in areas that matter to people and their lives. The message is always confirming the fact that I want to help everyday Texans have a better life.

Fight fiercely
Yours in victory

It wasn't signed, but the header at the top of the page said: "Bush, GW." He had typed then sent it from the fax on his home computer. And when I saw it, I realized I was going to work for a candidate who understood the critical importance of making his message relevant to people's daily lives.

That first week on the campaign trail, I watched his stump speech carefully. He had been giving virtually the same one since the start of the campaign, and it clearly connected with people. They applauded the need for better schools, tougher laws and welfare reforms. Their heads all nodded when he arrived at his signature call to restore personal responsibility and change the culture from one that too often delivered the wrong message: "If it feels good, do it; and if you've got a problem, just blame someone else." But one line rankled every time I heard it; it struck me as off-putting and out of character.

"You know in your speech, when you declare 'I am a capitalist!' " I said one day on the airplane. "It doesn't come across right. Why do you do that?"

"Because I am a capitalist," he said pointedly. "Aren't you?" His eyes narrowed suspiciously, as if he had unknowingly hired some Marxist to join his campaign and was only now discovering his mistake.

"Of course I am, but it just doesn't sound right when you say it that way," I said.

"How would you prefer that I say it?" he asked, a little mockingly, "given that I am a capitalist, and we live in a capitalist system where people risk capital — that's how our economy works."

I was undeterred, as I generally am when I'm on a mission. "Talking about the free enterprise system might sound better," I suggested. For the next few speeches, whenever he looked out in the crowd and noticed me watching from the back of the room, after he said, "I am a capitalist," he would follow it with, "I believe in the free enterprise system." As I watched the faces in the crowds, I was increasingly convinced that the declaration "I am a capitalist" just didn't work; people fidgeted when he said it. Clearly I would have to bring it to his attention again.

We settled onto the airplane, and took off for the next stop. I had finally figured out what was bothering me: the line sounded exclusive, not inclusive, totally unlike the rest of his speech.

"How was the speech?" he asked, and I had my opening.

I stood up, waving my arms dramatically

for good measure. "I am a capitalist," I said in my loudest, most exuberant voice, my finger punching into the air for emphasis. "I am a capitalist — a *rich business* guy, and *you* — why, *you* are *not!*"

He half glared, half-laughed, and pretended to ignore me, while Israel Hernandez, his young travel aide, convulsed with laughter in the front seat, trying to make sure George W. didn't see him.

"What's so funny, Israel?" George W. demanded. And he never said it again.

Looking back, it was my favorite campaign, in some ways more consuming even than the presidential race, because it was so personal, so close. Almost every morning, I left home before dawn and took the Southwest Airlines 6:30 a.m. flight to Dallas, to join up with George W. and Israel. The three of us spent the day flying around the state in the "campaign plane of Texas," an eight-seater King Air. Volunteers picked us up when we landed in a city, and usually brought several friends who wanted to meet the candidate.

George W. got the passenger seat as Israel and I crammed into the small backseats of cars and vans across Texas. At every stop, George W. would give a speech and shake hands and work the crowd. Israel and I would do anything else that needed to be done: move the stage so the sunlight didn't appear from behind the candidate, giving his eyes green raccoonlike shadows; form a wall with our bodies to help him make his way through a crowd so we wouldn't be late to the next event; explain his policy proposals to local reporters in English, or in South Texas, Spanish, with Israel there to help translate my halting attempts to remember words from my early life in Panama. The evenings brought fundraisers, mostly closed to the press, and usually we were close enough to an airport that I would fly home to Austin to tuck Robert into bed while George W. and Israel did the fund-raiser and then returned to Dallas; George W. also wanted to get home to see his wife and daughters after a long day on the trail.

From their conversations, I soon realized that Israel was living at the Bushes' house. I was touched when I learned why: His apartment had been ransacked early one morning by an intruder who had taken almost everything; when Israel called the candidate to explain why he would be late, George W. insisted that he move in with them.

The very first week, George W. invited me to stay in Dallas after a day of campaigning to have dinner and meet his wife, Laura. We went to the City Café, a charming New Orleans-style restaurant that has good food and service without being too pretentious about it. We talked mostly about our families: how Mrs. Bush and their twin daughters were handling the changes his campaign was forcing in their lives, how my husband would manage with me on the road so much of the time. I liked Mrs. Bush immediately. She was different from her husband — calmer, less kinetic — and she had a natural warmth and relaxed sense of humor. As a couple, the Bushes were open and welcoming; their affection for each other was obvious, and infectious; I felt as if I had known them for a long time.

On the campaign plane, in between stops, we talked and laughed and strategized. Israel later told me my arrival brought a big change: we started predicting that day's media questions, and talking through George W.'s possible answers, the best way to bridge from the question to the message he wanted to convey. Until then, the campaign had been handling the administrative end of press relations: putting out news releases and scheduling interviews; but no one had been at the candidate's side at every stop, helping prepare him for the reporters he would see and the questions they would ask. I've always felt it's one of the most important things I do: anticipate the media's questions and help think through the possible answers. This is where my early training as a reporter is invaluable. I feel I've failed to do my job if the candidate is asked a question we haven't discussed.

We shared stories about our families. One morning I noticed George W. was uncharacteristically tired, rubbing his face in his hands, and yawning. He had been up much too late the night before, he explained, waiting to pick up his twin daughters from a party. He had been under strict orders to wait in the car, outside; under no circumstance was he to venture inside the house. His girls were going through then what my son would experience later on a smaller scale: the teenage mortification that makes it bad enough even to have parents, much less parents who are recognized and pointed out by other people. Their dad was already visible in Dallas as the owner of the Texas Rangers; now that he was running for governor, his face was on television all the time, on the news and in ads. So he sat outside, waiting in the car, as he watched other parents approach the door, go inside and emerge with their children, until his daughters finally came out just before midnight, way past his usual bedtime.

We shared stress. I trace his aversion to beeping noises to the 1994 campaign. I'm not very capable technologically, and either I didn't know or didn't think to turn my beeper onto a vibrate setting. It was always going off, interrupting our conversations, the precious moments of relaxation between events. The pages never brought good news, only bad: Ann Richards had attacked George W. Bush's latest proposal, saying it would cost a billion dollars (everything we proposed in that campaign cost a billion dollars, or so they said); Ross Perot was going to endorse Ann Richards (She can have Ross Perot; I'll take Nolan Ryan and Barbara Bush, my candidate said); one of his business partners had ties to gambling or real estate or big insurance and therefore George W. Bush would be a lousy governor. Assassination by association is a time-honored campaign tactic; at some point, after yet another attack about yet another one of his partners in the Texas Rangers, I asked him how many partners he had.

"More than eighty, I think," he said, and I remember thinking it was awful news because that was so much potential fodder for the campaign mill. For months, Democrats and the press tried to force us onto the defensive, claiming George W. Bush was "owned" by one of his partners in the Texas Rangers, businessman Richard Rainwater. To this day, I have never even met Richard Rainwater, much less felt he had any influence on any policy or decision. He is a successful businessman who gave money to George W. Bush because he was his partner and friend; I always thought the reverse would be more telling — what would it say if a candidate's business partners and friends, the people who know him best, did *not* support him?

But the press never sees it that way, and neither do political opponents, who latch on to any potential avenue of attack. It's a great example of how some of the stories that dominate the front pages, and consume so much time and attention, later turn out to be nothing more than distractions.

Despite it all, we laughed. We laughed at bad jokes we had heard. We laughed at the silly things people say. We laughed about the hostess in New Orleans who took one whiff of the candidate who arrived at her front door after a hot and sweaty day of campaigning in East Texas and retrieved a bottle of her perfume: "Here," she insisted to Israel, "make him use some of this."

George W. laughed at my exuberance. "I'm so glad it's fall. I love fall . . . Look at the ocean; I love the ocean. Look at those magnificent palm trees . . . South Texas is beautiful. I love South Texas . . . Look at the mountain, and the way the light falls on it. I love El Paso . . . I love the state fair — the old carnies and the junky food and the midway games and the crafts pavilion with little old ladies' jams and jellies. It's so full of energy and life . . . I love small towns; the people are all so friendly . . . I love East Texas, the way the pine trees stretch to the sky . . ."

"You love everything," he told me once, laughing; "you love spring, you love fall, you love summer, you love winter, you love the beach, you love small towns, you love the mountains . . ."

And I guess I do. We all have different gifts; one of mine is joy. It springs from a grateful spirit. I am thankful for life and beauty and special occasions, and many seemingly normal things are special to me: the first day of fall when the air is crisp and I know the leaves will soon begin turning, the powerful pounding of the white foaming surf against the hot, grainy sand of the beach. As my pastor, Doug Fletcher, once put it, if you know that God loves every one of us so much that he sent His own Son to die for our sins, your view of life is not determined by whether you look at the glass as half empty or half full: your cup is overflowing.

I quickly learned that George W. Bush has an infectious spirit too; he finds the humor in life, embellishes and enjoys it. In charge of keeping us on schedule, Israel kept searching for ways to let the candidate know when he really had to wrap up his speech and stop shaking hands or we would be late to the next stop, versus when he had time to wrap up gradually, and linger a little on the way out the door.

"Maybe we could have some signals," Israel suggested one day on the plane. I seized the moment, embarking on a series of elaborate finger-to-nose points, mixed with ear tugs and body brushes that would have made a baseball manager proud; George W. joined in, to a growing swell of laughter. Off and on for the next several weeks, in the midst of a speech, he would innocuously brush his finger to his nose, continuing the private joke, and forcing Israel and me to choke down laughter in the back of the room.

I learned how fully George W. Bush threw himself into everything — laughing, working or exercising; everything was all out, never halfway. "Left it all on the field," he'd say, using the sports analogy as he sank into the plane seat, exhausted after hours of giving his all to individual encounters with each of the hundreds of people who had come out to see him. Later he did it in New Hampshire, and all along the presidential campaign trail too, driving himself, pouring his energy into greeting every person. He only needed to shake hands for a couple of minutes, enough to get good television pictures, but the schedulers learned back in 1994 that if George W. Bush was working the crowd, they had better leave enough time for the whole crowd; he always wanted to return the huge favor each person had done by showing up.

I realized then the one word that I would use if I were only allowed one to describe him: *engaging.* He engages intensely, looking you right in the eye, drawing you in. For the minute or two you talk with him, you command all his attention, every bit of focus. "He never better-deals you," his lifelong friend Roland Betts told me once, when we were talking about the president's ability to connect with people. "He never looks over your shoulder for the next person. When he's talking with you, he's talking only with you. He's been that way as long as I've known him, even in college."

At editorial board meetings in small towns, he'd talk for an hour when thirty minutes would have been more than enough, especially when only one or two writers showed up. He would give them the full load, every detail of his eighteen-point juvenile justice plan and his vision of an education system where schools were funded centrally but governed locally. I tried to write a new speech once, focused exclusively on criminal justice issues because he was speaking to a law enforcement group. I thought a new speech would give us an opportunity to make news, deviate from the standard fare reporters had grown bored with; he thought I just didn't understand what was important.

"Just because they are police officers doesn't mean they don't care about schools or welfare," he admonished me. "They have kids; they need to hear about my plans for schools. They want to know about welfare reform." If people took the time to come see him, they deserved to hear everything — all his plans to make Texas a better place.

I also learned that for all the fun and humor, he was a hard worker, serious about his job. The media has never quite understood this; later, during the presidential campaign, they seemed to think that because he took time to exercise every day, he wasn't working hard. I never understood the logic: because George W. pushed himself, running several miles at a very fast pace to keep his body fit and mind sharp, he was somehow goofing off.

And one of my biggest failures is that I've never figured out how to communicate effectively one of his greatest strengths, the thing all the people who work for him learn he does best of all: ask questions that bore straight to the heart of any matter. Our campaign policy office, led by a brilliant and thoughtful lawyer named Vance McMahan, was always sending us reams of material, background briefings on new policy proposals and important state issues. I had to read and absorb and try to remember it all; so did the candidate, and somehow, he always managed to stump us with his questions.

It became almost a game: when Vance or Dan Bartlett or others on the policy staff knew they had to brief the candidate on a proposal, or if we were on the road and I was trying to relay information on their behalf, we would all try to anticipate and answer every question he could possibly raise.

We never once succeeded. He has a laserlike ability to reduce an issue to its core. Many times his questions were fired at me on the way to an event. I would be able to answer the first couple, but eventually he would probe past my knowledge, and I would frantically call the campaign headquarters for help from the policy shop. They would scramble to find the answer, which I would deliver just before the next news conference or editorial board meeting.

Over the years, I've realized his questions allow him to ascertain quickly how much you know, and whether, therefore, your opinion should be considered and relied on as part of a decision, or whether you are uncertain, in which case he moves on to someone else.

His questions about new criminal justice laws taking effect on the first day of September 1994 had led to an early morning news conference where he critiqued them, and Governor Richards for allowing them to become law. We had the news conference in the dark because this was Texas and the first day of the fall campaign was — even more important — also the opening day of dove season. I like to say I had never been dove hunting before, and I still haven't.

I had opposed the hunt, not because I

have anything against hunting, but because September 1 was the day that new state laws made sentencing more lenient for certain drug crimes. I thought criticizing Ann Richards for weakening laws against drug dealers was a better political position than blasting away at birds with a shotgun. I also couldn't get past the remembered gag reflex of a ten-year-old girl who had seen birds falling bloody from the sky, then learned they were in her soup.

"No blood," I had said. "If you have to go hunting, let's not have bloody pictures on TV."

I thought the whole idea of a candidate for governor going hunting on the opening day of dove season was a Texas macho thing — for the women as well as the men. Ann Richards couldn't stand to let the guys outdo her at something a lot of women did, too; George W. Bush couldn't stand to let Ann Richards claim hunting as her turf when he had hunted birds as a boy. That summer, Ann Richards had been pictured on the cover of *Texas Monthly* magazine, shotgun in hand, a good old girl, even though she had vetoed a measure that would have allowed Texans to vote in a referendum on carrying concealed handguns. Some of our supporters thought her election-time interest in hunting was primarily a public relations stunt.

This September morning, she fired a few blank shots into the sky. We, on the other hand, had the bad fortune to hit something.

I thought it was amazing at the time. As we walked out into the field just before day-break, I couldn't imagine any self-respecting bird would come near a loud and boisterous group of wisecracking reporters and politicians. After waiting for what seemed like a very long time — we were all getting hungry and restless — our guide suddenly called out, "Dove, on left."

George W. Bush stood, anchored his shotgun against his shoulder and fired. Something fell. He walked out to retrieve it, picked it up, and handed it to the guide. No blood. Perfect. We had our bird: clean, neat, painless. We waited a little longer, then left. Back at the hotel, we had breakfast at Denny's, conquerors who had opened the fall campaign season with a bang. Then we returned to our hotel rooms to clean up for the next stop in Dallas.

I was in the shower when the phone started ringing. It wouldn't stop. I grabbed a towel and, still dripping, reached to answer it.

"Karen, that bird, are you sure it was a

dove?" asked Reggie Bashur, our deputy campaign manager and my colleague in dealing with the press.

"Of course it was a dove," I said confidently, then realized: how would I know? "I mean I think it was a dove. The guide said doves. No one said anything else; why?"

"We had a call from a TV station. They say it's some kind of endangered species."

An endangered species? I was horrified.

"Well, not endangered, exactly, like the golden cheek warbler, but some protected songbird you're not supposed to shoot," Reggie said.

I dressed quickly, walked across the parking lot and down to George W.'s room and knocked on the door.

"That bird — are you sure it was a dove?" I asked when he opened it.

We called the guide to find out. They had to track him down, and it seemed like forever before he called back. I remember hearing the one-sided conversation: "It was? Why didn't you say anything? I understand. Don't worry about it. We'll take care of it.

"It was a killdeer. He didn't say anything because he didn't know what to do," George W. Bush told me, after he hung up the phone. I had never heard of a killdeer before, but clearly it was not a bird you were supposed to kill.

We looked at each other in sync: we had to confess.

Out in the parking lot, George W. ran into one of the reporters: "I have a confession to make: the bird I hit, it wasn't a dove. I am a killdeer killer."

He gave Dan Bartlett a blank check and sent him to find a justice of the peace: "Have him set a fine, and pay it. I don't care what it is . . . make sure he assesses a fine and make sure you pay it, today!"

I dialed and he talked; we called every reporter who had been on the hunt with us. As we boarded our plane in Houston, it was already on television: "George W. Bush just called us to say he accidentally shot a protected songbird, known as a killdeer. He plans to pay a fine . . ."

For the rest of the day I felt as if I were holding my breath. In Dallas, Bush opened his news conference about the new criminal justice laws with a joke: "Thank God it wasn't deer season; I might have shot a cow." My friend Sam Attlesey, the veteran political reporter, told me he thought it would hurt us: "You never know with this kind of thing; it could stick."

I was outwardly calm, but inside I was

very worried until the next morning when I arrived at the Austin airport for my 6:30 a.m. flight to Dallas. A middle-aged man, probably in his late forties or early fifties, wearing a baseball cap and blue jeans and missing several teeth, was loading the morning newspapers into the rack at the airport gift shop. Standing there, waiting to get my paper, I watched him stop, and look at the huge picture on the front page: "A killdeer," he said, out loud to himself. "I shot a bunch of 'em myself."

We had looked forward to the fall throughout the long, sweltering summer. We were always hot; once, Israel and I decided we had suffered heat stroke after sitting on a blacktop in the city of Socorro, outside El Paso, while George W. and other VIPs sat under a tent and listened as city leaders droned on about their problems for what seemed like hours. The campaign plane was a furnace; it sat on the runway and heated up while we were at an event. By the time we boarded and were airborne long enough for it to cool down, it was time to land again.

I remember being disappointed that September seemed just as hot, and the campaign itself was getting hotter: we were coming down the stretch now, and every day counted. George W. still insisted on giving the same speech everywhere, and the reporters were bored. Desperate, I developed what we called inserts, a couple of paragraphs that he could read in the midst of his stump speech to drive news coverage that day, yet preserve his ability to give the people he was seeing his whole agenda. Looking back, I realize he refused to see the people who attended his events as props, that although he knew the media coverage would reach a lot more people, he also felt obligated to the individuals who had come out to see him. The only time I ever heard him criticize one of the advance men who set up rallies before we arrived was when one organized an event so that the crowd had to sit in the sun. He made the further mistake of requiring people to arrive way too early: "You don't treat people like that," George W. scolded. "Don't make them wait; we're not big shots here."

I started inviting reporters to ride on the campaign plane with us, one at a time. I had witnessed George W. Bush's passion about the issues, and I wanted the journalists covering him to see it for themselves. He cared about poor people: welfare moms who were trapped in a cycle of dependency they couldn't break; kids whose best hope of escaping poverty — education — was failing to provide that life raft; immigrants who came to our country to find work because, as he understood, they wanted to feed their families.

"Family values don't stop at the Rio Grande," he said, way back then. Reporters were often surprised to hear him say it, and the passion with which he obviously believes it, much later during the presidential campaign.

Laura Bush joined us one day to introduce her famous mother-in-law, Barbara Bush, who in turn introduced her son. The rally was outdoors in a football stadium; the audience thousands of school children attending an antidrug rally, not an easy setting in which to speak. I had never heard Laura Bush give a speech before and had assumed that she didn't like to speak publicly. She was terrific; her voice was clear and calm; it resonated throughout the stadium.

"You are a fabulous speaker," I told her after the speech, and she looked surprised.

"I'm a librarian," she said matter-of-factly, "and librarians are storytellers."

Suddenly it was October, and everything froze in anticipation of the big event: the first and only debate with Governor Ann Richards. For days, the reporters could talk of nothing else. They made giant press badges for the big event, featuring the two candidates with shotguns in hand: "These dogs can't hunt." When debate day finally came, I realized the pressure had been building inside me, and it exploded that morning at my bathroom sink. I was brushing my teeth, and my husband turned to me, "I hope he'll say —"

"Stop," I ordered, "don't say another word. Whatever it is, don't say it. I can't stand any more."

After watching his father endure lengthy debate preparations — so crammed full of information that it was hard to think — George W. had issued orders: "If anybody's got any ideas of what I should say, give them to Karen. We'll do a couple of informal practice sessions and one mock debate, but I don't want everybody chiming in with too many suggestions. Tell Karen, not me."

If I thought the ideas were important enough, I was supposed to pass them along. By debate eve, I had learned the wisdom of that strategy; I was about to pop. The afternoon of debate day, after our last prep session, I was at the Bushes' house, curled up on the sofa in his office.

"Look at Karen in the fetal position," George W. teased, and that's how I felt:

curled up to protect myself against the onslaught I had endured. That night at the hotel, just before the candidates prepared to go onstage, our campaign chairman, Jim Francis, suggested a line. I didn't want to be responsible for failing to pass along something that might be important, so I started to bring it up. George W. raised his hand to stop me. At that point, he was trying to clear his mind, not cram it full of even more information. I think George W. was disappointed in me; so was I.

George W. did a great job at the debate, more than holding his own against both Ann Richards and challenges from the "citizen panel" the sponsors had organized to question the candidates. Its members, at least the most vocal ones, seemed suspiciously more liberal and concerned about details of welfare policy than had the citizens we had been encountering on the campaign trail. The defining moment had come when Ann Richards had answered a reporter's question about the future with a recitation of her old campaign promises.

"The campaign speech we just heard . . . could have been four years ago," George W. Bush said, a perfect retort. Later that night, I talked up my candidate's success in the bizarre ritual known as postdebate spin in the hotel bar; Richards's campaign staffers were there too, spinning their "victory" just as strongly. The only surprise would have been if either camp's supporters believed their candidate had not won the debate; that never happens.

George W. later told friends that that was the night he knew he might win. The polls were showing a virtual tie, and he had been underestimated (for the first time, but definitely not the last) by an opponent whose campaign had worked hard to create the impression George W. didn't know anything about state government, and couldn't possibly even stand on the same stage with Ann Richards.

The morning after the debate the air was finally cool; after all the months of waiting, fall had arrived, and the crisp air and big crowds in East Texas buoyed our spirits. We were surging now, suddenly in striking distance of the unbeatable incumbent. We had a few late scares: Ross Perot endorsed Ann Richards, and no one was sure what it would mean. And after Houston was hit with heavy flooding, Governor Richards was all over the Texas and national news, delivering help and comfort to victims. The polls started to show her making a move, probably just from all the visibility; but I couldn't stand having our candidate left out of such a big news story. A scheduled speech in Houston was cancelled because of the flooding, so I started lobbying for George W. to get out and tour the disaster, help some victims — do *something* that would insert him into the news coverage. He was reluctant, as I would later learn he always is, to put himself in the midst of a tragedy.

I think his reluctance is born of humility; he feels his presence will distract from the victims and make it appear he is capitalizing on their suffering for his own political gain. But over the years, I think I've managed to persuade him that people want to see their leaders during times of tragedy, want the reassurance that their political figures care and sympathize.

I persuaded him that day, too, although he grumbled about it as we went out on an airboat with one of our Republican county commissioners, who was rescuing people stranded by the rising water. We got soaked, and cold, and George W. kept telling me that if he got sick for the final week of the campaign, it would be my fault; but the pictures of him in the water rescue boat were fabulous on CNN.

We had huge rallies the final day of the

214

campaign, and a bigger plane as Senators Phil Gramm and Kay Bailey Hutchison and our chief political strategist, Karl Rove, and others joined us for stops in Houston, San Antonio, Tyler and Dallas. Robert and Jerry came to Dallas to celebrate the end of the campaign with me; I was too exhausted and excited to sleep. We all crowded into George W.'s Town and Country van the next morning to vote, only to discover after we had arrived at the polls that he had left his voter registration card at home. He didn't need it; after all that television advertising, the election judge recognized and vouched for him.

I had my Election Day haircut for good luck after returning to Austin, and sometime later that afternoon, a reporter from a national television network called to let me know the initial exit polling showed George W. Bush would upset incumbent Texas Governor Ann Richards. I held my emotions in check, not wanting to believe it, not trusting the polls. I've always been suspicious of them, always relied more on my instincts than polling data.

"Karen, have you heard?" George W. Bush yelled at me, rolling down the window of the car as it headed into the garage of Austin's Marriott Hotel, where Joe Allbaugh and I were waiting to meet him. Jim Francis, the campaign chairman, was worried we would claim victory too soon. "We need more numbers; don't get carried away" was his voice of caution, and I listened, until gradually the numbers kept piling up to an inescapable conclusion: George W. Bush would be the next governor of Texas.

I was thrilled, and deeply satisfied; he had given the race his all, and so had I. We had prevailed against the odds, and the expectations, and the popular incumbent, and I knew my boss would be a great governor. He was gracious in victory, thanking Ann Richards for serving as a role model for so many people, and talking about his positive message of change for a better Texas. Jerry and I stayed up late celebrating; I felt that I had been a part of something important, and good.

I was almost sorry it was over; it had been so much fun. I realized that after six months of swapping stories and sharing stressful moments, I believed in this man. He was such a decent and thoughtful person, a person I would trust to make a decision for my own son or husband if I couldn't, because I knew he would listen, think it through, and do the right thing. Unlike so many bosses, he had never complained about the things I said in the newspaper. He had laughed at my antics, and listened to my advice. He was tough minded, challenging, and enormously fun. He had a great wife and daughters, and lifelong friends. He was secure and comfortable with himself.

I had joined the campaign not only with no expectations, but also with no intentions of working in government, which had always seemed bureaucratic, confining and reactive. I thought it was the difference between offense and defense; government offices tend to put people in a defensive crouch, reacting to incoming news; I was a road warrior, always on offense, driving the news.

I had expressed my misgivings about government to George W. Bush many times along the trail. The morning after his victory, he met with us individually. I arrived for my meeting and walked in the door. He was sitting at a table in his hotel suite, and he fixed me with his laser focus: "You are coming with me." It was a statement, not a question, and I just nodded.

"Always return each other's phone calls first," Governor Bush told us at our first staff meeting, and it set the tone for the collegial spirit that would dominate our years in the Texas governor's office. Joe Allbaugh, the campaign manager, became the governor's executive assistant, "first among equals," Governor Bush called him. Joe essentially functioned as a chief of staff, but the governor didn't want filters, so the rest of us reported to him directly, not through Joe, and we were all invited to walk into his office anytime we thought it was important. Vance McMahan, the policy guru, and Margaret LaMontagne, the education expert who would also become extensively involved in the appointments process, and deputy campaign manager Reggie Bashur and I had worked together on the campaign; now we were joined by Dallas businessman Clay Johnson, Houston lawyer Al Gonzales, longtime South Texas political activist and former Cameron County Judge Tony Garza, former state senator Dan Shelley, former state representative Cliff Johnson and Texas budget expert Albert Hawkins. Karl Rove ran the governor's political committee; under Texas law, state business and politics had to be conducted separately. My colleagues were all smart, thoughtful people and we had lively senior staff meetings, full of debate and discussion.

"You're so much different than I thought you would be," Albert Hawkins told me one day, "you're such a nice person." Then he realized what he had said, and tried to explain, and we both laughed and understood that all Albert had known about me had come from reading my tart quotes about Governor Ann Richards and the Texas Democrats in the newspaper. It was the first time, but not the last, that I would appreciate that the political process can create skewed impressions.

I may have taught Albert that people can be nicer than their quotes; Albert taught me the truth of the Watergate adage, Follow the money. He had worked with the Legislative Budget Board for almost twenty years, and I quickly learned that if I needed to know anything about state government, Albert was the best person to ask. In the process of reviewing agencies' budgets, he had learned almost everything worth knowing about what they did and how they operated. I learned a lot about the give-and-take of the legislative process, too, the inevitable tensions between the executive and legislative and judicial branches of government, all of whom try to protect their turf and authority.

And I learned a lot about leadership. Governor Bush led by setting a vision, then sharing credit for success. He asked individual legislators, both Republicans and

Democrats, what they most wanted to accomplish, and then worked with them to achieve those goals. He quickly forged a friendship with Lieutenant Governor Bob Bullock and House Speaker Pete Laney, both Democrats. They didn't always agree, but they learned to trust and respect and listen to each other.

I made an effort to get to know them too, the speaker and lieutenant governor, and committee chairmen like Mark Stiles and Paul Sadler and Steve Wolens, many of them larger-than-life personalities. Bob Bullock was legend. The stories abounded: staff members who were fired, rehired and fired again, all in a single day; people who threw up after being treated to what was known as a Bullock "drive-by ass-chewing."

I had never met Lieutenant Governor Bullock until I went to work in the governor's office, and wasn't sure I wanted to. During my tenure at the Republican Party I had publicly branded him Archie Bunker Bob after he had made an inappropriate comment suggesting a woman state senator would pass more legislation if she wore shorter skirts.

One morning I heard a voice boom through the marble hallways on the first floor of the Texas Capitol. It was a summons; there was no avoiding him now. "Karen Hughes, you said some pretty mean things about me," Lieutenant Governor Bullock said, grabbing my hand and refusing to let go as I stood there, uncertain how to respond. "And you are damn good at your job," he said under his breath.

"Thank you, sir," I sputtered.

"Come see me sometime," he invited, and I did, many more times than I ever would have imagined. He was smart, and cagey, and he developed a genuine affection for my boss. Although he was a proud Democrat, he made it clear he supported Governor Bush for reelection, even though Bullock was the godfather of one of the children of Bush's Democratic opponents.

In the 1998 reelection campaign, I was the verbal artillery. Governor Bush's opponent was Garry Mauro, the sixteen-year veteran Democrat land commissioner, who had chaired President Clinton's campaign in Texas. My goal was to make sure my boss, way ahead in the polls, never had to mention his opponent's name until they came down the final stretch in the fall.

During the early months of the campaign, Governor Bush traveled across the state giving speeches, shaking hands, talking about his plans for Texas, while I worked from campaign headquarters, responding to his opponent's daily attacks. Once, when Governor Bush was in East Texas, he met a woman named Karen Hughes who was running for judge. Governor Bush came back to Austin with one of her blue-and-white campaign buttons, but he crossed out the Karen Hughes "for Judge" and in his trademark black Sharpie, wrote: Karen Hughes "for Governor."

Later that summer, when I finally joined my boss on the road, I was distressed to find some of the younger campaign workers trudging along, appearing tired instead of eager, not giving it their all but just going through the motions. Logan Walters remembers me standing on the campaign airplane, hands on hips, lecturing them: "We believe in what we are doing; we have fun. This is the campaign of joy, dammit."

It became our joke; whenever people were complaining or things were hard, we reminded each other: this was the campaign of joy, dammit. But in truth, for me and many on our staff, the 1998 reelection campaign felt more like a must-do than a mission. The 1994 campaign had been a come-from-behind cause; this time we were the overwhelming favorites to win. Instead of scrambling to catch up, we were way out front, being shot at every day. You can never take an election for granted, and Governor Bush worked hard, wanting a big margin of victory to bolster his plans for more education reforms, teacher pay raises and additional tax relief. I wanted my boss to win big too, but this time it seemed harder to be on the road, away from Jerry and Robert.

The rhythms of work and home life had flowed smoothly during the governor's years. Jerry and Robert came with me to state celebrations; I took days off to lead field trips at his school. I worked long hours during the Texas legislative session and state crises or major events, but the busy times were balanced with slower ones. I had a very capable deputy, Ray Sullivan, and during our second year in the governor's office, I used vacation and accumulated compensatory time to take a month off in the summer, with the governor's blessing. I organized "Camp Karen" for Robert and his friend Alex; we visited caves and water parks and went to baseball games. During the school year, I spoke to Robert's class about the process by which a bill becomes a law (we debated a bill declaring pizza the official school lunch of Texas, and amended it to include a few other choices). Our daughter, Leigh, was living with her husband in West Texas, and when our granddaughter, Lauren, was born, we all drove there immediately. They visited us often on weekends and holidays. After my aerobics classes had left my joints aching, I took up swimming again, and became a regular at our community pool.

And Jerry and I went back to church. I wanted our son to be reared in the faith, as we had been. We had attended services sporadically during the early years of our marriage; when we moved to Austin, the director of the Presbyterian preschool program where we had enrolled Robert had encouraged us to get involved in the church. The first Sunday we attended services, the interim minister, Jack Lancaster, looked at Jerry's name tag: "One of my lambs," he exclaimed. Jack Lancaster had been the pastor of the church Jerry had attended as a child; he was back in Austin temporarily while Westlake Hills Presbyterian searched for a new pastor. Soon after we started attending, Doug Fletcher was hired as the new senior pastor. Doug has a wonderful ability to speak to a church full of people and leave everyone convinced he is speaking directly to each life, and each set of circumstances. He is a dynamic leader and we learned from and were inspired by God working through him.

Our first year in Austin, we went to a church picnic and I stood in line next to the director of children's ministries, Cindy Gangstad. Her love for children is inspirational; I have taught children's Sunday school off and on, mostly on, ever since. Eventually, I was asked to serve as an elder, a leader of the church. Presbyterians believe in a concept called the priesthood of the believers, that all of us who believe in Jesus Christ are called to minister in His name; elders of the church are ordained. Elders are also asked to serve on various church committees: I thought the education committee seemed nice, and safe. The only one I was not at all interested in was evangelism.

"I'd like you to serve on the evangelism committee," Doug Fletcher told me, the first weekend I went to the church leaders' retreat, and I was intimidated, forced out of my comfort zone. Later, when I chaired the evangelism division, we used to joke that we practiced evangelism "lite," but I gradually became more comfortable talking about my faith. I don't try to impose it, but I do wholeheartedly believe it; it's too important not to share.

Jerry and I had been looking for a greater

sense of community when we moved from Dallas to Austin, and we found it not only in church but also in the small-town feeling of our suburban neighborhood. We saw people we knew at the grocery store; we met the kids of our community through sports. Robert was in kindergarten when he signed up to play soccer; Jerry and I checked the box on the form offering to serve as parent volunteers. The night before the first game, we got the call: "Would you coach the team?" We didn't know anything about soccer, but Jerry understands games, and we bought a book, and he began years of coaching kids' soccer and baseball. He soon teamed up with our friend Steve Margolin. They specialized in the strategy; Janice and I handled the mothering. Jerry and Steve still laugh about the time a young boy on the team walked up to Steve after several practices: "What exactly is the point of this game?" he asked. Steve looked over at the sidelines: "See that tall woman over there?" he said, referring to me. "Go talk to her; she'll explain."

My husband became so involved in our community that he decided to run for the local school board. I was proud of him, and supportive. He knew a lot more about the issues than I did, but I knew campaigns: I helped him write a brochure and fill out the questionnaires. I called voters, and put up signs, and I learned how awful, and personal, politics can be when it involves someone you love: it drove me crazy when people questioned or criticized him. Several of our close friends who are Jewish were told they shouldn't support Jerry because he was a "member of the Christian Coalition" and was "pursuing a right-wing agenda." It was almost laughable: my husband was a Democrat when I met him, and it took me years to persuade him that he might consider voting for some of the Republicans I represented. Jerry is strong willed and opinionated; we are both Christians, but the idea that he is some kind of ideologue is ridiculous to anyone who knows him. He won, and served on the school board for three years, attending long hours of committee hearings and board meetings, but was defeated when he ran for reelection. He had advocated splitting the growing student body into two high schools, which he thought would result in better academics and greater opportunities for student participation, but others thought it might dilute the school's winning football tradition.

My husband's dedication had given me a renewed appreciation for those who give so much of their lives to serve the rest of us. A few days before Election Day, 1998, I realized that for the first time after so many years of serving the people of Texas, Lieutenant Governor Bob Bullock's name would not be on the ballot; he had decided not to run for reelection.

"I'd like to come visit the lieutenant governor on Election Day, to pay my respects," I told his administrative assistant when I called. The next day his chief of staff called back: "Governor Bullock wants you to join him for lunch. Can you come around twelve?"

I figured he was hosting a party, a gathering of those who had worked with him throughout his career. When I arrived for lunch, I learned that I was the only guest. The two of us sat at the big table in the dining room just off his office. We talked about the campaign and the legislative session ahead. When I got up to leave, he gave me an engraved gavel: "From your friend, Bob Bullock," and a signed picture: "To Karen — the toughest lady in Texas state government. From, sweet and precious." I treasure it.

That night, my boss won a huge reelection victory. It felt good: the voters had affirmed his hard work and bipartisan leadership. Yet we barely had time to celebrate because he was suddenly viewed as something much more — perhaps the next president of the United States.

Karen with sister, Beverly, and parents, Hal and Pat Parfitt. (*Olan Mills*)

Karen as a reporter for KXAS-TV, interviewing a protester in Dallas in 1979. (*Pete Petrisky*)

At home in Dallas with daughter, Leigh, fourteen, and son, Robert, four months, late summer 1987. (*Family photograph*)

Robert and Governor Bush in the garden at the Texas Governor's Mansion before the Capitol 10,000 Race, spring 1995.
(*Family photograph*)

Karen and Governor Bush working on a
speech in the Texas Governor's Office.
(*David Woo*, The Dallas Morning News)

Karen working in a traveling "office,"
the corner of a hotel ballroom during the
presidential campaign, 2000.
(*Glen Johnson* / *Associated Press*)

Karen and Governor Bush consulting before a news conference in Portsmouth, New Hampshire. Senator Judd Gregg, R-N.H., is on the left, and Lieutenant Mike Escalante, Texas Governor's Protection Detail, is to the right of Governor Bush.
(The [Nashua] Telegraph / *Don Himsel*)

In the governor's living room on the longest night, Election Night 2000. Robert is on the lower left. (*Brooks Kraft*)

A lighthearted moment in the Oval Office, late fall 2001. (*Eric Draper, The White House*)

Karen and Robert on Air Force One, flying home to Texas. (*Eric Draper, The White House*)

Karen and press secretary Ari Fleischer
checking in from the White House staff van,
May 2001. (*Eric Draper, The White House*)

Karen and President Bush at work at his ranch
in Crawford on the president's prime-time
speech on stem-cell research, August 2001.
(*Eric Draper, The White House*)

Karen briefs the nation from the Justice
Department on September 11.
(*Tina Hager, The White House*)

Karen with National Security Advisor
Condoleezza Rice, Mary Matalin, Vice
President Cheney, and members of the
national security staff in the emergency
operations center, September 11, 2001.
(*Paul Morse, The White House*)

Karen talks with President Bush before the
press comes into a Cabinet meeting the
morning of September 12. Secretary of State
Colin Powell and Vice President Dick Cheney
are on either side of President Bush.
(*Eric Draper, The White House*)

Communications staff meeting in Karen's
office in the West Wing the morning of September 12, 2001. Mary Matalin is seated on
the floor; White House communications director Dan Bartlett is seated next to the desk.
(*Paul Morse, The White House*)

Karen peers through the peephole before walking into the Oval Office to ask President and Mrs. Bush about music for the national prayer service, September 13, 2001.
(*Eric Draper, The White House*)

Witnessing the terrible devastation at the
World Trade Center with Federal Emergency
Management Agency Director Joe Allbaugh,
September 14, 2001. Carl Truscott, the head
of President Bush's Secret Service detail, is at
the far right. (*Eric Draper, The White House*)

Discussing the day's challenges with President
Bush, Chief of Staff Andrew Card and
National Security Advisor Condoleezza Rice
between meetings in the Oval Office.
(*Eric Draper, The White House*)

President Bush, Karen and Chief of Staff
Andy Card working on the State of the Union
speech in the president's office at Camp
David, January 2002.
(*Eric Draper, The White House*)

Karl Rove, always at work, as Condi Rice and
Karen try to nap in the senior staff cabin of
Air Force One during an international trip,
spring 2002. (*Eric Draper, The White House*)

Members of the American delegation greet
Russian president Vladimir Putin after the
signing of the nuclear arms reduction treaty in
Moscow. (*Paul Morse, The White House*)

The "girls with gloves," Karen, Mary Matalin,
Trainer Trish Bearden, Margaret Spellings
and Andi Ball, at the White House.
(*Susan Sterner, The White House*)

Reviewing a publication with First Lady
Laura Bush in her East Wing office.
(*Susan Sterner, The White House*)

A hug in the Oval Office from Secretary of
State Colin Powell just after Karen announces
she is leaving the White House, April 23,
2002. (*Eric Draper, The White House*)

Karen meets with her communications staff in
her West Wing office on her last day at the
White House, July 8, 2002.
(*Tina Hager, The White House*)

Karl Rove and President Bush playfully grieve
about Karen's departure photo the week she
left the White House, July 2002.
(*Susan Sterner, The White House*)

Karen is greeted by children in Afghanistan as members of the U.S. Afghan Women's Council arrive in Kabul, January 2003.
(*Daria Fane, State Department*)

Karen, Jerry and Robert at Camp David.
(*Eric Draper, The White House*)

Karen and President Bush confer in the
Rose Garden.
(*Eric Draper, The White House*)

CHAPTER 6

Great Expectations:

The Presidential Campaign, Part I

"I'm not going if you're not going," Governor Bush said to me one morning in his Capitol office. Don't get me wrong: I don't think that Governor Bush would have decided not to run for president merely because I didn't want to join the campaign. I brushed the comment off when a reporter asked me about it much later, saying my boss is a good salesman. But he is also a sincere person; I thought he was telling me that he would be more comfortable if I agreed with his decision, and wanted to be a part of it all.

We had talked extensively over the past year about our trepidations. He was worried about the bright spotlight the presidency would put on his family, especially on his teenage daughters during their college years; I was worried about how I could possibly fulfill my responsibilities to my husband and son during a campaign I knew would be a two-year, all-consuming, all-out fight. I was also worried about leaving my comfortable life in Texas to go to Washington if he won. The decisions were linked, my husband and I had agreed; we knew there was no way I could work for the campaign, then tell the new president no, our family wouldn't move to Washington if we succeeded. I had never wanted to live in the nation's capital; it seemed a place whose values were out of sync with my own. I worried that Washington is a workaholic town inhabited by people consumed with power, prestige and position, all jostling to gain or keep their place. I remember attending a party there once with Governor Bush; it seemed everyone in the room was looking over his or her shoulder for someone more important to talk to. I didn't like the feeling; it seemed fake and sadly hollow.

And my normal optimism had failed me when it came to the idea of a presidential race. I saw it as more of a burden than an opportunity, something to be endured, not enjoyed. But it meant a great deal to me that my boss wanted me to work on the campaign with him, even though I had no experience with a national race, or with Washington. I never told anyone about our conversation, and I was horrified almost a year later when a reporter asked about it: "Is it true that Governor Bush said he wouldn't run unless you joined the campaign?" Dan Balz of *The Washington Post* asked.

I went to my boss, upset: "Someone told Dan Balz about our conversation when you said you wouldn't run unless I came with you," I told Governor Bush. "I never told anyone about that."

He was amused. "It must have been McKinnon," he said, referring to our mutual friend who produced the governor's television commercials.

"Who told McKinnon?" I asked.

"I did," he replied.

My friend Jim Oberwetter used to say running a political campaign is like pushing Jell-O upstairs: You never know whether you'll be able to heave it successfully onto the landing or whether it will just slide down and suffocate you with its slippery, shivery weight. I thought of Jim's analogy often during 1999 and 2000 because many times I felt stuck in an odd game of someone else's making, uncertain how to break out.

I quickly learned that the first and sometimes most difficult opponent in any presidential campaign is the race against expectations: No one can really tell you who set the standards or even what, exactly, is expected. Expectations are mysterious, murky, undefined; they are born of conventional wisdom that becomes conventional after thousands of conversations, predictions and prognostications at bars and offices among political journalists, lobbyists, fund-raisers and campaign staffs. You always want your candidate to exceed the expectations and never fall short. That was a problem for us because we started our campaign with a huge stack of them: George W. Bush was the son of a president; the eldest child of one of America's most beloved women, Barbara Bush; and the successful governor of the great state of Texas. The conventional wisdom said that his name, connections with fellow governors across the country, and powerful home base gave him an entrée to contributors and voters, and made him the leader of the pack.

He viewed it a little differently: "I inherited all of my dad's enemies and half of his friends," he used to say. "I'm trying to pick off a few enemies and work on more of the friends."

I didn't know what to do with all these expectations, except poke fun at them. For our first campaign trip to Iowa, we christened our plane Great Expectations. I suggested that the governor welcome all the reporters on board with a funny announcement.

Mark McKinnon wrote a great script that Governor Bush embellished: "Please stow your expectations in the overhead bin . . . otherwise they might fall and hurt someone, like me."

By the time we boarded the campaign plane in June of 1999, Karl Rove had been at work for a couple of years researching, planning and preparing for a possible race. The rest of our senior staff — Joe Allbaugh, Elton Bomer, Albert Hawkins, Margaret LaMontagne, Vance McMahan, Terrel Smith, Clay Johnson, Margaret Wilson — had been busy with state business. The 1999 legislative session had just concluded, and the governor was still reviewing bills for signature and veto. But talk of the presidential race had hung over the legislative session, and the things that didn't seem normal had started happening more than two years before.

In August 1997, for instance, a reporter had called asking for my reaction to a poll. "What poll?" I replied, confused; it wasn't even an election year.

"The poll that shows your boss is the front-runner for the Republican nomination for president," he replied.

I did my usual sprint across the long, formal reception room that separated my office from his. The Department of Public Safety officers who sat outside his door used to laugh about my wearing a path in the carpet because I raced back and forth so many times each day.

I poked my head into his office: "I need to get your reaction to a poll."

"What poll?" he said, echoing my confusion as he looked up from his desk. "You've got to be kidding," he responded when I explained.

After that it started to snowball. He would get on an elevator, and someone would encourage him: "I hope you'll run for president." He would walk through a hotel kitchen and one of the workers would ask if he was going to be the next president. A television station from Denmark showed up in Beaumont to cover the Texas governor who might be a national contender; national reporters like Howard Fineman of *Newsweek* and Dan Balz of *The Washington Post* and Richard Berke of *The New York Times* started visiting Texas with more frequency. And once, late in the 1998 campaign, I felt it in El Paso: an electricity in the air. A huge Hispanic crowd turned out in that very Democratic city; the women were hugging Governor Bush and screaming and before I even realized what I was thinking, I

251

said it out loud: "You're going to be the next president."

He looked at me, surprised. I don't spend much time speculating or fantasizing; I'm too practical for that. "You felt it, too," he said.

My boss was a rock star at the Republican Governors Association meeting in November 1998, after his big reelection victory; fellow governors and party activists crowded around him, urging him to seek the presidency. His victory statement on election night had credited his "compassionate conservative" agenda for his success. The speech I had drafted used the phrase repeatedly, and he started to strike some of the references as repetitive, but I argued: "We need to make sure that whatever excerpts the media choose, it has that phrase in the sound bite. It's your signature."

The two words had first occurred to me in the middle of an interview, as a British reporter pressed the governor to describe his philosophy.

"I'm a conservative," the governor replied, but the reporter argued: "When you talk about educating children of immigrants, when you talk about leaving no child behind — that doesn't sound like a typical conservative."

"Well, then, call me a conservative with a heart," Governor Bush had said, which gave me the idea for the mantra I had been seeking. "Compassionate conservative" had been born of his philosophy, of Karl's frequent reminder that George W. Bush was a "different kind of Republican," and of my penchant for a focused message that says a lot in a few words. The phrase explained Governor Bush's basic philosophy, but even more important, it said he was different. This was not a grinchy old Republican of the "abolish the Department of Education" or "shut down the government" school of the past; this governor was a conservative because he believed his philosophy offered people — all people — the hope of a better life.

I later learned we hadn't coined the phrase "compassionate conservative"; it had even been the title of a book, but I don't remember having heard it before I first applied it to Governor Bush.

As the expectations that my boss would seek the presidency kept mounting in December of 1998, I ran into my pastor and friend, Doug Fletcher, at the Trianon coffee shop one morning after taking my son to school, the type of chance meeting Doug describes as a "divine encounter." We are both busy people, and on almost any other weekday, we would not have had time to talk; that day, we were both off. We sat in the shop and drank coffee and talked for three hours. When I finally arrived home, I found that my husband had been about to go out looking for me; he couldn't imagine where I had gone. Doug and I talked a little about church matters, but mostly about my doubts, and worries about my family, and the fact that I couldn't get over a sense of trepidation, even dread, about getting caught up in something as mean and unpleasant and all consuming as a national campaign.

The breakthrough came as I was telling Doug about one of our recent national policy meetings in which I had learned that almost 1.5 million American children have parents who are in prison. We talked about how those children's lives would be so different from those of our own children, and about our concern for their future. Doug saw the campaign — and helped me to see it — as a great opportunity: imagine what a president could do to touch and change those children's lives. Imagine the potential to extend the promise of our country to neighborhoods where children do not know that promise, to help others grow up with the certainty that I had that tremendous opportunities are available to you in America if you seek them and work hard to achieve them.

Doug and several members of our church had participated in a prison ministry to befriend and mentor people who are behind bars; I had never been brave enough to go, but I admired those who did, and through the ministry, my family had sent Christmas presents one year to several children on behalf of their father, who was in prison.

A prison also had been the setting for a moment that was one of the most memorable of our six years in the Texas governor's office. Governor Bush was visiting the juvenile justice facility in Marlin; he had advocated and signed stricter juvenile justice laws to try to turn around young lives with a clear message: you are responsible for your behavior, and you will face serious consequences if you commit serious crimes. The juvenile inmates at Marlin had to wear uniforms now, bright orange — no more gang clothing allowed, and their heads were shaved when they arrived. The rules and schedules were strict: inmates had to attend classes and perform chores and participate in drills; the Texas juvenile justice system was no longer an easy place to be.

After our tour, Governor Bush sat down to talk with a group of inmates. They had all committed serious crimes; a street-tough armor was their only body language. I would have found them menacing had I run into any of them in a dark alley at night, yet here they seemed vulnerable, and when I looked into their eyes, I thought I saw a glimpse of some scared little boys, not much older than my own son.

"Tell me what your schedule is like here, what you do during the day," Governor Bush said. "Have any of you been here before; is it different now?" The guards were watching and the conversation was awkward, the answers halting at first; the kids were being taught not to speak out of turn, and they had to raise their hands in a funny half salute in order to be called on.

"How many of you belonged to a gang?" Governor Bush asked, and most of the hands went up. "Why did you join?"

They seemed eager to talk about this: the gang was like a family, they looked out for each other, helped each other.

"Did any of your friends from the gang visit you after you were in prison?"

They shook their heads. The young men started talking more then, about how their mothers or relatives had been the only ones to come see them. Governor Bush has a natural way of putting people at ease; you could see the kids relaxing and opening up. This meeting that they had been required to attend was suddenly more interesting than an ordinary day in juvenile jail. Toward the end of the conversation, a young man who hadn't said a word the entire time slowly raised his hand.

When Governor Bush called on him, the young man's eyes bore straight into his and he asked quietly: "What do you think of me?" It was a haunting moment. I read the question as a desperate appeal: Do I matter? Do I count? What about me? Is there hope?

Governor Bush gave the young man a great answer: "I think you've made a big mistake, and you are here paying the consequences. But if you choose to learn from it, you can turn your life around. People here want to help you. Your teachers at school want to help you. You need to listen to them, and learn, and work hard, and don't commit any more crimes, and I know you can succeed."

"That was a powerful moment," Governor Bush said to me later.

"It broke my heart that he had to ask the question in the first place," I said. "He wasn't sure if an African American kid from a broken home and a terrible neighborhood had a chance."

"That's why we've got to fix the schools; it's kids like that who get shuffled through," my boss replied.

My discussion with Doug about the children of prisoners reminded me of that young man, and so many others like him, who doubt that the promise of America is meant for them. Just before we left the coffee shop that morning, Doug prayed that God would guide my decision and give me a sense of peace about it; as I left, I felt I already had a different perspective. I knew Governor Bush would be a great president; I believed his policies would make our country a better place. What right did I have to be selfish about my life in the face of all the little boys and girls who ask: "Is there hope for me? What about me?"

In the beginning, it was fun, challenging, maybe a little overwhelming when we left Austin in June 1999 with more than one hundred journalists on board, but in a good way, the way that stretches you to do better and learn more. The governor poured his heart into speeches and meeting voters at our first stop in Iowa, then handled press questions with humor and deftness at the first news conference in the fog in New

Hampshire. In between our work on the Texas legislative session, we had spent a great deal of time during the winter of 1998 and spring of 1999 preparing for the campaign. Governor Bush had hosted more than fifteen policy sessions at the governor's mansion, where we brought in some of the brightest people from across the country, experts in the fields of national defense, health care, social security, the economy. They were some of the most fascinating discussions of my career — full of new information and lively give-and-take.

Governor Bush asked questions that went right to the heart of the matter: "If you could design a health-care system from scratch, what would it look like?" (Sparking a lengthy discussion about access, affordability, competition and consumer choice.) "If the army didn't have any tanks today, would you build any?" (Yes, but lighter, faster.) "If you could do just one thing to most improve our military, what would it be?" (Invest in its people.)

At our economics sessions, we were warned that the economic bubble of the 1990s was about to burst, and that the taxes being collected from Americans totaled 32 percent of the gross domestic product — the highest tax burden the American economy had ever seen. Tax cuts were essential, the gathered experts agreed, to lift an anchor on the economy.

Much of the information discussed at those meetings proved prescient, some eerily so, after Governor Bush became president and inherited a recession. Then, after September 11, when I looked back at notes and realized that when Governor Bush had asked the collected national defense experts: "What are the biggest dangers facing us?" one had replied: "A false sense of security."

As these knowledgeable policy leaders came to Austin and met with Governor Bush, they left convinced he was a total dolt. I jest, of course, but that's what much of the press coverage would have you believe. The sessions were mocked as "tutorials," campaign school for someone who didn't know anything about national politics, an updated stanza of the old refrain from 1994, "lightweight," "not up to the job." We all felt the press was missing the story of what was really happening: our visitors were seeing for themselves the governor's laserlike ability to distill an issue to its core, his willingness to think differently, his knack for provoking discussion and thought. Some of the brightest, boldest thinkers in the country were coming to Austin and leaving impressed and committed to the governor from Texas.

It was the first of many times in the presidential campaign that I would experience an essential truth of political journalism: the perception is often far more important than the facts. Tom Wicker describes this phenomenon in his book *On Press* when he writes about being assigned to cover the national presidential campaign. He had wandered into the hotel bar on his first night, and asked a veteran reporter from *The Washington Post* for his advice. "Young man," the veteran said, "if you're going to be a political writer, there's one thing you'd better remember. Never let the facts get in your way."

Facts change: crime is up one quarter, down the next. Facts conflict: Republicans say the tax cut is too small, Democrats that it's too big. (The Republicans are, of course, right!) Much of the political reporting in America is dominated by speculation and perception: who's up, who's down, who is in, who is out, who has the candidate's ear, who won or lost a battle over legislation?

And the "tutorials" were a classic example of the great divide between perception and reality. During our meetings in Austin, Governor Bush and his advisers had begun to build a deep policy foundation for his presidency, yet the meetings had also aided and abetted a perception that he didn't know enough to be president.

That perception was only reinforced by the pop quiz, the second time in my career that I recall being completely stumped — unsure what to do, and in the end, unable to do anything. The first instance was back in the Dallas mayor's race, when Fred Meyer was being interviewed on live television on election night. The anchorman put Fred on a split screen with his runoff opponent, without letting us know in advance. Fred couldn't hear anything in his earpiece, and totally unfairly, it made him seem unable to stand up to his opponent because he couldn't hear a word anyone was saying. That was the week before I had Robert, and some of my colleagues thought I had been hesitant to step in and stop the interview because I was so pregnant. But that wasn't it: you can make the candidate look worse by doing the wrong thing on live television, and I wasn't sure how to stop an interview that was already in progress.

I had the same sinking feeling as I watched Andy Hiller of WHDH-TV in

Boston conduct his now-infamous "pop quiz" interview, in which he asked my boss to name the leaders of Chechnya, Taiwan, Pakistan and India. It was one of the few times during the campaign that I detected genuine anger in my boss; his eyes narrowed. George W. Bush knew he was being hit with a cheap shot.

I felt sick — that I had let my boss down, that he was paying for my own lack of experience. Hiller apparently had a reputation for pulling stunts; I hadn't known that, and had authorized the press office to book the interview after it was recommended by the New Hampshire campaign. We did several such local interviews almost every day; but it quickly became clear this one was far from routine. Sitting in the room watching, I was frozen: this was bad, but trying to interrupt or stop the interview while the camera was rolling might be even worse.

I tracked down Condi Rice afterward: "We've got a problem."

I called Andy, the reporter, and tried to persuade him that if he was going to run the interview, it was only fair for him to do the same thing to the other candidates in the race because once he had aired it, he would never be able to re-create the same surprise. The other candidates would come prepared for the game of "name that leader."

No, he told me — he had the tape and he was airing it.

I felt just as I had in the aftermath of the killdeer kill so many years earlier, only this time the endangered species might be our campaign. By the next afternoon, we had heard nothing but silence: no follow-up questions, no reaction. Someone dared to hope: "Maybe this won't be a big deal," but I knew better. At some point, the national press would see or hear about the tape, and all hell would break loose. It happened that night, and suddenly it was everywhere, running over and over again on cable, reinvigorating all the old questions: was he up to the job, did he know enough to be president?

That kind of interview will never happen again, because President Bush has now met most of those leaders personally, and once you meet someone it is much easier to remember a name, especially a foreign name. Like so many things in the course of a campaign, it was a huge story that I felt had nothing whatsoever to do with the candidate's qualifications to be president. For the rest of the campaign, I carried around a long list of names of world leaders, and we would read over them periodically, trying to memorize them. I could never remember most of them, either, until we started meeting them in person.

Nothing about a presidential campaign is normal: you travel too many miles to too many different places and eat too many bad meals, but life on the campaign trail soon settled into a mind-numbing routine, every day different but the same — up early, into a van, out to an airport, answer reporters' questions, on to a city, an event or speech or rally, work the crowd, more reporters' questions, back into the van, onto the airplane, on to the next city, another event or speech or rally, more handshakes, more reporters' questions, time for the candidate to exercise, back in the van, onto the airplane, on to the day's last stop, a final event, another crowd, another van, another motel, more questions, another night with not enough sleep. We quickly realized one rule of life on the road: the nicer the hotel, the less time we would get to spend there. My mom would sometimes ask whether I had called my aunt or cousin who lived in a city where I had been; it was hard to explain that I really hadn't visited the place, I was just at a rally and talking with reporters or listening to a speech and then we were gone; most of the time, I barely knew which state I was in.

Presidential campaigns ought to come with a warning label, the same admonition Juliee Bliss gave her husband after the birth of her first child: "Don't ever let me forget how painful this was." Reunions of the campaign team tend to be full of laughter and nostalgia; forgotten is that the reason you feel so close is because you survived so much trauma together.

Odd things stand out from the blur of events:

Karl Rove, who makes the Energizer Bunny seem lethargic, singing exuberantly in a van, the rest of us exhausted at 3:00 a.m. on our way to Kennebunkport, Maine, after a long day and night campaigning in Iowa, the pork capital of the world (lobster is the other, *other*, white meat); sweating through my clothes at a Fourth of July parade in New Hampshire, thinking a Texan is not supposed to come to New England and die of the heat; the collective gasp from reporters at the new conference where Governor Bush announced his first fundraising totals, the first time I realized exceeding expectations could be a double-edged sword (our fund-raising success helped establish Governor Bush as the clear front-runner, yet also undercut his image as an outsider); losing my temper and screaming at *Newsweek* reporter Martha Brandt, even though she was in the middle of an interview with Mrs. Bush, because one of her colleagues at *Newsweek* had written something wrong about me, but really because I just couldn't stand it anymore, the final weekend of the campaign.

At home, whenever we had a day or sometimes the luxury of a few days between trips, I went to meetings at campaign headquarters and washed clothes and tried to catch up on sleep. Jerry grilled chicken or picked up Mexican food because I was usually too tired to go out. We bought a new house just weeks into the campaign; we had outgrown our old one as Robert and his friends got bigger, and the new house gave us more room for family activities: we played Ping-Pong in the den and swam in our backyard pool, the first one I had ever had.

I went to strategy sessions or meetings with my staff at campaign headquarters downtown; we were a huge operation now. Joe Allbaugh, our campaign manager, oversaw a staff of a couple of hundred people; I had almost fifty people working for me in the communications, press, and speechwriting offices. Our territory was vaster — fifty states, plus territories, not just one — the issues different and sometimes more complex; but I found most of the skills were the same: discussing Medicare at the federal level was just as complex and mind boggling as describing Medicaid at the state level. We faced more reporters, and their questions covered a wider range of subjects, but answering them required the same mix of knowledge and discipline as it had in Texas. And my boss hadn't changed. We had a lot more people around us, but we still laughed and talked about what our opponents were saying, and what the press would ask, and how we should answer.

In late July 1999, a few weeks before the first test among real voters, the Iowa August straw poll, Governor Bush insisted that I fly home to Austin to watch Robert play in a Little League championship game. I had mentioned it the day before; that morning after sending one of the security officers to my room to summon me, he said, "I've been thinking; you need to get on a plane and go home to see that game."

I went home to help write his campaign biography, too, when it became clear we wouldn't get it done any other way. I had been the big advocate of the project; I thought a book would help explain his philosophy and leadership and management style. We were facing a September deadline, and no one else who knew him well enough to work on it had time. The day after Governor Bush won the straw poll in Ames with 31 percent of the vote, I did my first Sunday show, *Meet the Press*, then flew home to Austin and told my campaign staff they wouldn't see me for the next month.

Mindy Tucker, a savvy young woman I had lured from Washington to Texas during the governor's 1998 reelection campaign, did a great job of managing the communications shop while I was gone, and I was truly absent: I went to church, and to Robert's once-a-week middle school football games, but otherwise, all I did for the last half of August and the first half of September was write, working from audiotapes dictated by Governor Bush and notes from interviews he had done over the years. I got up early and wrote for an hour or two before getting Robert off to school. I wrote until lunch, took a break, and wrote again until Robert came home. I would get him a snack and talk about school, then write some more until dinner, which Jerry would pick up or help make.

Sometimes, in the evening, I would write for a few more hours until I fell into bed, exhausted. When I got stuck on one chapter, I opened another; when I got tired of writing in the living room, I moved to the dining room, or outside to the pool. Josh Bolten, our campaign policy director, had done me an incredible favor at the senior staff meeting when I told my colleagues I was taking myself off the campaign trail to write. As everyone sat there, stunned, Josh turned to me: "How can I help?" He lent me one of his policy deputies, Stephen Garrison, as a researcher and Stephen worked round the clock, finding memos, or copies of speeches, or newspaper clips to refresh my memory; he would deliver stacks of material to my house at all hours. It was one of the best times of my life: I was crashing on a project I cared about, and I was there every afternoon when Robert came home from school.

I spent most of the weekend of my wedding anniversary at the governor's mansion rewriting the chapters with Governor Bush to make sure it accurately reflected his thinking. "How did you know this?" he asked me occasionally, surprised at the accuracy of my description of his feelings about going to boarding school or learning his little sister had died; I had listened to him carefully over the years. At 8:30 p.m. on Friday night, September 10, I told the governor I had to leave. It was my wedding anniversary, and I wasn't about to miss dinner with my husband. We went to our favorite restaurant, Jeffrey's; the next morning I went back for another writing session at the governor's mansion.

After the book was finally finished and I had returned to the campaign trail in mid-September, the race felt different. The press was edgier, unhappy with what they saw as a lack of access, especially in contrast to the freewheeling, all-day bull sessions that were taking place on John McCain's bus in New Hampshire; our campaign team seemed somehow to be going through the motions. Governor Bush was systematically laying out innovative, comprehensive policy in a series of major speeches, but people were also starting to describe him as scripted. Mike Gerson and his speechwriting team were crafting beautifully written and frequently poetic speeches, but former secretary of state George Shultz pulled me aside after one of them and warned me we should avoid making the governor sound like something he was not. And then we missed the first debate in New Hampshire.

With our candidate seen as the favorite, we weren't in any hurry to debate with the other five Republicans in the race: Senators John McCain and Orrin Hatch, Steve

Forbes, Gary Bauer and Alan Keyes; we knew there would be lots of debates, and I was taken aback by the outcry about missing this one. I don't think we ever seriously considered attending because Governor Bush had a conflict: Laura Bush was being honored as a distinguished alumna by her alma mater, Southern Methodist University. It was important to her and she never asked for much, and we knew he wanted to be with her. One of the most affectionate and emotional moments I remember witnessing between George and Laura Bush, a librarian who loves books, had come when he dedicated a promenade at the SMU library to her.

We told the press that Governor Bush would have to miss this debate because of the ceremony honoring Mrs. Bush. I thought a candidate missing a political event because he wanted to be with his wife was a sign that he had his priorities straight, that he put his family ahead of his political ambitions; the press and many of the voters of New Hampshire thought he was ducking.

From then on, it got harder. The press was more suspicious; John McCain was surging; and we still didn't know what impact Steve Forbes and his money might have. I was learning that a presidential campaign is hours of monotony punctuated by moments of sheer terror. It's just another routine October day until the phone rings, and a reporter asks: "Was Governor Bush arrested in Houston back in the 1970s for using drugs?" Those are the allegations outlined in a new book about to hit the newsstands, the reporter told me; he had to know the answer, right then.

That was one of the low points, one of the times I felt the process was sick and sleazy. Governor Bush was campaigning in Washington state; I had sent a deputy with him so I could stay at the Austin headquarters for some strategy meetings. Imagine having to track down your boss and ask him, over the telephone: "How's it going? By the way, were you ever arrested in Houston for using drugs? And, for extra good measure, did your dad, the former president, intercede to get you off?"

"Of course not; what the hell is this?" was my boss's immediate response. The story was absurd, but we also knew it would suck all the oxygen from the campaign for days. The allegations came from out of the blue, from an author who turned out to be a convicted felon, but the legitimate media felt it had an obligation to follow up. Once something is in the ether, it has to be dealt with.

It's on the Internet, so the other reporters have to ask; and they are all afraid their competitors might report it before they do; and even when it is discredited, someone writes about it or something happens to make it news.

Many of the reporters were apologetic when they called me to ask for comment, as if it made them feel a little dirty, too: "You understand I have to ask," one said.

I didn't say what I really thought: yes, I know the game, but no, I don't understand, not at all. A reporter I respect a great deal once told me he believes he should publish everything, and let the public make its own judgments. I disagree. I worry that the obsessive interest in a candidate's past prevents too many good people from running for public office. And I think the public has trouble discerning what is true and what is not.

One of the most common questions people ask me now is how can they know what information or what media to believe? I have trouble answering that question because although I believe that most journalists strive to be accurate, I also feel much of the news that I see provides a skewed perspective, often because the time and attention the media give to certain stories creates a false impression. For example, I think most people in America have a mistaken impression that President Bush had a wilder past than he actually did. The media obsessed about what he meant when he honestly admitted, "When I was young and irresponsible, I was sometimes young and irresponsible." They chased all kinds of rumors and published many of them. I think the news media should do a better job of helping the public discern the truth by placing a much higher burden of proof on those who make allegations, rather than forcing candidates to disprove allegations or react to anonymous rumors.

I taught a seminar at my church that weekend and shared my disgust with people there. It was a sign of sickness in the political process, I told them, that someone can write a book alleging that a former president had used his connections to get his son cleared of drug charges when none of it was true — yet so many reporters had called the former president's office to ask about it that he had to put out a statement to repudiate it. The press then used the existence of the statement as an excuse to write stories, repeating the falsehoods. I was glad to be at church that weekend, glad to be reminded that in the grand scheme of God's plan, none of this mattered very much.

Throughout the campaign, I experienced church as a sanctuary in a way I never had before. It became a refuge from the conflict; people there cared about me, not about the campaign, but about me. How was I holding up; how was I surviving this madness? My minister's sermons spoke to me, too. I especially remember one: "We all face pressure in our lives," Doug said, no matter what we do, whether we are running a company or rearing children. Pressure is a part of life. What we should strive for as Christians, he said, was not to eliminate pressure, but to show grace in the face of it. I still pray that simple prayer before every speech or television interview: "Lord, give me grace under pressure."

Once during the campaign, a member of the congregation wrote me a nice note, telling me that he admired me for coming to church in the midst of the chaos: "I frequently see you on a Sunday morning show, then see you here," the note from Mike Hasler said. "It's been a witness to me." But I wasn't attending church to set an example. I felt I had to be there, to keep my priorities straight, to remember what was truly important in life, and most of all, to maintain perspective, a lifeline: this, too, shall pass.

I tried to maintain my sense of humor and natural exuberance despite the long and trying days; I was always reminding the young people on the campaign to look up from their pagers and out of the van windows at the spectacular sights of America: "Look at the beautiful mountain," "The sunset is gorgeous," "The trees are all turning," I would exclaim, pointing out fall pumpkin displays and, later, Christmas decorations, with such frequency that Logan Walters, the governor's personal assistant, and Gordon Johndroe, my traveling press aide, teased that they were on "Karen's holiday tour of America."

I was glad to spend most of my time on the road rather than back at the headquarters. Most communications directors work from the main office; I prefer traveling with the candidate. To me, it's the difference between offense and defense: at the headquarters, you take calls and respond to the grenades lobbed at you by your opponents or incoming press questions; on the road, with the candidate, you still answer questions, but you also make news and drive the agenda of the campaign. Tolstoy, in *War and Peace*, called it the moment of "contingency": the time when opposing armies meet, and the fog of war begins, and things do not go according to plan. At headquarters, they specialized in the plan; on the road, we took care of the contingencies. Obviously, we all had input on both; I was always proud that our campaign married the road team with the headquarters team better than any I had ever witnessed.

Governor Bush had placed three of us at the head of the campaign: he paid us each the same salary, and treated us as equals. Karl Rove was our political guru, in charge of the overall strategy; Joe Allbaugh was the campaign manager who liked to be known as "the enforcer"; and I was the communicator, responsible for the message. Joe called us "the brain, the brawn and the bite." The national media began calling us the "iron triangle," and attributed the moniker to people in Texas; I had never heard it before my boss decided to run for president. My friend Jim Oberwetter wrote me when he saw it appear in the stories: "The Iron Triangle! What's that? Some kind of weird chastity belt?"

The three of us had worked together for years; Karl and I since back in my days as executive director of the Republican Party; Joe and I since Joe had joined Governor Bush's first campaign in 1994, when the governor decided the mostly young campaign staff needed some adult supervision, and had brought Joe Allbaugh to Texas from Oklahoma. Karl and I were constant motion, loud and energetic; Joe was steady, slow to budge or yield, especially when it came to spending the campaign's money. Karl's hyperactivity could send me into fits of laughter and drive Joe crazy. We would get on an elevator, where Joe couldn't escape, and Karl would start a chorus of "Are we there yet, are we there yet?" He was like a kid on a car trip, and you could see the pink rise in Joe's face until it seemed steam would come out of the top of his head. All strong-willed people, we sometimes disagreed, even vehemently, but we respected and listened to each other. Governor Bush had insisted early on that members of his staff communicate, and whenever any of us was uncertain about something, we checked with the others.

At headquarters, Karl chaired meetings where representatives of the policy and press and political shops developed the calendar of speeches and policy announcements and events; on the road, we implemented and adapted, answered the questions of the day and seized opportunities as we saw them. One fall morning, Leslie Goodman, our senior press representative in California, was chatting with reporters to anticipate and prepare for their questions. Ron Fournier of the Associated Press was asking about that day's front page story in *The New York Times* outlining congressional Republicans' proposals to balance the budget by stretching out payments of the earned income tax credit, money paid out through the income tax system to low-income families. I had seen the story, and seen opportunity, and had called Josh Bolten, our policy director, because it didn't seem like something Governor Bush would agree with. Josh got back to me quickly: there was no policy reason we couldn't criticize the proposal.

I went to the governor's hotel room. "You're going to get asked about this," I told him. "It doesn't seem like something you would do." I had checked with Josh, I reported.

When Ron Fournier asked the question, Governor Bush answered: "I don't think they ought to balance their budget on the backs of the poor . . ."

The statement rankled some Republicans in Congress; but it was true to Governor Bush's heart and convictions, and the media coverage of Governor Bush disagreeing with members of his own party on a compassion issue did more than weeks of speeches or standard responses ever could have to help seal my boss's credentials as a compassionate conservative, a different kind of Republican.

I vividly remember another time I brought my "outside the Beltway" perspective to the campaign; I was on the phone talking with press secretary Ari Fleischer because we were being asked about the Medicare "lockbox." This debate could only happen in Washington. Trust me, no one in the real world would ever account for their money this way. Medicare is divided into two parts, A and B. (I always remembered the difference between the two because in typical Washington fashion, it's reversed: Part A is hospital, and Part B is doctor, even though in real life you usually go to the doctor before you go to the hospital.) Part A runs a surplus; Part B runs a big deficit, and when you combine the two, the government pays out far more in Medicare expenses than it takes in through Medicare premiums. Yet the lockbox refers to locking away what is essentially the fake "surplus" that exists in only one part of the program.

Governor Bush was in a classroom, talking with students; I was standing in a hallway, juggling a stack of papers and my cell phone, a position in which I seemed to find myself frequently in those days: "Forget the lockbox," I said to Ari. "Let's just say that every dime that comes in for Medicare will be spent on Medicare." It took a few minutes to explain what I meant; Ari was a federal budget expert who had worked on Capitol Hill for the Ways and Means Committee for years; he was used to looking at Medicare the Washington way.

"But the lockbox refers only to the surplus in Part A," he said, thinking I just didn't understand.

"I know, but there isn't really any Medicare surplus, not when you look at the whole program like real people do — when people like my dad talk about Medicare, they're talking about both parts, not just one — so every dime that comes in will be spent on Medicare, because we spend more on Medicare than we take in," I insisted.

"You're right," Ari said, "I never looked at it that way."

And that's what we said — one of my contributions to the political debate of the 2000 campaign. Now if only I could explain that there is no Social Security trust fund, no bank where they deposit all the money; the revenue collected from Social Security taxes is actually spent that year on other government programs, and the government then issues an IOU to Social Security. If more people knew that, I think, the personal retirement accounts the president has proposed would be even more popular. Then you could actually invest some of your own retirement money and know where it is, in an account with your own name on it, not just on a piece of paper held by the government.

The above, in a nutshell, is what I do for a living: take arcane matters and try to explain and communicate them in a way that makes sense. My other skill is writing sound bites, figuring out ways to crystallize important thoughts into quotable, newsy statements; both come in handy on a daily basis in a political campaign.

Governor Bush made a one-day, nineteen-hour, up-and-back trip to New Hampshire from Austin the week before Christmas, to visit that key state one more time before the holidays. Robert was already out of school for Christmas vacation, and the opportunity to see a presidential campaign up close doesn't come along very often; I had always wished my son was a little older so he could take time from school and travel with us, like several of the college students who worked on our travel team. I asked if Robert could come along for the day trip and it was fine with Governor Bush. Robert rode in the state trooper's car at the front of the motorcade, and watched Governor Bush speak to students at the high school, and played cards with the young men traveling on the campaign airplane.

By now, I had visited New Hampshire enough to have the feeling they didn't like us. I kept trying to talk myself out of it: perhaps we were just too loud and boisterous, while they are famous for that New England reserve. New Hampshire is a beautiful state; I loved the mountains and forests and little rock walls and charming cottage-style houses, but everything there seemed different. All my instincts were screaming trouble, especially when I asked the man driving the van how many people were volunteering at headquarters, and he said they were all from Texas. We kept seeing a lot of the same people at our events, again and again. One night in Laconia, I stayed in my hotel room and watched television for a couple of hours with an increasingly sinking feeling in my stomach. The first thing the next morning, I reported in to the campaign manager: "Joe, I'm really worried. I watched TV last night and our ads just don't look good; we're running that news-reel thing and McCain's ad is really good, patriotic; so is Bradley's, and even Gore looked better than we did." I called Mark McKinnon, in charge of our television spots, and told him my concerns: our news-reel ad seemed jumbled, and not nearly as compelling as the McCain spot; he assured me we were changing to a new ad, that day.

I called Karl, too: "We need to plan a big rally in South Carolina for the day after the New Hampshire primary; if we win, it'll be a victory rally, if we lose, we'll need a huge crowd . . ." I didn't like what I was feeling, but I didn't trust myself either. I didn't know anything about New Hampshire or its politics, and our New Hampshire people seemed to think everything was fine. As it turned out, it wasn't.

Jerry and Robert joined us in New Hamp-shire the weekend before the primary be-cause with the Iowa caucuses followed closely by the New Hampshire primary, I had been away from home for several weeks. I thought I would see them late at night, in the hotel room, but Robert surprised me.

Here's what he wrote about the experi-ence.

Robert: I remember going to New

Hampshire with my dad; he stayed in the hotel room but I wanted to ride around on the campaign bus because it seemed interesting. This is how we elected a president, and I wanted to see it. It was grueling. We had to get up early and stay out late; it was constant motion. On the bus, they prepared for the next event; you never had time to relax. There were some lighthearted moments. I remember standing backstage once at a pancake breakfast. Suddenly, a guy came falling backward through the curtain and the DPS agents all jumped because they thought somebody was trying to get to the governor, but it was just one of the candidates, Gary Bauer, falling backward trying to catch a pancake. I also remember going to the polls on election morning. It was interesting because they were starting to pick the president, but the voters didn't seem very excited about shaking the governor's hand.

Later that Election Day morning, Governor Bush decided to exercise and I found myself with unexpected free time: Jerry and I enjoyed the luxury of a peaceful lunch in downtown Manchester together while Robert, who was tired, watched television in the hotel room. The phone was ringing as I walked in: "Have you seen Karl?" the governor asked, not bothering with hello.

"No," I hadn't. "Why?"

"He's on his way to tell you we got the first exit polls, and they're not good," Governor Bush said.

"How not good?" I asked.

"Very not good, nineteen points down. Come down here in five minutes," the governor ordered.

I was stunned. My family could tell something was wrong; I remember Robert looked shocked when I repeated the numbers. "I have to go downstairs to meet with the governor," I said, and Robert wanted to come.

I hesitated, not sure the hotel room of a man who had just suffered a huge political setback was the place for my child, but Robert insisted, and I relented. He followed me into the room. "We're a team," Governor Bush started, "we got here together, and we're going to hold our heads up and go out and win this together," he said to Joe, Karl, me and Don Evans, his good friend from Midland who was serving as finance chairman for the campaign. "We got beat, and now we're going south and we're going to win. I don't want anyone pointing the finger of blame at anyone else. Karl, make sure the New Hampshire folks understand that, and call our political leadership, tell them we're headed south, which will be much friendlier territory. Joe, call the governors; Karen, you need to get to work on a statement for tonight." I hadn't even had time to think about what it all meant, and here was the governor, moving on, making sure his team didn't start blaming or undermining each other.

I still think the statement I drafted in my hotel room that afternoon was one of the best I have ever written for Governor Bush. It's not that the words were particularly elegant or poetic. But the most important part of my job is strategic positioning, and I think I was able to capture in words what I had witnessed in my boss: he was gracious but unbowed, humble in defeat yet strong and convinced he would win the Republican nomination: "I am proud of my supporters, and I am proud of the kind of campaign we conducted here in New Hampshire . . . the road to the Republican nomination is a long road. Mine will go through all 50 states, and I intend it to end at 1600 Pennsylvania Avenue. Mine is a campaign in every state in America, because mine is a message for every American. We must reform our public schools . . . I am a better candidate for having come to New Hampshire and waging this campaign, and because of this competition . . . If you think our politics needs a fresh start, a new beginning of idealism and optimism and integrity, come and join our team."

Governor Bush was phenomenal that night: his strength and grace in adversity convinced me yet again that America needed this man to be the next president. When I arrived back at our hotel, the clerk called me over to the desk. "Your mom and dad called; they were so nice I wrote it down," she said, handing me a message: "Your dad said to tell you it is always darkest before the dawn. They love you."

In my hotel room, later, I thought about it all, and was grateful that my son had been there to witness it. I was tired, and emotional. Thinking about it brought tears to my eyes, and embarrassed Robert: "Whatever, Mom," he said, a typical teenager even then.

Robert: It never felt right in New Hampshire; people didn't seem as

excited as they should have been. I had heard that New Hampshire was a quirky state, and Senator McCain seemed to fit that bill. He was running as a maverick, and I had heard Mom and others talking about how New Hampshire had a history of picking those kinds of candidates. So when we heard about the exit polls, I was surprised but not completely shocked. I was worried. This was the first real primary and to lose it was a downer for the whole campaign. We ran down to the governor's room after he called, and when we walked in, I was surprised that he seemed upbeat, real positive instead of negative. Instead of dwelling on the defeat, the governor and the rest of them looked forward to the next thing and what they had to do. He said not to blame anybody, that it wasn't any one person's fault. It taught me how to be a gracious loser.

We called John McCain's nineteen-point victory over George W. Bush in the New Hampshire primary a bump in the road. We knew the media would try to define the loss as a huge setback, and we wanted to put our own context on it, but it felt more like an avalanche than a bump. I was mad at myself for not seeing it coming; Laura Bush pointed out to her husband and a few of us that we had never really responded to, or fought back in the face of, McCain's criticisms. The governor's instincts had been to try to rise above it all, avoid intraparty warfare, but when you turn the other cheek in campaigns, most often you just get slapped, and we had been, hard.

Yet New Hampshire did not turn out to be the lowest point of the primary season for me. That would come later, after our loss in Michigan. I was too busy to allow myself to feel down, scrambling, trying to convince the press and our own team that New Hampshire was not the beginning of the end, but merely that bump in a very long road. We fought off attempts to force us to play the political rumor game: Karl was being fired, or I was, or Joe was, or McKinnon was, or we all were. We all knew we had to do something, or a series of things, to show that we had learned our lesson, that we were changing course after this setback.

I was back in Austin, on my way to get my hair cut, when I dialed Karl on my cell phone. It had finally hit me: I was steamed that John McCain, a longtime senator and powerful Washington committee chairman, had managed to steal our candidate's position as the Washington outsider in this race. George W. Bush was the real reformer, I thought, the governor who worked with Democrats and got things done. Our tremendous success at fund-raising, and the press coronation of Governor Bush as "front-runner," was undermining our own position.

"Karl, McCain has managed to steal our reform mantra," I said, "but he's never reformed anything. He's tried to reform campaign finance, but hasn't been effective. Governor Bush has reformed schools, reformed welfare, reformed the juvenile justice and tort systems . . . Governor Bush is the real reformer in this race; the difference is he's a reformer with results," I said, talking myself into the idea as I explained it.

"I like it," Karl said. They debated the new slogan at campaign headquarters. Some people worried it might be playing into McCain's hands, venturing onto turf he had already captured; but I was convinced it was right, and in the end, we put it on banners, and it became part of the new story line: the Bush campaign was changing course, retooling, digging out from the disaster of New Hampshire. Of course, our candidate didn't change one iota of his philosophy, or a single issue position, but the external perception of change (that is, that we had learned our lesson) was everything.

I saw the crucial importance of perception acknowledged very honestly as the 2004 presidential campaign got under way: in a story about Democrat John Kerry's campaign in the aftermath of his surgery for prostate cancer:

"Mr. Kerry has made fund-raising calls while convalescing. More important, his aides have let it be known that he was making fund-raising calls while convalescing, to drive a perception that he is a serious and driven candidate" (*The New York Times*, February 26, 2003).

As that story clearly states, the appearance is frequently more important in presidential politics than the reality. Acutely aware of that fact, we wrote a long list of things we could tell the press we were doing differently: a new slogan, new format, more audience questions for the candidate. Merely doing things differently is not enough. You also have to acknowledge you made a mistake, and explain how you are correcting it, before the press allows you to move on; there's not much glossing over under such an intense microscope.

Our first stop in South Carolina was at Bob Jones University. Karl had called me back a day or two after my worried phone call from New Hampshire to say the South Carolina campaign team wanted us to go to a campus that had a big auditorium and a conservative student body that would be very supportive. That wasn't what I had been thinking, I had told him; I thought we needed a big outdoor event, with families and music, very upbeat. That wasn't very realistic on a work day, Karl reminded me; it would be hard to turn out a large crowd in the middle of the day and the South Carolina people really thought Bob Jones University was the place to go. My lack of experience showed here, too; I had never heard of the school, and didn't pay attention. At some point, the South Carolina staff sent a memo, which I didn't look at until we were on the plane heading there. By then all I could do was brief Governor Bush in the holding room about the school's ban on interracial dating — not what he wanted to hear as he prepared to walk onstage. When the press asked about the ban, Governor Bush said he disagreed with it. The visit didn't become big news until later when Tim Russert asked on *Meet the Press* about several controversial statements the university's founder had made. I had never heard those, either; the briefing paper hadn't covered it, and we suddenly faced what we thought were terrible cheap shots accusing Governor Bush of being anti-Catholic.

I had the old feeling that I was holding my breath for the entire three weeks of the South Carolina primary campaign; it was a war every day, a dizzying barrage of charges, countercharges, debates and news conferences. We were in the South now; the sun was warmer, people's accents softer and more like our own. If we couldn't win here, it was doubtful we could win anywhere: we had to carry this state. Governor Bush answered seemingly endless questions from the audiences in the new "one on one with George Bush" town hall format; Karl and the political team poured everything into an all-out blitz of phone calls, advertisements, and television commercials. Later, we were blamed for spreading falsehoods about Senator McCain. I never heard or knew of anyone on our campaign circulating the ugly rumors, and Governor Bush never would have allowed or condoned it. Our criticisms were tough but focused on the issues. Governor Bush even made Mark McKinnon change an already-produced television commercial because he thought it was too tacky.

My favorite ad of the entire campaign was one we aired in South Carolina. It was developed by Mark and his ad team, then revised by Governor Bush during filming in a park the week before the primary. Senator McCain had gone too far in comparing Governor Bush to President Bill Clinton, and there was a hard glint in the governor's eye that gave voters a preview of the resolve and leadership he would display after September 11: "Criticize me, but do not question my integrity," he said in the ad.

The night we finally won South Carolina, Governor Bush did an exhausting round of television interviews. His position as the front-runner had been restored, and we flew to Michigan, happy and relieved to be back on track. But the good news would prove to be short-lived. The Michigan primary was only three days away and, suddenly, we would be derailed again.

We had already left Michigan when we learned we had lost the state. We had stopped in St. Louis for a rally, en route to California. The governor had just finished speaking and was headed back to the airplane when he got the news from a reporter: "Governor, Fox News has just called Michigan for John McCain," correspondent Carl Cameron said. We got on the plane, and I insisted that Governor Bush participate in some television interviews we had already scheduled, just so we wouldn't look the way we really felt: worried. This, the second loss in less than a month, was the low point for me. For the next week, a refrain played repeatedly in my head: What was wrong? What were we missing?

We all knew we couldn't survive many more setbacks, which made victory even sweeter the next week, in Virginia. Governor Bush was on-stage, shaking hands after finishing a speech at a high school there. He saw me walking across the room; it was early afternoon and he knew that I should have the first exit poll numbers. A reporter had called me, and I mouthed the good news to Governor Bush up onstage: "Up by twelve in Virginia."

His smile warmed the room: "Finally," he said.

Then the victories started adding up. Of course, they were a lot better than losing, but by now I had stopped fully celebrating wins, realizing the truth of Kipling's words: "If you can meet with Triumph and Disaster and treat those two impostors just the same." Victory is an impostor many times throughout a presidential campaign, because it only means you live to fight another day. Of course, that's much better than the alternative, as all of our primary opponents would learn.

We had a big party the night my boss clinched the Republican nomination. All our supporters crowded into a ballroom; we had music and balloons. I had worked with Governor Bush for several hours earlier that day refining his speech. People were congratulating me and applauding Karl and Joe, and the young members of our staff stayed up late partying. It was a fun evening, and an important moment, but I had that sense again: the celebration felt tentative, incomplete. The hard work, the work that really counted, was still ahead.

A week or so later, I went in to tell my boss that I thought he might want to replace me.

"What are you talking about?" he asked.

"The press doesn't like me; I don't play their game. That can't be good for your campaign," I told him.

I wasn't exactly sure how or why it had happened; I had always felt I worked well with members of the Texas press. I respected them, and felt they respected me: they knew that while I stayed on message and didn't always tell them everything I knew, I also didn't lie to them, or play games, or selectively leak information to favorite media outlets or try to play reporters against each other.

I'll never forget one of the first times I dealt with the national press corps, at an event in Cincinnati in 1998. I was talking with a reporter for one of the wire services, and he was looking very skeptical as I answered his questions. "You look like you don't believe me," I told him.

"Of course I don't," he replied. "I cover the Clinton administration. They lie to me all the time."

I was somewhat shocked: first, that he would think that, and then, that he would say it. It was one of my most basic rules: don't lie. You don't have to answer every question; you certainly don't have to answer the way the press wants you to, but you can't lie. I thought I had earned credibility: I knew the candidate, I knew his philosophy and principles and I had worked hard to learn the issues.

But I didn't do my job the way the Washington press expected. I was too "on message," they complained — they couldn't get anything out of me. I wouldn't give up on even little things; I wouldn't let my hair down and criticize my boss in the hotel bar at night once in a while.

Too serious, relentlessly on message, disciplined; thus the nickname Nurse Ratched, after the rigid, tyrannical nurse in the movie *One Flew Over the Cuckoo's Nest*. I always suspected Howard Fineman of *Newsweek* did the christening; he once told me I approached the press like a school marm, thinking I could herd and order them around. Based on that, and some unnamed sources, he's my suspect. If I were covering this story as some of my friends in the media do, I would perhaps just rely on anonymous "sources" to imply that Howard is responsible, but I'm putting it on the record: I think he did it. My apologies if I'm wrong; in any case, I'm sure he'll take the accusation as a compliment. In typical Washington fashion, no one ever said the nickname to my face, but it started appearing in the gossip columns and stories about the campaign. I don't see many movies, but I had seen that one, and I remembered the cold, controlling nurse. Of course the nickname hurt. You are not supposed to admit to having feelings in Washington; you are supposed to pretend that the mean things people say don't bother you. But I have found that most people don't like being criticized or called names, in grade school or in the newspaper.

I was also worried the media's frustration with me would hurt my boss. "Maybe we need to get someone who will play the game, schmooze with them more," I told him. "I want you to win; maybe we should think about hiring someone else to run communications."

I meant it, but he wouldn't hear of it: "We're going to win this our way," he told me emphatically. Then, unbeknownst to me, he called Jean Becker, his dad's chief of staff, who is a former reporter herself, and asked her to come to Austin to have breakfast with me and make sure I was all right. I was fine; I just wanted to make sure he felt free to do whatever was best for him. I wanted him to be the president, and I wanted to make sure he wasn't sticking with me out of loyalty, to the detriment of that goal.

"We'll do this our way," he said again later — the final word.

By the end of March 2000 we were all tired. I felt like I was on one of those rusty old playground toys that go round and round in a circle; the campaign kept spinning with no end in sight. I wanted it all to stop for a while, but Karl kept pressing: we had to use the spring to put out policy, win the issue debate. It was brilliant on his part; looking back, I still think we may have won the campaign because of the strong issue beachhead we established in the spring. Vice President Gore had all the advantages of incumbency; had he used them early and effectively to establish himself as the issue-focused front-runner, we might have spent the rest of the campaign playing catch-up. Instead, he kept trying to reinvent himself, and we gleefully pointed out every reincarnation: he's changing his clothes (Earth-tone-Al), his staff, his headquarters location and many of his positions.

I had learned an important lesson during the primaries: you can poke fun at your opponent; you can make fun of yourself; but you cannot joke at the expense of the press. One Monday morning, I got on board the campaign airplane in Austin and walked back to greet the traveling reporters. Over the weekend, *The New York Times* reporter assigned to our campaign, Frank Bruni, a thorough reporter and wonderful writer, had written a story our campaign team thought was terribly unfair, basically accusing our candidate of taking it easy, not working very hard. I'm a high-energy person, and I was exhausted; I knew the president gave the campaign his all, every day.

The rest of the media always follow the lead of *The New York Times*, so I wanted to shoot the story down before we ended up with weeks of bad stories, analyzing every move through the prism of this new context: that the Bush campaign was essentially lackadaisical. Frank wasn't on the plane, which I noticed right away. "Where's Frank?" I asked his colleagues.

"Taking a few days off; he's tired," one of them replied.

The irony was too delicious: "He's tired, after covering the campaign that's not working hard enough? How could he be tired?" I laughed. I thought I was making my point with humor; the reporters thought I was unfairly attacking one of their own, criticizing Frank to his competitors. I barely had time to walk back to the front of the airplane before my cell phone went off.

It was Dan Bartlett, the easygoing, unflappable communicator who was in charge of our rapid response operation: "Karen, did you say something criticizing Frank Bruni?" he asked.

"I was teasing about him taking days off when he said we weren't working hard enough," I told Dan.

"Well, I don't think some of them took it that way," he replied. "They told Frank you were attacking him behind his back." I called Frank to apologize, and told him I was trying to make my point in a humorous way. Later, the governor teasingly chastised me about it in front of the press, although privately I think he was glad that I had stuck up for him. I continued my mea culpa: "I've already apologized, do I have to grovel?"

I had learned my lesson: it's the reporters' job to write about us; we're not supposed to say anything about them. I should have known that, as a former reporter myself. Back in my Channel 5 days, I would not have liked someone trying to involve me in a story that I had been assigned to cover. I was not happy when a city councilwoman once asked me how I voted. Intellectually, I knew reporters are present as observers, but a presidential campaign blurs so many of those lines. It's almost impossible to view people who travel with you all the time, ask you questions all day long, eat with you and fly with you and stay in the same hotel for a year and a half as mere observers; they become a part of the whole experience. Not that they support you (on our plane, a reporter once took a poll that showed our traveling reporters thought Al Gore would win); but they do become a part of it all, almost like a huge tail that is supposed to follow along, but ends up weighing down and sometimes even wagging the dog.

We arranged our schedules to adapt to the media's deadlines and planned events to make the evening news. The news organizations paid all their own expenses, but we employed several full-time staffers to reserve the traveling journalists' hotel rooms, and order their food, and distribute information and make sure they had phone lines and filing centers from which to write and submit their stories. And sometimes it felt as if they, not we, were setting the agenda of the campaign: bored with talking about Social Security, or tax cuts, or our featured message of the day, they were always pushing, as is their job, to get us off message, while I was pushing back, trying to keep us on message, which was my job.

Yet sometimes, when we had enough time to go to dinner or talk over a glass of wine at night, we could take a break from our roles and enjoy each other's company. During the work day, I had many confrontations with NBC reporter David Gregory; one night, relaxing on the plane, we agreed it was because we had similar, aggressive personalities. At dinner, over drinks, at ball games, the reporters were intelligent, curious, irreverent and fun to be with. I thought most of the journalists who traveled with us regularly tried to understand and accurately present the views of Governor Bush and our campaign: people like Producer Mike Roselli and correspondent Candy Crowley of CNN; producer Nancy Harmeyer and correspondent Carl Cameron of Fox; Patsy Wilson of Reuters, covering her sixth presidential campaign; and Glen Johnson of the Associated Press, covering his first. The network producers who were with us every step of the way — Alexandra Pelosi of NBC, Susan Rucci of CBS, and John Berman of ABC — worked incredibly long hours to satisfy the demands of television news programs that started early in the morning and signed off late at night. I knew the reporters from Texas; they had covered us for years and brought interesting insight: Wayne Slater and Sam Attlesey of the *Dallas Morning News*, Clay Robison and R. G. Ratcliffe of the *Houston Chronicle*, Ken Herman and Jena Heath of the *Austin American Statesman*, Jay Root, of the *Fort Worth Star Telegram*. The reporters for the major daily newspapers — Frank Bruni of *The New York Times*, Terry Neal of *The Washington Post* and Judy Keene of

USA Today were thoughtful observers, as were the news magazine reporters. Although I didn't always agree with what they wrote, I felt they tried to be fair. And I owe them for teaching me to recognize "color," the tidbits of detail that bring stories to life, like the color of the furniture inside or the weather outside of an important meeting. When I started the campaign, I was terrible at chronicling color; the questions of journalists like Jay Carney and John Dickerson of *Time*; Howard Fineman, Martha Brant and Trent Gegax of *Newsweek*; and Ken Walsh of *U.S. News & World Report* taught me to be more observant. I have groused about stories written by almost all of the reporters mentioned, but I like them and respect the dedication with which they approach their jobs.

When I was executive director of the Republican Party of Texas, I used to tell political candidates that reporters were neither their friends nor their adversaries: they come to every event with one purpose in mind (candidates sometimes called out, "to screw you," but that isn't it, at least not necessarily); no, reporters come to every event to get a story. That's what their jobs and editors demand, what their newspapers and magazines and radio and television newscasts require — a story, the more colorful and controversial the better, because that means better placement on the front page or at the top of the newscast. And news, by its very nature, is about change and controversy: you don't see headlines saying PEACE AND HARMONY PREVAILED IN CONGRESS TODAY, although it might be news if they ever did.

I think the need for a sharper focus, a more dramatic headline, motivated Jay Carney of *Time* magazine to push me so hard in Iowa, in a moment captured on C-SPAN's cameras. Governor Bush had just finished a news conference where he had been grilled about abortion. It was just days before the Iowa caucuses, the starting gun of the presidential contest. Our campaign wanted to talk about tax cuts and education reforms and Governor Bush's plans for the future; the reporters wanted to talk about abortion, litmus tests for Supreme Court judges and FDA approval of an abortion pill. Jay stayed after the news conference to ask me about hiring gays. I repeated Governor Bush's position: he views a person's sexual orientation as a private matter — that's not a question he asks. It wouldn't come up in a hiring decision. But that was old news.

Jay kept pressing: "If he knew someone was gay, would he hire him?"

"How would it come up? It's not a question he asks," I replied.

In fairness to Jay, I think he just wanted me to make it clear. But in fairness to me, I knew the headline that would result if I answered the way he wanted me to: Bush would hire an openly gay person. I didn't want Jay to write that lead, because I thought saying it that way had the effect of making a person's sexual orientation an issue in hiring, when our position was that it is not.

Looking back at the tape today, I can see why reporters were frequently frustrated with me: I wouldn't let them cover our campaign their way. Perhaps I was too rigid. That question doesn't need to be asked anymore, because the Bush administration has hired people who are openly gay. But I don't believe it's my job to go beyond what I know my boss would say in response to a question; that's his decision to make, not mine.

I generally refuse to allow reporters to put words in my mouth. Occasionally, their questions are open ended; but most often, the questions try to shape the answer, define it for you and push you to a conclusion: "Are we fighting a guerrilla war in Iraq? Is the president fed up with the United Nations process?" It's hard not to repeat those words, or let the question define the answer. Sometimes, if I don't want to be associated with words in a question, I will say: "Those are your words, not mine."

I've learned it's one of the hardest things to resist, the temptation to agree or disagree with words journalists choose for you, therefore allowing yourself to be defined by their questions. It happened much later in the Oval Office when a reporter asked President Bush whether Ariel Sharon was a "man of peace." A reporter put the words in play, but the president repeated them. Later, he told me that he hadn't wanted to suggest that any leader didn't want peace, and he followed his statement with that thought: "Ariel Sharon is a man of peace . . . he has embraced the notion of two states living side by side." But the rest of the quote didn't get played much, and the question didn't get played at all. When my husband and pastor visited the Middle East recently, every Arab leader they met complained about the American president's calling Prime Minister Sharon a "man of peace."

The president is responsible for the words he uses; we all are. I am suggesting that the press has far greater influence on our national dialogue than it sometimes admits. I know from personal experience that it is very hard not to repeat a word or negative idea once someone has suggested it, "I am not a crook" being perhaps the most famous example, echoed not too long ago by then-Canadian prime minister Jean Chrétien as he tried but failed to distance himself from his spokesman's words, "George Bush is not a moron." Merrie Spaeth, who runs an international communications business based in Dallas, puts out a monthly "bimbo" list chronicling the dumb things people say. Almost always, the negative words or quotes are cases of people trying to repudiate, but in the process repeating, something that was asked in the question.

After winning the primaries, we went to work to drive home a perception that our Democratic opponent, Vice President Al Gore, would say and do almost anything to get elected: change the color of his clothes, flip-flop on issues, exaggerate about inventing the Internet. The conventional wisdom said that Al Gore was a good debater. He had participated in numerous debates over the course of his long career in Washington politics, and we reminded reporters at every opportunity that Governor Bush hadn't debated nearly as much as his

311

opponent, even as we started having practice sessions to prepare.

"You've become Al Gore; I really don't like you," I told Senator Judd Gregg after one of the sessions where he played Al Gore lecturing Governor Bush in vintage tones of condescension. Some intellectuals have a terrible superiority complex; they assume they know better than the rest of us what is good for us. It reminded me of an argument I had with an editorial writer for the *Houston Chronicle* during my years in the Texas governor's office. He was criticizing Governor Bush's proposed tax restructuring, and told me that most of the people in Texas had no understanding at all of how bad it was.

"All those people don't know what's good for them, but you do?" I asked him.

"Well, I did have a higher SAT score than most of them," he sniffed.

Something in me snapped: "What was your SAT score?" I countered; he answered with a number. "Well, mine was higher," I replied. "Does that mean I win — I'm right and you're wrong?"

I don't remember exactly how the conversation ended — quickly thereafter, and unpleasantly — and I was steamed as I went to a senior staff meeting and vented with my colleagues. "Can you believe this insuffer-

able prig? He presumes to tell me his SAT score is higher than most people's, and therefore he should tell them what to think?" The writer apparently recounted the conversation to some of his colleagues at his newspaper, too, and years later we apologized to each other. But I thought his attitude was symptomatic of the smug superiority conveyed by many elites — that the rest of us don't know enough for our own good — and Judd Gregg captured it perfectly in our debate practice sessions. In fact, I thought the senator did a better job of portraying Al Gore than Gore himself did when we finally got to the debates.

At one of our late-spring meetings, campaign chairman Don Evans had brought up the subject of debate preparation, and said he thought I should be in charge. I had read about elaborate presidential debate preparations in newspapers for years. Debates were tremendously important, and our opponent already had more experience; I thought we should bring in someone who had led national debate preparations before. But Don and Joe and Karl talked me into it: you know the candidate, you know what he likes and what he doesn't, that's what is most important, they insisted.

And so I helped oversee the debate prepa-

ration sessions. My role consisted primarily of suggesting sound bites and knowing when the candidate was fed up and didn't want to practice anymore. Much later I laughed at a *West Wing* episode featuring President Jed Bartlet at debate camp. He and his staff had holed up for forty-eight hours of preparation; President Bartlet was complaining because there were forty-seven hours and twenty minutes to go. The difference is, Governor Bush would have never agreed to a forty-eight-hour session; he wanted to strike a balance between preparing and being overly crammed with information.

Although I was nominally in charge, the real work was done by others: Josh Bolten and the policy staff, who prepared massive books, major points and questions and answers about each subject; Judd Gregg, who did a great deal of homework and had Al Gore's issue positions and mannerisms down cold; Stuart Stevens, who did a great job as our moderator preparing tough questions; Condi Rice, who led the foreign policy discussions; Bob Zoellick and Paul Wolfowitz, who attended several sessions and helped us work through issues and answers; and, of course, Governor Bush himself, who had to read and absorb, then

articulate all the information we were throwing at him. Despite all the preparation, we all knew debates frequently come down to one or two moments or key lines, and there was no way to know what they would be. We could not have imagined during our intensive preparations that the most memorable moments of the 2000 debates would be Al Gore's exaggerated sighs, and Governor Bush's quick grin and relaxed body language when his opponent confronted him, trying but failing to intimidate him.

The clock seemed to be ticking faster now as we moved into summer: months, then only weeks to select a vice president and prepare for the convention. One day, Mrs. Bush, the Bushes' friend Nancy Weiss and I were making sandwiches at the ranch while Governor Bush met in the other room with the chair of his vice-presidential selection process, Dick Cheney. Over lunch, Laura asked how the process was going. "The man I really want to be the vice president is here at the table," Governor Bush said, stunning us all with the seemingly offhand reply.

As we finished our sandwiches, the two men went outside to the back porch to talk some more. "He's the very best person for the job. . . . I think I might be able to convince him to do it," Governor Bush said, half to himself, half to me, later that afternoon as he walked me to my car before I headed back to my family in Austin. Their months of working together had convinced Governor Bush that he wanted the benefit of Dick Cheney's wisdom, judgment and experience — not just in selecting a running mate, but in running the country.

A few weeks later, Governor Bush summoned Joe, Karl and me to the governor's mansion late one Saturday afternoon. The atmosphere was heavy, somber, as we sat down in the library. "Dick wants us to carefully think through his health situation," Governor Bush told us, and Secretary Cheney explained that while he was active and vigorous, and ran a big worldwide business, he also had heart disease, and we had to understand what that meant in practical terms.

"If I have chest pains, or feel something is wrong, I have to go to the hospital to get it checked out," Cheney explained. "It could happen anytime, and you need to think through what that might mean if it happens during the fall, or the last couple of weeks — what impact it might have on the campaign."

We asked a lot of questions: How often

had it happened that he had to go to the hospital? Not very often, he replied, but that wasn't any guarantee it wouldn't happen at any time. How might this affect his ability to serve as vice president? He didn't think it would, since he had run an international business and been through lots of stress and intensity as secretary of defense during the Gulf War under former president George H. W. Bush.

At the end of a lengthy discussion, the president asked for our conclusions: I felt that if he wanted Dick Cheney as vice president, the issue was manageable. Many Americans live with heart disease, and Governor Bush was healthy and vigorous, which I thought would mitigate any concerns about the health of his running mate. We needed to make sure Cheney's doctors were convinced that he could fully perform the job and be prepared to brief the press, but I didn't think the issue excluded him from consideration.

We didn't leave with a resolution. Governor Bush wanted to think about it, and as chairman of the selection committee, Dick Cheney told him he felt an obligation to present him with other options.

At the end of the next week, my traveling press assistant, Gordon Johndroe, and I were driving to Austin from the ranch when my cell phone rang: "Karen, can you think of any reason why Dick Cheney would have changed his voter registration from Texas to Wyoming this afternoon?" asked Lisa Meyers, a savvy reporter from NBC News who had covered many campaigns before. The presidential and vice-presidential candidates can't be from the same state, and Dick Cheney had a longtime residence in Jackson Hole. I wish I had said something clever: it's just too hot in Texas, or he decided he was really a westerner, but I was taken aback: I hadn't known he was going to do it. "You'll have to ask him," I told Lisa.

Shortly thereafter, cell-phone and beeper hell broke loose, as Lisa went on the air with her story and all at once, all the reporters had to know: is Dick Cheney going to be the vice president, and if not, who is? Telephone reception between Austin and the ranch isn't good, and between Gordon's phones and beepers and mine, it was chaos all the way back to Austin.

Another candidate, former senator Jack Danforth of Missouri, was still in contention. Dick Cheney's selection process had identified him as well qualified, and the campaign had flown the senator and his wife to a hotel room in Chicago on July 18 for

Governor Bush to meet privately with them. I had advised the governor that if he wanted to make the announcement of his vice president and not have the media announce it for him, he shouldn't make a final call to his nominee until the morning he wanted to announce it. I was pretty sure which way my boss was leaning, but he didn't say it directly and I didn't ask, wanting to give him a chance to think it all through a final time. I wrote up a statement for all our senior staff and spokesmen to use: "Governor Bush is in the midst of making his final decision . . ."

I spent the rest of the weekend at home, floating in my swimming pool, but constantly interrupted by my ringing cell phone. The reporters were all hyperventilating, afraid they would get beat on one of the biggest stories of the year. I felt for them; I knew the pressure they were under. Getting the scoop on a big story like this one, or getting beat by the competition, can make or break a journalist's career. The night before the scheduled announcement, I was at the governor's mansion doing a round of media interviews, and Mrs. Bush offered me a glass of wine. I still had one more appearance to make, on the Larry King show. "I can't," I told her. "If I have a glass of wine, I might tell who I think the vice president will be . . ."

The governor called me just after six thirty the next morning: "Dick Cheney said yes." But CNN reporter John King had relied on a "senior campaign official" to break the news the night before, even before Governor Bush had made the official call, which made me mad: I didn't think it was right for anyone else to announce it before the candidate did.

I don't know how these kinds of leaks happen; I don't think, as some of the critics do, that reporters make it up. The way reporters frame their stories sometimes shades or colors them, but I do not believe that most of the journalists I know fabricate news. Someone gives them the information. The question is: who is that someone, how much does he really know, and what is his agenda? My friends in the press will say they rely on anonymous officials to find out what is really going on; I worry that some of those officials aren't very high ranking, and have their own skewed perspectives. Any one of a hundred different people at close to a dozen different agencies can be described as a "senior administration official." That gives their comment an air of authenticity, even though it may be a minority view, or one that was considered and rejected.

As I finished writing this book, the Justice Department was in the midst of a criminal investigation of who leaked the name and CIA employment of the wife of Ambassador Joseph Wilson, a critic of President Bush's policies in Iraq. I don't know who leaked the information to reporter Robert Novak; I don't know if the leakers knew it was classified. I suspect, since Novak reported that his sources were "senior administration officials," that they most likely worked at one of the agencies, not the White House; otherwise he would have called them "White House officials." But regardless of the source, the leak compromised the confidential identity of a longtime public servant, which was wrong, and unfair to her and those who worked with her. Whoever did it should come forward and not hide behind journalistic ethics for his or her self-protection.

As a former reporter, I understand journalists need to shield their sources; once they have given a promise of anonymity, they can't take it back. But the use of unnamed sources has become a convenient way for too many political operatives to hide and avoid accountability for their statements. And this problem will continue until journalists stop quoting anonymous sources, or at least enact much more exacting standards to restrict their use. A *New York Times Magazine* story in January of 2002 included a line that was very revealing: "There's a signaling problem between the White House and the press, and in the Bush White House it is worse than in most, because the Bush people don't speak to the press in anything but the official tone of voice. They've shut down the sneaky little off-the-record chats through which the truth finds its way into print." The assumptions that underline that statement are breathtaking: the "official tone of voice" must not be true; the truth comes only from "sneaky little off-the-record chats." My question is: what are the motives of the people having those chats, and who is holding them accountable? And if arriving at the truth is journalism's guiding ethic, why allow so many people to conduct their business in the dark? Being quoted anonymously contributes to the debasing of our political discourse; anonymity allows a speaker to be harsher and more critical than he otherwise might be, and even to say things he otherwise might never say. I have done it myself, occasionally, and when I did, I felt that I was participating in something a little underhanded. I hope that thoughtful members of the journalistic community will consider dramatically reducing their reliance on anonymous sources; it would be healthy for American democracy to put it on the record.

After Governor Bush had announced his choice of Dick Cheney as his vice president, we traveled to Wyoming for a spirited rally in Dick and Lynne Cheney's hometown. The future vice president was immediately attacked for several votes he had cast years before in Congress. It was initially difficult for those of us in the communications office; we were suddenly defending not just one candidate, but two, and we didn't know all the circumstances of those long-ago votes. But Dick Cheney is so reasonable and credible on television, just as he is in person, that the firestorm quickly passed. And with the vice-presidential suspense behind us, all eyes quickly turned toward the convention.

Andy Card was doing a great job overseeing the convention operation in Philadelphia. I had heard good things about him from mutual friends, but had never met him until we gathered in Kennebunkport in May for a convention planning session. I quickly learned that Andy is smart and thoughtful; he has a great sense of humor, and he's strong, but in an evenhanded way. I was also impressed with his vision for the convention: he outlined the concept of four P's. The convention had to be based on principle; conducted in the spirit of partnership; the policies had to be personified; above all else, it had to be presidential. I liked the P's, and even better, I liked that Andy was approaching his job that way; it mirrored my view about the importance of communicating under a strategic umbrella.

Mike Gerson had started work on the convention speech in May, about the same time we started getting serious about debate preparation. Governor Bush is a stickler for being prepared, a fact that a lot of people overlook because of his easygoing personal style. On big speeches, he wants to start work early; one of my deputy communications directors in the governor's office, Linda Edwards, still laughs about the time he jestingly crouched down toward his knees in the foyer outside his office, pretending to beg me to work on his late-January inaugural speech a couple of weeks before Christmas when I was equally adamant that I was going shopping.

Mike came back after two weeks of hibernating at the Bush library with an excellent draft and we began editing. When Governor Bush is working on a major speech, he's on a mission. The phone will ring at all hours: "Paragraph five on page two says the same thing as paragraph four on the page before"; "This whole page is too repetitive"; "That section is way too passive; I'm not bobbing along like some cork; I want active verbs." First he focuses on the structure of a speech, then he begins striking excess words. I used to tease him that he edits out most all of the adjectives.

We had talked about his vision of an ideal speech once shortly after he had been elected governor. He didn't like the draft speeches we had been giving him, so, frustrated, I asked him how he thought a speech should be written. He took the paper from my hand and finished the outline. A speech should have "an introduction, three major points, then a peroration — a call to arms, tugs on the heartstrings," he wrote on the piece of note paper I still have; then "a conclusion," which, he explained, is different from the peroration.

"Where did you come up with that?" I asked him.

"The History of American Oratory, at Yale," he replied.

He practiced the convention speech once in a big room in Austin, then a couple of times in the living rooms of friends on the way to Philadelphia. They invited their families and neighbors; we set up the TelePrompTer and Governor Bush would give the speech, tinkering with it, refining after each delivery.

Finally, after the long weeks of preparation, the first day of the convention arrived. I flew to Philadelphia with Mrs. Bush for her address; I had advocated her speaking on Monday night because I thought having Mrs. Bush open and Governor Bush close the convention was a way of figuratively putting their arms around the entire four days. It was the biggest audience she had ever addressed, and she was marvelous: calm, composed, sincere. She talked substantively about education and reading, yet only one of the television networks, ABC, carried it, which annoyed us all: who knows the potential president better than his spouse?

Late Monday night, after her speech, we flew out to rejoin her husband so they could arrive together in Philadelphia on Wednesday, the night before the roll call and formal nomination. Unlike previous conventions in 1988, 1992 and 1996, when I was a staff member from Texas and didn't know most of the people running the national conventions, this time I had all-access passes and invitations to all the best parties, but I was too tired and busy to attend any of them. Before I knew it, I was standing on the floor, proudly watching my boss give a powerful speech with great conviction. I was caught up in the clapping and excitement until I felt the brief, suffocating panic that I always feel when the balloons come down and stifle all the air and noise. My boss was the Republican nominee for president, a tremendous achievement, but there wasn't much time to celebrate. Early the next morning, we boarded a train, back on the campaign trail. We would travel thousands of miles, to dozens of states, but now we had only one destination: victory or defeat.

CHAPTER 7

On the Road with Robert:

The Presidential Campaign, Part II

Now I had company: the week after the convention, when I left my house before 7:00 a.m. to board the campaign airplane for California, Robert came with me. The idea had been brewing since his first trips to New Hampshire in December and January. Texas has a home-school law that allows parents to teach their children at home; perhaps I could use it to allow Robert to take advantage of this once-in-a-lifetime lesson in politics, geography, history and democracy.

Robert was only in middle school, preparing to begin the eighth grade. Jerry and I had long discussions: we wished our son were a little older, but decided that he was mature enough to handle life on the campaign trail. I would do my best to teach him along the way, but we were realistic: we knew that a semester away from his honors classes might leave him a little behind, especially in algebra and science, but decided the educational opportunity outweighed any other concerns. Robert was a good student; he could catch up.

"Maybe we could take you out of school this fall, and you could come with us," I suggested one day, and Robert was eager, enthusiastic. I half expected that as the time drew closer, and the thought of leaving his friends became more immediate, Robert might change his mind and decide to stay home in school and play football — after all, it was fall in Texas. But Robert never wavered, and by early summer I realized that if this was going to happen, I needed to talk with my boss.

"Can I get your reaction to something?" I said one day to my friend Joe, our campaign manager. "I've been thinking about asking the governor if Robert could travel with us this fall."

"You mean take him out of school?" Joe replied.

"I could meet with his teachers and have him keep up with most of his class work. I'm not too worried about that; he would learn so much on the campaign."

"What about other people who might want to do the same thing?" Joe asked.

"No one else who travels regularly has children," I reminded him. Joe's daughter

Taylor is a little older than Robert, but Joe almost always worked out of the headquarters in Austin; ditto with Karl, whose son Andrew was a year younger. The road warriors were mostly younger and single, except for me and Governor Bush.

"I hate being away from Robert so much, and this would take a negative and turn it into a great experience for him," I said. Joe knows me well, and he could see the benefits to everybody of having me happier to be on the road.

"I think we could make it work," he said.

How many people do you know who, preparing to embark on the most challenging endeavor of his life, would say "sure" when a staff member asks, "By the way, could I bring my kid along?" Governor Bush was not just supportive; he was enthusiastic.

"That's a terrific idea," he said, a tribute both to him and to my son — and we were off, a home-school adventure en route to the presidency.

Robert's first couple of days on the campaign trail coincided with a train trip in California with our former primary opponent, John McCain. I've always liked the feisty senator; maybe it's the free-spirited swimmer in me. He's not always popular among his colleagues in Washington because they think he grandstands and plays to the media too much. But the army brat in me says anyone who spent the time that he did as a prisoner of war has earned the right to be a little cantankerous. I also can't help but admire someone who stands up to the get-along, go-along spirit that so often prevails in Washington. Or maybe I'm just prejudiced because he was so nice to Robert: when Governor and Mrs. Bush visited John and Cindy McCain at their home in Sedona, the senator spent almost an hour showing Robert and me around the property.

Robert: It was really weird because he had been our enemy for so long. I didn't know what to think because I remember him attacking the governor and saying bad things. It was surprising because I wasn't expecting him to be nice to anyone, including Governor Bush, but he was. We walked around and he showed us his pond with all the fish, and he picked an apple from one of his trees and gave it to me to eat. It made me realize the campaign turns you into somebody you're really not; the candidates are trying to win and it

makes them say things that they normally wouldn't say.

My son adapted amazingly well to life on the road. Every night we would pick out our clothes for the next day and repack our suitcases, setting them outside the door or delivering them to a room so we could sleep as late as possible: morning bag call was always several hours earlier than we were scheduled to leave the hotel. We would get up and get dressed; me in a suit, Robert in one of the nice dress shirts and khaki pants we bought him for the campaign. Most mornings, we headed to Governor Bush's room, where he and my traveling assistant, Gordon Johndroe, were just finishing up the morning local radio interviews. We'd talk about the overnight news, the day's events, and Governor Bush would quiz me about his speech or proposals he was scheduled to make that day. If I didn't know the answers, we called back to the policy or speechwriting shop to ask questions and order changes. And then we were off to the first event.

By now, we were prepositioning on most days, which means flying to a city late the night before, so we could get an early start on the day's first event. I didn't like it, partly because it made the nights later, but most important, because it robbed us of preparation time on the plane the next morning. The reporters were asking me questions before I'd even had time to read all the thick news summaries and absorb all the news of the day. On the airplane, Robert would do his schoolwork. He always walked back to the press cabin with me when I went back to brief the press, and sat or stood beside me, listening and learning. On the ground after rallies, while Governor Bush worked the crowd, Robert and some of the young campaign workers threw footballs on the tarmac. He loved sitting in the front cabin with the governor and our staff, especially when Mrs. Bush was traveling with us. The Bushes have an affectionate, teasing relationship; they laugh a lot, and Robert enjoyed laughing with them. One of their favorite activities was making fun of me.

Robert: Everything was fast paced. At home, you can eat slow and enjoy your food; on the campaign, you had to eat fast and do everything fast or else you would get left behind. The governor is prompt; everything had a set time period and all the frantic activity had to fit into a day. We

stayed at some very nice hotels (the Breakers, the Waldorf-Astoria and the Regent Beverly Wilshire were my favorites), but after a while, it didn't matter how nice it was, if you got there early enough to eat dinner and relax, it was automatically a good place to stay. One night we had time to go out to one of Emeril LaGasse's restaurants in New Orleans with several campaign staffers. Several of us were debating whether to order the flounder or the snapper. The waiter convinced us the snapper was much fresher and the flounder was a little old, so we all went with the snapper. Then the waiter came back to the table. He said they were out of the snapper, but they had some wonderful "vintage flounder." It was one of the lighthearted moments on the campaign trail.

I loved having my son with me. The reporters called him the "campaign kid" and several wrote stories about our arrangement. One described it as either a "grand adventure, or a bizarre form of child abuse"; Robert and I viewed it as a wonderful opportunity. I realized how rare it is for our children, as they get older, to spend so much time with their parents; Robert got to watch me do my job all day long, in all kinds of circumstances. At night, in our hotel room, he would frequently ask questions, and I tried hard to be patient and answer them, although I know I was frequently way too tired and way too short with him.

Robert: One of the most interesting things on the campaign for me was watching my mom and Governor Bush edit speeches. I learned more about English watching them work than in all the English classes I had ever taken. I learned a lot about grammar as they corrected sentences. I learned not to use passive verbs, which was one of their pet peeves. I also learned a lot about campaign sound bites. Each speech had to have a perfect sound bite. It couldn't be too long or too short, and it had to have enough information to get the point across and have meaning.

When I look back at the pictures, I realize how much he saw and experienced: so many parts of our great country, so many political rituals: train trips, campaigning in New Hampshire, Labor Day parades, debates, election night. I don't know whether he'll end up liking politics or hating it; I do know that he regularly follows and often informs me about news as it happens. He also has greater insight into, and understanding of, world events than do most of his peers. It was interesting to watch how the different political leaders around the country reacted to the presence of the young man on the campaign plane; some were incredibly gracious and made a special effort to talk with and include him, but a few others completely ignored him.

Robert: The most fun was being around Governor and Mrs. Bush. They laughed a lot and they called each other Bushie. Governor Jeb Bush gave me a nickname: Homeschool. Governor Ridge talked to me about football and sports; Governor Celluci told me the history of Boston Harbor on the boat ride on the way to the first debate. I had a great relationship with Condi Rice and Josh Bolten, who taught me a lot and always took time to try to broaden

my horizons. And I had fun joking and hanging out with Logan Walters, Gordon Johndroe, Chris Gilbert, Curtis Jablonka and "check man," Eric Terrell, who paid the bills. All the Secret Service agents were nice guys; Nick Trotta and I talked about the Mets and the Yankees all the time.

Of all the different jobs he witnessed, Robert liked the role of the Secret Service agents best. He regarded the press with great suspicion, perhaps because it was hard for a young man to watch them question his mother with such intensity, perhaps because of the frequent disparity between what he observed and what he saw in their stories. Robert's English teacher had told me that her class would be practicing the use of quotes in writing that fall, so one day I asked Robert to write a news story using quotes from Governor Bush's speech on health care. His lead sentence said the governor had "attacked" Al Gore on the issue.

Robert: I wrote it in the way I thought the press would write it. I had been there for months and I would be at the events, and the next day I would

337

read about how the press had covered the event and it seemed so skewed; they twisted everything. A simple speech about Governor Bush's own policy would turn into a personal attack on the other candidate when you read it in the next day's newspaper. I think that the media's main goal is to make people read their stories, so they exaggerate things to make them more interesting and confrontational.

While those of us on the campaign trail spent life tightly wrapped in the bizarre cocoon of airplanes, fifteen-passenger vans and a succession of hotel rooms, our families' lives went on largely without us. Jerry felt he was in limbo, waiting for life's next chapter and uncertain what it would be; he did some legal work, kept the house running and helped us get ready to leave again whenever we stumbled back into town. He tried to monitor campaign news and give me an objective read on how it appeared to the public; but he couldn't watch too much because all the pundits and prognosticators drove him crazy. My daughter Leigh got divorced; our granddaughter Lauren started kindergarten at the same school Robert had attended. When Leigh and her husband had separated the year before, she and Lauren had moved in with us for several months, just as the campaign was getting under way. We were really proud of our daughter. She had gone back to school, studying nights and weekends to earn her certification as a licensed vocational nurse. Now Leigh had an apartment near our house, and a good job as a nurse with a group of ear, nose and throat doctors in Austin. Mrs. Bush and I had a glass of champagne with my longtime friend and her chief of staff, Andi Ball, to help Andi celebrate her twenty-fifth wedding anniversary; her husband Lonnie had sent it to our hotel in New York. The next year, when we were at the White House, Andi and Lonnie went out of town to a bed-and-breakfast to celebrate their twenty-sixth anniversary. I sent champagne, with a note: "Sorry I couldn't be there to celebrate with you; glad Lonnie was able to stand in for me this year."

Our days dissolved in a spin cycle of motion, all the hours of frantic activity geared toward the minute or so we would get on that evening's news, and the few quotes that would appear in the next morning's newspapers. Once, when a Washington magazine sharply criticized a number of the reporters covering our campaign, calling them everything from "clueless" to "dumb," I went back to the press cabin, tongue in cheek: "I just want you all to know you can't believe everything you read in the media. I've learned a lot of the hateful things they say about you are wrong, just wrong. If any of you needs someone to defend you, I'm known as a fierce advocate . . ."

Looking back now, it's hard to imagine that I maintained any sense of humor at all. The press was always questioning, always asking, always there. Whenever I went to their filing center or the back of the airplane, it was like sprinkling food in a fish bowl. One especially grueling day, when reporters had been grilling me for what seemed like hours, I climbed on board the airplane and saw the head of our Secret Service detail, Mike Pritchard.

"How about if we change jobs tomorrow, Mike? I'll look out for the candidate; you deal with the press," I suggested.

He looked at me, horrified: "No way. They can only shoot me; they torture you," he said.

Campaigns have cycles, up and down, and the giant sucking sound in September was our campaign, being pulled down,

down into the media drain. Al Gore had come out of the Democratic convention in late August with a huge surge, based primarily, as far as we could tell, on of all things, a kiss. I didn't get it; public displays of affection, PDAs as my husband calls them, are not greeted warmly around my house. But when Al Gore grabbed his wife and kissed her for a few moments too long on-stage, he looked real, which, as I had helped point out to my fellow Americans, was rare for him.

A new story line was being written: Al Gore was on his way up, while we were trapped in a swirl of our own making about debates. Our debate strategy turned out to be a huge miscalculation, as Governor Bush had warned from the moment we first suggested it. The Presidential Debates Commission had proposed three debates, which we thought were too many, especially since they were formal, stuffy affairs. In the previous twenty years, only once, in 1992, had the Republican and Democratic nominees for president debated three times. The presidential candidates debated twice in 1984, 1988 and 1996, and just once in 1980. Yet, predictably, the Democrats had started squawking that our campaign was "chicken," yet another variation on that old theme, "lightweight" — not up to debating.

We had hoped to catch the Democrats unprepared: on the eve of their convention, we announced that Governor Bush would participate in three debates, although we didn't say which ones, and refused to say that they would all three be sponsored by the Presidential Debates Commission. We thought we had a lot of choices because Al Gore had gone around promising various reporters he would debate on their programs; we naively thought the press would roast him if he failed to keep those promises. We liked the idea of mixing it up; including one formal debate, then a couple of different settings like *Meet the Press*, where we knew Tim Russert would challenge both candidates and refuse to let them get by with memorized speeches and practiced sound bites, and Larry King, who had moderated several insightful and interesting exchanges during the primary season. We were a little suspicious of the stuffy, formal commission debates, where the candidates stood behind podiums, governed by rules that were supposedly agreed on by both campaigns but were really mainly imposed and overseen by the commission. Governor Bush has little patience for things that strike him as fake; we felt he would be far more comfortable in a conversational give-and-take setting with reporters than from behind a podium delivering practiced remarks. I thought it would make for more interesting debates, too. Ironically, most of the press didn't see it that way: once again, they thought we were just ducking.

"I hope you all know what you are doing," Governor Bush had said, clearly thinking we didn't, when we proposed the strategy to him.

"We're going to announce that you will participate in three debates, then name which ones later," we told him.

"What are you going to do when he says no?" Governor Bush asked.

"The press won't let him," we assured the governor, "we've got him on tape saying he'll debate anytime, anywhere; they've got to hold him to his word," Karl and I were most vociferous; Joe agreed, and so did Don Evans, now our general campaign chairman.

Governor Bush was not convinced: "We're going to end up backing down," he warned, clearly not happy with our proposed debate strategy. But we were pretty insistent, and for some reason, he told us to go ahead, one of the only times I can ever remember him authorizing something that his gut told him was wrong. Then we failed, miserably.

We announced that Governor Bush would participate in three debates: one on *Meet the Press*, one on *Larry King Live*, and a final presidential commission debate. We quickly learned that there are certain institutions, like the Presidential Debates Commission, which have become a part of the process and are larger than any individual candidate in any given year. The press trusted the commission and resented our efforts to take control of the debate process. The stories were skeptical as we headed toward Naperville, Illinois, for its Labor Day parade.

Labor Day is the traditional kickoff of the fall campaign, another milestone we had eagerly anticipated. The crowd was huge and enthusiastic, the day sunny as Governor Bush gave a prepared speech, but suddenly, something was wrong. It began as a minor buzz, just after the event. I overheard a few people whispering: "Did you hear that?" "Did he say a bad word?" Maybe it was a rumor. I was talking with Diane Sawyer, who had come to Naperville to observe our campaign in advance of her interview with Governor Bush about education the next day. But then a reporter came to me:

"Karen, several people in the audience heard Governor Bush calling someone an asshole from the stage." I couldn't imagine it; I had heard his speech but hadn't heard anything like that. "It was before the event started, he said it to Dick Cheney," the reporter insisted.

I went to find out; the governor was already on the move, walking toward the starting line of the parade. I whispered to him: "Did you call someone an asshole?" I could see his brain computing: Karen is not supposed to know about this.

"Yeah, I did," he said, nodding. It turned out that he had spied a reporter from *The New York Times* that he thought had written some unfair stories about his dad, and had turned to his running mate, "There's Adam Clymer," he had said, speaking under his breath, "a major-league asshole." "Yeah," the future vice president agreed, "big time."

The powerful directional microphones had picked up and broadcast his comments. Governor Bush was subdued the rest of the day; he felt that he had let people down. He didn't want kids to hear him using bad language. It was one of the few times in the entire campaign that this disciplined man had made a mistake; there are no private asides in presidential races. The press wanted an apology, but he had said it, and meant it, and he's an honest person so he didn't back down: he was sorry that remarks he had intended to be private had been overheard by the public.

For the next several weeks, I felt we were slogging through a swamp of bubblegum in hiking boots; we couldn't get any traction or momentum. *Time* magazine's cover said it all: HUMPTY W.: HOW BAD A FALL?

I kept thinking this was the time when all good Republicans should rally to our side, point out that despite the devastating drumbeat of negative news stories, the polls were showing the race was a statistical dead heat: the CNN-Time poll that week had the race "too close to call," with Al Gore at 47, and George Bush at 46 percent. But you wouldn't know it from reading the stories. Our so-called friends and fellow Republicans were piling on, even helping foster the bad news: "Undeniable panic is gripping partisan Republicans," reported columnist Robert Novak; according to *The New York Times*, Republicans were calling the Bush campaign "defensive, bumbling, weary, detached or peevish."

"All in one sentence?" asked *Washington Post* media writer Howard Kurtz, questioning the sudden rush of negative stories.

Our campaign was "sliding in the polls and facing questions over strategy," *The Dallas Morning News* had reported on the morning of September 8, when we had a great event featuring retired Generals Norman Schwartzkopf and Colin Powell. Governor Bush even made news, hinting that Colin Powell would be a part of his administration if he won.

But that wasn't the news the reporters who swarmed me at the event wanted to cover; our campaign was losing, mired, stuck. "What are you going to do about it?" the reporters demanded.

Calmly facing the media storm in a moment that I think was one of his best of the campaign, Governor Bush met the press under the wing of his airplane later that morning, his unruffled demeanor helping regain control of the coverage. "George W. Bush embarked today on an effort to retool his campaign by showing new willingness to compromise on the presidential debate schedule and indicating that he will work more aggressively to connect with voters," *The Washington Post* reported. "Bush told reporters that he would negotiate with Al Gore over the debate schedule — a stark reversal of his earlier effort to impose a plan that the Vice President deemed unacceptable," the newspaper continued. The press had extracted its pound of flesh, we had reversed ourselves; maybe now we could move on.

Privately, Governor Bush was unhappy with us. He felt our misguided effort to commit to three debates of our choosing had left him in a position where he no longer had room to negotiate, and he was right. But he was also sanguine about the demands of the political process, describing the Republicans who were questioning everything as "people getting ready to jump out of the foxhole before the first shell is fired." I was furious with all the anonymous Republicans for making things worse, but I knew better than to say anything like that. I swallowed my pride. "We're listening," I made myself say. "We know it is well intentioned. Republicans want to win."

It was Laura Bush, a little removed because she had spent most of August and early September getting her daughters off to college, who saw it first. She called me down to their room one night: "Have you been watching the pictures on the nightly news?" she asked. I hadn't; mostly I read the summaries because we spent our evenings at events or on the airplane. "Vice President Gore is always surrounded by cheering crowds; George is on the plane, in his shirtsleeves, hunched over, talking to reporters."

I realized immediately that she was absolutely right; my boss's accessibility to the press at the back of the airplane was now hurting us. Given a choice between an excerpt from a rally speech and Governor Bush's answer to one of their own questions, journalists would choose his response to their questions every time; America was seeing George Bush jousting with reporters on a dark airplane, and Al Gore in front of balloons and huge adoring crowds. It was time to keep Governor Bush at the front of the plane. The reporters wouldn't like it, and he would miss the give-and-take, but the pictures were what mattered now.

Just when it seemed nothing more could go wrong, the rats came. The rats weren't all of those Republicans who were jumping off the ship, although that's what I secretly wanted to call them; these rats were letters in a campaign commercial. Mark McKinnon thought the story was so ridiculous that when he first got the call, he didn't take it seriously. The next morning, when it appeared on the front page of *The New York Times*, we all had to pay attention. I ducked behind a curtain at our morning event to place a cell-phone call to Alex Castellanos, who had produced the ad for the Republican National Committee. The reporters were all lined up outside, in full frenzy mode, waiting for my response: had the Bush campaign tried to unfairly influence voters with subliminal advertising designed to drill into their unsuspecting brains that Al Gore was a rat? Alex told me the suggestion was ridiculous, that he had used a video-streaming technique that brought the word *bureaucrats* up on the screen a few letters at a time, rather than all at once, to make it look as if the word leaped onto the screen. (When we were at the *Oprah* show a few weeks later, I noticed her name comes on the screen the same way at the opening of her program.) The combinations of individual letters were not visible to the naked eye, Alex told me; only if you watched the commercials in slow motion, frame by frame, for one-thirtieth of a second, could you see the letters forming the end of the word *bureaucrats*.

A slow-motion tape of the ad had been delivered to *The New York Times* by Vice President Gore's campaign; reporter Richard Berke had called various producers of campaign advertising, several of them rivals of Alex's, who suggested that we were using this technique to plant a subliminal message that our opponent was a rat. Of all the stories I could imagine would consume two days of our time in the final months of a campaign to determine the president of the United States, this one had to be the most bizarre. We were trying to focus on Governor Bush's plan to add prescription drug benefits to Medicare; but the press was in full frenzy about the letters in our ad. To show we didn't take ourselves so seriously that we couldn't laugh in the midst of a media crisis, I decided to greet the press as they boarded the plane with a plate of cheese. Some of the press got the joke; others, looking for the conspiracy behind every action, thought I was implying they were rats.

Robert: Sometimes my mom is funny, but this wasn't even close. She was trying to make fun of the story, but she just looked stupid walking around the plane with a plate of cheese. The reporters missed the whole point; no one was laughing. Gordon and I had tried to talk her out of it, but she stubbornly refused to listen to us. I thought she should have just ignored it; the

whole story was so ridiculous that it didn't seem worthy of a response.

The very same day, reporters started asking about a profile written by Gail Sheehy in *Vanity Fair* magazine suggesting that Governor Bush mispronounced words occasionally because he has dyslexia. At the news conference where he was asked about this medical theory and the rats ad, the governor mispronounced the word *subliminal* four times, adding a syllable to create a new word, *subliminable*, a fact we noted with great hilarity on the campaign airplane. Governor Bush generally laughs about his verbal gaffes; earlier in the campaign, he had picked up the airplane's public address system one night when he had confused an entire paragraph in one of his speeches, and addressed the press: "I know who the thems were, and the thems was you!"

"That's how Texans talk when we're tired," I told the press that night. My favorite excuse, though, was one I came up with later: "His brain faster works than his mouth does," I joked. A doctor later told me there's more truth to that than I realized when I coined it. A lot of highly intelligent people whose brains work quickly stumble over words, he told me. It makes sense, at least as much as a magazine trying to diagnose the medical condition of a presidential candidate — yet another reminder of what a long way from normal a presidential campaign truly is.

But rats and assholes and even dyslexia were distractions; the fall campaign is really dominated by debates. And our debates gained added intrigue when part of our debate preparation notebook and a videotape of Governor Bush participating in a mock debate were delivered to Al Gore's campaign. To their great credit, the Gore campaign immediately notified the FBI and our campaign chairman, Don Evans. Governor Bush and I were in California, at an Asian-American rally, and the reporters surrounded me: how could our debate materials have been shipped to Al Gore? I couldn't imagine; I was in charge of debate preparation, and I didn't know any more than the reporters did, except that this was very fishy. The one thing I knew, and kept repeating, was that no one who wanted George Bush to be president would have sent those materials to Al Gore. An FBI agent called me, and said he might need to ask me some questions. He never did: I don't think I was a very likely suspect. I did call Jerry at home that night and asked him to search the house until he found my debate notebook, to make sure I hadn't accidentally left it somewhere where someone might have grabbed it. The FBI spent time at our campaign headquarters, and at Mark McKinnon's office; eventually one of his employees was charged and later convicted of mail fraud for sending the materials to the Gore campaign.

Even without the added drama, we had all learned that debates freeze the campaign. Almost everything else — all the travel, all the speeches, all the rallies — is largely irrelevant in the days before and after a debate, as the press engages in the ultimate expression of the expectations game: Did George W. Bush do what he had to do? Did the vice president live up to his reputation as a great debater? Did George W. Bush put aside the doubts about his foreign policy knowledge? Can Al Gore shed his image as a candidate who changes positions as easily as he does clothes?

"He did what he had to do," Governor Bush kept jesting all week, mocking what the pundits would say about the debate results. "I think I'll just *be myself*," he would announce, mocking all his friends and staff who told him, again and again: "Just be yourself."

"Who do they think I might be?" he asked me more than once, laughing.

Debates may not elect a presidential candidate, but a mistake can sure defeat one. Governor Bush always tried to keep his head clear on debate days, no last-minute cramming, no staff debates about what he should say — just a low-key final review session, an hour and a half or so, to go over the day's news, possible new questions, a final discussion of any answers he didn't feel comfortable with or wanted to go over one more time. George Bush doesn't like commotion before big events. He likes order, familiar people, a familiar routine: up early, read the newspapers and have coffee with Mrs. Bush, read the Bible, as he does every day, find time to exercise.

Formal debating is not a skill a president ever uses; unlike members of Congress, presidents don't go to microphones to spar with their opponents except when they seek election or reelection. Debates do help gauge how a candidate responds to pressure, and to a lesser extent, how well he thinks on his feet: after more than a year on the campaign trail, candidates are accustomed to answering questions; normally they have their standard spiels readily available for speedy delivery. Debates can also be an unfair measure: they frequently come down to one memorable line or moment that may or may not reflect the entirety of the exchange: "I paid for this microphone, Mr. Green," Ronald Reagan memorably said in New Hampshire in 1980, chastising the master of ceremonies and graciously taking the side of his other opponents by allowing them to join what had been billed as a two-man debate between Reagan and George H. W. Bush; "I knew John Kennedy; John Kennedy was a friend of mine; and you, sir, you are no John Kennedy," Lloyd Bentsen memorably said to Dan Quayle in a perfectly delivered put-down. But lines like that are hard to come by. We had a few ideas, but never a showstopper.

The night before the first debate on October 3, a group of us went downstairs to the hotel restaurant with Governor and Mrs. Bush. The waitress was overwhelmed by the thought of serving a potential president; she fluttered around, then disappeared. After almost an hour, the salads still hadn't arrived at the table, and our patience-is-not-his-strong-suit-and-neither-is-waiting-too-long-for-a-meal candidate was fit to be tied. If Governor Bush had it his way, the plates of food would arrive as soon as he did; he's always the one who wants to order, now, and can you bring it fast. Don Evans kept going to the kitchen, urging the chefs along, but we ate way too late, and then the train whistles from the nearby tracks blew all night long; none of us slept well, especially the candidate. If you had to plan the worst possible predebate evening for a candidate who likes to eat early and sleep well, that night would come close.

A debate is a bizarre exercise: while the candidates joust onstage, people with computers work backstage, checking every answer against the facts and things the candidate has said previously, searching for inaccuracies and inconsistencies. The minute I heard Al Gore say he had visited Texas with James Lee Witt during the wildfires, I knew he was wrong. "He did not," I told Dan Bartlett, in charge of our rapid response operation. "I was there, so was James Lee Witt, so was Governor Bush: Al Gore wasn't." Our researchers checked and verified he had made other trips with Witt, but not this one. After the debate, in the media room, our campaign gleefully pointed up that fact, and several other statements we thought exaggerated or misrepresented the facts. Privately, I called the first debate "lies and sighs," because Gore's claims were frequently accompanied by condescending huffs as he chastised what Governor Bush had just said as one of the (sigh!) stupidest things he had ever heard.

Robert: It was tense on debate days; everybody was nervous. During the debates, we would sit in a room analyzing each and every word of the candidate's responses. But the real work for my mom started afterward when it was a war of who could best spin that their candidate had won. Governor Bush gave me the notebook he used to jot down his thoughts during the second debate, one of my favorite souvenirs from the campaign.

The second debate focused extensively on foreign policy. Before it, some had questioned whether a governor from Texas whose experience with foreign affairs had been primarily limited to working with Mexico would be able to hold his own against the incumbent vice president; Governor Bush was clear and forceful. I remember Condi Rice turning to me as the debate wrapped up: "I think he won the presidency tonight," she told me.

The most memorable exchange of the

third debate came not with words, but with body language. Early in the debate, Vice President Gore made a weird, sinister-looking move toward Governor Bush, as if he were physically challenging him; Governor Bush defused it with a congenial laugh and a relaxed shrug. There had been no knockout punches, no debate hall of fame moments, but we all felt Governor Bush won all three debates. I was so relieved the morning after the final one that I decided to poke fun at all the postdebate spin. I wrote a takeoff on David Letterman's top ten list, and shared it with colleagues and some of the reporters traveling with us:

"From the home office in Nashville, Tennessee (home of Gore campaign headquarters), the top ten reasons Governor Bush won the debates:

No. 10: The mikes were on.
No. 9: There are laws against stalking.
No. 8: Major league performance. Big-time.
No. 7: Al Gore finally stopped sighing about his record.
No. 6: Two words: subliminable messages.
No. 5: Nice guys finish first.

No. 4: Gore's dog likes Bush's prescription drug plan better.

No. 3: Texas: It's not a third world country.

No. 2: He's finally learned the difference between East Timorians and West Texians.

And the No. 1 reason why Governor Bush won the debates: strategery (the word *Saturday Night Live* had used to poke fun at Governor Bush's mispronunciations).

The debates behind us, it was now just a matter of time: we were counting the days, and rallies: a week to go, six days, only twenty-seven more times to crank up the music, give the speech, shake the hands, move on to the next event. And then, the Thursday before the Tuesday election, my beeper went off: CALL DAN, 911. This was before September 11, when 911 still meant just "emergency."

The president was in a routine interview; I called in to campaign headquarters. Our rapid response director, Dan Bartlett, didn't even say hello: "One of our spokesmen just got a call from Maine, asking about the governor being arrested for

DUI," he told me. Four days to go in the campaign, and all the air was suddenly gone.

The call had come from our New Hampshire office, where a local Fox reporter had confronted a member of the campaign staff: "I have information saying that Governor Bush was arrested for DUI in Kennebunkport." The New Hampshire office called Austin, and talked with our regional spokesman, Ken Liasius, who walked into Dan's office: "You're not going to believe what I just heard . . ."

Dan said he had felt the blood draining from his body. "Really?" he asked Ken. "Yeah, they claim they have some document that proves it; they're going to fax it down," Ken said. "Get Karen on the phone," Dan told his assistant, then walked down the hall to tell Karl Rove and Don Evans.

"Karen?" Dan said, questioning the silence on my end of the line; he later told me it was the only time since he had known me that he could recall me being speechless.

"We've got to acknowledge it," I said as soon as I could talk, thinking out loud: "That's what we always said we would do if we were ever asked, but I've got to talk to the governor first."

Dan and I both knew it was true: the governor had told me and a few others because he didn't want us blindsided or put in a position of lying about it; I had told Dan for the same reason. We had talked a few times about making it public, but there never seemed to be a way that was consistent with our candidate's wishes or previous statements. Governor Bush had always said he wasn't going to itemize irresponsible behavior as a younger man; he felt the media's obsession with candidates' pasts prevented good people from getting involved in politics. I had brought it up when we had written his autobiography: "If you want to get it out, you could talk about it in the book," I mentioned, but he had decided not to. The governor's daughters didn't know; they were teenage drivers, and he didn't want to set a bad example for them or other young people. He had been honest that he had sometimes had too much to drink in the past, and he had quit drinking.

Governor Bush was still finishing his interview, and Dan called back on my cell phone: "I've got Carl Cameron (the national Fox reporter) on the phone, he's thirty seconds from going on the air," Dan said.

"I'm standing outside the door waiting to

talk to the governor," I replied.

"He's going on the air," Dan reported.

"Confirm it," I said, making the decision, and the delay was only seconds: "A Bush campaign official has confirmed . . ."

"I've got to see you alone," I told the governor. I had told Robert to stay outside, the only time I had ever done so; I couldn't imagine how my son would react to this news. "A reporter in New Hampshire called to ask about the DUI," I told the governor.

His face didn't change, but his body slumped a little: "We've got to confirm it, then," he said.

"I just did," I told him. Laura Bush joined us; they began making plans to call their daughters. We were on the way to the airport; I knew I would have to talk with the press before we took off. This story wouldn't wait any longer. I scratched some notes on my legal pad: "Twenty-four years ago, Governor Bush was arrested in Kennebunkport after having several beers . . . drinking and driving is a mistake." A full frenzy was under way as I stepped into a huge swarm of reporters on the tarmac. I realized Robert might get lost in the shuffle, and called to Mark McKinnon. "Mark, grab Robert; make sure he gets on the plane." As the media pelted me with questions, Robert watched with Governor and Mrs. Bush from the airplane window; they said it looked like we had thrown blood to sharks.

Robert: I was with Logan and Gordon and we were just messing around in the hall juggling oranges. I knew something was up because it was weird that my mom didn't let me in the room. I usually went to all the meetings. When I found out what it was, I realized it was serious, but I thought it was all so long ago. I wasn't even born then. Everybody makes mistakes. People should be forgiven. I thought it was a cheap shot, and I thought that the Gore campaign had purposely let it out with only a few days to go in the campaign. The reporters were all swarming around my mom; we couldn't even see her in the middle of them.

Even as I tried to answer all the questions, I knew my briefing wouldn't be enough. At big moments like this one, the press and the public need to see the candidate. I talked to Joe Allbaugh, our campaign manager, and he agreed completely: Governor Bush had to address this himself. I went to tell the governor, behind the stage at the next event. He wasn't happy about it, but he knew it was the right thing to do. After his speech, four days before Election Day, he and Mrs. Bush walked over to the press to answer questions about his arrest twenty-four years before for driving under the influence of alcohol. "I've oftentimes said that years ago I made some mistakes. I drank too much, and I did on that night . . . I regret that it happened, but it did. I've learned my lesson."

The story dominated the air waves and ran nonstop on all the cable channels; reporters were all over me the next morning on the campaign airplane. Members of the media were trying to ascertain whether we had misled them; I reminded reporters that Governor Bush had been directly and publicly asked in 1996, after he had been dismissed from jury duty, if he had ever been arrested for drunk driving and he had replied: "I do not have a perfect record as a youth. When I was young, I did a lot of foolish things. But I will tell you this, I urge people not to drink and drive."

Trying to dampen the frenzy, I observed: "He recognizes that this is new news for the media and so the media have to cover it. It's also something that he thinks is not very new to the American people; I don't think there are too many Americans who are surprised that someone who used to drink too much, one night drank too much."

I believe the last-minute revelation hurt our campaign, ironically not so much because of the long-ago arrest itself, but because the public was so fed up with scandal after the Clinton administration. The reporters tried to make the comparison, asking me if it would have been okay for President Clinton to have denied involvement with Monica Lewinsky because he was concerned about his daughter Chelsea. That infuriated me: I saw absolutely no equivalence between a sexual act with a student intern that the incumbent president of the United States had engaged in while on the job in the White House, then lied about to the American people, and a long-ago arrest for drinking too many beers one night that Governor Bush had chosen not to voluntarily disclose. With great difficulty, I restrained myself: "The only time the governor was directly asked if he'd ever been arrested for drinking and driving, he replied, and I quote, 'I do not have a perfect record.' "

The news of the arrest came out at the worst possible time, with only four full days to go in the campaign. Many have suggested that I would have served my candidate better had I insisted he disclose it earlier; maybe so, but I had agreed with him that there is too much focus on the long-ago mistakes of people who seek to lead us. It's a fine line, and I'm still not sure where to draw it: how much do we really need to know?

We stumbled through the final days; the advance teams gave out Mickey Mouse hats at the hotel the last night: HUGHES and LITTLE HUGHES said mine and Robert's. Jerry flew to Florida and joined us for all four stops on our final day of campaigning; I was so grateful he was there. I felt I had been through the most trying, traumatic experience of my life and I was just glad it was almost over, and he was there to hang on to.

The only thing that gets you through something as grueling as a presidential campaign is the absolute certainty that come Election Day, win or lose — and by the end, you almost, but not quite, don't care — it's over. You cling to that certainty whenever it seems that you can't go to another rally or listen to another speech or answer another question: just two months, and it's over; just three weeks, and it's over; just ten days, and it's over; one more weekend, and it's over; just one more rally, and it's over.

Governor Bush met with our traveling reporters at the governor's mansion before he went to vote on Election Day. When they were escorted out, he asked me to stay, and he thanked me. One of the photographers tried to walk back into the living room to take a picture of us talking, but the governor shooed him away: this was private. Neither of us is a second-guesser: we felt we had given it our all, run a good campaign, and we had done it our way.

I couldn't help but think of one of his last interviews, with Alexandra Pelosi, an NBC producer who had carried a home video camera with her from the beginning of the campaign and later put together the HBO documentary, *Journeys with George.*

"What's happened since the first time I interviewed you more than a year ago?" she asked.

"Let's see," Governor Bush said. "What's happened: I've given some speeches, my girls went to college, it's rained on the ranch." That's not a typical answer for a political candidate wrapping up a presidential race, and it's one of the things I like best about him: it's not all about him. He's too normal to be the president, I remember thinking, in the very best sense of the word;

for Governor Bush, even the possibility of being the president was not all consuming, just a part of a much bigger life that includes family and friends and faith and that beloved ranch in Texas.

I walked to the courthouse with Governor and Mrs. Bush when they went to vote, and answered some questions, not hard ones, anymore: it was all over but the casting and counting. Of course, that morning, I had no idea just how excruciating the casting and counting would prove to be. "How do you feel?" some of the reporters asked me; exhausted, mainly; relieved that it was finished. Karl had been certain for days now that we would win with more than three hundred electoral votes; I'm naturally suspicious of polls and predictions and never allow myself to believe them completely, but I thought we had probably won.

Robert: I was exhausted. I had just endured five months of sixteen-hour days, a diet of airplane food and vending-machine snacks, and a group of reporters who refused to leave my mom alone. It had all started to hit me in the last two weeks on the campaign trail. I started getting tired, homesick, and

sick of all the annoying idiosyncra-
sies that go along with life on the
campaign trail. Throughout it all, I
had realized that on Election Day it
would all be over and I could finally
relax. So I was both excited and nervous. Excited that I could finally
sleep in my own bed and not wonder
what beautiful Tarmac I would visit
the following day. At the same time,
I was nervous about the outcome.
The campaign had been my life for
the last few months, although I was
not quite certain how I wanted it to
turn out. Of course, I wanted Governor Bush to win because he was
my friend and I knew he would make
a great president. However, I was
worried about the effects it would
have on my life. I would have to
move from a city where I had lived
for ten years, leave behind countless
lifelong friends and move to a
brand-new city in the middle of my
eighth grade year (not the best of sit-
uations for a thirteen-year-old). In
the end, I decided that it was selfish
to want the president to lose so that I
would not have to move, and I realized that it was important that Pres-

ident Bush be elected for the good of our country and millions of others throughout the world. The morning of Election Day, I decided to play golf with Mark McKinnon and two of his coworkers in a fruitless attempt to divert my mind from the election. After nine holes of playing in the cold and rain with very few good shots, we quit and went to have lunch at Hula Hut, a local restaurant that overlooks the lake. It would be the only food I would have for the next twenty-four hours.

My parents and sister had traveled to Austin and I met them for lunch; Karl called me toward the end to say the exit polling service was having trouble; the first sets of numbers were all messed up. Since I don't pay much attention to polls anyway, I didn't think much about it. I went for my Election Day good-luck haircut, and then went to cast my vote for my boss for president, a thrilling moment. It was quiet and ordinary at the polls, but not inside me: I had never expected to know or care so intensely about the person whose name I marked by filling in the oval with a number two pencil. I took my time, wanting to make sure the mark was perfect, then I picked up Robert, and drove back to campaign headquarters.

Robert kept quizzing me about the exit polls, so I called the office, and it wasn't good news: "That's interesting. Twenty-four states too close to call? Hmmm." It didn't make sense — one of them was Colorado, and we were supposed to win handily there. "We should get the governor to call in to some radio stations," I told Karl, to tell people it was going to be really close and urge them to vote. But I was really just going through the motions. I didn't think anything we could do at that point would have made much difference.

Robert: When Mom picked me up, she had a reporter in the backseat; he was following her around for the day. I wanted to ask my mom how she thought the election was really going, but felt uncomfortable talking about that in front of him. I bit my tongue and decided to wait until we were in private to ask. Unfortunately, I never got that opportunity. As soon as we walked into headquarters, my mom was told to rush into Karl Rove's office immediately. The exit polls looked terrible. I felt very

disappointed, even though we had not lost the race yet. I knew that those polls were pretty accurate, although they are wrong sometimes. I went to my mom's office and watched her make calls to several people, trying to make a last ditch effort to get people to the polls. It seemed like every minute another state was being called for Gore, and none for the governor. I honestly thought we had lost at that point.

A few minutes after seven, with the polls still open in Florida's Panhandle, the networks called Florida for Al Gore. It ruined the Bush family's election night dinner; the phone in my office rang a few minutes later.

"I'm going back to the mansion," Governor Bush told me, "come over after a while." He was supposed to stay at the Four Seasons and watch returns in a suite with family and friends; he must want more privacy, I thought, and started talking with Mindy and Dan and Gordon and Ari about how to explain his exit to the reporters who had seen the motorcade leave the hotel.

"Don't worry, Robert, it's in the bag," Mark McKinnon kept telling my son, "it's just a very small bag."

Karl and Mathew Dowd, our pollster, and Mark and others were crowding into Karl's office at headquarters; Karl was ranting about Florida: "This is wrong; the numbers don't support it; get CNN on the phone . . ."

My phone rang again. "Are you coming?" Governor Bush asked. I had stayed away to give him some privacy, but hurried over now. I walked up the back steps, Robert just behind me, and saw former president Bush on the sofa in front of the television. Without thinking, I blurted out: "Hello, Mr. President, how are you?"

"Not so good right now," was the quiet answer, and I spent the next hour kicking myself: some public relations person I am; a father is watching his son possibly lose the presidency, and I'm asking how he's doing.

Robert: I was overwhelmed by what we saw when we got there. The only people in the room were the governor, Mrs. Bush, former president Bush and Mrs. Barbara Bush. It was really quiet; I just followed my mom and tried to stay out of the way. I went to a back room to watch the television; my mom was asking how they could have called Florida when

we were fifty thousand votes ahead. Logan and I started working to add up combinations of electoral votes that would let us win without Florida.

I was looking for an opportunity to show the media that we were still in the race. When Al Gore's home state, Tennessee, went for Bush, I saw it. We invited the media up for a photo opportunity, with Governor and Mrs. Bush, his mom and dad watching returns. They answered a few questions: this would be a long night. The presidency was still up in the air; our people thought the numbers in Florida and maybe Pennsylvania were wrong.

Robert: It was awkward; there wasn't much to say, and the press didn't seem to know what to ask. No one was sure what was going on. I still thought we had a chance because I kept hearing all the numbers the networks were reporting and it just didn't look right — we were consistently ahead in Florida.

"We're still alive," Governor Bush said to Dick Cheney on the telephone at 9:30 p.m.

just after the press left; then minutes later, we heard the sound of someone taking the steps, several at a time:

"Back from the ashes," Governor Jeb Bush of Florida shouted, as he ran up the back stairs of the Texas governor's mansion just minutes after the networks pulled Florida back from the Gore column, declaring it once again "too close to call."

Robert: It was a chain reaction; once one network changed Florida, they all did. I didn't know what to think: it was so weird. I had never expected anything like this. It was funny when Jeb Bush came running up the stairs; one of the only times that night we were able to laugh.

For the next several hours, former president Bush watched the returns with his two sons, and I sat there with mine. Barbara Bush had retreated to a bedroom, but she wandered out occasionally to look at the television; so did Laura Bush, and her mother, Jenna Welch. I don't think any of us could believe this was happening.

Robert and Logan were still working on combinations that would deliver the 270 electoral votes Governor Bush needed to win the presidency. "Twenty-four more votes, that's what we need," Logan said. "Doesn't Florida have twenty-five?" he asked Jeb, tongue in cheek. The response was quick, and jesting: "Logan, shut up," the other governor Bush replied, not needing to be reminded of the stakes.

The numbers slowly rolled in: 10:56 p.m., my notes say, 99 percent from Duval, 130,200 to 96,000, a 34,000-vote margin with no absentees counted, we didn't think. Governor Jeb Bush was on his computer, tracking numbers from the Florida elections office, calling them out periodically.

Robert: I remember Jeb and his assistant, in the corner, huddled over his computer. They were looking at the secretary of state's Web sites, trying to get the numbers from the counties that hadn't reported yet.

At 12:17 a.m. we were getting precinct reports, as if we were adding totals for a county commissioner's race, instead of the presidency. "If they keep on counting 'em, and we end up with more votes, we win," Governor Jeb Bush announced once, stating the obvious to great laughter; but by then we were all exhausted, and nothing was obvious anymore.

Suddenly, Fox called it: Florida was in the Bush column, deciding the presidency.

Robert: I was in the back room; I walked to the main room and Logan told the governor that Fox had called the election. Suddenly, CNN did, too, and all the others.

We weren't sure whether to believe it; then another network agreed and we all started applauding. The new president-elect kissed his wife, shook his father's hand, gave his mother a kiss on the cheek, hugged me; but Jeb was still worried, looking at his computer, checking with Florida.

"I don't see it," he was saying, almost to himself, "where are they getting these numbers?"

Happy chaos was erupting around us. Vice President-elect and Mrs. Cheney and Don and Suzie Evans were on their way over from the Four Seasons Hotel. We needed to finalize the draft speech for the president-elect to give to the crowd in front of the Texas Capitol, but there was still confusion amid the congratulations. As the only senior staff member present, I felt responsible; I didn't want us to make a mistake or claim victory too soon.

Shortly after 1:30 a.m. our time, 2:30 on the East Coast, the call from Vice President Gore came in.

Robert: Logan had Vice President Gore on his cell phone; he asked me to help him find the governor. He was in the kitchen with the makeup lady, getting ready to declare victory. Logan handed him the phone and we stood there and listened.

Governor Bush wrote a few notes from the conversation and handed them to me:

VP: Congratulations.
GWB: You're a formidable opponent
        and a good man.
VP: We gave them a cliff-hanger.
GWB: I know it's hard, and hard on
        your family. Give my best to
        Tipper.

Jeb was still worried about the numbers; I decided to make sure as many reporters as possible knew that the vice president had called to concede the race. I talked with Ron Fournier of the Associated Press, and

Candy Crowley of CNN, and it started being reported: Vice President Gore has called to congratulate the new president-elect. . . .

It seemed we could believe it, then, as people poured in downstairs, laughing and cheering and congratulating the governor. Then we waited. And waited some more.

Robert: My mom and the president-elect were trying to edit his speech in the front hallway. Everything seemed rushed; we never really had a chance to celebrate.

Our chairman, Don Evans, got a call from the Gore campaign chairman, who said they were double-checking some numbers. Governor Bush had walked back upstairs; I went up to join him. When I walked into the living room, he was on the telephone, once again, with Al Gore. Governor Bush's posture was stiff, his voice incredulous as he pressed the telephone to his ear: "You mean you are calling me to retract your concession?" I heard him say.

"Well, you've got to do what you've got to do." Governor Bush put down the phone. "He says he's retracting his concession," the governor told us. Vice President Gore later described the governor as "snippy"; he clearly wasn't happy, but this was unprecedented: the incumbent vice president was calling to retract a concession call he had made only an hour before?

Jeb was still at the computer, looking at numbers. "They think it's going to be a long time before we know," he reported. Governor Bush asked Don Evans to go out to speak to the crowd; Don and I huddled and worked on a quick statement.

"I'm going to bed; we'll reconvene in the morning," Governor Bush announced, his last words as we walked out of the house. Chairman Evans addressed the crowd waiting in the rain across the street. Robert and I returned to the hotel room where Jerry was waiting, where we had planned to celebrate election night at the Four Seasons downtown.

Robert: When we arrived at the hotel we were just quiet. I don't remember my mom and me doing a lot of talking. There was a picture of us in a magazine leaning against a column in the governor's mansion because we were really tired — that's how the night was.

Jerry was up and we talked briefly. Just as I managed to fall asleep, exhausted, the phone rang. It was Alicia Peterson, who booked television interviews for the campaign: Could I do the *Today* show? I couldn't; I didn't think I could even move; there was just no way. Ari Fleischer, to his credit and earning my true gratitude, stayed up all night and did the morning shows. I got back over to the campaign headquarters about eight thirty: Governor Bush and Dick Cheney summoned me, Joe, Karl and Andy Card to a meeting at the mansion at eleven. Gore's team had flown to Florida the night before, we learned; this was a new campaign and we were already behind.

We needed a statesman and a lawyer to handle our effort in Florida; former secretary of state James Baker was the immediate consensus choice. Don Evans went to call him, and shortly thereafter, Joe Allbaugh left to pick him up and fly him to Florida. Surely this would take only a day or two; the rest of us would handle things in Austin and start initiating the transition, which Clay Johnson had already been working on for months.

I spent the first few days feeling sorry for myself. I felt like a marathon runner who had just done the hardest thing in her whole life; then, just as she fell across the finish line, someone tapped her on the shoulder and said: "By the way, keep running; we'll let you know when you can stop." But it quickly became clear that this would become in many ways the fiercest fight of all, and I had to man my battle station.

Karl, Don Evans and I did a news conference the next day; it was packed with hundreds of journalists. For the next several weeks, I was on television every time I came in or left the governor's mansion. Once, a camera crew followed me down the hall on my way to the restroom, another time I was photographed as I went to buy a sandwich for lunch. The reporters who had covered our campaign were annoyed that I wouldn't spend more time talking with them, but our statements were being carefully coordinated now with the legal team in Florida.

Robert: This is when people started recognizing my mom everywhere. We couldn't go anywhere without people interrupting us or talking to her. I just tried not to pay attention. It was weird; I just tried to stay away, and walk way behind her in the malls.

Governor and Mrs. Bush went to the ranch, where he was on the phone, early and often, considering the legal recommendations, making decisions, giving instructions. My family was in limbo: Robert had been out of school and had become part of the campaign team; he wanted to be at campaign headquarters so he would know what was happening; there was no sense putting him back in school if we were moving to Washington, but we weren't sure we were moving. We had to sell our house if we were moving, but we couldn't put it on the market: the press would find out, and read it as the Bush team being overconfident.

It was awful, and just when I thought things couldn't get any crazier, my phone rang a little after five on the Tuesday morning of Thanksgiving week: "Secretary Cheney went to the hospital early this morning with chest pains," Don Evans told me. We were both worried, but Don reported he seemed to be feeling better now; he gave me daughter Liz Cheney's phone number and asked me to call her to coordinate.

I worked on a statement based on the facts we were able to collect: "Secretary Cheney was admitted to the hospital early this morning with chest and shoulder discomfort. His EKG shows no change and initial blood work shows that his cardiac enzymes are normal . . . He is now free of discomfort, and remains hospitalized for further tests and evaluation . . ."

My family had been scheduled to go to Dallas for Thanksgiving at my parents' house; the day before, with Secretary Cheney in the hospital, I canceled the trip. Our friends Steve and Janice Margolin insisted we join their family for Thanksgiving dinner and wouldn't let us bring anything. I was so grateful to their family for taking us in, and for helping remind us that there was a part of our life that was still somewhat normal.

At the end of the next week, we were still waiting; arguments were scheduled in the Supreme Court the following Tuesday. "You need to get out of town this weekend," Governor Bush insisted, "You haven't had a break; you need one."

I nodded, not convinced.

"Have you decided where you're going this weekend?" Governor Bush asked a few hours later; when I didn't have an answer, he called to his assistant: "Make Karen reservations to go to Mexico this weekend."

"I don't want to go to Mexico," I protested.

"Well, the next time I see you, you better have reservations to go somewhere or I'm sending you to Mexico," he said.

I called Jerry: "The governor is really serious about this," I said. "Can you call the Margolins and see if they'll keep Robert while we go to Santa Fe?"

The number of people who recognized and stopped me had exploded during the high-profile weeks of the Florida recount; when I had dashed into the grocery store on my way home from the campaign earlier in the week, at least fifty people had stopped to ask me questions or encourage me. It surprised me: during the campaign, Republicans and political junkies occasionally recognized me; suddenly, everyone seemed to as the country waited and watched to find out who would be the next president. "Maybe it's just Austin," my husband had said: "The governor lives here, so people are really focused on it. You'll be incognito in Santa Fe."

After we got off the airplane, Jerry went to get the rental car, and the skycap at the baggage claim pointed at me and exclaimed: "Hey, you're the lady who works for George Bush!" People yelled at me from across the street while I was shopping, and they came over to our table at dinner at night. They didn't want to bother us, but they wanted to know: how was it all going to turn out? They were all nice, and thanked me for what I had done for the president, but it was a shock to be so visible: my new life wasn't normal at all.

The weekend away did boost my spirits: I read, and shopped, and tried to catch up on sleep. But by the end of the next week, the rest from the three-day hiatus had worn off, especially by Friday afternoon, when the Florida Supreme Court issued its ruling allowing the recounting (I called it re-creating) of the vote to begin once again. It made me sick to think about: election officials holding up ballots, trying to read the minds and discern the intentions of the people who had cast them. Their judgment seemed arbitrary, based on whether a tiny bit of light appeared through a hole that might or might not have been poked, and how would they ever know whether a voter had started to vote one way, then changed his or her mind? It's not very popular to say so, but invalid ballots are invalid ballots: if they are not properly cast, they are not counted. Years before, as a reporter, I had witnessed numerous recounts: the fact is that a lot of ballots are discarded in every election because they are improperly

387

marked. The difference is that the presidency doesn't usually depend on it.

We couldn't believe it when we learned this bizarre exercise was going to begin again. Robert was upset and I called Jerry to come get him, but uncharacteristically, I couldn't find my husband for more than an hour. Jerry had been so sickened by the ruling that he had left the house, walking aimlessly, unable to stand it anymore. Governor Bush also seemed worn down — for the first time — when I talked with him that night. "The country can't stand much more of this; it's not good for the country," he told me.

"Have we won yet?" Governor Bush's chipper voice asked when the phone rang just after six thirty the next morning, his good humor obviously restored. I hedged, not certain — could I have missed something during the night?

"Not yet, not that I know of," I replied to my boss, who was checking in, cheering me on for what he knew would be a long, trying day. Overnight, Joe Allbaugh and Karl Rove had marshaled hundreds of people and sent them to sites across Florida to monitor the recount. One of our traveling press assistants, Jill Foley, was marrying another campaign worker, Cliff Angelo, later that day.

They had scheduled the wedding for December 9 to give everyone plenty of time to recover from the campaign. Jill and Cliff are good friends and I really wanted to attend their wedding, but with counting resuming in Florida, I realized I couldn't leave headquarters. The church was much emptier than they had planned because many of their friends were still in Florida or at work; the minister had just declared them man and wife when the best man handed Cliff a note that had made its way to the front of the church: "The U.S. Supreme Court just stopped the counting."

I was at the office when it happened; Robert was watching television at home. He ran and told his dad. I called my lawyer husband: "What does it mean?"

"It means we're moving to Washington," he replied.

Monday night, the Supreme Court issued its ruling. The correspondents were standing by on live television, trying to read it and determine what it meant at the same time. At first, it was hard to believe the long ordeal was over.

"Congratulations, Mr. President-elect," I said to my boss when I talked with him, just minutes after the ruling. "We've got a lot of work to do," he replied. I was happy, and relieved, but it had all been too grueling for exuberance; also, we recognized the need to unite the country after a difficult ordeal. Jerry and I sat up late, in front of the fire, talking about all we had been through, and all that was ahead. To make matters even more surreal, a rare ice storm hit Austin during the night, coating the trees and power lines, knocking out my phone and alarm clock; when I awakened at 8:30 a.m. I got my cell phone and immediately called my boss, knowing he was probably looking for me.

"Where are you?" he asked. "You need to get over here; we have to work on the statement."

"I'm not calling back this time," Al Gore said later that day, his ability to muster some humor earning all our respect when he called to congratulate the governor; it must have been very hard for him to joke when it had to hurt so much. Finally, Governor Bush was President-elect Bush, and my family knew our future.

Oddly, Governor Bush and I had first talked about my role in the White House on the day of his third and final debate, when I thought his mind might have been on more urgent matters. "I'm thinking I'm going to ask Andy Card to be the chief of staff," he had told me, inviting my reaction as we walked around the lake at the house where he was staying. "He's a great guy, a team player; he's fair and everyone respects him. He knows Washington and how the White House works. I want you involved in everything and I want you to have direct access to me." I had listened as he talked it through; it hadn't seemed quite real then: now, it was about to happen.

I thought of a time along the campaign trail, when Governor Bush had given a speech about education. Excited about expanding opportunity for all children, his speech was about watching their "dreams take wing." But the governor mistakenly transposed the words, saying instead that "wings take dreams." I wrote it down, because I couldn't think of a better description of the year and a half on the campaign airplane. It had been his dream, not mine, but I had believed in him and wanted to help, and now he was going to be the president.

We had traveled a long way from normal, and when it was all over, and President-elect Bush announced I was coming to Washington with him, the headlines in my hometown newspaper, the *Austin American Statesman*, read: THE VOICE OF LOYALTY . . . BUSH'S STAUNCH DEFENDER TAPPED

TO "SPEAK HER MIND."

When she saw the announcement, one of the members of the campaign advance team, Kathy Becker, sent me a block of wood with a note: "I thought you might like this as a paperweight on your new desk. Please notice the beautiful grain of the wood. You can see it so clearly because it is 'unvarnished.' "

CHAPTER 8

Counselor to the President

"I promise I will always give you my unvarnished opinion," I told the new president-elect.

"No question about that," he interjected, to knowing laughter from the colleagues and reporters gathered in the formal yellow living room of the Texas governor's mansion.

It had become my trademark; I would definitely let everyone, including the new president, know what I thought. Send Karen "into the propeller," our media director Mark McKinnon always teased, meaning send me to deliver news our boss might not want to hear, news that might provoke a hot reaction, a sudden rush I knew would later turn to more thoughtful deliberation: George W. Bush almost always called back to talk about it further, even after he had gunned down an idea.

I've always had a reputation for telling it like I think it is. Blunt, some might call it. "You talk to everyone the same," my husband teases, "like a dog."

Of course, I love my dog.

As we prepared to move to Washington, my Texas colleague Terrel Smith sent me a picture with President-elect Bush in the middle, Terrel on one side, and me on the other. Terrel had written some dialogue:

Terrel: "Here's how I see it . . ."
President-elect Bush: "No, here's how I see it . . ."
Karen Hughes (to self): "I'll listen in one ear to him, in the other ear to him, then tell both how it really is."

We had gathered at the governor's mansion on this December Sunday afternoon for President-elect Bush to name three new members of his White House staff: Al Gonzales as legal counsel, Condi Rice as national security adviser, and me as counselor to the president. Our new chief of staff, Andy Card, had first suggested the title, saying he modeled it on the role and title given Ed Meese in Ronald Reagan's administration. I liked it, especially its biblical connotation, where "wise counselors" are expected to speak the truth to those in power. I hoped it would remind me of two things: my great responsibility to my boss, and my ultimate identity, which rests not in any title or position, but as a child of God.

It was a wonderful moment, standing with my friends Al and Condi. The three of us were on our way to one of our country's highest platforms, the White House, yet each of us came from a very ordinary background. Al grew up in poverty, the second of eight children reared in a one-bedroom house in Houston. Condi was the daughter and granddaughter of Presbyterian ministers; I was the daughter of an army officer and a stay-at-home mom, the granddaughter of a coal miner and railroad engineer. Jerry and Robert were there to watch the announcement, in the familiar house where I had attended so many festive events during the president-elect's six years as governor. We had gathered there for a toast just the week before, the night Al Gore finally conceded and my boss spoke to the nation for the first time as president-elect from the chamber of the Texas House of Representatives. I had advocated the setting because it was grand without being pretentious, and it gave the new President an opportunity to talk about the way he had worked with members of both political parties in Texas, and intended to do so nationally. After the speech, we had returned to the governor's mansion and finally uncorked the Dom Pérignon that the governor's father had sent on Election Day to celebrate his son joining him as a U.S. president. The champagne had been on ice ever since, along with the rest of us. The president-elect doesn't drink, but most of us had a glass, and it was sweet, but it didn't taste quite like victory. It had been too long, and too hard, and there was too much to do.

When my two friends who know the most about Washington, Margaret Tutwiler and Mary Matalin, called to congratulate me about being named counselor, they both asked the same question, a very weird one. You would think they would ask something logical: Are you sure you know enough to do this job? What do you know about foreign policy? But that wasn't what they wanted to know.

"Where is your office going to be?" Margaret asked me.

"I have no idea," I replied; it hadn't even occurred to me.

"You have to find out; this is im-*portant*," Margaret said, drawing out the syllables, underlining them by raising her voice, as she does when something is, well, important. "You need to be close, on the first floor. You should be in that little office where Stephanopoulos was, right next to the Oval Office. It's not very big, but that doesn't matter. Who's in charge of assigning the offices?" she asked.

"I don't know," I replied, not particularly interested in what I saw as an administrative matter.

"You have to find out," she ordered. "Trust me. This is a *big deal.*"

I had learned to respect Margaret's Washington knowledge and instincts. We had become good friends, although we had only met the month before, during the trauma of the Florida recount. When President-elect Bush had asked former secretary of state James Baker to lead our legal efforts in Florida, Margaret had seemed the perfect choice to handle communications there; she had been his spokesman and senior strategist at the State Department. I knew of her, but I didn't know her, so I asked Condi Rice to call and introduce me so I could ask her to go to Florida. Our friendship got off to a rocky start with an early morning phone call the Sunday after the election. I heard only one end of the conversation — my normally good-humored husband snapping: "She's asleep. Don't ever call us again this early on a Sunday morning."

"Who was that?" I asked sleepily, looking

at the clock, which read six thirty, assuming it was probably a reporter; my husband hates it when they call at home.

"I don't know," he said, "some woman I never heard of named Margaret Tutwiler." My husband had just slammed down the phone on a woman who had dropped everything to go to Florida, was doing me a *huge* favor, and was now just trying to find me before Secretary Baker went on the Sunday morning talk shows. Jerry felt terrible, but he had no way of knowing; he was trying to protect me and knew I desperately needed sleep. Jerry and I had barely even seen each other since Election Day.

Ironically, after that embarrassing first call, my friendship with Margaret had been forged on the telephone. We talked for hours each day, she in Florida, me in Austin, weighing strategy in the communications battle that was occurring minute by minute on live television as the lawyers fired their shots in court. Our instincts were remarkably similar, yet she brought a different perspective and great insight into the ways of Washington and Washington journalists. I found myself wishing I had known her during the campaign; I was relying on her now to help me avoid making stupid mistakes in my new job.

Later the same afternoon, after Margaret's congratulatory call, my friend Mary Matalin, the longtime Bush loyalist and former host of CNN's *Crossfire* called. "I'm so proud of you. You'll be great. Where's your office going to be?"

I was a little confused. Mary and Margaret had been enormously successful in Washington power circles, which were not often occupied by women. I had watched Mary from afar for years; when I was the executive director of the Republican Party of Texas, I had greatly admired her loyalty and fierce advocacy of former president Bush during his 1992 reelection campaign. I had called on her for advice several times during our campaign. I knew Margaret and Mary were much savvier than I was about the ways of Washington. But the president was in the midst of naming his senior staff and selecting a cabinet; I was trying to help him along with setting up the White House communications operation, and choosing my own staff. Jerry was making all the arrangements to move our family to Washington. Christmas was coming, and I hadn't bought a single present. The location of my office had to rank near the bottom of my concerns, if it even made the list.

But Margaret wasn't about to let it drop.

She called several days later. "Have you found out where your office is going to be?" Most of my meetings these days were with the president-elect, the vice president-elect, the chief of staff, and Karl as we went over lists that included names of some of the most prominent people in our country. I couldn't imagine bringing up something as small and petty as the location of my office.

"No," I told her, "I don't even know whom I would ask."

"Karen, listen, I know you don't think you care about things like this — but this town does," Margaret explained, in her you-really-need-to-listen-to-me tone of voice. "This will have an impact on how well you can do your job. It's a *huge* signal." And I finally realized what my friends were really asking: not so much where my individual office would be, but how close to the Oval Office it would be, how close to the seat of power.

It reminded me of a classic political power play, chronicled not in *The New York Times* or *Newsweek*, but in Matthew in the New Testament. The mother of two of Jesus' twelve disciples, the sons of Zebedee, James and John, pulls an end run. She goes behind the back of the other disciples to ask Jesus to guarantee that her boys will be closest to His seat of power in heaven: "Declare that these two sons of mine will sit, one at your right hand and one at your left, in your kingdom," she asks. I love the audacity of that request. It comes from a mom — and how typical of a mom. She obviously thinks it's important, but she doesn't ask for herself: she asks for her kids. This mom wants a favor, just a small one — the best seats in the house for her boys, for eternity.

It's classic human nature, isn't it? what Dr. Martin Luther King described as the "drum major instinct." We all want to lead the parade, to be out front, to finish first, have the office that is the closest to the most powerful. But that's not the end of the seat-arrangement story. Jesus doesn't say "sure," or "no way," or "here are the seats you can have." He tells the mom she's got it all wrong: that's not the way to look at things. "You know that the rulers of the Gentiles lord it over them, and their great ones are tyrants over them. It will not be so among you; but whoever wishes to be great among you must be your servant . . ." There was the lesson of how to approach my job: I was going to the White House to serve — to serve the president, to serve the country and, always, to try to serve in keeping with my faith.

I saw the office question as my first test: would I succumb to Washington's definition of power, or would I rise above it? Moving to Washington did not mean I had to play the Washington game. So the more my friends insisted, the more I stubbornly refused to ask. Yet as hard as I tried to avoid it, occasionally I would catch myself wondering why people who hadn't been with the president nearly as long as I had were making this decision; or I would start thinking that I "deserved" an office close to the president. Then, I would banish those thoughts; I told myself it wouldn't matter. But the fact that I had to put up a fight, to force myself not to care, made me realize what a struggle it would be to maintain my balance in the status-conscious world of Washington.

And the truth is I wasn't being either noble or clueless. I knew the president. I knew if he wanted my advice, he would seek it — no matter where my office was. He had gone to great pains to set up a structure that would allow longtime advisers like Karl and me to have full access to him. He had witnessed the frustration of senior people in his own father's White House when access to the president had been strictly limited by an overbearing chief of staff.

And the new president understood Washington, too, a lot better than most people gave him credit for. During one of our early weeks at the White House, we were discussing something in the Oval Office; it was a beautiful afternoon and he took me outside to show me the swimming pool, the golf green, the tennis courts. As we walked around the track that encircles the south lawn, he told me, "Access to power is power in Washington. And you have access. By tonight, everybody in town will know you were out here walking with me."

My boss was bestowing clout, helping to make it clear that he considered me an integral part of his administration. He did something else to send a signal in the early days, too: he invited me to be his guest at the annual dinner of the Alfalfa Club, the ultimate Washington insiders' group. Alfalfa is a spoof; the club exists for a once-a-year dinner at which the Marine Band marches into the ballroom and plays patriotic songs. Then the assembled guests nominate a "presidential candidate." Each year the club adds new members, known as sprouts, and Alfalfa's presidential nominee delivers a speech, the funnier the better. To succeed at Alfalfa earns respect; to bomb can be fatal. Governor Bush had been the nominee a couple of years earlier, and had worked with speechwriter Landin Parvin on an acceptance speech that was hilarious and had wowed the crowd. I had been home in Texas when my boss gave that speech; tonight, I sat at the head table, next to the chairman of the Joint Chiefs of Staff, and watched as a convivial *Who's Who* of Washington filled the room, laughing and talking, seeing and being seen.

"It's a little overwhelming, isn't it?" I asked my new boss one morning, thinking of both the complexity and the sheer volume of the subjects we were now responsible for handling.

"You don't seem overwhelmed" was his quick reply. I was handling my new job the only way I knew how: throwing myself into the work, attending meetings, asking lots of questions, stating my opinions. I had been given two hats as counselor: one an advisory role, the other managing the message of the White House, which meant overseeing all its communications functions. During the transition, Clay Johnson had given me organizational charts from previous administrations. I reviewed and borrowed some ideas from them, but set up our White House a little differently from most because I wanted us to be as proactive as possible, rather than merely reacting to the daily news and questions.

I asked Dan Bartlett to join me as my deputy. I had been impressed with his effectiveness in handling some of the toughest media queries during the campaign, and his good judgment often led me to talk with him first when I called in from the road. Ari Fleischer was the obvious choice for White House press secretary after having done a great job as our Austin-based press secretary during the campaign. Ari's professionalism and effective advocacy had first attracted our attention during the summer of 1999 when he was working for Elizabeth Dole's campaign. When she dropped out of the presidential race that fall, I flew to Florida for an airport meeting to recruit Ari to our team. I knew the national White House press corps would command Ari's main attention and focus, as well as that of his two deputies in the press office, Scott McClellan and Claire Buchan. So we made the Office of Media Affairs a separate entity and gave it the mission of outreach to regional and local media around the country. Tucker Eskew and his deputy, Nicolle Devenish, assembled a great team of spokesmen who were responsible for establishing relationships with important regional and local reporters, delivering the White House message and staying abreast of major news in their assigned regions.

We set up a communications office and split its deputies, recruiting a new talent, Jim Wilkinson, to oversee the development of events and talking points to convey the White House message, and, perhaps the best decision of all, putting Scott Sforza in charge of the picture. Scott was a former television producer who had come to work for us during the campaign; he is incredibly creative and one of the hardest-working people I have ever met. My own days in television had reminded me of the truth of the adage "a picture is worth a thousand words," and that has proven true time and again as Scott creates powerful backdrops to showcase the president and his policies.

The eloquent speechwriter we had hired during the campaign, Mike Gerson, agreed to head up the White House speechwriting office. He recruited a wonderfully insightful thinker and writer, Pete Wehner, to serve as his deputy, and convinced Matt Scully and John McConnell, two great writers who had been with us during the campaign, to join us in Washington.

The senior members of my staff gathered in my office every morning, joined by Margaret Tutwiler and Mary Matalin, to brainstorm the day's news and events. I believe in collaboration and don't like to put people in a box, so I always encourage the people on my staff to chime in with ideas and opinions — the speechwriters may have a great idea for an event, and the spokesmen may offer a great line for a speech. I was proud of our staff and continue to believe the communications team we assembled was the best in the history of the White House.

My other role at the White House was an advisory one that I sought to clarify with the president the first week. "What exactly do you want me to do?"

His answer was short, the job huge: "Go to the meetings where major decisions are made. Make sure they're thinking about it the way I would; let me know what you think."

So I was attending a dizzying blur of meetings: senior staff; regularly scheduled meetings on domestic policy, economic policy, legislative strategy; message meetings; and specially called meetings on specific issues: climate change, energy regulations, logging rules, nuclear waste storage. We had meetings on speeches, and meetings on strategy, and at one point, meetings to discuss the size and structure of our different meetings. Every day seemed to bring a new crisis, or several.

One morning I woke up to a story alleging the Bush administration was proposing weakening regulations on the level of arsenic in drinking water. I was apoplectic: how did this happen? No one else at the White House seemed to know about it, either; the arsenic regulation had been one of thousands that had been proposed by the Clinton administration and had routinely been placed on hold by the new administration for our own review of the science and facts. Someone, somewhere in the bureaucracy, obviously recognized the public relations value and flagged the press: the horrible, terrible, no-good, very-bad Bush administration was obviously going to wreak havoc with the environment and undo the Clinton legacy by (gasp!) allowing dangerous levels of arsenic in drinking water. Of course, lost in all the hype was the fact that the proposed regulation was talking about making the existing standard stricter; therefore, even if nothing happened, the level of arsenic would only stay the same as it already was, but I knew better than to fight that battle. Arsenic in drinking water is simply not defensible, even if it's already there.

I learned two lessons: some people in the bureaucracy were not our friends, and suddenly, "the Bush administration" was responsible for everything that happened in the federal government, even if those of us at the White House knew nothing about it. And then we learned that there were dozens of similar regulations, on hold at several different agencies, a veritable minefield ready to explode, one at a time. Our policy staff quickly convened meetings to review potentially problematic regulations in the pipeline: snowmobiling in national parks, rules prohibiting roads in the national forests, a kaleidoscope of new (at least to me) issues and problems.

The work was frequently fascinating, as my friend Margaret Tutwiler had predicted when she wrote me in December:

This experience will, like all Presidents' staffs before and those to come, have incredible peaks and valleys. You will learn so much and be exposed to so much that you never really knew much, if anything, about. Your perspective on our country and the world at large will be changed. No one can experience what you are embarking on and not be broadened by it. There will be much that will be incredibly hard and frustrating, but the opportunity to participate and serve has no other match in our professional lives. The opportunity to make a difference in people's lives both here and abroad will create emotions and experiences you will never forget.

I had persuaded Margaret to join us at the White House for six months to help me learn the ropes. It was a huge sacrifice on her part; it meant leaving the private sector, losing money in the process and having to show up once again for those awful, early morning senior staff meetings. I was enormously grateful for her help, and her experience helped ease the way for all of us. She knew the traditions; she knew when it was appropriate to use the Rose Garden or the East Room, or when that would signal that an event was more important than we intended for it to be. She had great instincts for when the president should personally respond to events, and when it was more appropriate for a cabinet secretary or spokesman to carry the message. It was also fun to work with a friend: we laughed and she helped me keep the challenges in perspective. Margaret's presence made life easier at the office; at home I was experiencing the "hard and frustrating" part she had warned me about.

I felt as if a tornado had sucked us up, tossed us in the air, then belched us out at the house we were renting in Arlington, Virginia. Our first week in Washington had been total chaos: our daughter Leigh had joined Jerry, Robert and me for the inauguration, and the four of us stayed crammed in a crowded room at the Four Seasons Hotel because there were no extra hotel rooms in Washington during inaugural week. Jerry and Robert had driven to Washington a week earlier so Robert could start school at the beginning of the spring semester; my sister did me an incredible favor and drove my car to Washington so I could fly up with the president.

My journey to the White House did not get off to a very good start. "Whose dog is that?" the president-elect demanded as my golden retriever barked ferociously from her travel kennel at the president's springer spaniel, Spotty. My dog, Breeze, had been sleeping quietly until Spotty got on board, but I wasn't about to say that; I was embarrassed that my dog was there in the first place. I had been busy working, Robert and Jerry were en route to Washington and I was worrying out loud at the office one day about how to get my dog and cat to Washington: even if I could get them to the airport, who would pick them up? A member of our advance team suggested I should put my pets in the hold of the air force plane and take them with us as we flew to Washington; my friend Andi Ball said the man who was transporting Barney and Spot to a kennel for inaugural week would be glad to take my dog and cat, too. It was all arranged, until I arrived at the airport that morning and the nice air force flight crew member told me the hold wasn't pressurized; my dog and cat would have to stay in the passenger cabin. I was mortified, but stuck. It felt a little like Noah's ark as I boarded the airplane, me and my animals, two by two. I couldn't help but think what the air force crew must be thinking: these Texans, bringing along everything but the chickens and the goats.

To make matters worse, when we arrived in Washington, the advance staff member in charge of the motorcade told me to wait on the plane with my animals. I did what I was told, watching as everyone else scrambled into cars and vans, then suddenly realized I was about to be left behind. I ran down the back stairs of the plane, my dog on a leash in one hand, my cat in his carrying case in the other. The president-elect of the United States watched from his limousine, waiting, as I transferred my pets to the man who already had Barney and Spot, then raced to the staff van. "Thanks for holding up the whole motorcade," the president said, not really teasing, when we arrived at the Blair House where he was spending inaugural week.

"I'm sorry, I did exactly what the advance person told me to do; she told me to stay on the airplane; the only reason I came down was I saw you were ready to leave," I protested.

"I don't have much to do; didn't mind at all waiting for you to get your animals taken care of," said the soon-to-be president of the United States, a man who hates to wait. During eight years of working for the president, I could think of only one other time when he had had to wait for me, in New York, during the campaign, when I had been meeting with the president of CBS News. The police shut down the streets for Governor Bush's motorcade, and my cab got caught in the traffic. The person in charge of the motorcade arranged for the press bus to stop and wait for me, outside the Holland Tunnel, and when my cab got stuck in traffic again, I got out and raced about twenty blocks through the streets of New York, convinced I would have a heart attack by the time I scrambled onto the bus. When we arrived at the plane, the president had been there almost twenty minutes: "Did you have fun shopping?" was the only thing he ever said about it.

I arrived in Washington with my suitcase and my animals; everything else that we owned in the world that was not already in our jammed hotel room was on a moving van making its way from Texas to Washington, including my husband's winter coat and all our rain gear. My son didn't own a coat; he hadn't needed one in Texas. We were supposed to move into our new house on the Friday before the Saturday inaugural, but it was pouring rain and the move was postponed until Monday. We didn't have access to any of our things; my husband wore a garbage bag on his head to keep dry at the inaugural. ("I hope nobody knows he's related to Karen," my friend Janice Margolin remembers thinking when she saw him.) The night before my boss became the president, when we realized the weather was going to be rainy with the temperature in the low twenties, we set out to find Robert a coat. The hotel bellman gave us directions to a downtown department store, but it was five o'clock on Friday, and the streets were frozen with inaugural traffic. By five thirty we had advanced only several blocks; I got out and started walking, and had already found a coat for Robert to try on by the time he and Jerry arrived, just minutes before the store closed at six.

Our senior staff members had each been given two tickets for the stage where President Bush would take the oath of office. Jerry and I had been planning to use them, and give our audience tickets to my parents and sister, and the friends who had joined us for this special occasion: Bob and Juliee Bliss; Steve and Janice Margolin, and their son, Alex, Robert's best friend. But Robert protested: "I was the one who was there all during the campaign; I should get to sit with you," he told me. Jerry and I talked about it, and agreed that Robert's long months on the campaign trail had earned him the seat on the stage. It was freezing, and raining, and miserable, but nothing could dampen our joy and pride as we watched the president take the oath and give his inaugural address, at least not until several hours later when my feet were almost numb and we left the inaugural parade early, cold, wet and exhausted.

The West Wing was open for members of the staff and our families to visit our new offices on Sunday. Nothing but blue carpet and a refrigerator holding a broken bottle was in mine when I arrived, but I thought it was beautiful: lots of light and windows, which I had worried about. When we had come to visit our counterparts in the Clinton administration, I met with the communications director, whose office was a windowless room in the basement. So I was delighted to have been assigned the big airy second-floor office that looked out on the White House residence, with a view of the flag proudly waving above it. And many of my friends from Texas were upstairs, too: Karl Rove, and Margaret LaMontagne, and Clay Johnson and Al Gonzales. The small office near the Oval Office that Margaret and Mary had talked about was assigned to our deputy chief of staff, Joe Hagin. It was small, and looked confining; I liked my open, spacious office much better.

I walked down the hall on the first floor and peeked into the familiar oval room that we have all seen so many times on television. The world's most powerful office looked familiar, yet different: a lighter rug had replaced the dark blue one, a desk and different furniture had been placed there.

Yet the Oval Office seemed empty, not yet reflecting the personality of its new occupant. I realized how many difficult decisions my boss would be asked to make in this room in the years ahead. As I thought about the monumental task in front of us, my eye settled on a familiar painting, which had also hung in my office in Texas. It portrays a horseman leading a charge up a steep, rocky hill, a look of purpose and determination on his face. The painting is based on a Methodist hymn, "A Charge to Keep I Have." The hymn speaks of serving a cause greater than self; many hymnals associate it with a Bible verse: "Now it is required that those who have been given a trust must prove faithful" (Corinthians). I looked at the painting and felt reassured. Everything was going to be okay, I realized; President Bush would be the same person on the day he left this place as he was on the day we arrived, because he has his priorities straight.

The next morning, Monday, January 22, I woke up early. I was brushing my teeth in the bathroom, trying not to make any noise so I wouldn't wake the kids, when my husband walked in. "I'm going to work at the White House today," I told him, marveling at the thought. He looked at me as if I had lost my mind. I could see him thinking, what does she think this has all been about? He went over the map with me again, and I set off nervously: I had never helped run a country before.

Driving into the White House was a stark reminder that nothing at my new workplace was normal. We had been told which gate to use, but nothing more; after showing my new photo identification card, known as a hard pass, I was waved into the complex. I had already passed the white line when the man standing by it yelled that I was supposed to stop there and turn off the engine and open my trunk so the bomb-sniffing dog could inspect it. Then I drove through several more heavy steel gates, waiting each time for the guard to compare the picture on my hard pass with my face, before I finally arrived on West Executive Drive, where I parked and walked into the basement. The officer sitting at the desk by the entrance helped direct me to my office; although the West Wing is small, its three floors are each laid out very differently, and it's confusing until you get used to it.

Members of our staff were sworn in that morning in a very nice ceremony in the East Room; Jerry had to take Robert to school, then he and Leigh went to meet the movers, so he couldn't come, but my parents and sister came, and got to say hello to President and Mrs. Bush and meet some of my colleagues at the coffee that followed. I learned that along with my new title came a rank, assistant to the president, which suddenly entitled me to be addressed as the Honorable Karen Hughes, the appellation that would appear on all the formal invitations I received in Washington. (I later jokingly suggested that from now on, Robert and Jerry could refer to me as the Honorable Mom; they didn't think it was very funny.) Mostly, I was mortified that this new rank, assistant to the president, was roughly equivalent to that of a three-star general; my dad had retired after thirty-six years and three wars as a two-star general, and I didn't think that my service could possibly approach what my father and other members of the military have done for our country. I still don't.

That morning, the president asked us to uphold the highest standards of ethics and to serve the people with humility and respect: "I want it said of us at the end of our service that promises made were promises kept. On a mantelpiece in this great house is inscribed the prayer of John Adams, that only the wise and honest may rule under this roof. He was speaking of those who live here. But wisdom and honesty are also required of those who work here. I know each of you is capable of meeting that charge."

The first day passed in a blur of meetings with my new colleagues, my own staff and the president. That night, I navigated the maze of Washington bridges long after dark, struggling to find my way to the house we were renting, which I had seen only once, in daylight. I finally arrived home about nine to utter chaos. Jerry and Leigh had done the best they could; Leigh had spent a day of her vacation helping us move, but egged on by my husband, whose mantra was "get everything out of the boxes," the Christmas glasses we used once a year were in the cabinet where the everyday dishes should have been; the drawers were full of all the wrong stuff, and boxes still lined the hallways and filled the garage. I didn't get to spend any time there until Saturday, when I worked like a madwoman all morning, trying to restore some order.

"I'm hungry," Robert announced that first weekend morning about eleven. The two grown-ups looked at each other, completely stumped. We didn't know where a grocery store was, much less any fast food places. "What do you feel like?" I asked, gamely. "Schlotsky's," he replied, naming the Texas-based sandwich chain. I got out the phone book and looked, but there was no Schlotsky's in Arlington, Virginia. I think we all wanted to cry: we were hungry, tired, out of place and out of sorts in the messy house that wasn't ours, in the new city we didn't know.

Robert wasn't saying much about his new school or about anything. I had talked with him, and perhaps said too much. I tried to explain that I would have to work more than I had in Texas, that my hours would be long and there wasn't a great deal I could do about it, but I loved him and he would always be my most important priority. I think he heard the first part, but not the last. I picked him up from school one afternoon, and ran into the director, who told me Robert was doing well, but was worried about me: "I asked him how you were and he said he wasn't going to see you very much, that you had to work all the time," he told me. "He seemed sad about it."

It broke my heart. I had to do something to show Robert that working at the White House had not supplanted my love or concern for him. So my second week at the White House, I instituted a new policy: Midweek Moment, named for a program my church had on Wednesday evenings. On Wednesday afternoons, I would leave work at the unheard-of-for-Washington hour of 5:30 p.m. so I could spend the evening with Robert and Jerry, a way to demonstrate, by walking away from it all, that my family still mattered most. January 2001 had been so crazy that I didn't have time to write my appointments down; my calendar is almost empty. It notes a parents' meeting at St. Albans on Tuesday morning, January 30, then on Wednesday, January 31, in addition to all the regular White House meetings, appointments with Brit Hume of Fox News and *The New York Times* Washington Bureau, an ethics briefing with Al Gonzalez and at 5:30, Midweek Moment with Robert.

But it wasn't enough for me to make a little room for my own family; as one of the senior women in the White House, I felt an obligation to set an example, to let others know they could make their families a priority as well. Throughout my career, I have noticed one difference between most women who work and most men (warning: a sweeping generalization is ahead; it's probably not entirely right or fair): when women leave work to take a child to the doctor or go to a school event, they generally explain why; when men leave for a family errand, they either don't say what they are doing or just say they are headed to a generic "meeting." I have always felt it is important to state what I am doing, so that others who are more junior know that they have the option of leaving for family events, too. I talked openly about my Midweek Moment, and a reporter from *The Washington Post* heard about it and wrote a story.

I was stunned by the reaction: a couple of dozen people stopped me in the halls of the West Wing and Old Executive Office Building that day. "Thank you for speaking up," one administrative assistant said. "Thanks for saying it's okay to go to your child's school," another longtime White House career employee told me. I told them all that I was able to do so because our boss, the president, believes that if you are a mom or dad, that's your number one responsibility in life.

During the campaign, Robert had decided that if we moved to Washington he wanted to attend St. Albans; our policy director, Josh Bolten, had graduated from the private boys' school and told Robert what a wonderful education it offered. Josh is an incredibly intelligent, kind, thoughtful man, one of the most decent people I have ever met. During the campaign he had taken time to explain issues to Robert; his gentle, low-key style reminded me of scenes from years earlier, when Robert's grandfather had patiently explained the different purposes of all those construction vehicles. Josh also has a great sense of humor, and Robert decided that when we moved to Washington, he wanted to be a St. Albans man, like Josh.

The week that we finally knew we were moving to Washington, Jerry had called the school. They politely explained that they usually don't take students in the middle of the year; they could count on one hand the number of times they had made an exception. "Could you send me an application?" my husband replied. Robert took the entrance exams during Christmas vacation, and when he did extremely well, the school seemed slightly more interested.

I tried to suggest that Robert might want to consider other options, but he wouldn't hear of it, so when Jerry went to Washington to find a house, he rented one in Arlington, which has good public schools, a backup in case St. Albans turned us down. But getting into the school was so important to Robert that I did something unusual for me: I asked my boss for a favor. He knew Robert well; his own brothers had gone to St. Albans; would he mind writing one of the recommendation letters the school required? I

424

hated to bother him, especially since I of all people knew how busy he was, but I was also a mom wanting the best seat for my son. A few mornings later, when I arrived at the governor's mansion, the president-elect handed me a sheet of paper.

December 21, 2000
Austin, Texas

To the admission officers of St. Albans school,

I write to recommend Robert Hughes for admission to St. Albans.

I know Robert very well. During the campaign for the presidency, Robert Hughes traveled with me every day. His mother is one of my most trusted advisors. Early in the campaign, she asked permission to have Robert by her side for the summer and fall months. In short, Robert would be "home schooled" on the road while his mom fulfilled her duties to my campaign.

So I saw the boy every day from the early morning until late at night. He is an extraordinary person. I never heard him complain about lack of sleep or lack of attention or lack of a

425

normal meal (this distinguished Robert from most of the adults on our plane). He was remarkably composed and polite. He listened and he learned a lot. Not only did he do well in his assignments from the Austin school system, he learned invaluable lessons on the campaign trail.

Robert observed victory and defeat. He watched and listened as his mom and I made hundreds of decisions. He absorbed a lot of information and did so in a way that never bothered the stressed out and harried adults.

Robert would make a great addition to your school. He is thoughtful and smart. He will work hard and take advantage of the fine education your school offers. Plus, he will make a contribution to your sports teams.

I appreciate your consideration of Robert Hughes and hope that you accept him.

Sincerely,
George W. Bush
President-elect

P.S. This letter is self-typed, late at night. Obviously I could not find the proper stationery. Please forgive the informality.

I was overcome by the thought that our country's new president had taken time to type by hand such a thoughtful letter for my son; the president-elect had captured our campaign experience far better than I ever could have. He made an extra copy for me; I sent one to the school, and saved the other for Robert's scrapbook. Josh did us another great favor by accompanying us to St. Albans for Robert's interview, and we were all thrilled when Robert was accepted. Despite all the changes in our lives, at least the uncertainty was behind us: we had a new address, a new phone number, a new school, a friend who was president of the United States; I had an office at the world's most prestigious address, and an exciting new opportunity to make a difference.

Yet from the opening days, the thrill and privilege of working at the White House competed with a shadow. I felt it every morning as I drove to work in the dark, leaving my husband and son still asleep, sneaking out the front door so I wouldn't wake up the dog in the garage. Sometimes, the headlights and noise roused her despite my attempts at quiet, and Breeze would bark, and my husband would have to get up and let her out, not the best way to start his morning, since he hadn't wanted the dog in the first place. The mornings were cold and dark and we found them depressing.

Another mom on our staff, Margaret LaMontagne, had called me during the transition to talk about her concerns about moving to Washington. She had been asked to head up the domestic policy office, a challenging and important job, but she was single at the time and had two daughters, and she was struggling with her decision, especially after a meeting with Andy Card, where he outlined the expectations for the White House staff. "He said you don't go home until late at night, you work every weekend, and when he worked there during the last Bush administration, he didn't have a day off for several years," she told me. "I can't do that; there's no one else to get the girls' dinner or check their homework. You aren't going to do that, are you?" she asked.

I most certainly was not. I remembered my own advice — before accepting any new job, always make the ground rules clear. I hung up the phone and called the president-elect.

"I just want to make sure you know I'm always going to do my job, but I am also going to spend time with my family," I said, barely giving him time to figure out what I was talking about. I explained about Margaret's phone call, and our concern about the office hours that had been described. "You know I'll sit up until midnight writing a speech, or go out of town or be there any time you need me or it's important, but I am not going to sit at the office every weekend if I can get my work done at home, or stay until eleven at night just to show the light is on," I told him. He knew that, he assured me, and later cautioned our new chief of staff: "Don't run off my mothers."

But Andy had just been trying to be realistic about what was expected; he had served in the previous Bush administration, and he *had* worked for several years without a single day off. And his warnings proved to be valid. Although I made a deliberate effort not to spend too much time at the office, between out-of-town trips and important meetings, and weekends spent working on big speeches, I ended up working two or three weekends a month during my eighteen months at the White House; I tried to reserve Sunday for church and family as much as I could. And that's not very much by usual White House standards, or those of my own colleagues. Andy Card, Condi

Rice, Karl Rove and a whole lot of other people you never heard of work almost all the time to keep the White House going. They make enormous sacrifices. Andy gets to the White House about five thirty in the morning and is frequently there after ten at night. He goes to Camp David with the president most weekends; when he doesn't, he is at the White House all day Saturday and usually on Sunday afternoons, too. Condi arrives early and leaves late, and gets calls day and night, around the clock; I know because we have shared the guest house at the ranch and someone's always knocking at the door bringing "message traffic," news about events around the world that she needs to know about and, frequently, act on. Harriet Miers, the attorney who served as staff secretary in charge of all the paperwork that goes into and out of the Oval Office, and later as deputy chief of staff, regularly works eighteen-hour days and never complains; I don't know how she does it. Karl works incredibly long hours, meets people for breakfast and dinner, travels the country for political events and, his wife tells me, sends Blackberry messages from his bed at night. I'm a high-energy person, but after I've poured myself into a twelve- or fourteen-hour day, I come home and want to do something different because my brain is pretty much shot.

And I am emphatically not a morning person, which made working at the White House especially difficult for me. I have a simple test about this important matter: if you wake up at 7:45 a.m., but you don't have to be up until 8:00, and you go ahead and get up anyway, you are a morning person. If you roll over and close your eyes, taking every last second of opportunity to stay in bed, you are a nonmorning person, just like me. When Condi Rice wakes up, she has to get up. So does my husband; so did my roommate after college. I would never, ever, do that.

I have a lot more energy than most people I know; I work hard; I work long hours, but I don't like to work early in the morning. When I was younger, I used to sleep until 10:30 or 11:00 on Saturday mornings. I no longer do that, but I sure like to stay in bed until 8:00 or 8:30. By that time, the president has run three miles, walked two more, made coffee, read the papers and had his morning intelligence briefings.

I was especially out of sync in Washington because I was a nonmorning person in a White House full of early risers. The president usually arrived in the Oval Office by

6:50 a.m.; by then, Andy Card and Harriet Miers had been at the White House for more than an hour, and Karl was usually at a breakfast somewhere. Condi arrived by 7:00 a.m.; our first meeting was at 7:15 a.m., usually about the time I first begin stirring, long before I want to be up and dressed and at the office, in makeup and hose. This meeting was optional, a super-senior staff meeting in Andy Card's office, and after attending for a few months, I opted to miss it most mornings for the extra fifteen minutes of sleep.

The mandatory senior staff meeting started at 7:30 a.m. It began with the scheduler reading the president's schedule for the day, which always struck me as a little ridiculous, since it was printed on two pieces of paper placed in front of each of us: one of them an ordinary size, 8½ by 11, the other a smaller pocket size. The chief of staff communicated anything he needed to, then the press secretary reported: a litany of where we have been kicked in the teeth overnight, stories we would have to respond to or manage. This was the first opportunity for Ari Fleischer to get guidance from the senior staff on how to respond to specific stories or issues; we would discuss them in more detail in my meeting with our communications staff at 8:30.

And we would go around the room: Nick Calio, the legislative director, filled us in on issues, decisions or problems confronting us on Capitol Hill; Mitch Daniels gave a budget update — and now for the bad news — here was Larry Lindsey with the latest economic reports. (We teased that the economists always brought bad news, especially that first year, with the economy in recession.) Condi would have an update on foreign policy and the latest tensions throughout the world; Lewis Libby and Mary Matalin briefed us on the vice president's activities; Clay Johnson told us about personnel announcements; Josh Bolten highlighted pending domestic policy issues and Karl and I would bring up anything we needed to discuss with our colleagues. I usually left the meeting with a long list of things to do, complicated issues and problems that we had to manage or determine how to communicate. And the senior staff gathering was only the first in a day full of meetings; I would frequently not have any time in my office to return phone calls or review documents or speeches for the next day until after six at night.

I enjoyed my colleagues and felt privileged to work with them. When they assembled the staff, the president and vice president and Andy Card did a great job of balancing people from Texas, people who knew how the president worked, with people who knew how Washington worked. Legislative Director Nick Calio had a quick smile and a great sense of humor; he was a straight shooter who somehow managed to deal with all the big egos on Capitol Hill and earn their respect. Budget Director Mitch Daniels also was quick with a quip. He earned a presidential nickname, the Blade, because he was always looking for ways to cut and control the budget; he guarded the nation's pennies like his own. I had gotten to know Larry Lindsey and Andy Card and Condi Rice from working with them during the campaign. Condi and I had become good friends, enjoying many dinners and attending church together on several occasions. She is brilliant, always perfectly put together; she's so talented that you would expect people to resent her, but nobody does because she's so gracious. Larry is a big bear of a man, always jolly, even when delivering the bad economic news; I admired him and his wife for adopting children from overseas. Our chief of staff, Andy Card, set the tone for the White House. He is honest and fair, strong without ever being mean, and one of the hardest-working people I have ever met. His wife Kathi is a Methodist minister who marries strong convictions with a quiet, gentle manner.

Unlike what I had read and heard about infighting among previous White House staffs, ours was remarkably collegial. We weren't split into various factions or camps; we were all part of a team assembled to serve the president, and the team included the vice president and his staff, too. Vice President Cheney is wise and reflective, quieter and lower key than President Bush. The amount that he says is inversely proportional to the number of people in the room; he speaks much more openly in small meetings than in large ones. People always sit forward and listen intently whenever he says anything. He is a thoughtful and insightful man; he combines strong convictions with a pleasant and reassuring manner that makes him particularly effective on television. The interactions between his staff and ours were seamless; his counselor, Mary Matalin, came to all my communications meetings. I wanted her input on everything, and she became a dear friend.

One of my immediate message priorities was the president's first big speech to Congress. It wasn't called the State of the Union that year because incoming presidents instead give what is called a joint-session address. We felt this speech before Congress and the nation was especially critical because of the close election. The speechwriters worked, and we revised and edited, but I didn't have a good feeling about the result. The president still teases that I told him "this is unacceptable" the Thursday before he had to give the speech the following Tuesday. I don't think I was quite that harsh, but I was worried that we didn't have it right.

"Come up to Camp David this weekend; bring your family, and we'll get it done — you always do," he told me. Camp David is a wonderful retreat, with all kinds of outdoor activities, a bowling alley and a movie theater and a big dining room where we all ate family style around a large table. We all enjoyed spending time with the president and first lady and it was thrilling to be at the "presidential retreat," but I didn't get much recreation that weekend: I sat in a little office in the back room of the main lodge and wrote, then met with the president and discussed and revised, then wrote some more.

I always focus first on the logic and structure of a speech; I had worried that the initial drafts of the address had led with the proposed tax cuts, the same tax cuts that had propelled us to a resounding 49 percent victory. I felt we had to explain them differently, so I reversed the logic, beginning with all the places the government would be spending money, on programs ranging from health care to Social Security to education to the environment, and ending with a pile of money left over that could be used for bigger government or returned to the people who had earned it in the first place. "Some think the tax cut is too big," the president said, giving the Congressional Democrats a chance to stand and cheer, and "some think it's too small," allowing the Republicans to go wild. "I think it's just about right . . ."

By early April, just as I felt we were beginning to get a handle on our new jobs, a Chinese fighter plane hit one of our big, slow air force intelligence-gathering planes, sending the Chinese jet spiraling to the ocean and its pilot to his death. Our pilot did a fabulous job bringing his damaged airplane in for an emergency landing on China's Hainan Island. We knew the plane had landed safely, but we didn't know what had happened after that. SPY-PLANE STANDOFF screamed the big banner across *Headline*

News; it was jarring to me. When you work in a governor's office, not much that you do makes headlines on CNN.

I remember thinking: we are responsible for solving this, and for saving the lives of the young air force crew. We all remembered how the Iranian hostage crisis had paralyzed the Carter presidency; our national security team's first goal was to avoid allowing this to escalate into a confrontation. I started meeting with the president, vice president, Andy Card and Condi Rice every morning after their intelligence briefings, evaluating the latest information, discussing what we should say and when. The meetings proved so valuable that shortly thereafter, we added a daily communications meeting to the president's schedule. Karl joined the group and it became our opportunity to talk at the very highest level about our daily message, scheduling and strategic plans.

During the "spy-plane standoff" I felt it for the first but certainly not the last time: the huge weight of responsibility for other lives — in this case, twenty-four men and women whose faces and families we were getting to know on television every day. In the midst of it all, the president had a speech in Delaware. Steve Hadley, the deputy national security adviser, and I flew to the event with him, but we never made it into the auditorium to see the crowd or hear the speech: Steve and I spent the entire hour standing out by the swimming pool, the only place we could get a cell phone signal, as he talked to the American who was being allowed in to visit the crew for the first time since their emergency landing. I remember the big smile on the president's face when he came off the stage and Steve was able to report: "We've seen the crew; they all seem to be in good health; they want to come home."

"I *hate* working for the federal government," my son's voice protested loudly from his bedroom across the hall as the phone rang shortly after 5:00 a.m. It was Condi: "I think we've got this resolved, can you come in?" she asked. When I arrived at the White House, Condi was optimistic but guarded, worried that the situation could change at any moment until the crew had actually left the country; I advised we not say anything until we were absolutely certain.

Ari spoke up; he had already confirmed the news to the Associated Press White House reporter, Ron Fournier, based on the

439

information that Condi had given him. It caused some nervous moments; we didn't want something the White House had said to cause any last-minute complications. This time, it turned out fine; we soon learned the crew was on its way home. That's always a tension in the White House: when to confirm information. Frequently, the media is already reporting something, and it puts the press secretary in a difficult position. The reporters are pressing; the public deserves accurate information; yet once the White House confirms something, the story changes. It's no longer just the facts of the story; the news becomes that the *White House* has released or confirmed or announced the facts, which can sometimes be sticky when other countries are involved and want to make announcements on their own terms.

There was some discussion of sending President Bush out to Hawaii to welcome the crew home, but the president shut it down: "The spotlight should be on them, it's their reunion with their families. I'm not going to insert myself into the story, we can have them here later," he said, and that was that. It was a wonderful moment when he welcomed them into the Oval Office several weeks later, and personally thanked them for upholding the honor of our country under difficult circumstances.

I felt things were moving so fast it was still hard to believe; months into his presidency I was still having what I called pinch-me moments — moments when I heard the band play "Hail to the Chief" and I would look up and feel I had to pinch myself because it still surprised me: that's the president of the United States and I know him, and he knows me.

I had a pinch-me moment during one of our first foreign trips, to Mexico. I was sitting on Air Force One in the senior staff cabin, which has four big leather chairs, the kind that swivel and recline so you can turn to work at the desk behind you, or try to sleep on a long international trip. I looked across from me: there sat Colin Powell, the former chairman of the Joint Chiefs of Staff, and now the secretary of state. On my right sat Dr. Condoleezza Rice, the former provost of Stanford University and now the national security adviser; to my left was Andy Card, the former secretary of transportation and now the White House chief of staff; then there was me. My first thought was what am I doing here? My second was that here, in one of the most powerful rooms in the world, half of us were African American, and half of us were women. I'm proud that the Bush administration had more women in senior positions than any administration in our nation's history. People ask me what difference it makes, and that's hard to answer. It's like asking whether I see the world differently because my eyes are blue. They've always been blue; I've always been a woman. I do think I brought a mom's perspective to the White House, a sense of practicality, a sense of the impact our decisions might make on people's everyday lives.

I remember one early meeting in the Roosevelt Room, the big conference room in the West Wing where President Theodore Roosevelt's Nobel Peace Prize sits on the mantel and flags commemorating all the times the United States has committed military forces into combat stand at attention against the walls. We were discussing the impact of proposed energy regulations on the price of household appliances like washing machines. I think I was the only woman at the table, and I remember looking around at the collected Ph.D.'s and economists and experts, and thinking: "I bet I'm the only person at this table who regularly *uses* a washing machine . . ."

In the midst of all the meetings, one stood

out: the president and vice president asked me, Margaret Tutwiler and Mary Matalin to join them for their weekly lunch; they wanted to hear from the White House women. We sat in the lovely small dining room in the White House residence and talked about a host of subjects, from tax cuts to the Middle East to the environment; at one point, the president mentioned he wanted to do something to promote baseball: "It's America's pastime, our national sport," he said, and the idea for T-ball on the South Lawn was born.

When people asked me later: "Why T-ball?" I said, "They can't break windows," but that's just part of it. Some of my favorite pictures of Robert are from T-ball, a beginner's baseball game where the ball is hit from a rubber tee instead of being pitched, everyone gets to bat and you don't keep score. Kids that age are so innocent and engaging. Hosting T-ball gave President and Mrs. Bush the opportunity to celebrate teamwork and good sportsmanship, and to salute the volunteers across America who coach and work with kids. Jim Wilkinson on our communications staff took the idea and ran with it. We invited two local Little League teams, and asked Bob Costas to do the play-by-play: "It's the fifth out here in the first inning, but we're not really keeping track." The San Diego Padres' Chicken came, and so did the players' families, and we had a big barbecue. I learned that nothing is done halfway at the White House: instead of merely throwing out bases, they had an architect sketch the diamond; I had the plan framed and it still hangs in the reception area of my old West Wing office. A picture of President and Mrs. Bush from that first T-ball game hung there for a long time, too; the smile on the president's face as he watched those children was the most relaxed and happiest I had seen since we'd arrived at the White House.

T-ball was one way the president's interests and values were permeating the White House; there were many others. The first several months, dozens of members of the support staff — motorcade drivers and military personnel and the air force flight crew — commented to me about how the president was always on time. They appreciated it because they thought it showed a respect for their time; if the schedule said the motorcade was leaving at nine or Air Force One was departing at ten, the president was there on time, or a few minutes early; dozens of support people didn't have to sit for hours in hot cars or on airplanes waiting for him. And we all said thank you, many others commented; the president said please and thank you, and treated members of the staff with respect, and we all followed suit. It would be hard for me to imagine doing otherwise. When the marine guard at the front gate of the West Wing watches you approach and turns to open the door, I always said, and think everyone should say: "Thank you, sir."

A lot of wonderful people work at the White House no matter who the president is. We considered them part of the team, too: the doctors and nurses who make up the White House medical unit and took care of us when we were sick; the Secret Service officers who protect the president and are always courteous and professional; the fabulous White House operators who always helped me track down the people I needed on holiday weekends; the mess stewards who served coffee and meals; the florists who make the White House special every day with lovely arrangements of fresh flowers; house staff in the residence who work so hard to make guests and staff feel at home there; the cleaning crews who visited our offices every day. These people will still be at the White House, still serving with the highest standards of professionalism long after the rest of us are gone, and I always tried to remember that.

The president was flying home to Crawford for Easter weekend, and he offered to give our family a ride. I was thrilled to have the opportunity for Robert and Jerry to ride on Air Force One and spend the weekend at home in Texas, but the trip was also a reminder of what we were missing: we spent time with Leigh and our granddaughter, Lauren; celebrated Easter at our church; went to dinner with our friends the Margolins for Robert's birthday. The bluebonnets were even prettier than we remembered, and as we stepped off the plane, my husband exclaimed: "Look at the sky; it's so big. You can't see it in Washington; it's closed in by all the trees." Texas was open, welcoming, *home;* it was hard for all of us to get on the plane on Sunday and go back to Washington.

My journal calls the week beginning May 20, 2001, "the most significant week of his presidency so far." It included three commencement speeches, at Notre Dame, Annapolis, and the president's alma mater, Yale; and ended with a dramatic change of power in the Senate and passage of one of the president's campaign priorities, the tax cut.

It had threatened to rain all week. At Yale, the skies were overcast; as President Bush and Senator Jim Jeffords met in the Oval Office on Tuesday afternoon, clouds were gathering outside Washington. The lightning and rain wouldn't hit the capital city until later that evening, but in the Oval Office, the storm had already begun.

I had been at an afternoon meeting of a Weight Watchers group some of the women in the White House had organized and when I returned to my office, I had a call from CNN's Candy Crowley: "Did the president meet with Jim Jeffords this afternoon?"

"I don't know," I told her, "it's not on his schedule; I'll find out and let you know if I can help you."

When I arrived in the Oval Office, the president, vice president and chief of staff were there discussing what had just happened: Senator Jim Jeffords had met with the president and left him with little doubt that he intended to leave the Republican Party.

Senator Jeffords seemed nervous, the president told me, "and I wasn't exactly warm and fuzzy."

"Here we are in the Oval Office," President Bush told me he had said to Senator Jeffords, "and you are contemplating something that's going to have a profound impact on the country — something that will affect my ability to get things done on behalf of the American people, and I just want to know: Why? This is a historic move; can you tell me why?"

Senator Jeffords was all over the map, the president said: upset with Senator Judd Gregg about the education bill, that there wasn't enough special education funding in the budget. "I told him, you're in a perfect position to work for what you want," President Bush said. "You are the swing vote — you can have enormous influence."

But then Senator Jeffords went on and on about how he had the opportunity to assume the chairmanship of the Environment and Public Works Committee. Those in the room were left with the impression that Jeffords had negotiated a better deal with Democrat Leader Tom Daschle, although Jeffords later publicly denied that in a carefully worded written statement: "In my conversations with the Democratic leadership over the past two weeks, a lot of possibilities have been discussed, but nothing has been or will be final until the Senate acts," Jeffords wrote. The president told me he had asked Senator Jeffords directly whether the White House had done anything that had offended him, and the senator had responded that he had "the utmost respect for you, Mr. President; you've done nothing to cause me to leave."

Our legislative director, Nick Calio, called me from Capitol Hill the next morning: "Someone in the leader's office got a press call saying the White House is blaming him (Senate Majority Leader Trent Lott) for not handling Jeffords better; we need to shut that down."

I organized a conference call with Republican staff members and communicators on the Hill: "We are a team; we're all in this together," I told them. "If Senator Jeffords decides to leave the party, the only person responsible will be Senator Jeffords. We need to treat him with respect . . . I want to personally assure you the White House is not going to engage in finger-pointing or name-calling; we shouldn't play the blame game." Susan Irby from Senator Lott's leadership office called me afterward to say how much she appreciated it. "We don't want a circular firing squad," she said.

The White House didn't point fingers or accuse anyone else, so in typical Washington fashion, we got the blame. Anonymous Capitol Hill staffers and those ubiquitous "Republican strategists" said the White House was responsible for Senator Jeffords's decision to leave the Republican Party, even though he had personally told the president a different story.

On the morning Senator Jeffords announced he was leaving the Republican Party, we traveled to Cleveland. We heard his speech while we were on Air Force One; listening to him frame his decision as a matter of principle made several of us in the staff cabin sick. We felt he had sold out his party in exchange for a committee chairmanship and that sure didn't seem like a matter of principle to those of us on the White House staff. (Shortly after the Senate changed hands, Jim Jeffords became chairman of the Environment and Public Works Committee.)

On the return flight, the president asked me to join him for lunch. "So what do you think?" I asked, expecting him to talk about the impact of Senator Jeffords's decision. "My focus is on the tax bill," he told me, already moving ahead. "We were elected to get a job done, and I'm getting it done."

As we picked at cold salad plates, he made calls urging legislators to get moving and get an agreement on tax relief. He also called to thank the House members who had voted with him on his sweeping education reforms. Everyone knows about the Jeffords switch; what went virtually unnoticed was that earlier the same week, the president had met with about twenty House conservatives who were concerned that the administration had been listening too much to Senate moderates in building consensus on the education bill. I thought it was a great example of the complicated tensions of Washington, a place where compromise often means conservatives are expected to move toward a moderate position, rather than the other way around. It's like when Tom Daschle suggests Democrats ought to have greater input on President Bush's judicial nominees; I don't recall anyone ever suggesting that Newt Gingrich and Trent Lott should help pick judges for President Clinton. Or when *The New York Times*, in a front page story, wrote: "Bush, looking to his right, shores up support for 2004." What, exactly, had the President done to look right? He had worked to enact the conservative principles he believes in and on which he campaigned, things like tax cuts and a strong national defense. This, the newspaper reported, has given him "significant latitude" to appeal to moderate voters on issues like expanding Medicare to cover prescription drugs for seniors, an issue on which President Bush also campaigned. Several years into his presidency, the media still seem surprised that you can be a conservative and be compassionate, and that President Bush has worked in office to enact the proposals on which he campaigned.

Nick Calio and his legislative team; Chief of Staff Andy Card and our deputy chief of staff, Josh Bolten, Karl Rove and our economic advisers were working day and night on Capitol Hill to enact the tax cuts; the recession that Larry Lindsey had long predicted seemed to be happening. (The numbers later showed the economy had actually fallen into recession in early 2001 but because of the lag in reporting, we didn't know that yet.) The president had a bad cold; he delivered his Annapolis speech in a nasal tone, and by the time I called him at Camp David on Friday night, after the House and Senate had reached an agreement on his tax cut, his voice was so hoarse I could barely understand him; he sounded terrible that night, and even worse the next day when he returned to the White House.

In the East Room, when the tax relief bill was signed on May 26, the audience didn't want to stop clapping. It included a number of the tax families who had met us along the campaign trail and supported his plan by publicly saying what it would mean for their families. At that moment it struck me: the tax plan had never been especially popular, not with the press, not in the polls, yet the president had not let any of that deter him. He believed it was right, and important for the economy, and he just kept pushing.

"He achieved this through sheer force of will — it was incredible leadership," I whispered to Karl Rove, who was sitting next to me.

"You mean it wasn't because of the mandate from the election?" Karl jokingly replied.

Later in the Oval Office, the people who had helped make it happen lined up for pictures with the president: Nick Calio and the legislative staff, and Larry Lindsey and his economic team, who had initially developed the plan during the campaign, when then Governor Bush had sent them back to the drawing board several times to make the cuts more generous for lower income people, especially single mothers. In addition to cutting all tax rates, he added a new lower rate of 10 percent and increased the child credit.

"One more with Karen and Karl," Andy Card said to the president. "Oh yes," the president said, opening his arms to invite us into the space, "I have to have one with the people who drove Jim Jeffords from the Republican Party," joking about official Washington blaming the White House for Jeffords's defection.

A couple of weeks later, I was late for work; Jerry and Robert were joining Jerry's sister and nieces and nephews at a family reunion in Florida, and I wanted to see them off. My telephone rang: "Mrs. Hughes, this is Signal; I have the president trying to reach you from Air Force One," the operator said.

"Two things," the president told me as he came on the line: "I want you to call *People* magazine and tell them that putting my girls on the cover, doing that to nineteen-year-old girls, crosses the line between news and sensationalism; they are trying to sell magazines at my girls' expense, and you need to let them know that I don't appreciate it. Also, the Europe speech needs editing; I want you to focus on it." I told him I had just left a voice mail for our chief speechwriter, Mike Gerson, letting him know I thought it needed a more compelling signature and focus; it needed to advance our policy beyond our current support for a

Europe "whole and free." Mike e-mailed back: "Karen, I strongly agree with your voice mail. We need a summary at the end of the speech that fits the ambition of the speech, not just a united Europe but a Europe linked to America by deep values and great goals, a Europe partnered with America and active in the world . . . We need a brainstorming session . . ."

That afternoon, and the next day on a conference call, we worked on the speech; Ambassador Dan Fried of the National Security Council staff found a wonderful Churchill quote about a "house of freedom." I felt the house needed windows; I liked the metaphor, and especially the contrast with the Iron Curtain that had closed so much of Europe in the past: "Now we plan to build the house of freedom, whose doors are open to all of Europe's peoples and whose windows look out to global challenges beyond," the president concluded. Meeting by meeting, I was learning, even contributing in a small way to, America's foreign policy.

I had eagerly anticipated our first trip to Europe; I kept a travel journal, the old reporter in me, wanting to notice and write down everything.

My watch said 3:00 a.m. as we arrived in

Madrid, more than eight hundred of us, a huge entourage that required several planes and a forty-five car motorcade (I know because the president always asks, and grumbles when he thinks our entourage is too big, which is always.) I couldn't help but think of the time just three years earlier, in June 1998, when we had flown into Grand Saline, Texas, for the Salt Festival, on a King Air carrying four of us and the pilots: Governor Bush, his travel aide Logan, a member of the governor's security detail and me. We landed on a little runway that the governor, a former pilot, quickly realized was too small: "We're not going to be able to stop," he said, as we ducked our heads and the security agent flung his body around the governor, prepared to shield him in case of a crash. As we finally careened to a stop just inches from the end of the runway, the cows in the field looked very surprised. It turned out we had landed at the wrong airport; the longer strip where we were supposed to have come down was two miles away. We wouldn't be landing on the wrong runway anymore, and I couldn't help but think about how far we had come, and not just in miles, as Air Force One began the long descent into the sunny blue skies of Madrid.

On the helicopter ride to the president of Spain's ranch, we saw huge olive tree groves resembling odd Chinese checkers boards. The tents that had been set up to house the traveling press were huge: "There's the Forbes tent," Ari joked, harkening back to the Iowa caucus, where Steve Forbes had tried to curry votes on a hot summer day with an elaborate air-conditioned tent that must have cost a fortune; then again, he had one.

"Karen, have you met el presidente?" President Bush asked, introducing me to our host, Spanish president Jose Aznar. "Karen *es la voz* [the voice] *de la administración*, and Ari *es la cara* [the face]."

That night, as we arrived at the American embassy, it was profoundly reassuring to see the Stars and Stripes: "It's so special to see the American flag when you are abroad," Ari said, and it's true. We too often take it for granted at home; overseas, it stands out as the beacon of freedom that it is. I was tired after the long plane trip, but I made myself wander outside of the hotel room that night to experience the summer evening in Madrid. In nearby Santa Ana Plaza, people were out, everywhere, walking their dogs; grandmothers sat on benches, watching, as the grandchildren played nearby; young couples wrapped themselves around each other, people sat at small cafés, enjoying cerveza and tapas. "The bad news for you is I really like Europe," I told my husband on the phone that night, before falling, exhausted, into bed.

"You'll get the question, what do you hope to achieve with Belgium as the capital of the EU," Condi tells the president the next morning on the way to Brussels.

"Endive," was the quick, jesting comeback; then he turned to me: "Karen, how many countries in the EU?"

"Fifteen," I replied. I had read the briefing book. "And nineteen in NATO."

"Very good," the president nodded, approvingly.

"The ABM treaty constrains us; I ask for your understanding and support as we undertake research and development to improve all our security; we need a new security framework for a new century," the president told his colleagues at the NATO meeting. It was fascinating to watch the different reactions. Denmark's representative wrapped nice words around big doubts, saying he welcomed the "assurance of continued discussion," as we "need time" to develop a new framework because "no one wants a new arms race." Czech President

Havel took the opposite view: "We are a defensive alliance; the argument that an antiballistic defense will lead to a new round of weapons development is not valid." German Chancellor Schröder was skeptical, welcoming "dialogue" but with a "host of questions." French President Chirac felt there was no harm in a "fresh look" at security arrangements. (I was thinking he meant look, don't act.) Prime Minister Blair was prescient, compelling: "The world is changing around us. There is a need for us to develop, and develop as a matter of urgency, our own defenses . . . weapons of mass destruction pose a real threat, and it is growing, not diminishing . . . Iraq, Iran, Libya and Syria have potential . . . the debate that has been launched by President Bush is right." President Kwasniewski of Poland was supportive: "Missile defense is visionary, courageous and logical . . . walls have come down and unleashed the devils . . . it would be a mistake to ignore these demons who do not know borders." President Aznar of Spain was also prescient: we face "new problems, new threats . . . this is of the utmost importance in building security appropriate for the twenty-first century." The different approaches were fascinating at the time, even more so in the aftermath of September 11 and President Bush's effort to hold Saddam Hussein accountable for his promises to dismantle his weapons of mass destruction program. I didn't know it then, but I was already witnessing the deep differences in how the leaders of the world would view and respond to that threat.

"You're the straight talker," a man at my table said, as we enjoyed a delicious lunch of salmon with whitefish roe at a lovely country inn filled with the smell of lilacs. "I've been reading about you," one of the Swedish representatives told me; it was an odd feeling. We had briefing books; they did, too, and I was apparently in them.

At our next stop, in Poland, the soldiers lifted their boots knee high, toes out, as they marched around the square in front of the presidential palace. Condi told me how different it had been the last time she was there, in 1992, when Poland was just emerging from Soviet occupation. The building that used to be the Communist Party headquarters is now the stock exchange, we learned; Poland was the only place in Europe where we saw protesters with signs *supporting* missile defense. In the square, the NATO flag waved beside the Polish one, and as the Polish band played

"The Star-Spangled Banner," Condi's bottom lip quivered; she brushed away a tear, and I reached over and patted her on the shoulder.

The clock said 9:12 a.m. as I rolled over in bed the next morning, the ringing of the phone startling me awake in my room at the Marriott Hotel in Warsaw: "Karen, are you coming with the motorcade?" Of course I was. What a dumb question.

"Well, we're downstairs and we're leaving right now," Logan Walters told me. The hotel had not placed my wake-up call, or I hadn't heard it; my body clock was completely out of sync, and I was about to miss the plane to Slovenia for President Bush's first meeting with Russia's president Putin.

"Don't worry, you can probably catch up; we have a wreath-laying on the way to the airport," Logan said, and I frantically jumped up and pulled on my clothes. I had left my suitcase outside my door the night before because the bag call was in the middle of the night, so at least I didn't have to pack.

One of our advance men, John Horne, stayed behind to rescue me and we drove frantically toward the airport. He had a radio: "They didn't stay long at the wreath ceremony," he reported; a few miles from the airport, we saw the motorcade. When John tried to join it, waving his official credentials, the policeman wouldn't let him; finally, after all the cars had driven by, we were allowed through the barricade and we sped toward the airplane, going about ninety. I arrived in time to get on the plane and join my colleagues in the senior staff cabin.

"Where have you been? I didn't see you at the wreath laying," Condi said.

"You almost didn't see me at all," I replied.

"When we come out of this meeting, what do we want to have accomplished?" President Bush asked those of us in Air Force One's conference room — Colin Powell, Condi Rice, Andy Card and me — launching a lengthy discussion of the issues he expected to raise in this, his first meeting with the Russian president. I remember a sense of great anticipation: "Even now, it's still *the* moment when the president of the United States meets the president of Russia for the first time," Condi told me.

As the doors opened, and President Putin walked into the room of the restored palace, with its gold formal drapes and huge flat glass prisms that cover almost the entire ceiling, President Bush turned to the chief of protocol, his old college friend Don Ensenat, and whispered: "Enzo, we're a long way from Yale."

"Mr. President," Enzo intoned, "President Putin of the Russian Federation."

I couldn't hear what President Putin said, but I could hear my boss's response: "I *did* play rugby . . . *very* good briefing." It struck me as a sign of both the scope and the limitations of intelligence briefings: President Bush had played rugby for a short time in college, but it would never be one of the things I would first mention to him.

"I had a nine hour flight," President Putin replied. "I watched a movie about you and your family."

"I hope it was one we made," my president responded.

"They must be really hitting it off; it's been an hour," I said to Andy Card as we waited outside the room; just the two presidents and their national security advisers were in the meeting. "Either that, or they gassed the room," he deadpanned.

Outside in the hall, anxious security and advance men paced and talked into their cell phones and radios as the meeting stretched past an hour and a half, far longer than scheduled.

"They've agreed on a new Louisiana

plan," someone cracked; "we gave back Alaska and they're going to drill in Anwar." On trips, the staff and advance team and doctors and security personnel spend hours waiting while the principals meet; only afterward do the rest of us spring into action.

I thought about my impressions of the Russian president. He was shorter than I had thought from seeing him on television, and blonder, and he seemed hard: hard body, hard eyes. I couldn't help but think how different his blue eyes were from those of President Bush's. Our president's eyes exude a twinkle, a sparkling warmth; President Putin's eyes looked deep, almost bottomless, as if you could look into them forever and still not discern anything.

The two leaders looked much more relaxed as they emerged from their private meeting laughing and talking easily with each other. They joined us in a larger room, where our American delegation sat across from our Russian counterparts at a large circular table. As the two presidents talked, it became clear that President Putin was concerned about Russia's economy. He talked a lot about trade and investment; he wanted the secretary of commerce to bring a delegation of American business leaders and investors to Russia. I couldn't help but think, here is the president of Russia, the former seat of communism, saying to the president of the United States: please send me your capitalists.

"I think I made progress getting him to trust me," the president said afterward. "He's a student of history, I'm a history major, but I told him, 'Let's not get stuck in our history; we're making history together.' "

"Interesting about the intelligence briefings; President Putin knew you had played rugby, but he didn't have the context. I mean you just played for one semester in college, right?" I said, dismissing it.

"I played for a year," the president corrected me, "and it was the varsity."

At home in Washington, the rest of June seemed slow, lethargic; we seemed to be skipping from one little event to another, with no coherent or consistent message. One of the keys to delivering an effective message is consistency and repetition; whenever we had too many things jumbled on the president's calendar, I used to joke that we had "message ADD." The president always thought it was funny, and laughed heartily every time I said it. But he recognized the serious point: we needed a more focused message.

One of the tugs of the presidency is that the president has to do so many different things: speak out to help win approval for (or kill) a specific piece of legislation; highlight holidays and special occasions; comment on the latest Supreme Court decision, or natural disaster, or economic news or events in a foreign country. It gets even trickier when you have to depend on the media to deliver much of your daily message: news is change, not repetition. It's not news for the president to keep talking about the economy, or pushing for his education reforms, over and over again; you have to make it fresh.

Message discipline is hard in a place as busy as the White House, and in late June 2001, I felt we were drowning in an alphabet soup of little messages — what President Bush calls "playing smallball" — with none of our activities big enough or important enough to carry the day. I'd been making the argument at meeting after meeting; my team was frustrated. I wrote a lengthy memo to the president, rare for me: I wanted him to take time to think about the need to outline broad themes and develop better communications story lines.

The same week, *Time* magazine ran a

story: "With Bush slipping in the polls, his message shop — led by Karen Hughes — tries to remake his image." It quoted an anonymous GOP consultant: "Karen gets it, a lot of others don't." I was mortified: the story made me look good at the expense of the president and my colleagues. The story led with comments I had made in a senior staff meeting when I had argued against Legislative Director Nick Calio's recommendation that the president should publicly threaten to veto a flawed Patients' Bill of Rights being considered in Congress.

"Once he says veto, that's all anyone is going to hear," I had worried out loud. "We can't just be against something; we have to be for something."

The bill was headed in a bad direction, Nick countered, and the only way to fix it was to threaten a veto. I was appalled that someone had quoted comments I had made in a private senior staff meeting to reporters from *Time*, and although the story was sympathetic to me, I was described as having "lost" this battle, because the president subsequently issued the veto threat. That wasn't the way I felt: it wasn't a battle, more a great example of two White House staffers doing two very different jobs. I'm paid to worry about perception and message; Nick is paid to shepherd the legislative process and get good laws that are consistent with the president's philosophy to the president's desk for his signature.

We're all expected to speak up and represent our different points of view; then the president has to weigh the different perspectives, and decide which is right or most important in each case. Once the president decides, my role changes. Before he makes a decision, my role is to give him my best advice; after he decides, my role is to advocate and defend the decision. My quotes, which showed that I had argued against what the president ultimately decided, weren't helpful for anyone.

The president called my deputy, Dan Bartlett. He hadn't read the *Time* story, he told him, but Mrs. Bush had seen it and didn't like it. I was surprised the president had called Dan instead of me, and I asked him about it. The president responded that he thought "junior bird men" were talking too much. He wanted to send a signal through the organization that he was paying attention.

"Please let Mrs. Bush know that I don't like it any more than she does to see things I say in internal meetings printed in a national magazine," I told the president. I was sick about the whole thing: that someone had leaked my comments, which only breeds suspicion and mistrust; that it appeared that my staff and I were trying to make ourselves look good at everyone else's expense; that President and Mrs. Bush thought my people were talking too much.

"This is a terrible place," I said to the president, distressed.

"How about last night; that wasn't so terrible was it?" was the president's quick comeback.

Mrs. Bush had surprised her husband with a party celebrating his birthday and the Fourth of July. He had returned from a trip and walked into the state dining room to find his family and good friends: college roommates, friends from Texas, some of our staff. We had fried chicken and watched the fantastic fireworks from Washington's best setting, the Truman Balcony in the White House residence. My whole family was in town for the week; Leigh and Lauren had joined us for the Fourth of July celebration on the White House lawn, and we had visited all the monuments the day before, an all-American Fourth in our nation's capital.

"Last night was spectacular," I said, honestly. But the idea that we couldn't trust fellow staff members not to repeat things we said in internal debates, so different from the pattern of trust and respect that had prevailed during our years in the governor's office, troubled me. I found it corrosive, both to morale and to good decision making. Everyone worried about leaks, so the larger the meeting, the less anyone talked. Karl once suggested that we have a premeeting before message meetings so we could discuss and agree on things without so many people in the room; that may have been smart given the ways of Washington, but it would have changed the nature of the meeting. I like brainstorming sessions where different members of the staff toss around and feed off each other's ideas; because of the fear of leaks, many White House meetings became merely venues to distribute marching orders. And that's pretty much what the message meeting became, a meeting to get everyone on the same page. I gradually quit going and sent my deputy. We instituted a new meeting where the real decisions about schedule and message could be made in a smaller, more leakproof group.

The very next week, on Friday, July 13, a new poll came out in *USA Today* showing the president's job approval rating was back up to 57 percent. "I notice the White House has revived my image," the president teased me, as I walked into the Oval Office that morning. I always marvel at his ability to let the ups and downs of the media coverage roll off his back; during the campaign, he often joked about a "news blackout," meaning he wasn't reading the stories or paying any attention to them. He would shoo Mrs. Bush and me to the back of the plane if he heard us grousing about an article: "Out of my earshot if you're going to talk about that; I don't want to hear it," he would complain whenever he heard us complaining about the coverage. But I often found he knew more about the stories than he let on; I would mention a point from an article, and he would counter with another one, making it clear he had read it even though he sometimes pretended he hadn't.

We worried that the headlines on our second trip to Europe would be dominated by protests; thousands of protesters were expected to descend on Genoa for the meeting of the leaders of the world's largest industrialized nations, the G8. But first, we were stopping in London for another pinch-me moment: lunch with the queen of England. My army family upbringing had taught me that all people are equal; I had never paid a great deal of attention to the royal family. The grace and elegance of Princess Diana had intrigued me, as it did so much of the world. We were out of town at one of my son's soccer tournaments the night of her fatal car wreck and I stayed up for hours watching the coverage, saddened by the death of a young woman who had put such a human face on royalty. But other than that, I didn't know much about the royal family and I certainly never imagined I would ever be invited to dine with them.

My first thought was, What will I wear? Something pastel is good for lunch with the queen, we were told (I bought a pretty light green suit); and by the way, don't touch her unless she touches you first.

I was scheduled to appear on the morning television shows the day of our luncheon, and one of our press staffers told me I would be asked about the meeting with the queen. I panicked and spent hours scrambling to find the right answers to questions; the last thing I wanted to do was offend our hosts or cause an international incident. "Why don't we curtsy; what if I'm asked about that?" I asked a member of the national security staff; the real answer is Americans don't curtsy, I was told, but that seemed a little rude to our hosts, so I decided I would say that those who were not British subjects are not expected to curtsy — which was a good thing, since I had not the first idea how. Of course, the question was never asked: I was grilled about missile defense, the Kyoto treaty, funding for the World Bank, would we allow Russia into NATO?

It was pouring rain when we arrived at Buckingham Palace; the queen had someone bring a towel to dry the drops off President Bush's suit. In the receiving line, the president introduced our delegation. When he got to Karl and me, he stopped and turned to the queen: "These two have been with me since the beginning." At the luncheon the president sat next to the queen; Mrs. Bush sat beside Prince Philip and I sat between the British ambassador, a delightful man named Sir Christopher Meyer, and the Duke of York, whose name I had not seen on our advance briefing paper. Mentally, I tried to place him: "He's the one who was married to Fergie; whatever you do, *don't* mention that." He was charming; we talked about education and account-ability, and found common ground de-crying the intrusiveness of the media. They were all incredibly gracious, yet I felt unso-phisticated and out of place. I really wanted to look around the palace, but I was trying to be polite and make sure I didn't drop anything.

We visited Prime Minister Blair at his country residence, Checquers, and I was again struck by the special nature of the friendship between the United States and the United Kingdom. Meetings with other foreign leaders frequently have the feel of a delicate dance; each leader comes prepared with certain moves, specific subjects that need to be broached in a certain way, and at the proper moment, before the next step is introduced into the mix. But meetings between President Bush and Prime Minister Blair were much more casual, as if neither needed to worry about what he said to the other. The prime minister practically bounded through the rooms, showing President Bush his library, filled with the familiar smell of old leather. "It's hard to keep up with you," said President Bush, who is frequently hard to keep up with himself. The two talked easily, openly, hopscotching from Macedonia to Northern Ireland to the Middle East. "I don't have good news for you," President Bush said to the prime minister. "I'm worried Arafat, maybe, doesn't want to make a deal; maybe he wants to get rid of Israel, in which case he's got a real problem with us and with you. A lot of this violence is provoked by Arafat's inactivity; we've got to send a very strong signal that the terror must stop . . ."

What struck me as we arrived in Genoa for the G8 summit was what we didn't see: people. The downtown had basically been evacuated for this meeting of world leaders. Security was so tight that most shops had closed; no one was on the streets. It reminded me of an earlier trip to Quebec City for another gathering of international leaders: several square miles of the city had been cordoned off; it looked as if a bomb had exploded and killed all the people but left the vacant buildings. It was sad, I thought, that because of security risks and the huge crowds of unruly protesters, leaders had to be isolated from the people they represented. The cities seemed hollow and lost much of their charm without residents filling the streets. Genoa was particularly unsettling with police officers everywhere, and U.S. Navy SEAL divers in black wet suits periodically emerging from the water next to our hotel at the harbor.

President Bush met with the leaders of the G8 and again with president Putin: "He understands he's got an opportunity," President Bush told me later, "The chemistry's great — he gets it; very few leaders have had the chance to refashion how the world thinks about security."

"Mr. President, you just made a breakthrough," was Condi Rice's assessment.

"I hope someday you can tell your grandchildren: I was at the table at the groundbreaking discussions that led to a more peaceful and stable world . . . ," President Bush told members of our two delegations. "Titanic changes are under way in the world," he said to me and Andy Card later, in the limousine on the way to the airport, "the question is whether we will be able to influence the shape of the new architecture."

We walked slowly up several long flights of marble stairs on the way to our audience with the pope at his summer residence; I felt as if we were literally climbing the "stairway to heaven." The pope hadn't been feeling well that morning, we were told. His voice was clear, yet occasionally trailed off as he read his statement; his hands were shaking. "Karen Hughes, Your Holiness," President Bush said, introducing me and the other members of the delegation. The pope handed me a medallion, an image of Peter casting his nets into the deep, and as he reached out and gripped my right hand, it was almost as if a current went through my arm, the grip surprisingly powerful for such a frail man; I felt this was truly a man filled with the spirit of God.

We quickly came down to earth, donning bulletproof vests for our flight to Kosovo, where the president would visit American troops who were part of the peacekeeping force there. We were told not to step off the concrete because the grass might contain land mines. The president, Andy Card and Condi Rice flew to Kosovo on one small plane; Karl and I were on another identical one. Our plane crossed through the mountains into the valley first, and then did a long series of elaborate circles and maneuvers that made our stomachs churn. Karl and I looked at each other; no one admitted it when we joked about it later, but we knew: we had been a decoy; if anyone wanted to shoot at the president's plane, our aircraft would have drawn the fire first.

During our European trip, I had asked the president to compare, after six months, the presidency to his service as governor: "The stakes are higher and the range of issues more complicated . . . it's harder to interface with legislators; people ossify in their positions," he told me. "There's a lot more politics: witness the fact that the majority leader of the Senate [Senator Tom Daschle] would intentionally criticize the president as he left on an international trip. What makes the job more complex and interesting is the foreign policy; because of our standing in the world, the United States is expected to be active everywhere in the world: right now in Macedonia, Ireland, Korea, the Middle East, Iraq. The irony is that Europe is anxious for our help, yet at the same time, they want to tie our hands; they are trying to bind us to international treaties that restrict our capacity to act, and I'm not going to let them do that. In the Middle East, especially, there is the expectation that only the United States can solve the problem. Both sides expect us to be involved, but to different degrees . . . My attitude is we have to be patient, press the parties to be realistic, press dialogue, insist on an end to violence . . .

"I don't feel any of the so-called loneliness of the job; Andy Card understands the chief of staff role as well as anybody conceivably could; information gets to me in an efficient way and he does not feel threatened that I have close friends as part of my inner circle, so people have access to me and I'm not cut off. The Cabinet seems to be working very well; my home life is good . . ."

My own home life, or more honestly, the

lack of one, was my major concern. Jerry and Robert had been to events at the White House, to Camp David and on Air Force One, but they weren't seeing much of me. I was traveling, learning new things, working long hours; when I was home, I was tired, and I found myself not wanting to go out. When I left in the morning, my family was still asleep; by the time I got home from work, Robert was hibernating in the downstairs den, watching television or doing homework and emphatically not interested in talking with me.

I was eagerly anticipating our annual vacation at the beach in late July, not only to see our friends, but also to spend time with my family. Congress was still in session, but we had already bought our airline tickets, and I wasn't about to stay behind in Washington. I had missed our annual trip to South Padre Island the year before during the 2000 campaign because it conflicted with the Republican National Convention. The vacation is our version of *Same Time, Next Year*; every summer, the Berkowitz, Margolin, Gunter and Hughes families, occasionally joined by a couple of others, meet for a week to relax, catch up with each other and measure how much all our kids have grown since the year before. The

Berkowitzes and Margolins started the tradition when Steve and Ellis graduated from medical school more than twenty years ago. The two oldest children in our group, Leah and Anna Berkowitz, weren't even born then; they are both in college now. We all stay in the same condominium complex, and the biggest decision we make each day is where to meet for dinner. We have a rule: we don't talk about work unless the person involved brings it up. It was wonderful to be with people who cared about me, not my job, and although I was interrupted a few times by White House phone calls, it was a great break. I was struck by how happy Robert was to be back in Texas; he and Alex Margolin laughed, and ran, and played in the surf. Far too soon, the week was over. We visited my parents in Dallas, then Jerry went to Austin to visit Leigh and Lauren while Robert came with me to meet President Bush in Crawford.

I was there to work on the president's first prime-time speech, about stem-cell research, perhaps the toughest decision of his presidency to that point. He had been wrestling with its moral and ethical implications for months. The stem-cell issue came down to a question no one could really answer: is a fertilized human egg that is alive, but only in a laboratory, a human life?

As Doug Melton, one of the scientists we met with, put it: "This issue is a philosopher's dream and a lawyer's nightmare. Who are we to decide when life begins?"

These fertilized eggs, or embryos, are created during the process of in vitro fertilization, which has helped so many couples have children. A woman's egg is fertilized in a test tube by a man's sperm; the result is a human embryo that clearly has at least the potential for life: if it is implanted in a woman's womb, it will become a child. If the embryo is not implanted, but remains in a test tube, it will not become a child — but it is still the seed of a child and is capable of becoming one. These fertilized embryos are the source of stem cells. The problem is, the process of extracting the stem cell for research kills the embryo. The question thus becomes, Is it acceptable for the government to fund research that will destroy this potential for human life?

The issue sparked a series of fascinating discussions. "We are here on behalf of our children; I'm defending my family," said a representative of the Juvenile Diabetes Research Foundation, a father whose child has that terrible disease. "One hundred million people would be affected by this. We do not believe these are living embryos; no one knows what to call these cell clusters," he said.

Doug Melton, of Harvard, said: "It's arguable that something frozen that has the potential for life is, in fact, life. People who know more about research than I do say this is the area of research that can revolutionize medicine. Only the embryonic cells can make any cell in your body."

But again, we faced those nagging ethical questions. "They are not a person, they are not alive," Doug Melton told us, "on the other hand, they are not to be treated cavalierly: part of this is the mystery of biology."

"I must confess I am wrestling with a difficult decision," President Bush had told a group of ethicists meeting with us in the Oval Office one afternoon. "On the one hand, it offers so much hope; on the other, so much despair. I worry about a culture that devalues life. I think my job is to encourage respect for life; on the other hand, I believe science and technologies have enormous potential to help solve a lot of problems and save lives. What do you say to the argument that these embryos are going to die anyway; that we are practical people; why shouldn't we do some good with them?" President Bush had asked.

"The fact that a being is going to die does not entitle us to use it as a natural resource for exploitation," one of the ethicists had answered.

"We at least owe them respect and not to manipulate them for our own purposes," another answered.

"Do we know that it's a human being?" one asked out loud. "We don't mourn when it dies, but since we don't know, shouldn't we err on the side of treating it with as much respect as possible?"

"One goes with a heavy heart when we use these things," Leon Cass said, "We are dealing with the seeds of what could be the next generation."

President Bush wanted to know more about the potential of funding research on existing stem cells that had already been extracted from the embryo: would allowing research on them to pursue the scientific promise be morally defensible?

"If you fund research on lines that have already been developed, you are not complicit in their destruction," Cass responded.

I could see the president considering it. This approach would allow the federal government to fund research and further science without crossing a moral line by promoting the additional destruction of life.

President Bush stopped me as I was leaving the office: "Are you comfortable with this?"

I nodded, still thinking.

"No, you're not, I can tell," the president pushed. "I want your opinion."

"I'm increasingly uncomfortable with additional destruction," I said.

"Me, too," the president nodded.

The president ultimately made the decision he had first explored in this meeting, avoiding government-sanctioned destruction of life while funding research on stem cells where the life-and-death decision had already been made; I thought it was principled, and saw it as a preview of the many difficult moral judgments that will face policy makers in the future as science and medicine advance.

I had started drafting the stem-cell speech in Washington in July, before my beach vacation; at the ranch in early August, President Bush and our policy expert, Jay Lefkowitz, and I revised and edited it. We all enjoyed working in the more relaxed setting, under the open Texas sky; the afternoon before the speech, Robert got to go fishing with the president. That night, in prime time, the president gave what I thought was a powerful speech, explaining a difficult issue in clear terms and giving the American people an insight into his decision-making process.

When my family returned to Washington after two weeks in Texas, we walked into a flood. The District of Columbia had been hit with big storms and had what was described as a hundred-year rain; the garage and basement of Margaret's house, where we had stored most of our boxes after moving from the rented house in Arlington just a few weeks earlier, was standing in a foot of water. It took weeks to dry everything out, and we wondered, What else could make this year more chaotic?

As we prepared for the fall of 2001, two things were foremost in the president's mind. "Get Mike and the speechwriters working on a big foreign policy speech to outline our strategy and goals. I'm tired of being labeled an isolationist because I won't agree to treaties that aren't good for America," he told me. And the second, by far the most important issue, was the budget. We had to fund the president's priorities yet control spending; federal revenues were down dramatically because of the recession, so we had to insist that Congress restrain from excessive spending and give the tax cuts time to boost the ailing economy. The president had given us our marching orders, opening a budget meeting with a lecture: "We've done the nation a great favor; we've removed $1.35 trillion that would have been spent on bigger government. We've redefined the debate: this is the appropriators versus the fiscally responsible people, and in round one, the fiscally responsible people are winning. At a time of economic downturn, the other side wants to raise taxes. They are the spenders; we are the guardians of the people's money. Anything else on the budget?" the president had asked, making it clear there was nothing else to say. The fall would be dominated by the battle of the budget, and he had just issued the war plans.

I almost missed the arrival ceremony for our first state visit, welcoming the president of Mexico, because I had been at the back-to-school chapel service at Robert's school. I always try to attend school events, to show Robert his school is important to me as well as to him, and I wanted to pray for him to feel more at home in Washington. Traffic was terrible when Jerry dropped me off downtown; I had to run through the streets for blocks to get to the White House just before the ceremony began at 10:00 a.m. That night, the fireworks celebrating the state visit filled the night sky; when you order fireworks for two presidents, people tend to go overboard. The display was supposed to last ten minutes; after twenty, the sky was so bright you could barely look at it, which seemed to defeat the purpose. "We were testing the new missile defense system," Condi joked; "There goes the last of the surplus," said Senator Phil Gramm.

"A fairy-tale day," Andy Card described it at the next morning's staff meeting, and it had epitomized the dazzling aspects of my new job: meetings with foreign leaders, pomp and ceremony, wonderful entertainment.

That weekend, I e-mailed my friend Kevyn Burger, one of the Amazon women from my Channel 5 reporting days:

Sept 9, 2001

We are having a little trouble adjusting to washington — the job is incredibly challenging and demanding, as you might imagine — i struggle to find time for family/myself — my son does not like washington, and, it's all my fault we came here — Jerry is ter-

487

rific as always — but trying to figure out what he wants to do — he was in charge of the move, and now that we are settled in D.C. he is ready to find something to do — but it's a little harder than usual because we have to worry about conflicts with my job — but of course it is thrilling for all of us to go to events at the White House and the President and Mrs. Bush continue to be most gracious about sharing special times with us — robert got to fish with the president in Crawford, which meant I wasn't in quite so much trouble with him for at least a day or so — We'd love to have you come visit — bring your kids and I'll take you on a tour of the west wing — I am sincere — the best part of all this is the opportunity to share it with friends.

CHAPTER 9

September 11

When I think of that morning, I still hear the sound: so routine, and thus so shocking, so totally out of place. Horror had rained from a brilliant blue sky on September 11, 2001, yet from the second floor window of my Northwest Washington home, the steady drone of a leaf blower several yards away dared to suggest that things were somehow normal.

It was definitely not normal that I was even at home that morning; almost any other weekday of my entire eighteen months in Washington I would have been at the West Wing or on the road traveling with the president. But September 10 is our wedding anniversary. I had never missed an anniversary dinner with my husband, not during a presidential campaign, not through campaigns for governor, nor for any other reasons during our almost eighteen years of marriage, and I wasn't about to start just because I worked at the White House. It's not that my husband would have been angry (in fact, he said we could celebrate another night if I decided to go to Florida with the president), or that I think that couples who have to be apart because of work or any other reason are somehow putting their marriage in jeopardy; I do believe that life is a series of small choices through which we sometimes communicate big things. I decided that while I wanted to travel to Florida, site of our postelection trauma and an important state for the president's future, it wasn't essential — at least, not as essential as spending that evening with my husband, who had left his daughter, granddaughter and much of the rest of his life behind in Texas to move to Washington with me.

We had dinner at Jeffrey's, a longtime favorite restaurant of ours in Austin, which had opened a Washington location at the Watergate shortly after the president's inauguration, thinking it would attract a lot of business from the Texans now in the nation's capital. I remember debating what to wear. Early September is a hard time of year, still warm, although summer is passing. I chose the light green suit, the one that had been perfect for lunch with the queen, but was a little too pastel and a little too summery for early September. ("How can you remember things like what you wore?" my husband always asks. The same way he remembers it was Cotton Spreyer who made the catch against Notre Dame that led Texas to victory in the 1970 Cotton Bowl. "But that's important," he protests.) The restaurant was not crowded. We sat by the window, and surveyed our life. We had weathered the worst of the upheaval, we thought on the night of September 10; we had survived the campaign, the transition, the move to Virginia and then into the District of Columbia, and the flood in the basement. Robert was starting ninth grade and a number of other new students would join the class; surely, this year he would settle in and feel more at home in Washington.

Jerry had dealt with the phone companies, cable companies, moving companies, utility companies, vehicle registration and license offices two different times in two different cities now; he was ready to find something more interesting and challenging to do. We knew it would be difficult: almost any law firm he could join would have lobbying business, and clients whose interests could pose a conflict with my job. Our major, ongoing worry was a financial one: our house in Texas had been on the market since January but had not sold, and making two house payments, one for the rent in Washington, the other for the mortgage back home, plus paying for private school tuition, was eating into our savings at an alarming rate.

I was scheduled to represent the White House at a Habitat for Humanity home-building event near my neighborhood in Washington on the morning of September 11. I needed to come prepared to swing a hammer in blue jeans and a T-shirt, not appropriate West Wing attire, and knowing I would be out late for my anniversary, I took advantage of the opportunity to skip the morning senior staff meeting and sleep in. I was in the shower when the phone rang a little before nine; my husband answered and told my assistant that I was upstairs getting ready.

"Would you tell her that a plane has hit the World Trade Center, but we don't know much about it yet," my assistant, Jill Angelo, said.

"I think you had better talk to her yourself," my husband replied. Jerry has been asked to deliver many messages over the years, and he doesn't like it, especially when he knows the message will provoke a long list of questions from me. He brought the phone upstairs, and handed it to me as I stepped out of the tub.

"Karen, a plane has hit the World Trade Center and I think it's pretty bad," said Jill.

"How bad?" I asked, trying to envision a plane crashing into the building.

"Pretty bad. They think it involves ten or twelve floors," she said.

"Has someone told the president?" I asked.

"I called Dan just before I called you," she said, referring to Dan Bartlett, who had traveled to Florida with the president when I decided to stay home. I hung up with Jill and dialed Dan's cell phone. Condi Rice had talked to the president just after they arrived at the school in Florida, but they didn't know any more than I did. We all assumed it was some kind of weird accident; at that point terrorism didn't occur to us.

"He'll need to call the mayor," I said to Dan. I yelled to my husband to turn on the television, then walked over and flipped on the one in the upstairs dressing room of the house we were renting from Margaret Tutwiler. Unlike me, Margaret is a news junkie. She had a TV in every room in her house, and had left them for us to use. As I turned to finish getting dressed, I saw the large dark shape of an airplane heading right toward, then crashing into, the second tower. Horrified, I dropped to my knees and said a quick prayer: "Lord help those poor people in that building," then dialed the cell phone again.

"Another plane just flew into the second tower," I told Dan.

"What kind of plane?" he asked, shock in his voice.

"I don't know, a big plane, like a passenger plane," I replied.

"A passenger plane?" he asked incredulously. I was trying to reference the size of the airplane; it never occurred to me that passengers were actually in it. I don't know why; maybe it was just too awful to imagine.

Dan and I didn't say it out loud, but we didn't need to: we now knew that this was a planned attack. As Secretary of Transportation Norm Mineta would say later that day: "Once is an accident, twice is a pattern, three times is a program."

The local television station I was watching interviewed an aviation expert: "Our lives will never be the same; nothing will ever be normal again."

I wrote his comments on my notebook, along with an excerpt from the Bible: "For such a time as this." In the Old Testament story of Esther, a young woman who found favor with the king was made queen. The king did not know that Esther was Jewish, and when one of the leading noblemen in the kingdom hatched a plot to destroy the Jewish people, Esther's cousin Mordecai sent word that she had to intervene on behalf of her people. She was reluctant, and Mordecai chastised her: "Do not think that because you are in the king's house you alone of all the Jews will escape. For if you remain silent at this time, relief and deliverance for the Jews will arise from another place, but you and your father's family will perish. And who knows but that you have come to royal position for such a time as this?" Who knew, I thought, whether my boss had won one of the closest elections in America's history "for such a time as this"?

"Do we need to cancel the event?" Dan was thinking out loud on his cell phone from the school in Florida, where the president was in a classroom reading a book to the school's children when Andy Card entered the room there and whispered: "A second plane hit the second tower; America is under attack."

"You have to cancel it," I told Dan. "You all need to get back here as soon as you can."

The next thirty minutes were a blur. I stayed on the phone from the second floor of my house, on the line with Dan in Florida or Jill at the White House, watching a nightmare on television, with the drone of the yard man's leaf blower as background noise.

Dan and Karl Rove and Ari Fleischer were in a back room at the school in Florida; I talked with them through Dan. The president needs to make a statement before he leaves, we agreed. The president didn't want anything written out, Dan reported: "He'll just say something quick so we can leave."

When Air Force One took off, I thought it was headed for Washington; Dan and I didn't know that the vice president, Andy Card and Condi Rice had recommended the president stay away from Washington because we didn't know exactly what we were dealing with, and they knew this crisis would be even worse if something happened to the president.

I lost cell phone contact with Dan shortly after Air Force One took off from Florida; I was on the phone with Jill, who was in our West Wing office coordinating my staff, when she said suddenly, her voice shaky but composed: "Karen, the Secret Service is yelling at us to get out of here."

"Go, then, get out," I ordered and hung up the phone. Suddenly, I was oddly disconnected: the White House was being evacuated, the television reported, employees were being told to run. Chaos, then silence. I knew I had to get to work, but where? And how? The television reported that downtown Washington was shutting down; barricades were being erected and perimeters extended to prevent anyone from getting close to the White House or major government buildings. Someone reported the State Department had been hit by a car bomb (which later turned out to be false) and an airplane had crashed into the Pentagon. The White House switchboard wasn't answering; the operators had been evacuated.

Suddenly, I realized my son would see the news reports and worry; he frequently called me at work between classes to ask about breaking news. "Jerry, would you call Robert's school and let him know I'm okay at home," I called to my husband, who was looking up the number when the phone rang.

"Come get me," Robert said to his dad, and I realized I hadn't stopped yet to consider how horrifying this must be for our children. The grown-ups could barely comprehend what was happening; the kids must be terrified. Robert's school was only a short drive away. I would go with my husband to pick him up and get my family home safe; by then, maybe I could figure out how and where to get to work.

Traffic was terrible; people were fleeing downtown and jamming the streets of Northwest Washington. As we approached the school, my pager started beeping:

10:07 A.M. EDT MESSAGE 01: YOU ARE NEEDED IN THE SHELTER ASAP. I had never been to the shelter and didn't know where it was. I tried calling the White House repeatedly, but got no answer. My pager was vibrating again:

02: PLS CALL NOW; DUPLICATE MESSAGE; but the number they gave was busy. As we turned into Robert's school, I handed my cell phone to Jerry and jumped out of the car.

The school chaplain was outside, trying to make sure the boys didn't leave unless with a parent; he looked at me quizzically, perhaps wondering why I wasn't at work. Inside, boys were running through the halls; I asked several people if they knew where I might find Robert.

"Down in Trapezoid," one said, referring to the theater.

As I headed there, Robert walked up the hall toward me, his body rigid and controlled. He looked pale and frightened: "Let's go home," he said, and repeated several times in the car: "I want to go home." He didn't mean home to the rented house on Klingle Street; he wanted to drive to Texas, right then, with no stops. St. Albans is located on the grounds of the National Cathedral, the highest point in Washington; the students had been frightened that their campus might have been a target.

My cell phone had been ringing, Jerry told me; he had tried to answer it but couldn't make it work. Another page: 03: PLEASE GO TO (DOWNTOWN ADDRESS) MOST OF SENIOR STAFF IS THERE ASAP. As we worked our way toward home, my cell phone finally rang; it was Josh Bolten, our deputy chief of staff. My cell phone was beeping, and I realized the battery was almost dead. (My cell phone battery is almost always dead, especially when I need it most; I am not good about mechanical matters like remembering to charge the battery.) I asked Josh to call me back on Jerry's cell phone before we lost each other again.

"The vice president is looking for you to make a statement," Josh said. I told him I would be glad to do so, but I wasn't sure how to get into downtown Washington. The vice president would send a military driver to get me, Josh reported. My pager kept going off:

04: CALL FOURNIER URGENTLY; that was the always-on-top-of-things Associated Press White House reporter looking for somebody who could tell him what was happening;

05: (CODE NAME FOR VICE PRESIDENT) WANTS TO TALK TO YOU, CALL SIGNAL 11:11 AM EDT.

When I called the number Josh had given me, Transportation Secretary Norm Mineta answered, sounding surprisingly calm and unruffled. He had ordered the airlines to land their planes; the vice president was on the phone but he would get Mary Matalin for me. Mary said the vice president wanted me to call Air Force One; they were working on a statement for the president. I was surprised; I had thought the president was on his way back to Washington.

"No," Mary told me, "they're landing someplace in Louisiana."

The vice president got on the line; he was worried that perhaps the president shouldn't make a statement until we knew more about what was happening and he encouraged me to check in with the plane. I called Air Force One and asked for Ari.

"The president feels strongly that people need to hear from him directly," Ari told me. "We're working on a statement."

When he read it, the first line made me apoplectic: "America today was the victim of . . ."

"We are not victims," I interrupted, "we may have been attacked but we are *not* victims." Ari agreed, and put Dan on the phone, but we lost the connection.

Back at home, I put a toothbrush, an extra pair of blue jeans and a T-shirt in a bag to take with me; I had no idea how long I might have to stay at the White House. Jerry and Robert were watching television, listening to reports about the airplane now embedded in the side of the Pentagon; they didn't say anything about my going back to the White House, a place that was obviously a target, but I'm sure they were worried. It was unspoken: we all knew that I had a job and I had to do it.

Heading back into the heart of Washington became more than a duty; it was also an act of faith. Like a soldier going into battle, or a patient who learns he has a life-threatening disease, I had to confront my mortality, decide whether I truly believed what I said I did. It wasn't that I thought God would save me from the terrorists, or from death: there's 100 percent incontrovertible evidence that all of us are going to die, even though we often don't spend a lot of time thinking about that moment. But if I truly believed that God had offered me eternal life through faith in His son, everything else was just short-term thinking. I had to trust Christ's promise: He would be with me always, even till the close of the age, which might be closer than it usually appeared, especially if people were going to start doing crazy things like flying airplanes into buildings.

It seemed to be taking forever for the driver to get to my house, and for the president to make his statement. I called Mary again, concerned: "Mary, on TV it looks like the government has shut down . . . the White House was evacuated, the State Department was evacuated; it looks like we've just closed and gone home . . . we've got to get somebody out to calm people down and let them know that the government is functioning and responding."

Mary and the vice president agreed; I should call the president to get his permission for me to make a statement: emergency response plans were being implemented, airplanes were being grounded, our military had been ordered on high alert.

"This is a terrible day for our country," I said to the military driver who had finally worked his way through the traffic to get to my house. "Yes, ma'am," he said. I could see the smoke from the Pentagon rising on the horizon: "You probably have friends there," I said, and he nodded. I thought about how much life would change for the men and women in our military in the days and weeks ahead.

The drive back into downtown Washington was surreal. Everyone we passed was headed the opposite way, away from the city, toward someplace, anyplace, that might be safer. It reminded me of the time much earlier in my career as a reporter when my photographer and I had to drive toward Galveston Island to cover the hurricane, while everyone else was fleeing to the mainland.

"I need to talk with the president," I told the operator at the military switchboard; I knew if I could talk with my boss he would understand and approve the need for me to brief the press. The operator put me on hold, then came back to the phone, and grimly reported: "Ma'am, I'm sorry. We cannot reach Air Force One." It was one of the scariest moments of the day; this had never happened before. I had seen the elaborate communications equipment on Air Force One and had watched the president make and receive calls from all over the world. During one of our phone calls, Mary had told me that there had been a threat against the president's plane; surely, I prayed, nothing had happened to him.

As we got closer to the city, the traffic thinned. Then there was nothing: no one on the sidewalks; no one in the streets; no people, no cars, no signs of life in the nation's capital. From a distance, I saw something too bizarre to contemplate: men dressed in black brandishing machine guns. It felt like a scene from some foreign capital after a coup. In many ways, it was the most chilling image of the day: downtown Washington, the home of freedom and democracy, suddenly turned into an armed camp, the only sign of life, men in black holding instruments of death.

When our car was stopped at a barricade several blocks from the White House, a man in black, weapon drawn and pointed toward the car window, walked toward us. "I have Karen Hughes; I'm supposed to take her to the vice president," the military driver explained.

When the man talked into his radio, I could hear the voice on the other end: "Are you sure it's Karen Hughes? Do you recognize her?"

The man in black peered into the car at me: "Yeah, it's her; I've seen her on TV."

We were stopped twice more, then finally arrived at one of the entrances of the White House. "Where do I go?" I asked some of the officers standing outside.

"Just head in, and someone will show you," he said.

I walked into silence. No marines guarded the doors, no one was sitting at the desk. No receptionist, no Secret Service — no one in sight. "Hello, is anybody here?" I yelled, and I heard the heavy steps before I saw them, two men whipping around the corner, guns drawn. "I'm Karen Hughes; I'm supposed to meet the vice president," I explained, and one of them took me on a long, long walk, through heavy doors and tunnels, and more heavy doors, each of which closed behind us with a loud metallic bang and a pressurized sound like the seal on the hatch of a submarine.

When I finally reached the emergency operations center, the atmosphere was even heavier than the doors I had come through to get there. The vice president was on the phone; so was Secretary Mineta, overseeing the grounding of airplanes all across the country. Condi Rice was sitting next to the vice president; Mrs. Cheney was also there, so were several of our senior staff members, the director of the Secret Service, and a number of National Security Council and military personnel I didn't know. A number of airplanes were still unaccounted for; others were being tracked because they appeared to be somewhat off course, and no one was sure what had happened to an airplane that had disappeared over Pennsylvania. Unconfirmed reports kept coming in: a plane had crashed into Camp David; another had struck the president's ranch in Crawford. I was impressed by the strength and decisiveness I was witnessing as the vice president coordinated with the president and issued instructions to various agencies.

By early afternoon, waiting for the president to make his statement from Louisiana, Mary and I were frustrated knowing we had to get someone out to communicate with the public. I was watching as the government functioned quite well: the calm, decision making I was witnessing there in the emergency center was far different from the chaos I had imagined while listening to the news reports at home. That reminded me I should check with my family. I wanted to tell them that I was safe, but I realized that might not be true. I settled for the facts: "I'm at the White

House," I told Jerry, "I'll talk to you later. I love you."

Vice President Cheney kept saying I was the right one to do a briefing; I suggested perhaps it should be Condi, but they all insisted, no, people were familiar with me, I was viewed as someone who could speak for the president. Albert Hawkins, the White House liaison with the Cabinet agencies, was in the bunker with us and he began helping me collect information: the airports were closed, the banks were open, the Federal Emergency Management Agency had sent eight search-and-rescue teams to New York. I started writing, at first on a note pad, then someone took me to another room that had a computer. Facts and action were good, I thought, action would be reassuring: "The federal government is acting to help local communities with search and rescue and emergency management operations . . ."

The president's statement from Louisiana finally aired; it was short and the video quality was not good, but it freed us to get out the technical information. I decided to check with him directly. "I've been pulling together a briefing on what different agencies are doing to respond; do you want me to go out?" I asked my boss directly, not wanting to waste his time by asking what I really wanted to know: how was he doing, what did he think about all this?

"That's good, yes, I want you to do a briefing," he replied. "Don't you think I need to get back there?" the president asked me.

"Yes, as soon as possible," I replied; the Secret Service was adamantly against it, he told me. At this point, Air Force One was on its way to Nebraska so he could convene a meeting of the National Security Council by teleconference; he thought he needed to come back to Washington as soon as the meeting was over.

He practically came through the television screen an hour or so later as he opened the meeting: "We are at war against terror, and from this day forward, this is the new priority of our administration," the president told his senior team, assembled at the White House, the Defense Department and the State Department. It was reassuring to see him: he looked calm, confident, in charge. President Bush was carrying us through this crisis, lifting us all through his sheer will and strength of personality. At the end of the meeting, although the Secret Service and others had warned against it, he brooked no more discussion: "Get ready for me; I'm coming home," he said.

I left the shelter while the national security meeting was still in progress; the Secret Service hadn't thought it safe to brief from the White House, so my staff had gathered the press at the nearby FBI headquarters. The Secret Service moved me out of the White House and into a car; I had never been surrounded by agents with their weapons drawn before. I remember feeling vulnerable as we walked outside: we didn't know who the enemy was, or where they might be lurking. Mary Matalin came with me, and I was grateful to have a friend by my side. She says that I was uncharacteristically nervous; I'm always nervous before I go on live television, always aware that a single mistake could have major consequences. That day, I did feel an enormous responsibility, a special obligation to try to be calm and reassuring for a badly shaken nation. I prayed the prayer I always pray, but harder than usual and several times: "Lord, help me have grace under pressure."

I delivered the statement, reading from a typed text that was faded in places; the printer in the shelter had been low on ink and some of the letters were barely legible. "I'm Karen Hughes, counselor to President Bush, and I'm here to update you on all the activities of the federal government in response to this morning's attacks on our country . . . the federal government is acting to help local communities with search and rescue and emergency management operations, to take all appropriate precautions to protect our citizens and to identify those responsible for these despicable attacks on the American people . . ." The vice president and Condi and I had discussed whether I should take questions and agreed I shouldn't. My statement included all the information we had confidence in, and my inability to answer questions beyond that would only defeat the purpose of reassuring people. When I got back to the White House, the director of the Secret Service told me his wife had called to say my briefing had made her feel better for the first time all day; my friend Margaret Tutwiler e-mailed my assistant with a message from Morocco: "Please tell her (karen) that she did an excellent job for our country tonight — I watched her press statement and SHE WAS THE ONLY PERSON TO DELIVER IT — I kept thinking all day — Karen has got to be on top of this for the president and for our country — her command of the podium — her compassion — her strength — ALL came through." But in

Washington, no good deed goes unpunished. An "anonymous" Republican on Capitol Hill disparaged my remarks in the newspaper the next day: "She told us the president was okay; we needed to know that we were okay." Of course, that was a guarantee that I could not give.

The president had to address the nation from the Oval Office that night, we had all agreed; I talked to Condi Rice and the president several times about the contents. Reassurance was our primary mission, the president told me; we also had to present a policy of no tolerance for terrorists or states that supported them. The Secret Service finally allowed us to return to our offices about six that evening. I had an e-mail from my pastor, Doug Fletcher: "Dear Karen, I am in disbelief. You are in my prayers as is the President. I realize that were a country behind this, we would now be at war. We have services today at 12:45 AND 5:30. We will keep you in our prayers. I am attaching some notes from my meditation on Psalm 23. I love you, Doug."

Doug's notes talked about how Psalm 23 had been prayed during the destruction of Jerusalem; in foxholes and at deathbeds; by those who were very afraid, and those who knew where to turn with their fears. "Christian faith doesn't suggest that life is easy," he wrote, "The empty cross, a symbol of victory, is also a reminder of evil and violence. There are valleys, some of them dramatic and some of them less so. We do need a shepherd in those valleys. And we are not simply promised safe journey. We are promised a banquet. It is one thing to live bravely underestimating the danger. It is another fully to understand the dangers and live with the confidence of faith in the promises of Him who promised never to leave us or forsake us."

Psalm 23 should be a part of the president's remarks that evening, I realized, and started looking for a Bible. I always kept one in my briefcase, but it wasn't with me; I had left it at home. I called Stuart Bowen in the staff secretary's office; he brought over a Bible, but it was an unfamiliar translation. I wrote it in, figuring I could change it later: "I pray for them the comfort of a power greater than any of us, spoken through the ages in Psalm 23: 'Even were I to walk through a valley of deepest darkness, I should fear no harm for you are with me.'"

It had been chaotic in my office as we put the statement together; the president called with his thoughts; the speechwriters sent a draft; Condi Rice and her deputy Steve

Hadley had policy points they wanted to include; several other members of the communications team offered ideas. I walked down to the Oval Office with the draft we had assembled and waited on the patio with our legal counsel, Al Gonzales, as my boss arrived by helicopter, the wind thrown off by its giant blades causing the lush green grass to ripple like an undulating carpet.

Watching Marine One land, then seeing the president salute the young marine at the helicopter steps and stride confidently across the South Lawn brought tears to my eyes: the scene was so normal, yet so different. The world had changed since he had left the White House the day before, but the president was back, and in charge, and my job was to stay calm and help him do his.

We met and revised the speech, and the president noted the odd wording of Psalm 23 on the draft: "What's this — you need to get a good translation," he told me. Several members of our staff felt the president should declare we were at war; I had discussed it with him on the telephone and he had said no. There would be plenty of time for that later; he felt tonight's mission was reassurance.

Today, our fellow citizens, our way of

life, our very freedom came under attack in a series of deliberate and deadly terrorist acts. The victims were in airplanes, or in their offices; secretaries, businessmen and women, military and federal workers; moms and dads, friends and neighbors. Thousands of lives were suddenly ended by evil, despicable acts of terror . . . I've directed the full resources of our intelligence and law enforcement communities to find those responsible and bring them to justice. We will make no distinction between the terrorists who committed these acts and those who harbor them . . .

I watched from the next room as President Bush addressed the nation; after a harrowing day, a day none of us could have envisioned when he had been sworn in less than eight months before, the president had arrived back in Washington and steadied a shaken nation. Dan Bartlett and I walked back into the Oval Office, where President Bush was shaking hands and thanking the television producer and crew. As we walked out through the French doors onto the colonnade outside the Oval Office, the president turned to me: "I'm sorry you weren't there today."

I didn't know if he meant as the reliable note-taker and keeper of Bush history, or just as the longtime staff member who had traveled with him through most of the big moments of the last eight years — perhaps a little of both: "I'm sorry, too," I told him: my decision to stay home with my husband for our wedding anniversary had kept me from the president's side on what was no doubt the most difficult and important day of his presidency. Life does not always work out the way you expect it to: you make choices, and they have consequences. In this case, I had been able to brief the nation and pick up my son from school, but I had missed some of the most historic moments of the Bush presidency.

"Well, I'm here now," I said to my boss, as we walked across the patio to a meeting of the National Security Council.

I finally went home about eleven that night; it felt good to be there with the people I loved. I sat up and talked for about an hour with Robert and Jerry. I don't remember what we said, but I know I was trying to re-assure Robert as parents across America were trying to reassure their children: we were doing everything we could to keep them safe and try to find those who were re-sponsible. I had trouble sleeping, and got up extra early for me; I was back at the White House before seven the next morning.

At our senior staff meeting, we cancelled the president's planned schedule for the next week, and began adding national security and congressional meetings. I went to the Oval Office worried about what the president would say the first time he saw the press that day. He stopped me in midsentence: "Let's get the big picture. A faceless enemy has declared war on the United States, so we are at war. We are going to wage this war; it requires a strategy, a plan, a vision, a diplomatic effort and the understanding of the American people . . . This will require a complete focus; the command structure in the White House has to coordinate the response of the government," he told us.

"You're in charge of communicating this war," the president said, giving me my marching orders, then turned to Condi: "This Saturday, have everybody come to Camp David; we'll develop the plan."

"From this day forward, this is my main focus; this is the focus of our administration. We have to explain it to the nation; we have to prepare for another attack," he said. Every day for those first several days, we expected another strike, at any moment, perhaps an even worse one. "The likelihood is that somebody's going to get blown up today," the president said later that morning in the Cabinet Room. I remember marveling at how calm everyone seemed in the face of this new threat, especially the young people on our staff who had come to work as though things were normal.

Minutes after I left the Oval Office, my phone rang, summoning me back. When I walked in, the president handed me two pages of notes written with his black Sharpie pen: "This is an enemy that runs and hides — but won't be able to hide forever. An enemy that thinks its havens are safe — but won't be safe forever." I misread his handwriting, so the president's statement that morning said "harbors," not "havens" — even though Al Qaeda operates from caves, not boats.

Later that morning, the president met with congressional leaders from both parties. "These guys are like rattlesnakes; they strike and go back in their holes; we're not only going to go after the holes, we're going to go after the ranchers," he told them, explaining the new Bush doctrine to go after those who harbor terrorists as well as the terrorists themselves. "There will be no safe harbor for terrorism," the president told the congressional leaders. "Who knows where this will lead . . . we're talking to Pakistan in a way we've never talked to them before . . . Afghanistan, maybe Iraq."

"This is a different type of war than our nation has ever fought," the president explained, already plotting the course of history the morning of September 12. "We will use our resources to find the enemy, we will rally the world, we will bring patience and focus and resources . . . we will not let them win the war by changing our way of life," he said. "This is more than a particular group, it is a frame of mind that threatens freedom — they hate Christianity, they hate Judaism, they hate everyone who doesn't think like them."

President Bush was powerful, and tough; it made the contrast with Majority Leader Daschle so clear as he cautioned the president to back off: "War is a very powerful word," Daschle warned; "the last time we declared war was after Pearl Harbor; we don't know who the opponents are." I remember thinking, not for the first or last time, how grateful I was that President Bush had won the election; how much weaker and less decisive our nation's response might have been had the election turned out differently.

At the end of the meeting, Senator Robert Byrd, a veteran Democratic lawmaker who can be sharply critical and cantankerous, reminded us that he had served with eleven presidents, through the Cuban missile crisis and the assassination of President Kennedy. "I congratulate you on your leadership in this very difficult, unique situation," he told President Bush, then moved many of us to tears with his closing words: "There is still an army who believe in this country, believe in the divine guidance that has always led our nation. Mr. President," he said in that stentorian voice, "mighty forces will come to your aid." I still get choked up when I remember it.

The acrid, unpleasant stench of smoke hung over the Pentagon as we arrived there later that same afternoon. Sadness and anger hung in the air, too, on what otherwise would have been a beautiful late-summer day. "It's a whole different world in there, breathing it," a rescue worker told me, fighting back tears and losing. He had pulled out several bodies already, and the recognition was dawning that bodies were all that would be coming out of the jagged hole in the side of the Pentagon.

"Coming here makes me sad on one hand," said the president; "it also makes me angry . . . our country will not be cowed by terrorists," he declared, as firefighters unfurled a huge American flag down the side of the building.

Around the conference table inside the Pentagon, the commander in chief addressed the nation's military leaders: "We've just seen the first war of the twenty-first century. It's difficult to comprehend because there's no capital to attack, no Navy fleets are moving . . . All of us as leaders must work to help our nation understand this enemy is intangible . . . The emotion may die down; I don't intend to forget and I don't want you to, either. The declaration of war against us will require a response that will affect future generations . . .

"We want to make sure when we do something, we are not pounding sand . . . We want it to have consequences . . . Those who provide haven, we're going to go after them too. That's a change of American policy and a significant change. I appreciate you all being ready to go. I wish it was tomorrow, but this is a long struggle across a broad spectrum of the world. We're not trying to remove a mole; we're after a cancer . . . and we will win."

My sister came over that evening to spend the night at my house; she had been in

Washington at a conference and was now stranded. Beverly and I were sitting in the living room late that night, talking, when we saw a man drive up and park across the street. He got out and walked up and down in front of my house, talking on a cell phone. It was odd, and after an hour or so, I decided to call the Secret Service. They sent the police over, which panicked Robert; they arrived quickly but the man had left shortly after I had called. They searched the area and called for several hours to check on us.

I didn't sleep well that night, and the next morning, I went to see my boss. "I'm worried about my family," I said, telling him about the incident the night before. "If I die in a bombing at the White House, well, I signed on to serve, but I don't want my job to put my family at risk. I'm high profile, on television, and I don't want that to put Jerry and Robert in danger." Leigh and Lauren were in Austin, where I thought they were safe, but too many people knew that I had rented Margaret Tutwiler's house and thus knew where we were living in Washington. President Bush called in the head of his Secret Service detail, Carl Truscott, who reported that the Secret Service thought the man in front of my house the night before had been there to see neighbors.

"That should make you feel better," the president said, although I still thought it was weird. The neighbors put their house up for sale and moved out several weeks later. The president asked Carl Truscott to have someone check my house occasionally, and those of some of our other staff members, too.

Vice President Cheney had pulled me aside early Thursday morning to suggest the president needed to visit New York as soon as possible. I agreed; we had been holding off only to avoid interfering. In times of tragedy, people want their leaders to experience what they are going through, but moving the president, especially with the elevated threat of terror, required a major security presence and we didn't want to complicate the rescue operation. But now officials in New York didn't expect to find any more survivors; rescue crews were worn out; a visit from the president would be a big boost.

"Maybe we should go tomorrow after the prayer service," the president said. I thought our advance teams would have heart attacks about the short notice, but during a telephone call with Mayor Giuliani and Governor Pataki, the president announced that he would visit New York the next day, Friday, September 14. When the assembled reporters asked him how he was personally handling this crisis, I saw not just the president, but the person I knew so well.

The president looked down, and his eyes were full of tears as he looked back up at the reporters: "Well, I don't think of myself right now," he said. "I think about the families, the children. I'm a loving guy," he said, struggling to control his emotions, "and I am also someone, however, who's got a job to do and I intend to do it. This is a terrible moment, but this country will not relent until we have saved ourselves, and others, from the terrible tragedy that came on America." Gordon Johndroe, our press assistant, looked at me and couldn't hold back his own tears as he saw tears streaming down my face at the back of the crowd.

The press filed out of the Oval Office, and the president walked to the back room for a few minutes: "Sorry about that," he said to me when he returned. "You don't need to apologize for having a big heart," I told him.

We visited Washington Hospital Center later that morning to see some of the Pentagon employees who had been severely burned when the plane crashed into the building. "How are you, sir?" the president asked, saluting the army major in the bed in front of him, holding his salute for a long time as the major struggled to raise his hand to his forehead to return it.

"I'm sorry I'm not snapping to," the major said to his commander in chief.

"You're snapping to as far as I'm concerned," the president replied.

"This is my nurse; she's taking care of me, pumping me full of drugs," the major said.

"Do you remember what happened?" the president asked.

"There was a huge explosion and the wall fell in on me," the major replied. "There were lots of flames; I headed one way, then I heard somebody screaming about a baby and went over that way, then I found a way out," he replied.

"I talked with my buddies at Bragg today; they're waiting for orders," the major told the president.

"Don't worry, when we hit, we'll hit hard; I want it to mean something. Thanks for your service . . . are you a ranger?" the president asked.

"I'm special forces," the major replied, his physical injuries obviously not dampening his spirit. "My IQ is too high to be a ranger."

Toward the end of the tour, the president's assistant Logan Walters was handed a note that had been relayed from Andy Card, the chief of staff, who was back at the White House: "Don't delay coming back." When we pulled into the drive, Andy walked out to the limousine and got in, which was very unusual. They sat inside for several minutes, then got out and walked to the Oval Office, where the Secret Service director was waiting at the door. There'd been another threat against the White House, Director Brian Stafford told us; the vice president had already been taken to a secure location, and the Secret Service wanted the president to evacuate. The president called Condi and me into the Oval Office with Andy Card: "I'm not letting them force me out of the White House," the president told us. I brought up our responsibility to our employees, especially the junior members of the staff. We agreed the Secret Service would double-check the intelligence, then we would send the nonessential personnel home. The president opened the door where Director Stafford and Carl Truscott, the head of his Secret Service detail, were waiting.

"I'm not leaving," he told them tersely, "if a plane hits us, I'll just die. And, Ferdi, I'm hungry," President Bush said, turning to the mess steward. "I'll have a hamburger," said the president, who had been eating mostly fruit plates and salads as he tried to lose weight.

That was it; we would stay in the White House: "You might as well add cheese," I told my boss.

Later that afternoon, I brought the program for the next day's prayer service at the National Cathedral to President and Mrs. Bush for their approval. The president had asked me to check with Mrs. Bush as we began planning the service the day before. We had talked about including leaders from different faiths, and "a lot of music," Mrs. Bush suggested, "music is very soothing." When Tim Goeglin, our liaison to the religious community, brought me a draft program, I focused first on the hymns.

"We need familiar music," I said, and started thinking of hymns with a sweep of history. "O God, Our Help in Ages Past" was perfect; it described God as "our shelter from the stormy blast." We also needed a note of defiance, I thought: "The Battle Hymn of the Republic" would be a great way to end the service, but I wanted to check to make sure that was all right with my boss.

"It's been taken out of some hymnals because some modern churches think it's too warlike, but I think it's perfect; we need some resolve and defiance," I told him.

"Defiance is good," he said, and Mrs. Bush nodded. Tim had selected a great New Testament verse from Corinthians; he asked me to choose a verse from the Old Testament, perhaps something about leadership. Upstairs in my office, I flipped frantically through my Bible, which I now kept in my purse, when I realized I should ask the author for guidance. I said a quick prayer, and it leaped out at me as I turned to Psalms. Psalm 27: "The Lord is my light and my salvation; whom shall I fear? . . . though war break out against me, even then will I be confident."

Downstairs, my friend Jay Lefkowitz looked over my shoulder at the draft program as I waited outside the Oval Office. "Psalm 27, that's perfect," said Jay, who is Jewish. "We're saying it every morning now to prepare for Rosh Hashanah."

I tried, but failed, to keep from crying throughout the service in the National Cathedral. I was so sad for the families who had lost loved ones, and the service was my first opportunity to grieve. Billy Graham was so comforting, the music was lovely, and Mike Gerson and his speechwriting team had worked with the president on a beautiful and eloquent speech. And at the end, as five U.S. presidents and the nation's other leaders sang "Glory, glory hallelujah, His truth is marching on," Condi told me it felt like the mood had shifted from sadness to readiness; the hymn steeled us for the difficult job ahead.

And we needed that strength because later that afternoon, we traveled to New York. We saw it from the air first, but even that couldn't prepare me for the sight as we rounded the corner in the motorcade: a massive pile of steel, twisted like giant tinker toys. My hand went involuntarily to my mouth; it was more horrible than I had envisioned, even after seeing it so many times on television.

I stood next to my friend and colleague from the Texas governor's office, Joe Allbaugh, now, as the director of the Federal Emergency Management Agency (FEMA), in charge of the cleanup. "This is even more awful than I imagined," I told him.

"It doesn't get easier, either," he said, "It's harder every time I come."

The rescue workers were clearly exhausted, fueled only by emotion and anger; they strained to see the president and started chanting: "USA, USA." We hadn't planned for him to speak, but one of our advance team members, Nina Bishop, realized the crowd was eager to hear from their president, and she went to find a bullhorn. Firefighter Bob Bechtel was standing up on the charred, flattened wreckage of a fire truck. "Stay there," she ordered, to mark the spot for the president, and President Bush climbed up next to him and took the bullhorn. "America today is on bended knee in prayer; this nation stands with the good people of New York City," the president started to say.

"We can't hear you," voices began calling from the crowd, and President Bush reacted from his gut: "I can hear *you;* the world hears you; and the people who knocked down these buildings are going to hear from all of us soon."

I knew immediately that this was historic, and it was all George W. Bush. I turned to Joe Allbaugh: "They just saw the George Bush we know."

This was the first time I realized something I would think many more times in the days and weeks ahead: America was finally seeing the decisive leader those of us who worked for him knew so well. September 11 changed a lot of things; I don't think it fundamentally changed the president. We all grow and learn from our experiences, especially one so shocking and challenging; I'm sure I did, as did Condi and Andy and Karl and President and Mrs. Bush. I say the attacks made him more so. He has always been decisive; he was more so. He has always been focused; he was more focused than I have ever seen him. He's always in charge of meetings; now he was barking orders like a drill sergeant.

"Thank God the election turned out the way it did," Mayor Giuliani told me, watching the president that day.

We would see yet another side of my boss that afternoon, at the Javits Center, as he consoled the families of police and firefighters who had been trapped at the Trade Center. When the president first entered the makeshift room, created by curtains hanging from huge steel rods, it was silent, suffocated by agony, the only noise an occasional sob. "I've been working presidential advance for more than twenty years and this is the saddest thing I've ever seen," Bruce Zanca said, coming out of the room, wiping tears from his eyes. The president walked first to one family, then another, looking at pictures, asking about their loved ones.

"It takes a special kind of guy to do this, be this patient," the Reverend Kirbyjon Caldwell said to me as we watched. Kirbyjon is a friend of ours from Texas who had come to Washington for the prayer service and traveled to New York with us: "He does it better than a lot of pastors."

I couldn't stand it; I had to walk out after about twenty minutes with a terrible headache from trying to keep from breaking down. When I returned an hour or so later, the room felt much lighter. People were talking, even laughing occasionally as they shared happy memories. I saw a little boy clutching a teddy bear; the president hugged him and signed a picture of his missing father. The little boy just sobbed, and a couple of the Secret Service agents had tears running down their faces. I thought of Robert, and how grateful I was that his father and I were alive to hug and love him. A man had approached me outside, saying the mother of a Port Authority officer killed in the attacks wanted to present her son's badge to the president; I told him that I was sure the president would be honored to accept it. At the end of the visit, that mother, Arlene Howard, gave her son's law enforcement badge to President Bush; I watched as he told her he would treasure it and placed it in his coat pocket.

After the trip, I e-mailed a friend in New York:

Claire — I was with the president in New York and had three major reactions: 1. Horror — it's hard to imagine such evil. I can't fathom what kind of person, no matter what their training/fanaticism/mission, wouldn't pull up or turn sharply at the last moment before flying into a building full of innocent people. 2. Terrible sorrow. So many lives lost, so many families grieving, so many children who have lost a parent. There is quite literally a hole in the heart of Manhattan. (The president spent almost two hours consoling families of the firefighters and police officers who died — it was so sad I couldn't stay in the room — but he was incredibly strong and I think really helped console them.) 3. Inspiration. I cannot describe the incredible feeling as our motorcade drove down 42nd Street leaving the city Friday night — to look out and see thousands of New Yorkers — New Yorkers! — holding candles, shouting *God Bless America* — in many ways, that was the most emotional moment of the day. The president is awesome — the rest of us are taking our lead from him. I am holding up well — my faith helps sustain me — and as I was standing next to a formidable, concrete block building in downtown New York on Friday, looking at the remains of what had been two even bigger buildings, I realized that so much of what we take for granted, assume is permanent, is not. Ultimately, only God and His love are enduring — and another neat thing about this week has been to see so many Americans of different faiths come together to say that. I'll be thinking of you this Rosh Hashanah — Happy New Year to you and yours, I pray your daughter's fears and the fears of all America's children will be comforted. I've moved my Bible from my briefcase to my purse. Love, Karen

The next day, Saturday, I went to the funeral of Barbara Olson, the conservative commentator whose brilliant smile and joyful presence had made her a favorite guest on cable television. Barbara and her husband, Ted, had been so welcoming to

Jerry and me when we moved to Washington. The minister started talking about Barbara's call to Ted from her cell phone from American Flight 77. Ted is the solicitor general of the United States, yet there was absolutely nothing he could do as he learned his wife was on a hijacked airplane, knowing that two others had already been flown into buildings in New York. I made the mistake of letting myself think about the horror he must have felt, and I started sobbing. Karl put his arm around me, and pulled me close. I couldn't make myself go back to the White House after the funeral; I called in to the message meeting, then tried to act normal for an hour. I took my dog for a walk, but even the neighborhood seemed different. It was almost fall now, the leaves were skittering across the pavement, I noticed, brittle, just like everyone's nerves.

I went home and wrote in my journal, knowing I was witnessing history, and wanting to write it down before the memories faded.

How to begin to describe the five days since our world changed? So many emotions, all so powerful. So strong a sense of duty — my responsibility to the president and to our country . . . such a powerful sadness for so many lives lost, so many families shattered. For some moments, earlier in the week, I had to will myself not to be afraid — but the last several days, with God's help, I think I've settled into an understanding of what it truly means that nothing is permanent but God and his love and his faithfulness. He truly is our rock — and we must count on that, and as importantly, we must not put our trust in other things that may appear to be rocks, but are in moments rubble . . . Just returned from Barbara Olson's funeral. Her birthday is the same day as mine, December 27, one year earlier. For all my worry this week about my family — whether my job has put them at risk — I realize that she lost her life in this attack, and her job hadn't put her at risk — she was just on an airplane.

The sanctuary at our church, National Presbyterian, was already full when we arrived a little before eleven on Sunday. The minister nicely asked an usher to find a space for me, but when I got in, I realized Robert and Jerry hadn't followed because there wasn't enough room, so I had to sit by myself. Craig Barnes delivered a fantastic sermon: Where was God in this crisis? He was in the "midst of the city," as the psalm says, in the midst of the suffering, holding the people who were crying and dying. After the benediction the organ played "The Star-Spangled Banner"; I don't recall ever hearing it played in church before, and I thought it was a wonderful reminder that America is indeed "one nation, under God."

Outside, in the foyer, a young woman came up to me in tears. "Tell the president I'm afraid to go back to work," she said, sobbing. "I'm a flight attendant; he has to do something." She was young and frightened. I tried to assure her that we would do everything we could to make her job safer; I thought of her later when I argued in favor of putting the national guard on duty in the nation's airports. The sight of people in uniform would be comforting, I thought, a visible reminder that security had been improved.

I met President Bush at the White House that afternoon; we had talked earlier in the day about the statement he would make to the assembled press as he returned from Camp David. When he finished, he asked Dan and Ari and me to join him in his office. Condi was there, too; he was making calls to foreign leaders. He had spent the day before meeting with the National Security Council to begin developing military plans for action to close down Al Qaeda's base of operations in Afghanistan. "We are in a period where people's lives are going to be at risk," he told us; "leaks could be treason." He and I went over an outline for a proposed speech to a joint session of Congress; Karl and I were advocating the joint session as the best venue to show the world a united front and outline the case against the Taliban. But in typical fashion, the president didn't want to commit to the speech until he saw a draft, which meant we would have to work overtime to produce one.

It was early evening when I left the White House. I didn't call our chief speechwriter, Mike Gerson, that night; he has young children and I always try to keep Sunday a family day to the greatest extent possible. I didn't think he would start writing that night, anyway; I could talk with him the next morning.

Of course, the next morning I saw the president before I saw Mike.

"How's the speech coming?" he asked.

"I'm going to get with Mike and go over it this morning," I told him.

"Good," said the president, "because I

want to see a draft tonight."

"Mr. President, that's just impossible," I protested; major speeches usually take at least several days and often a week or more to draft.

"By seven," the president replied, smiling.

I called Mike frantically. "I've made a huge mistake; the president and I went over an outline late yesterday and I didn't call you; now he wants a draft tonight," I said breathlessly.

"That's impossible," he replied.

"I've already tried that. He said by seven."

The writers crashed all day, and got us a draft that night, not by seven, but by eight or so. The language was remarkably good given the short lead time; still, I didn't think the threat to our nation was described vividly enough and the president didn't like the conclusion; he called me three times that evening, wanting sections revised and rewritten.

The next morning, I ran into him in the hall. "How's the speech coming?" the president asked.

"I don't know, sir. I've been in the senior staff meeting," I replied.

"And you'll be focusing on it now?"

"Mr. President, I'm on my way to a message meeting," I protested.

He leaned over, and smiled, his blue eyes twinkling only about three inches from my face, and spoke in slow, exaggerated tones: "And you think a message meeting is more important than my speech to a historic joint session of Congress when our nation is at war?"

Not anymore, I didn't.

The president had just clearly focused my priorities for me. I think September 11 had that effect on all of us: we went to houses of worship; we held our children closer; we were kinder to those around us. I remember strangers talking with each other while standing in lines; it was a good feeling. Neighbors came out of their houses and said hello, and stopped to wave; the feeling of community was powerful.

Despite our numerous edits and revisions, the president still wasn't satisfied with the speech and hadn't agreed to give it. Congressional leaders were pressing for a decision, but Andy Card told them they could wait. "The president doesn't have to be rushed," he said. "He needs to be comfortable with this. We still have time." We agreed we would have to make a decision no later than Wednesday if the president was going to address the nation on Thursday night.

It had hit me as I walked out of an economic meeting: "The badge," I said, turning back into the Oval Office and looking at the president. I had seen him pull it out of his pocket on Sunday afternoon, and realized he was carrying it as a personal reminder of the tragedy, and of his duty. Larry Lindsey, our economic policy adviser, looked at me as if I had lost my mind, but the president was nodding. "The badge is the way to close the speech," I reiterated; the Port Authority badge that Arlene Howard had given the president.

The next day, we observed the one-week anniversary of the attacks with a moment of silence on the White House lawn. I had interrupted the president's morning intelligence briefings to suggest it, and he had agreed. The president was obviously not hearing good news: the atmosphere in the Oval Office was tense; when I asked for thoughts about what message we wanted to communicate from the White House today, the president answered tersely: "Continued vigilance."

By Wednesday morning, the president still didn't like the peroration of his proposed speech, and I was worried it didn't make the cruelty of the Taliban clear enough. Condi agreed, and offered to send two experts to my office.

"What's it like to live in Afghanistan?" I asked Dick Clarke and Zal Khalilzad when they arrived. Little girls weren't allowed to go to school; women weren't allowed to leave their homes without a male relative; even flying a kite or listening to songs on the radio was banned. The seeds of my passion for the women and children of Afghanistan were planted that day as I learned that this brutal government had smothered even small displays of joy.

Later that morning, the speechwriting team of Mike Gerson, Matt Scully and John McConnell gathered in my office. They had captured the president's convictions and developed a fabulous peroration: "Great harm has been done to us. We have suffered great loss. And in our grief and anger we have found our mission and our moment. Freedom and fear are at war. The advance of human freedom — the great achievement of our time, and the great hope of every time — now depends on us . . . We will rally the world to this cause by our efforts, by our courage. We will not tire, we will not falter, and we will not fail." And they had taken the badge and given it power: "Some will carry memories of a face and a voice gone forever. And I will carry this: it is the police shield of a man named George Howard, who died at the World Trade Center trying to save others. It was given to me by his mom, Arlene, as a proud memorial to her son. This is my reminder of lives ended, and a task that does not end."

"You are all smiling. That's a good sign," the president said when we walked into the Oval Office with a new draft early Wednesday afternoon.

"Mr. President, we think we have a great speech now," I was able to tell him.

"Let's tell the Congress," he said, giving his final go-ahead to schedule the speech after our edit session.

Condi distributed the speech for clearance and reaction, and people began calling in with comments and suggestions: the secretary of state, secretary of defense, the CIA Director, our senior staff. Karl Rove and Nick Calio stopped by; my office was chaotic as people proposed changes. We made the factual changes and tried to give the rhetorical ones a fair hearing.

The president stopped in midsentence at his next teleprompter practice: "This is new. You're not supposed to be putting new lines in here without my approval."

"You've been in meetings, sir," I replied, also explaining the rationale for the line.

He came to another new sentence: "No, I don't want this in here; it interrupts the flow. Are you just letting people stick things in my speech?" he asked.

"No, sir," I protested, "I probably rejected a hundred suggestions for every one we took."

"Well, you took too many," he complained.

"I had to use my judgment," I protested again.

On the way back to my office I stopped in to see Andy Card and fill him in on our progress. "When you see the president, tell him I put six new lines in his speech," I joked.

That afternoon, Paul Begala, the Democratic consultant and former adviser to President Clinton, e-mailed me a couple of paragraphs of suggestions. It was a very nice gesture; he's a partisan, but he's also an American, and he wanted the president to succeed at this important moment for our country. I e-mailed him back to thank him, and explained that this highlighted a fundamental difference between our two presidents: President Bush wouldn't take any more changes this late in the process, I explained; President Clinton would be making changes up to the minute he gave the speech, Paul told me.

The president was tired at his last teleprompter practice Thursday afternoon; he read through the speech, and was completely unaware that he had transposed a couple of words at the top of page six. It was my job to tell him, to point it out so he wouldn't repeat the mistake on national television that night. "Mr. President, you accidentally said the 'Homeland' of Office Security, instead of the Office of Homeland Security," I told him.

"I did? Are you sure?" he asked.

"Yes, sir."

"Maybe that woman was right," he laughed, jokingly referring to Gail Sheehy, the author of the *Vanity Fair* profile that had suggested the president might be dyslexic.

I decided to watch the speech from home, instead of going with the president; there was nothing I could do at the Capitol, but there was something I could do at home: be with my family. I also wanted to see the speech the way the rest of America would — on television. I had a lump in my throat the whole time.

"I ask you to live your lives and hug your children . . ."

I had fought for that line to be included; some had argued it was too simplistic and should be taken out. But above all, September 11 had given us great clarity about the precious nature of life, had reminded us to value and appreciate time with those we love.

"The course of this conflict is not known, yet its outcome is certain. Freedom and fear, justice and cruelty, have always been at war, and we know that God is not neutral between them," the president concluded.

"Thank you, I couldn't have done it without you," he said minutes later when he called from his motorcade on the way back to the White House, graciously sharing credit as he always did; he called to thank Mike Gerson, too. "You were superb," I told him.

Condi called, too, to tell me it was terrific, that Tony Blair had told her it was the best political speech he had ever heard. "Andy and I were laughing that just yesterday morning it was a nonstarter," she said.

"Our children and our children's children will remember tonight as the night the world declared war on terror," the anchor on the local ABC station said as the news came on that night. I would remember it as the night my boss gave the best speech I had ever seen him give, at a critically important time for our country.

The next morning, Margaret Spellings, our domestic policy adviser, was in the Oval Office briefing the president on the progress of his education reform package. "Great job," the president told her as she left. "How are the girls holding up?" he asked about her two daughters.

"Good, they're hanging in there," she replied. Margaret and I talked about it later: in the midst of planning a war, he took time to ask about her children.

That weekend, I was in a Sunday school class at church when my cell phone started ringing; it was deep in my purse and I couldn't get to it in time. I left the room and called home: "The Camp David operator is looking for you," Robert said.

I returned the call, and President Bush came on the line: "This financial action is the first battle of the war," he said. "Why am I not announcing this?" he asked me. I didn't really know what he was talking about; Dan had attended a meeting the day before because Condi had asked us to help coordinate the Treasury secretary's announcement about freezing terrorists' funds.

"We've got to think differently; this war is going to be fought on a lot of fronts — the financial war is part of it," my boss told me. I talked with Dan; we realized that everyone had made the assumption that since the Treasury Department was taking the action, Treasury would announce it.

"How did this get to be a presidential announcement?" the policy person working on the event, Gary Edson, asked the next day after we drafted a statement and added the event to the president's schedule.

"The president is how this got to be a presidential announcement," I replied.

Later that week, we were sitting in the Oval Office hearing bad fiscal news. "Mr. President, we had planned to bring your economic advisers back on Wednesday for —"

"A hanging?" the president interrupted, to laughter.

"We may have to deficit spend," Larry Lindsey told him. During the campaign, a reporter, I think it was Dan Balz of *The Washington Post*, asked then-candidate Bush whether he would ever allow deficit spending. "In case of war, a recession or some national emergency," the president had said, and I remember it vividly because I had worried it might result in a headline:

BUSH: DEFICIT SPENDING MAY BE NECESSARY — not the message we wanted to see when we were advocating a tax cut during a time of surplus. But the media had apparently not considered it newsworthy; when we tried to find the quote later, we could find no record that anyone had reported it.

Now the president reminded us: "I said war, recession or emergency; we've got all three."

"We've also got to rebuild New York," Vice President Cheney added.

"Now's the time to deficit spend if we have to," the president replied. "We've got to be bold; this is a leadership issue," the president said. "We'll do what it takes to protect the country and help the economy grow."

We were having economic meetings all the time now; the airline industry was in big trouble in the aftermath of September 11; consumer confidence was shaky. "Already a recession is baked in the cake; recovery is predicated on consumer confidence," the chairman of the Council of Economic Advisers, Glenn Hubbard, told the president. "If it stays low, you could have a severe recession through next year," Glenn said, beginning a discussion that would continue and ultimately result in a stimulus package, and later, another tax cut to boost economic growth.

We scheduled events to boost the hard-hit airline and travel industries, too. Members of the cabinet flew on commercial airlines to Chicago; President Bush invited congressional leaders to join him on Air Force One to travel there. On board, he urged them to avoid the temptation to blame the CIA or its director for the terrorist attacks, warning it would demoralize the very people we were depending on to guard against another attack.

"I'm pleased with the intelligence I'm getting," he told congressional leaders. "We cannot be second-guessing our people and I'm not going to. This attack was well planned; the terrorists had burrowed in for several years. What we don't know is how well planned future attacks might be."

They talked about Congress, and its past funding for intelligence operations against the terror network. "We didn't take it seriously enough," Minority Leader Dick Gephardt admitted.

"This is so nonconventional, it requires nonconventional thinking," the president said. "The Pentagon and FBI were set up in a cold war mind-set, but the biggest threat is not Russia, it's Al Qaeda. I think the CIA has already evolved way beyond other organizations to help us face the new threat."

And it struck me again, how the president saw hope in the ruins: "I believe this provides us a great opportunity to refashion alliances. This really shocked a lot of folks in the Middle East; we may be able to shake some of them loose of their terrorist sponsorship. This crisis will show the world that America is a spiritual nation, based on more than materialism, a nation of prayer and faith, a tolerant nation of many faiths. It's also an awakening among ourselves about how fragile life is; the importance of self-sacrifice. It's sick and terrible and sad, but it also presents us a great opportunity to reach deep in our soul and respond."

It reminded me of the minister's words at Barbara Olson's funeral. "Faced with this act, what did Americans do? We didn't take to the streets, waving fists and shouting death to terrorists. We went to blood banks, we gave food, we went to church, we prayed." I had even made myself pray for the terrorists; it was hard to do, but I knew it was right. I prayed that the Lord who had hardened the heart of pharaoh would soften the hard hearts of this terrorist organization.

I had talked with the president in our communications meeting earlier that morning about his use of the word *folks;* I had seen a quote in a newspaper, and I thought it conveyed the wrong impression.

"Mr. President, I'm not sure you ought to be calling the terrorists folks. It sounds like the nice people next door," I said.

"Folks aren't all good," he protested, "there are a lot of bad folks in the world."

"But it just sounds too familiar, too folksy." I wasn't giving up. "These are trained killers and it just doesn't sound right to call them folks."

"Anybody else not like anything else I say?" the president asked, making it clear he did not want an answer from Andy Card, Condi Rice, Karl Rove — the folks who gathered for our daily morning briefing. "Ari was in here earlier this morning complaining about me calling them evil."

"Evil is fine, they are evil," I said. "You've always said this is a contest between good and evil, but they aren't evil folks."

In Chicago, President Bush stood in front of two United and American airplanes and urged Americans to get back in the air and on with their lives. "The spirit of America is strong," he said, and an airplane took off behind him, its lettering clearly visible above his shoulder: SPIRIT, causing the crowd to applaud and chant, "USA, USA."

"Did you plan that?" a pilot leaned over and asked me.

"Not that I'm aware of," I replied; the advance team later told me they were good, but not that good. The president's speech was emotional, powerful.

"Mr. President, that was terrific," I said, as he stepped off the stage.

"I say any words wrong?" he asked, teasing. I winced inside. Actually he had, but I was reluctant to tell him. His statements had been so much more passionate, so much more convincing after September 11 that I realized in hindsight that he had been holding himself back during the early months of his presidency, perhaps worried about making a mistake. I liked seeing in his public statements the dynamic, energetic, passionate George W. Bush I saw in private; I didn't want him to go back to checking himself, but I had promised to always be honest.

"Well, you said 'mis-underestimate,' " I said hesitantly.

"I did not," he protested, looking at Andy Card to help him dispute my assertion.

"Three times," Andy said, nodding helpfully, "I counted."

The president shook his head: "A man stands up there and pours his heart out, gives a great speech and all you all can talk about is three words," he said, "a bunch of dang critics, that's what they are, Logan," he said to his aide as he walked away to pose for photos with the hosts of the event.

Less than thirty minutes later, I was sitting in the senior staff cabin on Air Force One when I suddenly felt two hands land on my shoulders. "I'm going to *mis-underestimate folks*," the president of the United States announced jovially. He shook my shoulders a few times, then said in a quick, underbreath aside: "You correct me whenever I screw up, always. I want you to."

It had been another emotional day. At lunch, when we stopped at a restaurant outside Chicago, a man stood up and led the crowd in singing "God Bless America." The crowds that lined the streets were clapping and cheering.

"Normally people get mad when we stop traffic," a Secret Service agent told me. "Now, it's a different time."

" 'Smoke 'em out, Mr. President,' that's what the guy yelled at me," President Bush told me, defending another line that I had worried about. "Just an average American guy, identifying with his president," the president teased.

"You mean he didn't yell, 'Disrupt them,

cut off their finances'?" I replied.

"Let me tell you how to do your job today," the president said to me another morning, when I walked into the office for the daily briefing; he had an idea for an event to communicate our progress in the war against terror. He was on top of all our jobs in the weeks and months after the attack, asking questions, issuing orders, demanding answers.

He wanted to know about a new proposal to help the unemployed. "Does a busboy at a hotel qualify for this? Exactly how much money over the eighteen-month period would a person get?"

"Make it happen," he ordered our legislative director, when he reported that a member of Congress was causing trouble on the budget. "Make it happen; then reconcile it."

"You have to understand his personality," Nick Calio protested, warning that the congressman was stubborn.

"He's about to find out about mine," President Bush replied.

On Tuesday morning, October 2, President Bush called me to the Oval Office. "Close the door. I'm going to launch a bombing strike later this week. I want you to start working on a statement; I want an explanation of why we are enforcing our doctrine, why we are destroying terrorist training sites." It struck me again: the tremendous weight of his responsibility. He would order young Americans to war, and some of them would die.

The same day, he called me on the phone. "Write this down, this is code. Six things," he said, without a hello, in the shorthand I knew meant he didn't want to discuss details on the telephone: "(one) the action; (two) the objective — including humanitarian aid; (three) the mission — restate what's at stake; (four) the nature of the campaign — this is yet another step; (five) patience — this is a long struggle that will require (six) sacrifice. End with the story of the little girl." The president was referring to a heart-wrenching letter Defense Secretary Rumsfeld had forwarded to me; I had shown it to the president thinking he might want to use it for a speech committing troops to combat because I thought it beautifully demonstrated the American spirit of sacrifice for a larger cause. A fourth-grade girl, her father in the military, had written: "As much as I don't want my Dad to fight, I'm willing to give him to you."

New security measures were being instituted at the White House; we were issued gas masks and hazmat suits; interns and nonessential staff members were moved to another building; the number of people in the West Wing was severely restricted. The medical team had counseling sessions for White House workers; I urged the president to greet employees one day, to thank them for coming to work in the midst of this threat. Some of our meetings were about things too terrible to contemplate; for instance, how we would respond if the terrorists detonated a nuclear or radioactive device in a major population center. The world seemed dark and threatening, and the president's job terribly difficult.

I decided to drop by the Oval Office one particularly grim day; I figured I was one of the few people he could let down his guard around. "How are you doing?" I asked him. "This has to be hard; are you okay?" He looked at me and stabbed his finger on the desk, not willing to indulge in even a moment of that kind of thinking: "I have never been more clear eyed about what I have to do."

We were all working long hours; I realized that Condi Rice was almost never leaving the White House. "Condi, have you had a meal anywhere outside of here?" I asked her one day.

"No, not since September 11," she replied. I insisted that she come to our house the next night for dinner. Jerry did the shopping, as he did almost all the time now. I made one of my quick recipes, corn pudding, and a salad; Jerry grilled salmon outside, with a Secret Service agent standing in the backyard and several others out front protecting the national security adviser. Jerry felt a little uncomfortable, leaving the man in the backyard. "Don't you want to come in?" he asked him. No, he couldn't, he was on duty.

I was rarely seeing Robert now; by the time I got home from work he was downstairs doing his homework and didn't want to be bothered. Robert was starving when he got home around six, after his afternoon school athletics; Jerry fixed dinner, sat down with Robert while he ate, then waited for me. I began to realize that the career-family balance was even harder with a teenager than with a toddler; when he was little, Robert was delighted to spend time with me whenever I got home. Any parent of a teenager knows that just doesn't happen. Once his stomach is full and he has retreated to his room, you can't drag him out unless the house is on fire, and even then, he would be annoyed by the interruption. I knew I should be talking with him more; we had talked about September 11 a couple of times, but I didn't know what he was thinking now. I would walk into his room, and he would tell me he was doing homework and ask me to leave; if I insisted on staying, I couldn't get anything out of him. He still wasn't going anywhere on weekends, or doing anything other than going to school. I was worried about him, but I had to push those thoughts aside: we had a national crisis, and it was consuming almost all of my waking thoughts and attention.

In the midst of it all, a box arrived in the mail from our church in Austin. It was full of letters, hundreds of them, from people we knew well and people we didn't know at all: they were praying for us, and thinking about us. Jerry and I stayed up late several nights; even he had trouble reading them without getting choked up. Such love and support from so far away.

We scheduled a second trip to New York as the military continued planning for an assault on Al Qaeda sites in Afghanistan. "There's an act of treason in the newspaper this morning," President Bush told me and Karl on the airplane on the way there, referring to a story that claimed our military would target thirteen training camps in Afghanistan. "Whoever did this is a traitor; they're putting lives at risk." We had never liked leaks, but now they could have deadly consequences.

Later that day his natural optimism returned: "This is a country that is in prayer, and I feel it," he told business leaders in New York. "These people have helped redefine our culture in some ways from one that was fairly selfish; there's now a reassessment taking place all over America. Moms and dads are reassessing how much time they spend with their kids; people are reassessing: what can I do to help? I truly believe that out of this will come greater opportunities for peace; peace in the Middle East. This is a fantastic opportunity born out of sadness, and the question is — can we seize it?"

"The job of a leader is to define reality and give hope," businessman Ken Chenault said at a press conference after the meeting, and I thought: that's exactly what the president has done in the weeks since the attacks.

We toured a school in Manhattan that day, and there was something incredibly tragic about seeing the unimaginable in children's pictures, graphic images of airplanes flying into buildings. "Some people in a different country don't like our country, so two men on two different planes killed the drivers on those planes and crashed the World Trade Center. I feel sad because I miss looking at the World Trade Center at night," wrote second grader Jillian Holch in an essay pinned to the bulletin board; "I feel worried because I think more people will be found dead," wrote first grader Raymond Chow. I realized these images are forever seared on our children's souls; I pray they will fade, but I know they will always be there, and I can't help but wonder: will their lives ever feel as normal as we once thought ours were?

I stayed home the morning of October 4 to work on the president's statement to announce military action in Afghanistan. It's hard to write at the White House; you go from meeting to meeting, from crisis to crisis. You act and react, but you don't have time to reflect.

My home phone rang just after eleven; it was President Bush: "I'm here with Ari. Are you on a secure line?"

No, I wasn't. Until that day, I had never needed one; I had one installed shortly afterward.

"Well," he said, deciding to tell me anyway, "we may have a case of anthrax in Fort Lauderdale, Florida; we don't know the source, it appears to be a high concentration in one person. This is a critical moment. We'll need to calm people. I may need to make a statement."

"I better come on in," I said.

"That's what I'm trying to tell you," the president replied.

"I'm on my way," I said.

When I got there, I went to Condi's office. Having the president make a statement was too high profile and might frighten the public more than necessary, we agreed; Health and Human Services Secretary Thompson was the appropriate person to brief the press.

As we worked on his statement, we all felt the gravity of the moment. It appeared to be an isolated case, but we couldn't be sure. The press wanted answers, but the answers weren't easy: no one had experience with anthrax used on humans.

That weekend the president asked me to go to Camp David with my family; he invited Mike Gerson and his wife to join us, too, so we could finalize his speech announcing military action in Afghanistan. The president's brother and sister and their families were there, and Andy Card and Condi Rice. At 9:30 Saturday morning, just before I arrived, the president had to give the military the preliminary authorization to put its planes in the air, the initial start of the operation; throughout the day, he placed calls to Prime Minister Tony Blair and congressional leaders to brief them.

We all tried to act normal, but we didn't succeed. We couldn't talk about it in front of the others, but our families knew from our somber demeanor that something was happening. The football games were on in the background, but no one paid attention; the president was about to send America's sons and daughters into combat, and that decision is always hard, even when it is absolutely right and necessary. Mrs. Bush had planned a dinner of comfort food: chicken-fried steak with mashed potatoes, and banana pudding for dessert; afterward, we edited and revised the speech.

Sunday morning, October 7, was a crisp, chilly fall day. "Get Condi on the phone and find out any final changes for the speech," were the president's first words as he boarded the helicopter that morning at Camp David; Condi had returned to Washington several hours earlier, where she would do a final clearance check with members of the National Security Council. We flew to a previously scheduled memorial for firefighters, then returned to Washington, where President Bush addressed the nation from his office in the White House residence.

On my orders, the United States military has begun strikes against Al Qaeda terrorist training camps and military installations of the Taliban regime in Afghanistan . . . A commander in chief sends America's sons and daughters into battle in a foreign land only after the greatest care and a lot of prayer . . . I'm speaking to you today from the Treaty Room of the White House, a place where American presidents have worked for peace. We're a peaceful nation. Yet, as we have learned, so suddenly and so tragically, there can be no peace in a world of sudden terror. In the face of today's new threat, the only way to pursue peace is to pursue those who threaten it . . . The battle is now joined on many fronts.

"What do we do now?" I asked Condi, after he finished, as we all gathered in the West Wing conference room.

"Now, we wait," she told me.

It was hard to tell exactly how the war was going in late October as we headed for an Asia Pacific Economic Conference (APEC) summit in China; both the fighting, and our targets, were so unconventional. We thought we had destroyed the Taliban's air capability and a number of terrorist training camps, but Afghanistan was full of caves and mountains. This would be a long struggle as America's military tried to find and fight a loose collection of individual killers who had for years scattered their operations, not only throughout Afghanistan, but also throughout the world.

We had received awful news the day before we left Washington: some of the anthrax that had been mailed to offices on Capitol Hill might be resistant to treatment with antibiotics. It was yet another horror too terrible to contemplate: the idea that a biological weapon might have been unleashed on our country, and we might be powerless to act against it. But on the helicopter, on the way to Air Force One to go to China, we got the call: "It is responding to antibiotics," the president reported as he hung up the telephone, to smiles from Condi and me. "That's the best news you've had as president," Condi said.

We all felt the strain of being out of the country, halfway across the world, with so much happening at home and in the war. The attitude of other world leaders toward the president had changed, I noticed; the president of South Korea called this the Bush summit, as fellow world leaders commended my boss for bringing the world together to fight terror. "He's gone from being the new kid on the block, the one they all think they need to give advice to, to being the leader they all hope they would be under the circumstances," Condi said. We were standing in a hotel room in China, watching on television as the troops of the Northern Alliance, supplied and joined by American special forces, attacked the Taliban in northern Afghanistan.

"It's the first war of the twenty-first century," Condi said to me, marveling at the pictures. "We're the world's only superpower, and our troops are on horseback."

September 11 changed far more than the way our military has traditionally fought wars. Condi described it as an "earthquake" across the international security environment: if we can no longer count on our oceans to protect us, it changes the way we have to look at everything. The attacks of that day turned many things upside down: the openness that allows people to visit and move freely around our country was used in an effort to undermine our freedom; religion was used as an excuse for murder. That day reminded us of our responsibilities as citizens, yet made our rights seem less secure.

Our nation went from peace to war; our budget from surplus to deficit as the combined blow of the attacks and the recession slowed the economy, and we dramatically increased spending for defense and homeland security. Any sense of invincibility was erased, replaced with a reminder of sudden vulnerability. America is the world's only superpower. The most skilled military and most advanced weapons in the history of the world defend us; yet we have learned that our strength is not an impenetrable shield.

"The poor people on top of those buildings . . . they were the living dead; there was no way we could get to them," a firefighter had told the president when we visited New York, and I realized it was going to take a long time to stop reliving the horror. Vice President Cheney started talking about a "new normalcy," a back-to-business mentality that would allow us to go about our everyday lives even in the face of the terrible knowledge that terror could strike us at any moment.

My minister wrote me, "People are both worried and longing to return to normal," but I realized there would be no returning to normal, at least not if normal means the way we were before September 11. We have been violated. A boundary was shattered, forever crossed that terrible morning. Like the victims of violent crime, we will recover. Time will ease the pain, but we will never view ourselves as invulnerable in the old way again. The world is not necessarily any more dangerous today than it was on September 10, 2001; in fact, it's probably less so because we have killed or captured so many terrorists. But we are still under threat, and we are now much more cognizant of the danger. And somehow, we must learn to live lives of joy and confidence despite the presence of that dark shadow.

CHAPTER 10

The New Normal

"You all go out too much," Robert protested as Jerry and I were dressing to go to a Christmas party one Sunday night in early December 2001.

"Robert, do you know the last time your mother and I went out without you?" Jerry replied.

"No," Robert shrugged, not about to let the facts get in the way of a good complaint.

"September 10," Jerry replied; it had been almost three months since our wedding anniversary.

I was surprised; I knew I had been incredibly busy, but the days and nights since September 11 had passed in a blur of work and worry about terror, anthrax in the mail and on Capitol Hill, homeland security, an economy that had been dealt a terrible blow and concern about how many people across the world seemed to harbor hatred toward America. It was so hectic that I had joked with my assistant about scheduling time for me to breathe. In many ways, everything about my job had changed. My focus shifted suddenly and completely to the attacks and their repercussions; my audience changed from the American people to the entire world. I dispatched members of my communications team to Islamabad, London and Afghanistan. My morning conference calls now frequently included Alastair Campbell, Prime Minister Tony Blair's communications guru; Ambassador Clinton Key in Pakistan; Torie Clark, the communications chief at the Pentagon; and Charlotte Beers and Richard Boucher at the State Department.

Alastair Campbell had come to see me at the West Wing in October, worried that we were getting killed in the international press coverage of the war in Afghanistan, and I agreed. From London, he saw more of the European and Arab media coverage than I did, but I knew I was waking up in Washington to find our administration on the defensive against wild verbal charges launched by the Taliban ambassador ten hours earlier in Pakistan: we had killed babies, looted hospitals, done things too awful to imagine. The accusations were almost always false, but they had played across the Arab world, cementing impressions while we slept. Mindful of the quote from Nazi war propagandist Joseph Goebbels that a lie told a thousand times becomes the truth, I wanted to fight back. Alastair suggested we model our efforts after an information campaign that had been conducted during NATO's bombing in Kosovo, setting up offices in different time zones to manage and respond to the news. We formed coalition information centers to communicate our actions in the war against terror. I described it as a communications wave around the world, beginning in Pakistan and Afghanistan, rippling across the Middle East and Europe and finally arriving in America. My staff put up a sign: "You either start the news wave, or you are swamped by it."

This communications job was harder than most because unlike our opponents, we were constrained by the facts. The Taliban ambassador seemed to feel no obligation to prove his charges, but if the White House or Defense Department or any American official said that American bombs had not hit a hospital or killed any innocents, we had to be darn sure that was right — and verifying what had happened in a war zone half a world away often took several days. We developed a "catalogue of lies" to pull out in response to the newest allegations, reminding the press about earlier

Taliban claims that had since been proven wrong.

I put Jim Wilkinson, our deputy communications director, in charge of the daily operations of our new coalition information centers, and he did a fabulous job, setting up the Indian Treaty Room in the Old Executive Office Building as a communications command central, with representatives from Defense, State, Treasury, Health and Human Services, the Agency for International Development and the British embassy. Having all the parties represented in one location allowed us to make and implement decisions quickly. We had daily briefings in Islamabad and began aggressively booking American officials on foreign media. We also highlighted our humanitarian efforts to deliver food, medicine, supplies and other necessities to the people of Afghanistan. Working with Karl Rove's public liaison office and the State Department, we hosted Ramadan dinners at the White House and at embassies throughout the world to demonstrate our country's respect for the Islamic faith. To keep the world's focus on the war against terror, we organized events in more than seventy countries and at the international space station on the three-month anniversary of September 11, and invited representatives of all the nations in our coalition to a ceremony at the White House on March 11.

I was searching for a way to communicate to the wider world, especially the Muslim world, that the views of the Taliban and terrorists were extremist, an aberration that was not representative of the teachings of Islam. I found it in the Taliban's mistreatment of women, which went far beyond cultural or religious differences. In many parts of the Muslim world, women are educated and work outside their homes; the Taliban didn't even allow little girls to learn to read. Women were not allowed to be treated by male doctors without a male relative present. And while many Muslim women cover their heads, the Taliban-imposed burka was a full-length robe that entirely covered a woman's head, body and even her face. The only opening was a small slit for the eyes, and it was covered by a fine mesh that limited a woman's view of the world, and made it impossible for anyone to look into her eyes.

Greg Jenkins, a member of my communications staff, brought me back a burka from Afghanistan. The beautiful silk material belied the horrible nature of the garment; when I put it on, the burka was hot, suffocating and it made me feel invisible, which was apparently part of the point. As my staff worked to communicate the urgency of the war against terror to an international audience, I thought focusing on the plight of Afghan women and girls was a way to highlight the cruel nature of the people we were up against.

"What would you think about Mrs. Bush joining you for the radio address this week?" I asked the president one morning as I walked into the Oval Office. "We'd like to focus on the Taliban's mistreatment of women, as a way of showing how the terror network threatens all of us," I told him.

"What do you need me for?" he replied. We didn't know it at that moment, but we were making history: Laura Bush became the only first lady ever to give the president's weekly radio address. She also organized an effort to send hundreds of thousands of yards of cloth and sewing machines to Afghanistan for making school uniforms for young girls. Boys wear uniforms to school there, and we learned many parents might not send their daughters unless they had appropriate attire. Mrs. Bush helped publicize efforts to send school supplies from America to Afghanistan, and President Bush created America's Fund for

Afghan Children, calling on the children of America to send in their dollar bills to help the children of Afghanistan.

That effort grew out of a discussion in the Oval Office one morning; we knew the American people wanted to help in the war against terror and we discussed what we could ask them to do. Karl reminded us that the March of Dimes started with an appeal from President Franklin Roosevelt for Americans to send their dimes to help fight polio; the modern equivalent of a dime was a dollar, we agreed. This new project had a dual purpose: it would raise money to help Afghanistan's children, and by asking American children to earn and give these dollars, we would teach them an important lesson about America's responsibilities in the world. And as our children responded, organizing lemonade sales and washing cars and doing chores to raise millions of dollars, a dollar at a time, I was reminded yet again of the generosity, the fundamental goodness, of the American people — and the huge gap between the way our country truly is, and the way much of the world sees us.

I worry that we have lived too long in the afterglow of World War II, and it has faded. For many years, people around the world knew America as the country that helped lead the world to defeat tyranny, then rebuilt what the war had destroyed, helping Germany and Japan become strong, productive countries and friends.

Many people still look at America and see a symbol of hope, a bright beacon of liberty and opportunity. But others look at our country and see only power, money and sex. They see the might of our military, and worry that there is no comparable force to check or balance it. They see the materialism of our consumer culture and our 24-7 work ethic. They see the sex and violence of our movies and television shows. An Arab scholar came to the White House and told us *Baywatch* is a favorite of young men in the Arab world — that is what they are learning about us. In the aftermath of September 11, I called my friend Margaret Tutwiler in Morocco frequently to get her perspective as an ambassador in a Muslim nation. "We've got to fight for the hearts and minds of this next generation," she told me, "and talk more about American ideals. We need more people-to-people exchanges; too many in the Arab street think of us as one big money machine." And the world looks at our murder rate, divorce rate, teenage pregnancy rate and abortion rate and sometimes concludes we don't value life and family.

These are all significant problems, and we must do a better job of addressing them, but the America I know is a far different place. In the America I know, adults volunteer at homeless shelters and rape crisis hotlines and Habitat for Humanity house buildings, and children send their money to children a half a world away. In the America I know, senior citizens volunteer their time to help school kids learn to read, and adults at my church volunteer their time at a weekly program to give a few hours of respite to those caring for Alzheimer's patients. In the America I saw on the presidential campaign trail, volunteers in Iowa give clothes and food and love and hope to families who need all of them; a woman in Minnesota washes the feet of the homeless; and workers at Teen Challenge help young people overcome lives of addiction and despair. People in downtown Los Angeles offer job training and education and another chance for those who want to turn their lives around.

This is the America I want the world to see: an America full of decent, loving people who care about their families and who care about each other. We know we can be this loving and responsible country because we were reminded of it in the aftermath of September 11.

Americans enjoyed a rebirth of patriotism in the days and weeks after the attack, and it felt good. We displayed our flags, and came out of our houses and found camaraderie among strangers. The unexpected challenge to our freedom reminded us, as it reminded generations before us, that we are part of an American story that is so much larger than our individual lives. And we were reminded of the responsibilities of freedom.

President Bush visited Fort Campbell the week before Thanksgiving. Members of our senior staff joined soldiers in the mess hall for an early holiday dinner of turkey and trimmings. I asked those at my table what they needed from their government. Most just shrugged, not sure what to say. I pressed, "Come on, it's not very often you get to tell someone from the White House what you need — better housing? More equipment, higher pay?" A young man, not much older than my own son, looked straight at me, his eyes full of steely determination: "Orders to go, ma'am."

That young man understood freedom's obligations, and September 11 reminded me of America's obligations in the world. We will make the world safer as we pursue and capture terrorists and confront governments that support them, but long term we cannot make it safe enough without winning the battle for hearts and minds abroad.

During my brief flirtation with libertarian thought, I remember believing that perhaps government should take out the garbage and defend the borders, and otherwise stay out of our lives. My mother used to criticize foreign aid; from her travels around the world, she thought we gave money to other countries and only bought their resentment. But I have become convinced that we have both a responsibility and an urgent interest in sharing the enormous fruits of America's resources with others around the world. First, it's the right thing to do. We believe in freedom and dignity for all people — not just Americans, or those of certain class or stature, or gender — but for everyone, because we believe those are the gifts of the God who created us. And it's in America's own interest to make sure the citizens of other countries have the opportunity to be educated and live productive lives. People who are educated and see a future of hope are more likely to be tolerant and less likely to become agents of terror. When we act to fight AIDS in Africa, to liberate Afghanistan and Iraq, to lead the way toward peace in the Middle East, we are acting on America's founding conviction: that human beings are created equal and endowed by our Creator with rights to life, liberty and the pursuit of happiness.

In the aftermath of September 11, we have seen that our national security and our democratic values are inextricably linked. Only when people around the world have greater freedom and more opportunity is the world likely to be a safer place, a place less likely to produce people so full of anger and resentment that they are willing to fly airplanes into buildings. Until September 11, the hate and resentment fostered in the Middle East was something that spilled blood "over there"; now we have seen it can explode in American cities as well.

I've always thought that dealing with the Middle East is like an elaborate chess game. The two sides are faced off against each other; the United States urges them to sit down and play. American presidents can nudge, warn, cajole, even threaten, but only the parties themselves can actually make a direct move. For many years in the Middle East, our country's policy focused on keeping the pieces in approximately the same places, preserving stability, but President Bush's speech on June 24, 2002, recognized that only if the values America cherishes most — democracy, freedom of speech, religious tolerance, rule of law, respect for the dignity of every human life — flourish in the Middle East will that region cease to be a source of terrorism and suicide bombers.

"Of the three of you in this room, how many think I should give this speech?" the president had asked, and four hands went up: Condi's, mine, Mike Gerson's, and most important, the president's. Others weren't sure the time was right for a speech, the president told us: the vice president and secretary of defense were concerned that it might look as if we were rewarding recent acts of terror; the secretary of state was worried for a different reason. He thought, given the anger and angst in the region, the impact of a presidential speech might be like a tree falling in the forest with no one there to hear.

But President Bush saw opportunity. I was struck that he had seen it even in the terrible days following September 11. Meeting with a group of Muslim leaders that month, he told them: "We have a chance to bring brothers and sisters together to fight terrorism . . . terrorists know no boundaries, we must win this . . . I think we have a chance to get peace in the Middle East out of this . . . I think this is going to be a transforming experience . . . a cataclysmic event that can transform a lot of relationships . . ."

During the first few days of June, as security council members considered a possible presidential speech, Condi asked Mike Gerson and me to sit in on a series of meetings in the small wood-paneled conference room known as the Situation Room. Tensions and violence in the Middle East were escalating and members of the National Security Council were discussing how to get the Palestinian Authority to change its ways and crack down on terror.

"Reform is essential, the prerequisite on which all is built; the question is how best to achieve it. If we fail to get reform, we're doomed to another train wreck; it's just a question of when," Vice President Cheney said.

President Bush listened to the discussion, and at the end spoke out: "I believe strongly that two states are critical for Israel's survival. . . . We have to lead on the issue. . . . Other Arab nations have got to be responsible, too; they have to be an integral part of any solution. In all the speeches we have given, we have impressed on the Arab world the universal value of human dignity. Our role as a nation is more than bringing an end to terror; our role is to stand up for the values of human dignity and human life. Imagine how effective it would be if right in the midst of all these undemocratic governments, a little flower begins to blossom. If we can take the Palestinians and make their lives better, we've roped the rest of the Arab world into the need to reform their own societies by putting a nice little laboratory in their midst . . ."

Leaving the room, we were all struck by his vision. "He loves to be a change agent," Deputy National Security Adviser Steve Hadley told me.

"We could have missed about forty-five minutes of that meeting," George Tenet said, "all we needed to hear was the president."

"So here's how the speech is going to go," the president told Condi and Mike and me in his office in the White House residence late that June Saturday afternoon: "A few hold many hostage . . . It's untenable for Israeli citizens to live in terror. It's untenable for Palestinians to live in squalor and occu-

582

pation. So I'm going to give the rationale for stepping in: things must change, and I believe there's a better way. Then we need to step back and say the first step to peace is for the world to fight terror . . ."

Later, as we revised and edited in Mike Gerson's West Wing office, we discussed why some members of the Security Council were concerned about a presidential speech. We all knew the president shouldn't speak out unless it would make a difference. "They're worried that passions in the region are so inflamed that people won't listen," Condi said.

"If Lincoln had worried about passions being too inflamed, he wouldn't have given the Gettysburg address," I replied, and she nodded: "Exactly."

Condi joined Jerry and Robert and me for dinner at a local Italian restaurant that night after we finally left the White House. The next morning she called me early, "The president wants us to have a conference call at eleven to talk about the speech," she told me. "He knows that's when you go to church, but he wanted me to ask if you could be on the call, or if not, could you talk to the vice president and secretaries of state and defense to hear their opinions, then talk to the president?" Condi asked.

I assured Condi I would be on the call, and got out of bed to go to the early service at church. When Jerry and I arrived at National Presbyterian, Condi was there, and we all sat together. I was there to worship, but my mind was also on the speech. During the service, I wrote a note on the Sunday church bulletin and passed it to Condi: "I think the central question is: if we think the policy in the speech is right, then it's just a matter of timing . . . and don't we have an obligation to help bring about the right time — to lead toward it?"

Condi wrote back, in a much prettier script: "Your Gettysburg comment yesterday was right on."

The sermon was about leadership: "The greatest leaders inspire us by speaking eternal truths," Pastor Craig Barnes said, and Condi and I exchanged glances. What could be more eternal than the right of all people, Israelis and Palestinians, to live in peace and dignity?

On the call, the issues came into sharper focus: the goal was reform and new leadership for the Palestinians because the group had concluded peace was not possible with Arafat in charge; the question was which actions would best achieve that result. The secretary of defense questioned whether this might be a time for diplomacy, working behind the scenes, while the secretary of state eventually came down on the side of a presidential speech.

"There is a great expectation he (the president) is going to say something," Powell told his colleagues. "I've been agonizing over this, recognizing the situation on the ground is not the most fertile . . . if you give no speech, I think things just drift . . . maybe it will take root, maybe not, but we have to try to move forward," he said.

It was a fascinating discussion: tough, smart, experienced people talking it through, what Condi calls "working it," letting the principals chew on the issue until the process resulted in consensus, or at least, clearer lines of disagreement. The president insists on this, prodding and asking questions of his team until he is confident he has considered the widest range of debate, the broadest possible information, the most thoughtful analysis. That night, the president decided to follow his initial instincts and give the speech. He felt he had an obligation to set the vision, and lead toward the circumstances that would give it the best opportunity to become reality.

Two of the major conditions that the president laid out in the speech seemed very distant that day. Yet they both became reality within a year, as a new prime minister was named to lead the Palestinian people, and Israeli prime minister Ariel Sharon publicly said that the Palestinian people should have a state of their own.

Achieving peace in the Middle East will be a long and difficult process; we will continue to encounter both setbacks and opportunities. But that goal has never been more important for our country, and our actions to remove Saddam Hussein from power in neighboring Iraq have greatly enhanced its prospects.

I have always been perplexed by those who questioned Saddam Hussein's ties to terror. He paid the families of suicide bombers, thus encouraging young people to kill themselves and others and fostering terror and continued hatred in the Middle East.

"This is going to be really hard," Condi Rice had told me, at dinner one night in California in late August 2002. The president had asked us to talk through a strategy to rally America, the United Nations and the world to confront Saddam Hussein.

"Did you ever think you would be here, Karen, talking about something that could literally decide the balance of power in the world for years to come? The stakes are huge. This is freedom," she told me. I had a lot of questions: after twelve years of tolerating his defiance, why did we have to act now? Why was Saddam more of a threat than others in places like North Korea? Condi told me she and other members of the Security Council felt Saddam was unique, not for any single reason, but because of a confluence of them: in the aftermath of September 11, our nation could not allow that kind of tyrant, with those kinds of weapons and a history of using them, to operate in that volatile region of the world. And we knew from what we had found in caves and on computers in Afghanistan that Al Qaeda was aggressively trying to acquire weapons of mass destruction; our nation had a responsibility to do everything possible to prevent the marriage of those who wanted these terrible weapons with those who had them.

"We cannot allow Saddam to continue to flout the world; it will embolden others, and we'll have problems all over the world . . . but this will be really hard," she said again.

"But is it right?" I asked her.

"Absolutely," she said, looking directly at me, convincing me with her certitude. I had the same discussion much later with the president. He knew his decision to take military action in Iraq would be controversial. "Is it right?" I asked him.

He used exactly the same word Condi had: "Absolutely."

Much of the criticism on the nation's editorial pages would have you believe these weighty decisions are made cavalierly, as if the leaders of our country wake up one morning and decide to go to war. Nothing could be further from the truth. No decision is more profound, or more agonizing. I watched over the course of a long year as smart, thoughtful people considered every option; debated strategy; worked hard to convince other nations that the world should present a united front. Ironically, the reluctance of nations such as France and Germany to join us in challenging Saddam probably emboldened him and made war more likely, not less.

I traveled to Camp David in early September for meetings with Prime Minister Blair and his national security and communications team; I remember thinking that it was profoundly reassuring that our closest ally in the world saw the threat in exactly the same way as we did. Philosophically, Prime Minister Blair and President Bush are miles apart: Prime Minister Blair is a liberal; President Bush is a conservative; yet both viewed the threat from Saddam Hussein in the same way. We all hoped that after its unanimous vote calling on Saddam Hussein to disarm in the fall of 2002, the United Nations Security Council would finally hold Hussein to account. But when the council would not back its words with action, President Bush made the toughest decision of his presidency thus far: to join with those nations who were willing to act in the interests of the civilized world's security and credibility by removing Saddam Hussein from power.

We are living in an amazing time; I saw it called a "hinge moment in history." Dramatic change is sometimes hard to see when you are living in the midst of it. Democracies are emerging where tyrants once ruled; former enemies have become friends.

"We are seeing a historic change in relationship between Russia and the United States," President Bush said, toasting his house guests. "Usually, you only invite friends to your home, and I feel that is the case here."

President and Mrs. Bush were hosting President and Mrs. Putin at the ranch in

Crawford. We had all flown to Texas earlier that day from Washington; the Putins were staying at the guesthouse right next door to the main house, and they walked over at six for the seven o'clock dinner. Despite the elaborate attention to detail on every presidential event, especially a foreign visit, the president of the United States had to tell the president of Russia about the time change between Texas and Washington. "I ought to apologize, but it's just so funny," Condi said, as we burst into gales of laughter once again. We were all in high spirits because just a few minutes earlier we had received wonderful news.

I was on the telephone talking with Karl Rove when Condi burst into the room. "We got them out!" she exclaimed jubilantly. The American military had rescued eight humanitarian aid workers in Afghanistan, including two young American women, Heather Mercer and Dana Curry. Many of us had prayed for their safe return, although at times it had not seemed very likely. Huge bolts of lightning were striking the ground near the ranch house, and the skies were pouring rain as we took the president to a nearby building to meet with the press pool and make a statement. "I am delighted they are safe, I welcome them to freedom, and I am proud of our military's successful mission."

The weather outside was miserable, but the atmosphere inside the ranch house was warm and festive. We were all touched by Mrs. Putin's gracious gesture; she wore a sequined vest in red, white, and blue. Ambassador Dan Fried and Condi Rice danced to "Cotton-Eyed Joe" performed by a western swing group, The Ranch Hands. Concert pianist Van Cliburn talked about his affection for Russia, "I would say to my Russian friends, please come to Texas because our personalities are so close."

"I've never been to the home of another world leader, and it's hugely symbolic to me and my country that it's the home of the president of the United States," President Putin said, toasting his host. "The United States is fortunate at such a critical time in its history to have a man of such character at its helm."

The next day, as the Russian and American presidents answered questions from students in the gymnasium of Crawford High School in one of my favorite events of the Bush presidency, I couldn't help but remember crawling under my school desk as a little girl in Jacksonville, Florida, hiding my head under my arms in a disaster drill to prepare in case of a Russian nuclear attack.

"I never thought I would see this in my lifetime," my mother said, putting it all in perspective. She and my sister had driven down from Dallas for the event; a group of friends from Austin also came to witness this special occasion. And that morning, the president of the United States invited the president of Russia to join him for his daily intelligence briefing from the Central Intelligence Agency. I couldn't help but think of my first impression of the Russian president and how wrong it was. What I had taken for distance in his eyes was caution; now I had seen his warmth and good humor.

"Write this down," President Bush told me on Friday morning, December 7. "Today at 8:25 a.m. I informed President Putin we are withdrawing from the ABM Treaty. I told him the reason is that the world has changed to where we need to address the real threat of today — terrorism — and our relations are strong enough to withstand such a significant change. We need to make sure the spirit of Crawford continues . . . we are doing the right thing for world peace."

Relationships are being transformed; yet we still see some reminders of the old world order. The Korean Peninsula is perhaps the most striking. "Too bad we have to have it, but that's the way it is — a fine line," President Bush had said during our visit to South Korea, when the American general briefing him asked what he thought as we stood at the DMZ, the area two kilometers on each side of a line demarcating the boundary between North and South Korea. It's one of the few places where the cold war has not yet thawed. The North Korean government blasts music and propaganda from loudspeakers toward the South; the South raises huge flags so they can be seen for miles from the North. Soldiers on both sides of the line glare at each other defiantly through binoculars, weapons holstered but ready.

The president was referring to the fine line between tyranny and freedom; I couldn't help but think of the huge difference those few kilometers would make in the life of a child: how very different a young boy's or girl's opportunities would be merely because he or she was born on one side of the line or the other. After leaving the DMZ, we stopped at nearby Dorasan Station, a new train station where a sign reads:

Pyongyang   Seoul
<—— 205 Km   56 Km ——>

But the sign points to a dream, not a destination: there are no tracks heading left to North Korea's Pyongyang. The Dorasan Station is beautiful and modern, but nobody uses it; trains don't come here because there's no place to go.

Later that night, I stood at a reception at the presidential palace in Seoul thinking how long it had been, how far South Korea had come since my father had fought here against the communists in North Korea. I was talking with a group of South Korean businessmen when something felt odd; when I looked down at my hand I was sickened to see a gaping hole where the center diamond of my wedding ring should have been. I tried to steal furtive glances at the floor as the two presidents entered the room and gave their toasts. As soon as they left, my colleagues helped me look for the missing diamond, but the room was huge and the carpet was light; we couldn't find it. On the way out, I showed the hole in my ring to the man in the coat-check closet. He didn't speak English, and I didn't speak Korean; I didn't think I would ever see my wedding diamond again. But back at the hotel, only thirty minutes later, a message came over my pager: STONE FOUND.

I knew the workers must have been on

their hands and knees with a comb to find it. I wrote them a thank you note, but it could never adequately express my appreciation.

My own gratitude reinforced my impression that the South Korean people have a profound and ongoing gratitude toward America. I felt it more clearly there than I did anywhere else we traveled; perhaps because South Koreans live in the shadow of a clearly defined line, they have not forgotten those whose sacrifice kept them on the side of freedom. When people I met learned that my father had fought in the war, they all thanked me, even though I hadn't done anything but live in America, and they asked me to thank him. Dad was among the veterans invited to visit Korea in July 2003 for the fiftieth anniversary of the end of the Korean War. He found much has changed: the cities are now bustling with commerce and trade; people no longer fear that their lives, or property, or independence will be stolen from them. Yet the threat is never too far away: South Koreans live with the knowledge that North Korea's MiG-29 warplanes could deliver missiles from the DMZ to downtown Seoul in less than two minutes.

So many things are erasing lines in the world: the Internet, the ease of international travel, greater freedom of trade and commerce are all making borders and boundaries less significant. During our visit to Beijing, members of the White House staff were served lunch from the new restaurant that's all the rage: McDonald's. There's a Schlotsky's in Beijing, too, and a Kentucky Fried Chicken. Many of the knickknacks in American stores are "made in China"; the labels in our clothes tell us they came from Korea, or Costa Rica, or Indonesia. Walk into your closet and look; you'll be surprised.

As the world gets smaller, I believe it's important that Americans reach out to those in different countries and cultures, listen to their ideas and opinions and respect their values and traditions. "We are all part of the human race," Afghanistan's minister of women's affairs, Habiba Sarabi, said as she stood in my living room one evening. I had explained to her that my guests included Muslims, Jews and Christians and that we all had much to offer and learn from one another.

Pastor Doug Fletcher reminded us in a sermon recently that there is a simplistic temptation to divide the world into good people and bad people, and think we would be fine if only we could get rid of the bad ones: Saddam Hussein, Adolf Hitler,

Osama bin Laden, and Joseph Stalin. But the more complicated truth is that the capacity for good and evil exists within each of us.

To win the war against terror, our country must do a better job of communicating and extending our values — liberty, tolerance and respect for others, dignity for every life — but not just with our words or even with our weapons, as important as our military strength is to keeping the peace. Ultimately, the best way to maintain the fine line between good and evil, right and wrong, civilization and chaos, is to do our best to maintain it in each of our own lives.

CHAPTER 11

The Decision

I ran up the stairs from the senior staff meeting and into my West Wing office at 8:20 one morning in April of 2002 and crashed into that day's warring priorities.

"Larry Lindsey needs you at a meeting of the economic policy advisers about oil supplies this morning at 9:45," Krista Ritacco, my assistant, reported, thrusting a stack of papers in my direction. "Here's a memo you need to read before the meeting — it's pretty long, five pages; this is a letter that Al Gonzales wants you to look at before he sends it to Senator Daschle this morning; Clay Johnson needs to see you for ten minutes — the president told him to get your reaction to nominees for the Medal of Freedom; here are two sets of remarks for tomorrow — Dan approved one for staffing last night but no one has looked at the other one yet; here's a red dot (an urgent document for senior staff review) that's due by noon. You have a message meeting," Krista continued. As usual, I'm behind and the day has barely started. "And you have policy time with the president this afternoon on aviation and transportation security and bioterrorism, and then he has interviews with Bob Schiefer and Hugh Sidey."

I had already seen the president this morning; I had stopped in the Oval Office after his FBI briefing and before he left for his road trip to suggest some additions to his speech. The 7:30 a.m. senior staff meeting had been a long one; a lot was happening on Capitol Hill and Nick Calio spent fifteen minutes briefing us on all the votes and issues coming up; then Mitch Daniels, the budget director, led a long discussion of potential changes in student loan policies.

I did the same thing I did every day at the White House: listened, debated, decided, edited, suggested and asked. But this day was different; I was nervous and time was short. Somehow, amidst the chaos, I had to find a time to talk with the president privately, to tell him that I had to leave the White House.

I had gone to bed relieved, that night a month earlier, after my husband and I had first talked at the kitchen sink about moving home to Texas. Over the course of that conversation, I had convinced myself: moving back to Austin for Robert's last three years of high school was the right thing to do. Driving east on MacArthur Boulevard toward the White House the next morning, reality hit me along with the harsh rays of the early morning sun. What was I doing? I couldn't possibly walk away from the president; how could I have raised my husband's hopes? I couldn't abandon my boss and my colleagues; our jobs were too important. My stomach was churning; I felt physically ill as I waved and showed my pass to the guard at the first entrance on E Street, then drove up to the white line for the bomb dogs to sniff my car.

I walked into the West Wing just in time for the start of the senior staff meeting, ready to greet my colleagues and that morning's problems in the world. "The Russian chicken boycott is significant, and we're not making progress in resolving it," Condi reports. "The supplemental budget request has to go to Capitol Hill tomorrow," Mitch says. Ari asks about a newspaper report: "Is it true we have U.S. troops in Indonesia?" We were all in our assigned seats, Andy Card in the middle of the table, flanked by his two deputies, Josh Bolten and Joe Hagin. Condi Rice sat directly across from Andy, with Karl on one side and me on the other; others sat around the table and at seats along the sides. This is not an accident: in the early weeks, elaborately calligraphed place cards told us where to sit, until it became a habit.

I'm still ashamed that I once blurted out: "You're sitting in my seat," to a newcomer just joining the senior staff when I saw him in the chair that had been assigned to me by that elegant, anonymous card. I wanted to take the words back as soon as I said them. How small and petty, as if I owned that chair or had bought into the hierarchy of the place.

But this morning, even the problems of the world seemed to take a backseat to my all-consuming decision: Washington or Texas? Stay at the White House or move back to our house? I looked down at the stacks of paper at my place at the table: the president's daily schedule, a thick summary of that day's newspaper clippings and a report from the White House Office of Strategic Initiatives analyzing recent trends in American culture. MORE MOMS MAKE KIDS THEIR CAREER OF CHOICE, read one of the headlines.

A mighty tug-of-war had taken place inside me for weeks: by day, consumed by crises at the White House, I knew I couldn't leave; by night, at home with my family, I knew we had to move home to Texas. I had never felt so torn: where did my highest responsibility lie? How much did I owe to my boss and my country? Wasn't my family more important than anything else? How could I make this impossible decision?

One mid-March weekend, I traveled with the president to Mexico, Peru and El Salvador. I loved the overseas trips, and was especially looking forward to this one because a different one that I had hoped to make the week before had been abruptly cancelled. I had been planning to lead a delegation of prominent women to Afghanistan for the first day of school there, the first time little girls would be allowed in the classroom since the Taliban had forbidden education for women eight years before. We had recruited a great group of women to travel with us and final planning was underway as I walked into the Oval Office one morning.

"I don't want to go to your funeral," President Bush said bluntly, looking up from some papers on his desk.

I was taken aback. I couldn't help but think that going to my funeral wasn't at the top of my to-do list for that day, either.

"I'm really concerned about your safety going into Afghanistan," the president continued and proceeded to read out loud selected excerpts from the intelligence threat assessment on his desk. "I don't want your plane to get blown up."

"Well, Mr. President, the whole point of this trip is good public relations for you and our country, and it wouldn't be very good PR if our delegation got blown up," I replied.

"I'm not worried about PR, I'm worried about you," the president said.

"My husband will appreciate that," I replied.

"How's Robert?" my boss asked, as he so frequently did. "Is he worried about your trip?"

"He's in Florida playing baseball. I'm really worried about him; he's not happy," I replied. "And of course, it's all my fault because we moved here."

"He's a teenager," the president reminded me, "Jenna said some of the same things to me back during the campaign. I'll talk to Robert if you want, pull him aside and tell him how important what you're doing is for the country."

Andy Card walked in. "I'm worried about your trip to Afghanistan," he said as Condi joined us, too.

"So I heard," I replied.

"We'd all be so sad if something happened to you," Condi said.

"It would really mess up the president's schedule," Andy joked.

How could I leave my friends and colleagues, these people who were so dedicated, yet perform their jobs with humor and fun?

That weekend, a bomb was detonated at an international Protestant church frequented by Americans in Pakistan. I learned about it when the phone rang at 7:22 on Sunday morning; it was Ed in the Situation Room calling to get my approval for a presidential statement. I turned to my husband in bed: "There goes my trip to Afghanistan." Several hours later, Condi called: "We think you need to cancel the trip."

It was clearly the right thing to do, but I had looked forward to it, so I was disappointed. It made me even more eager for the South American trip — eager to get out of Washington, away from the incessant meetings, to get on the road, where I always feel more comfortable.

Yet even in Mexico we couldn't escape Washington politics. We had to make a decision about how the president would sign the campaign finance bill that was headed to his desk. It was one of the times Karl and I most vehemently disagreed, but it wasn't personal; it never is. We are both strong-willed, forceful personalities and we advocate our positions. But I have enormous respect for Karl, and I know he would say the same about me. We are friends; most of our disagreements are born of our different jobs and perspectives.

My primary job is communication: the big-picture public message and perception; one of Karl's primary jobs is stitching together a complex network of different constituencies, whether to win an election or to assemble the votes we need to enact the president's agenda in Congress. That's why I had told Andy Card, back when we were organizing the White House, that I didn't think the Office of Public Liaison belonged in my purview. Some thought it showed my naïveté, because influence in Washington is judged by the size of your portfolio. But I knew that given a choice between attending a meeting with an important constituency group that was supporting one of President Bush's proposals, and resolving a communications crisis, I would choose the intensity of a communications crisis over a meeting every time. I told Andy that I thought I would give public liaison short shrift, that

Karl would be much better overseeing that office.

From Mexico, on the conference call about the legislation overhauling the system of funding political campaigns, I argued that the president should sign the bill publicly, invite the sponsors, be gracious to his former primary competitor John McCain, not allow the pettiness that had dominated the debate on Capitol Hill to spill onto him. Karl argued he should sign it quietly, with no ceremony, if he had to sign it at all, which Karl didn't think was a very good idea because he thought it was bad policy, and unconstitutional to boot. That discussion was behind us, though, because the president had been emphatic: the reform bill might be a long way from perfect, but he was signing it because he was disgusted with the current campaign finance system and all its loopholes.

"This would be the biggest mistake we ever made," Karl said to me on the conference call when I advocated a public signing ceremony, and Nick Calio, our legislative director, agreed: "This could be a disaster beyond which you cannot imagine." Feelings about the bill were so raw on Capitol Hill that some veteran legislators had been reduced to tears, they told me; we just couldn't poke a stick in the eye of its opponents, some of our biggest supporters. Purely in terms of public perception, I believe I was right to advocate a signing ceremony; in terms of our ability to work with members of Congress whose support we needed to enact the president's proposals, Karl and Nick were absolutely right. That's why it's healthy and good for the president of the United States to surround himself with different people and different perspectives. In this case, the president also called Speaker Hastert to take the temperature of Congress, and he ultimately chose to sign the legislation privately.

When I called home from Mexico, my husband reported that Robert had checked in and was enjoying the sunshine and warm temperatures in Florida. "He sounded really happy; he said he thinks he's just a southerner," Jerry relayed. The pendulum of my decision swung yet again: we had to take him home. Tim Russert, whose son also played on the team, called me, too: "Robert made a great play at second," he told me. "The other coach told us it was a major-league play." I felt a twinge of regret that we hadn't gone to Florida; Jerry and I had initially planned to, but Robert didn't want us to. We acquiesced, hoping the trip might be a turning point, that Robert might come back feeling more connected and better about living in Washington.

That night, president and Mrs. Bush asked me to ride with them on our way to a dinner our Mexican hosts were throwing for the assembled world leaders. As usual, we arrived early.

"Mr. President, you have to hold for President Fox to arrive so he can greet you," the Secret Service agent in charge, Eddie Marinzel, reported. The president suddenly lunged across the limo and threw his arms around Mrs. Bush: "Hold Mrs. Bush, you say Eddie? No problem."

We were in high spirits the next morning on the way to the airport, with two stops still to go but most of the hard work of the trip behind us. I had had a long talk with Ambassador Davidow about the changing nature of Mexico: "It's almost becoming two countries," he told me, divided dramatically by income and opportunity. "In the northern area of Monterrey, for example, the average income is about ten thousand dollars a year, while in parts of the south, the average annual income is eight hundred dollars, more comparable to other countries in Central America," he said.

We settled into our cocoon on Air Force

One for the long flight to Peru. Airborne, we can laugh and talk, only occasionally interrupted by a ringing phone or sudden crisis. Condi and I were still laughing about the first night of the trip, when she and Colin Powell and the president had met outside the president's suite on their way to a United Nations dinner.

As they walked toward the elevator, the secretary of state looked down: "Condi, you have a huge run in your hose."

Condi looked for herself: "You're right; I'll have to change them."

"How long does that take?" asked President Bush, impatiently.

"Two minutes," Condi assured him.

"We'll wait," said the president who hates to wait.

"I'll hurry," Condi replied, then raced back to her hotel room, frantically dug through the suitcase and found another pair of stockings. We laughed for days, calling this the only time in the history of our country that the president of the United States and the secretary of state waited while the National Security Adviser changed her hose.

Making history? Or making my family happy? I'm usually good at weighing options. I had prayed for guidance about the right thing to do; I had talked with my husband and several friends, but the more I agonized, the more impossible this decision seemed. I had called Margaret Tutwiler in Morocco earlier in the week to let her know I was thinking about moving back to Texas; I didn't want to leave her without renters to take care of her house.

"Don't worry about the house," she had told me, "we can find someone else to rent it. Just worry about what's right for you and your family."

The struggle to balance home and family had become one of the main topics of conversation at our workouts in the White House gym. I had organized the exercise group, late the year before, after becoming frustrated by my inability to fit exercise into my Washington routine. I've always enjoyed exercising; I did aerobics for years until my hip and knee and various other joints started hurting all the time, then I switched back to lap swimming. I was a regular swimmer and walker during my years at the Texas governor's office. I had managed to keep up fairly well, walking regularly and occasionally swimming during the presidential campaign until the final months, when I no longer had time to do anything but travel and work.

I couldn't figure out how to keep exercise from taking away from my already limited hours with my family in Washington until one day when Mrs. Bush invited me to join her at a personal training session when her sister-in-law couldn't make it. I loved it immediately. The trainer, Trish Bearden, was both knowledgeable and a great deal of fun; she had a joyful spirit that was contagious. I asked whether she would consider training a group of us in the employees' gym during lunch, and she agreed.

I recruited my friends Mary Matalin and Andi Ball, and later Margaret Spellings. We lifted weights, and did countless sit-ups and push-ups and planks. Most of all we laughed. We laughed at each other, and how ridiculous we looked in Trish's various yoga poses. We still laugh about the day I was trying to hold myself up in a plank position and my arms were so tired that I was shaking like a bowl of jelly. We laughed about the time we were doing push-ups with our feet against the wall and I accidentally hit a hidden panic button with my foot; we only found out when a White House guard came running into the workout room with his gun drawn. We immediately gave that exercise a new nickname: panic push-ups. The exercise we hated most, the wall-sit, where you crouch in a sitting position with your back against the wall and hold for a minute until your legs ache, we named the Taliban torture. We christened ourselves the "girls with gloves" after Trish bought us some black Nike weight-lifting gloves to protect our hands. President Bush, forgetting the exact name, once asked Mary how the "chicks with mittens" were doing.

It was great exercise, but most of all, it was mental therapy while we laughed and talked through the business of the day, and complained about how difficult it was to have a life while working at the White House. Mary and I especially talked about it; she has two young daughters and felt they needed more of her time. She wanted to leave at some point, too, but wasn't quite ready yet. Moreover, on one of Margaret Tutwiler's trips back to Washington, she had reminded us it wouldn't be good for two high-profile working mothers to leave the White House at the same time. Margaret had said that I should make my decision first, since my life had been chaotic far longer, since even before the official start of the presidential campaign, and at least Mary's family were in the city where they wanted to live.

Condi and I had talked about it, too.

While she doesn't have a husband or children, she has friends and family, and she understood how concerned I was about mine. The people who work in the White House know their jobs are a great privilege, but they also give up a great deal to perform them. They have no semblance of a normal life. Condi and Andy and Karl are constantly pulled in all directions: an important senator has to talk with them right now, a foreign leader needs to get a message to the president, a world crisis commands their immediate attention. And I always marvel that they don't seem to mind. They are amazing people, always in high spirits; they love what they do. Andy starts the day with a big smile, eager to delve into the work ahead; I've never seen Condi even once speak curtly to yet another messenger who is delivering yet another message requiring her response.

Air Force One is one of the few places where the interruptions aren't quite so constant; it's a rare calm place to have a conversation. One Saturday morning, Condi and I were talking about the next day, which was the Sunday before Easter, Palm Sunday, the start of the most important week of the Christian calendar. We realized we would be airborne, flying from Peru to El Salvador, and would miss church.

"Holy Week just doesn't seem the same if you don't start with Jesus' entry into Jerusalem," I said, and Condi, the daughter of a Presbyterian minister, agreed.

Maybe we could lead a church service ourselves, we mused. "You could do the music," I told Condi, who is an accomplished pianist and has a beautiful voice, "and I'll do the message."

"You all have a nice service. I'll just read my Bible like I do every morning," the president said when we asked him about it.

"Mr. President, it's a community of faith, not a read-my-Bible-by-myself faith," I teased him.

Late that night, in my hotel room in Peru, I read the Palm Sunday scriptures in all four gospels. I woke up early with an idea: I could talk about the different ways all the participants — the disciples, the Roman and religious leaders, Jesus himself — must have felt as Jesus approached Jerusalem that long-ago morning.

"Are you still having a service?" the president asked, sticking his head in the senior staff cabin just after we boarded Air Force One. We were, we told him; he and Mrs. Bush wanted to come.

We asked Andy Card to open the service;

Dr. Dick Tubb to read a psalm from the Old Testament; Colin Powell to read Matthew 21:1–9, describing Jesus' triumphal entry into Jerusalem. Condi worked with Reed Dickens, a staff member in the press office whose father is also a minister, and Harriet Miers; they selected songs and put together a song sheet with the words to several hymns: "Crown Him the Kings of Kings," "Amazing Grace," "Holy, Holy, Holy." We invited anyone from the staff or crew who wanted to come to join us in the conference room. We talked about inviting the small contingent of press with us at the very back of the airplane, but decided not to. I felt bad about it because I didn't want to leave anyone out, but we decided that even if we made it off the record, someone would talk about it and try to ascribe a political motive to what we intended as a genuine opportunity for worship.

"The Bible tells us that wherever two or three are gathered in His name, He is there," Andy Card started, "so this is a church and we are here to worship."

Condi led us in singing; Dr. Tubb read Psalm 121.

I gave a short message:

We don't really know what the disciples were thinking on the way into Jerusalem that Palm Sunday morning; the Bible doesn't tell us. We can guess. They were probably thinking: "Finally! For three years we've been traveling with this Jesus. He has done amazing miracles — raised people from the dead, healed the sick, given sight to the blind — but he never got the credit he deserves. And we haven't, either! Finally, we will show them. Finally, he is going to triumph. People are waving palm leaves, shouting hosannas, spreading their cloaks in the road to welcome him. He will be the King of Israel, and we will be some of the most powerful people in the world."

We do know what the Pharisees and religious leaders were thinking. They were worried. People were lining the streets, shouting hosannas, and calling this carpenter, this itinerant preacher, the King of Israel. "Look, the world has gone after him," one said. This was out of control, a threat to their authority — they had to get rid of him, fast.

And we know what Jesus was thinking. He was agonizing about the pain and suffering that was ahead. As he says in John 12:27: "Now my soul is troubled, and what should I say? Father, save me from this hour? No, it was for this very reason I came to this hour. Father, glorify your name." Jesus knows the tremendous cost of what is to come. Yet he responds with obedience — obedience to the will of the Father. Not grudging obedience — No, he says, it is "for this very reason" that he came — and so, "Father, glorify your name."

The joy of Palm Sunday faded fast. The crowd is fickle. The cries of hosanna became cries to crucify Jesus in five short days. To put that in terms we understand, that's a world-record drop in your favorable/unfavorable ratio. Yet what the world saw as death and humiliation, Christ knew was ultimate victory. And He knew that the only real power lies in obedience to God, and sacrifice and love for others. The joy of Palm Sunday is short-lived. And only the sacrifice and love of the Savior make the joy of Easter eternal.

Harriet Miers gave the closing prayer.

"That was a very nice service," the president said. "Thank you all for doing that."

"I think Karen missed her calling," Condi said; "she can preach."

"Like all good sermons, it was short," the president joked. I felt a great wave of affection as I looked at all the people leaving the room. I realized how much time I spent with them, from the Air Force crew to the Secret Service agents to the medical and advance teams; they had become my family, too.

Air Force One landed in the bright sunshine of El Salvador, and I felt the same sensations Robert had described to his dad from Florida: the brilliance of the sun, the lazy breeze that gently stirred warm air, the sense of light and openness that one does not feel in the eastern United States.

"I love Central America; most of my early memories come from the tropics, from my years in Panama," I told Condi.

El Salvador is busy, bustling; its transformation is inspiring. "The peace accords have been concluded and democracy is succeeding in El Salvador," President Flores proudly tells President Bush. It's hard to believe that just a decade ago, this country was embroiled in civil war.

"What can we do to help you?" President Bush asks.

"On trade, we need to walk at the pace of the fastest, and not at the pace of the slowest . . . The fact that you announced a trade agreement is changing Central America completely . . . there is a different mindset since January, when you announced it," Flores tells my boss. There it was again: another reminder of the vital importance of trade; we heard the same message from so many leaders, in so many places.

"A leader is a dealer in hope," President Flores told us he had said during his campaign, and in so many parts of the world, I had realized, trade is hope. It first struck me at a meeting of Central and South American nations a year before: Americans view trade as commerce; the leaders of developing countries see it as a lifeline. For a democratically elected government to succeed, it must provide economic opportunity and a better life for its people, and trade is the vehicle that drives that growth.

Later that week, back at the White House, I wished the president a happy Easter as I left the daily briefing on Thursday morning.

"I won't see you again?" he asked.

"Well, you're leaving early tomorrow, and I won't see you again today," I replied.

"I'm sure you'll find some reason to come storming back in here," he deadpanned.

"Storming?" I asked.

"Hurricane Karen," he replied.

But the real storm was brewing in the Middle East. "It was a very rough weekend," Condi reported at the Monday morning staff meeting after Easter Sunday. "The Middle East is a black hole; people go in there and nothing comes out. The president's statement on Saturday was well done, but then a bomb went off. It's a moving target; we need a diplomatic strategy, then a press strategy."

"Do you have a sense Prime Minister Sharon has a strategy?" someone asked.

"I'm not sure anyone would have a strategy," Condi replied. "He's got people strapping on explosives and blowing themselves up . . . people are worried; they want us to pull a rabbit out of a hat. The Israeli offensive is continuing; we have to decide whether we want to move into a situation that is very unstable."

"It's a terrible situation," Steve Hadley concurred; "the two sides are taking us over the edge."

I spent the days after Easter in high-level meetings, arguing that Secretary Powell needed to go out on the news shows and travel to the Middle East, encouraging the president to give a major speech and working with Mike Gerson to write and edit it after Condi's office provided the policy points.

"I feel strongly that you have to give this speech," I told the president by midweek. "When faced with the international terrorist threat, what did we say? We didn't just throw up our hands and say that so long as terrorists are willing to attack our country, there's nothing we can do," I argued. "There is always something we can do. We are the United States of America: we can work for peace; we can stand up for the values that we know bring peace."

"You're right," the president said. "You've had a good day — not bad for somebody who doesn't know anything about foreign policy," he teased.

That night, as I was leaving, I stopped in Condi's office. "Thanks for the Herculean effort," she said.

"It was kind of fun," I responded; it had been one of the most interesting weeks of my time at the White House.

"You need to get out more if this was fun," Steve Hadley joked.

A chilly wind was blowing in the Rose Garden the next morning; the cherry blossoms were in full bloom as Secretary Powell and President Bush walked out of the Oval

Office and up to the "Blue Goose," the large presidential podium: "Conflict is not inevitable. Distrust need not be permanent. Peace is possible when we break free of old patterns and habits of hatred. The violence and grief that trouble the Holy Land have been among the great tragedies of our time. The Middle East has often been left behind in the political and economic advancement of the world. That is the history of the region, but it need not — and must not — be its fate."

"From the time of the Passover massacre to the president's speech this morning was the hardest week I've had since I've been here," Condi Rice told Harriet Miers and me in the cabin of Air Force One, on our way to Texas. Prime Minister Tony Blair and his wife and children were visiting the United States; President and Mrs. Bush had invited them to the ranch and asked Andy, Condi, Karl and me to join them for the weekend. "September 11 was harder emotionally, and sadder, but we knew what we had to do and we did it. In terms of policy, this situation is much more difficult."

The ranch was beautiful, lush and green; Texas bluebonnets were everywhere. We had planned to go for a long walk early Saturday morning. The president was eager to get going, but Condi was being interrupted by constant calls and Mrs. Bush had gone back into the house to get her sunglasses: "Bushie, this is the slowest departure I've ever seen," the president complained.

"The timing on the speech was absolutely right," the president told me as we walked. "You've always had a great instinct for timing, sir," I replied, knowing the rest of us can give our opinions, but he's the one who has to pull the trigger.

We met with Prime Minister Blair and his staff later that morning; the afternoon was free until dinner. The night before, I had called our good friends in Austin, Steve and Janice Margolin, to check in. "Does Alex have a soccer game tomorrow?" I asked Steve.

"He does, early afternoon. Why?" Steve replied.

"I thought I might come watch him play," I said. "I have to work in the morning, but I have some free time in the afternoon and I haven't seen you all in a while."

The game was in far north Austin, only ninety minutes from Crawford. I left the ranch when we wrapped up, just after eleven, and stopped at the Coffee Station, the bustling all-in-one gas station, restaurant and convenience store that has been doing a booming business ever since Crawford became the home of the Western White House.

My friend Andi Ball had stopped, too, on her way back to Austin, and we stood outside and talked for a few minutes. Andi was part of my White House workout group, and had listened tolerantly for months as Mary and I had agonized about the work/family juggle. Andi's only daughter was grown and married; her husband had stayed in Texas to run his business, and they commuted back and forth. The arrangement had worked fairly well for her, but she didn't have children at home.

"I just can't stop thinking about this," I told her. "We're in the middle of critical stuff at the office, but I am so worried about Robert."

"I can only imagine how hard it is," Andi replied.

"What I can't get over is that he only has three years left in high school," I told her.

"And you won't ever get to do this over again," she said. "It's not like you can see how it turns out and change your mind later. This is it." Her words hit me, hard.

Standing on the sidelines at Alex's game felt familiar, as if I were putting on my old life, and it fit loosely, comfortably. For many years, our fall weekends, especially Saturdays, but also many Sunday afternoons and Labor Day and Thanksgiving weekends, had been spent at soccer tournaments — sometimes sweating, sometimes freezing — cheering Robert and Alex and their friends on to victory, or to a good game, which is what we always tried to say, no matter how bad the final score.

I watched as the players moved the ball up and down the field, but my eyes were not nearly as focused as my mind was, thinking about how much we were missing. I was missing the opportunity to watch my friends' children grow up; my son was missing the opportunity to be around his friends and their parents. I remembered my own high school years, when I had sometimes found it easier to talk with my friends' parents than my own. After the game, Alex rode with me to Rosie's Tamale House for a late Tex-Mex lunch. He filled me in on his school and sports activities, and Janice and Steve and I caught up over tacos and enchiladas. Another thing I missed about Texas besides my friends and their kids — good Mexican food.

On the drive back toward the hotel in Waco late that afternoon, I saw a large red-and-white Target sign from the highway. I exited the highway and turned left under the freeway, then pulled into a huge and mostly empty parking lot. I drove right to a space near the door, parked, went inside and picked up two three-packs of white socks. I walked to the front of the store, waited while the person in front of me paid, then handed the clerk my charge card. I was in and out in less than ten minutes. I realized this would never happen in Washington.

I had needed socks for months; I didn't know where to get them and I never passed a store like Target. A trip to the mall was twenty minutes away, and who had time? Even if there had been a sportswear store anywhere close to my house, I would never have been able to find a parking place; parking was always a problem in Washington. It was yet another reminder of how much easier and more normal life seemed in Texas.

"It all comes down to this," I wrote in my diary on my way back to Washington.

"If I had prayed and felt it was right to go to Washington, am I abandoning it because it's hard — or am I so uncomfortable because I've done what I'm supposed to do, and now it's time for me to step away from the power and the politics and to fulfill my other God-given responsibilities to be a good wife and mother? I truly feel my family will be better off in Austin, and that I need to free more time to spend with them, and for faith and friends, but I also feel a responsibility not to make the president's life any harder than it is in the midst of war . . ."

"Your family needs you," my husband had said gently to me the week before, about the closest he came to offering direct guidance. Several of Craig Barnes's sermons spoke to me, too. "Are you looking for direction in life? Then you don't need a lot more direction than Jesus' call to follow him. You can follow him as a banker, homemaker, student or the president. I don't know that God cares so much as long as you follow Jesus there," he said in late February. On Easter Sunday, in March: "Stop obsessing over the right career move. Stop pressuring your kids to be perfect. Stop fantasizing about what the latest diet will do for your body, because it is all going to die anyway. Just stop it. And go to the empty tomb, where there is the promise of a new life that will never die and the freedom to become committed to things that are eternal. Things like justice, caring for the poor, beauty, and worship."

Craig talked a lot about freedom that spring, the freedom to live your life without being trapped in worry about your job, or health, or guilt or problems. His sermons helped me realize that the life I was living was not the life I wanted to live — a life with virtually no time to reflect, no time to go to Bible study, not enough time to love my family and friends — not enough time to do the two things God said we had to do most of all: love God, and love one another. A life without time for those things was not a life God required or wanted for me, either.

"It must be hard for you to hear so much about freedom, when you're feeling trapped," Doug Fletcher said to me after attending church with us in Washington in early April. Doug, my pastor from Austin, was in Washington with his son Samuel to visit American University. We had had dinner at his brother's house on Saturday night, and all my worry and anxiety spilled over as I told him how torn I was. I realized I *had* been feeling trapped, pulled between conflicting responsibilities, and it was time to exercise my free will to make a different choice.

Doug had lunch with Jerry on Monday. Monday night, when I picked him up to take him to our house for dinner, I turned to him: "What do you really think?" I asked him.

"I think you all want to come home," he said. It was an enormous relief; hearing him say it out loud was like a permission slip to make my final decision. "Robert doesn't want to be blamed," I told him. "I'll help you all talk it through, if you want, tonight at dinner," Doug replied.

Doug led us in a family discussion of all our concerns about life in Washington and our desire to move home. I had realized it really didn't matter what the world thought, what the political pundits thought, even what my colleagues or anyone else thought, even, hardest of all, what the president thought. I had to do what *I* thought was right. And I didn't need any vain conceit that God or anyone else needed me to be the counselor to the president; God can work through people to achieve his purposes wherever they are. And I didn't need to think that I could accomplish more or better from the White House than I could from Austin Texas; I could make a difference wherever I was. Dr. Martin Luther King said, "Everyone can be great, because everyone can serve." I could serve God in my community in Austin at least as well and perhaps better than I could in the White House.

People still ask me whether the decision

was hard. Of course it was. Any life-changing decision is. I worried — no, worried is too light a word — I agonized about whether I was being selfish, doing what was right for me and my family at the expense of everyone else. I worried about my colleagues. Mary really wanted to leave and her children were even younger than mine; I worried about my fellow Texans, especially those who had moved children to Washington: Margaret Spellings, Joe Allbaugh, Don Evans, Al Gonzales and Albert Hawkins. I could only imagine the scenes my decision would prompt with their children: "Robert gets to move back; why can't we?" I wasn't worried about Karl's family; his son Andrew loved his new school and they were happy in Washington. But I knew Karl wouldn't want me to leave. We both care deeply about the best interests of the president and I knew Karl would be concerned about what my absence would mean to our team, just as I would be if he decided to leave.

I worried most of all about the president. I had seen up close the enormous demands of his job. How could I do anything that might make his life even a tiny bit more difficult?

On the other hand, I knew I could die tomorrow and life would go on. The West

Wing would make do without me, so would the president, so would my colleagues. My family would miss me most, and they were already missing me. I love President and Mrs. Bush; I would always be their friend; I would help whenever they needed something, and if they wanted me to, I could watch the news and make suggestions and work on speeches from my house in Austin, Texas, just as readily as I could from Washington, D.C.

That was a lot easier to rationalize than it was to verbalize. I had made the decision, but how in the world was I going to tell the president of the United States? I agonized all week about what, exactly, to say. My business is the message, but I could not imagine how to begin that conversation.

Jerry and I faced a fixed deadline, May 1, to pay next year's tuition for Robert's school. A number of reporters had children there; I knew if I didn't enroll Robert, word would get out quickly. I also felt I had to give the president time to think it through; it wouldn't be right for me to wait until I was bumping up against the deadline to tell him.

One afternoon, the president and I walked through the White House with former *Time* editor and president of the White House Historical Association, Hugh

Sidey, who was interviewing him about the meaning of various rooms in the residence and West Wing. It was a relatively quiet day and I realized this was my opportunity; as Hugh left, I told the president I needed to talk with him about something.

"What do you need?" the president asked. He already had his tennis racket in hand and was eager to walk outside to play with the dogs, yet he knew I wouldn't bother him unless it was important. "Come on outside," he said, walking out to the South Lawn, hitting the ball for Spot to retrieve. The Secret Service started clearing spectators away from the fence along E Street, where they gather to peer at the White House, hoping for a glimpse of my boss, who was now walking across the jogging track onto the lush lawn.

I looked at him, my head hurting and my heart beating way too fast, and said the words I had wrestled with for so long: "I love you, Mr. President, but I need to move my family home to Texas."

I hadn't been sure what to expect: I knew President Bush well enough to know he wouldn't be mean, or angry; he knew me well enough to know I had made up my mind, so there was no point in trying to talk me out of it. Most political leaders would

have had one thought: what about me? Can't you just stay through the next crisis, the next year, the next campaign? But that wasn't what President Bush said.

He stopped walking and turned toward me. He was thinking, but I couldn't read anything else on his face: "Will you still be involved?" was the first thing he asked, and those words were better than any I could have imagined. I realized as he said them how much I still wanted to be a part of his team, how much I wanted to continue helping my boss to be the best president he can be.

"Of course," I told him, eagerly, "I want to be involved." We talked for several minutes more and agreed that I would gain a different, outside-the-Beltway perspective by living in Texas, one that could be valuable. Yes, I would visit Washington regularly, and stay in touch with my colleagues and help with the reelection campaign. I was grateful that he understood that this was right for my family, and he didn't try to make me feel guilty or that I had let him down. "I respect your decision," he told me as I turned to go back to the West Wing and he headed toward the White House residence. I was enormously relieved that he understood, but I still felt bad: with all the

worries I knew the president had to deal with, I hoped I hadn't just given him one more.

The next week, I met Mary Matalin and Margaret Tutwiler for dinner to strategize about how to tell the press and the world about my decision to move home.

"This is going to be a *big deal*," Margaret said, her voice lingering on the last two words for emphasis. "You're close to the president; you're the highest-ranking woman ever to work at the White House; you're the first high-profile person to leave the administration — don't underestimate this," she warned.

I didn't back off my contention that while my decision was important to me and my family, it wasn't that big a deal in the grand scheme of things. It might make the front page of *The Washington Post*, and the Texas newspapers almost certainly would pick it up, but other than that, I didn't expect much attention. My only other experience was in state government in Texas, where members of an officeholder's staff are not considered big news.

I had already considered, and rejected, several ways of making the announcement: I could issue a written statement; I could have Press Secretary Ari Fleischer an-

nounce the news for me during his morning gaggle with the press or during his afternoon on-camera briefing; I could sit down with one reporter I trusted and give that reporter an exclusive in an attempt to shape the rest of the coverage with a favorable start. Ultimately, I rejected all those approaches, and decided I should announce my departure in the style that felt most comfortable: direct, blunt, myself. No games or orchestrated leaks. No exclusives. No picking favorites among reporters. I would go to the White House press room at the end of the morning gaggle, when Ari met with all the White House reporters to talk through the day, but not on camera. I didn't want to elevate the story, or make it any bigger than it had to be.

Now, over dinner at West 24, the restaurant Mary owned along with the other half of her political odd-couple marriage, James Carville, we talked through exactly what I should say. Political professionals would call this the spin. I always hated that term and its offspring, spin doctors, because they implied, I thought unfairly, that we concocted our message. I view my job differently. What I do begins with the facts. I try to communicate the facts in the best light possible, but I don't create the meat of the message. In this case, the facts were that I was leaving the White House of my own volition because I wanted to move my family home to Texas. I didn't want my decision to be seen as any reflection on the president or my White House colleagues, a great group of talented and dedicated professionals. I would continue to be involved and advise the president and the administration because the president had asked me to do so, and I wanted to.

We all knew communicating this message would be an uphill battle. Washington tends to view someone leaving a position of power for family reasons the way columnist Maureen Dowd later described it, as the step just before that person is indicted. My parents had worried about that very reaction when I told them I was going to leave: "They'll try to act like you were forced out," my dad had said.

My biggest concern was my son. He hadn't said a whole lot since I had talked with him about moving home, but he was clearly worried. The very first time I had broached the subject, I told him I knew he was not happy in Washington and we could think about moving home to Texas.

"That's okay, Mom," he replied, with words that sliced my heart, "I'm just looking at it like I'm away at boarding school."

Boarding school! I had been horrified. Living in a beautiful rented house in Northwest Washington with my husband and me was like being away at boarding school? He must feel even more isolated, more lonely than I had realized. He was standoffish, cautious even in our family discussion with Doug. No, he didn't like Washington. Yes, he missed his friends in Texas. But it was clear he didn't want to become the central figure in this decision, didn't want to be blamed for something that could be seen as bad for the president. It's hard to imagine being fifteen years old and having where your family lives or whether you are happy make any difference whatsoever to the president of the United States.

I couldn't fail to state the real reason I was leaving; but I knew there was a fine line between explaining it and making it sound as if my family was somehow to "blame," I told Mary and Margaret over dinner. We ate salmon (our trainer, Trish, would approve), but Margaret and I also had bread and butter (Trish would have preferred vegetables). Mary, as usual, skipped the bread, which is why Mary is thin and Margaret and I only want to be — but not enough to stop eating bread and butter.

I also worried about how to characterize my departure. I didn't want to use the word *resigning* because it communicated something counter to my main message — that I would continue to be involved. I finally decided to say that I would be "changing the way I serve the president," which I felt more accurately conveyed the central fact: I was leaving, but I would still work for the president; I would continue to travel back and forth between Texas and Washington.

It's amazing that the news stayed secret as long as it did. By the time I went to the press room the next morning, a lot of people had known for a fairly long time: President Bush, of course, and Mrs. Bush. She had made me feel best of all when I'd gone over to the residence to tell her. "I would have done the same thing if it had been Jenna and Barbara," she said. Mary and Margaret knew; so did Andi Ball, the first lady's chief of staff, whose comments in Crawford had been so instrumental to my decision. Immediately after my conversation with the president, I had told Andy Card, keeping my promise always to keep him informed whenever I had private conversations with the president that might affect the White House or its operation. I had told Condi, and Karl, who were sad but understanding. Karl had suspected something was going on; the day after my initial conversation with the president, Karl had walked into the back office as the president and I were talking, and Karl could tell from the looks on both our faces that something was up. The guilt had hit me, that day, and I felt terrible.

"Don't be guilty," my boss had ordered. "The key is to come up with a structure that keeps you involved, so people here know when something happens, they need to call you to talk it through."

I told the rest of my colleagues on the senior staff at our morning meeting, and that was hard. Most people looked stunned. A few looked as if they might cry, and I felt as if I might join them. No one said a word; they just listened. As the meeting broke up, Josh and Margaret and a few others came over and hugged me. My communications team seemed shocked when I told them at our regular 8:30 meeting; many of them were people I had hired long before, and I told them I knew they would continue to do a terrific job; they were ready to do it without me. My dad had always taught me that the real hallmark of a leader is how the team functions when the leader isn't there.

Finally, I went down to face the press. As

I did, unbeknownst to me, Mary Matalin made a quick telephone call to Tim Russert; she felt he would report the facts in a straightforward fashion. I have a sort of naive view that the truth will come out; Mary knows that sometimes you have to help it get there.

"My husband and I have made a difficult, but we think, right decision to move our family home to Texas," I told the reporters in the press room, who looked shocked, too. "As you all know, our roots are there. I have a daughter and granddaughter in Austin. My son is going into his final three years of high school before he goes off to college, and we want him to have his roots in Texas as well. At the same time, the president has asked me, and I have agreed, to continue to be involved, to continue to serve as a key adviser to him, to help develop his message — to give him advice on strategic communications and to continue to work on major speeches. I've talked with both the President and Mrs. Bush, and they're both very supportive of my decision . . ."

Most of the reporters were surprised; they had thought I, the loyal advocate, would be among the last to leave, not the first. As I looked around the packed press room, I saw the faces of many journalists whom I consider friends. I don't agree with some of the things they write — the difference between their jobs and mine often puts us at odds — but I respect them as individuals and professionals. I know they are paid to be skeptical, to question and push. I even think most of them try hard to be objective. They have difficult jobs, and they play an important role in our democracy. I like them as people, and I hope the feeling is mutual. Although we are often thrust into adversarial roles, we also share the privilege and challenge of doing our jobs in one of the hardest places to work in the world, and that forges a bond. One reporter who had traveled with us throughout our campaign even had tears in his eyes as he wished me the best on my move.

During the press conference, the reporters asked me several versions of the same question: what will this mean for the White House communications operation and the president? "I'm confident, with Ari Fleischer and Dan Bartlett and Mike Gerson and Mary Matalin in the vice president's office, and Jim Wilkinson and Scott Sforza in Communications, and Nicole Devenish in Media Affairs and Tucker Eskew working on our global communications effort that he (the president) will continue to be served in an outstanding way by the members of the great communications team that we have here." I was asked another variation of how the White House communications operation would function without me. "We have a great team of people in place who are fully capable of serving the president very effectively."

"But you run it," a reporter interjected, to laughter.

"Well, the president runs it," I corrected. "And he's staying."

CHAPTER 12

Back to Texas

The doves wake me most mornings now instead of an alarm. I stir gradually as the first light sifts through the bedroom windows. Griffey, our cat, hears the birds, too, and stretches, then lazily climbs toward me from the foot of the bed. I feel the weight of each paw against each rib until he finds a spot he likes and collapses against my chest, close enough that I can reach to scratch his ears. Breeze, in her dog bed next to my bedside table, looks at me and wags her tail. She knows better than to join us until Jerry gets up, but as soon as he does, she leaps onto the bed and curls beside me, glaring jealously at the cat and pawing at me if I don't immediately begin scratching her ears, too. Jerry makes coffee, and reads the morning newspaper; I talk to the animals, thank God for the new day and eventually get up to meet it.

Other mornings are different: the alarm clock rings early, and I head to the airport and fly off to give a speech, or go to Washington for meetings at the White House or reelection campaign office. One of the things I like best about my life now is that I've recaptured the rhythms: some days are hectic, others are not; most days I still work long hours, but some afternoons I float in my swimming pool and read a book. I work on a laptop in the little office at the front of my house, writing and reading; the White House sends me transcripts of all the president's remarks, and I get daily news summaries and political updates. Other days I give speeches, or travel, or work on projects to improve education in Afghanistan; sometimes I see friends or shop or putter around my house. I go to the grocery store, and fix dinner, and make countless scrambled eggs and turkey and grilled cheese sandwiches, trying to keep my growing teenager full. A friend came by one day and laughed at the large, erasable monthly calendar on the wall; it had two starred appointments: Robert's orthodontist and the president's State of the Union speech. That pretty much sums up my life these days.

Days and nights at the White House had a mind-numbing sameness about them: always busy, always chockful of meetings about important subjects, always too much to do and not enough time to do it. The Wednesday before Thanksgiving in the

West Wing felt the same as the Tuesday after Labor Day or the week before school was out; the only time that was noticeably different was August, when the president worked from Texas. Washington had lovely seasons, and I noticed the trees turning and the buds swelling, but I never had time to savor them. Back in Texas I appreciate daily beauty more, take time to enjoy the unexpectedly cool breeze on a late summer morning, or the brilliant warmth of the sunshine on an otherwise chilly winter day. My days are much more attuned to the school and church calendar. I feel the kids' anticipation when spring break is near or we are preparing to celebrate the birth of the baby Jesus.

I'm home a lot more these days, although I also travel fairly often and have spent quite a bit of time in Washington. When I left the White House in the summer of 2002, Jerry insisted that we spend two weeks at the beach at South Padre Island in Texas, and we did; I also talked with the president or colleagues at the White House almost every day. I spent the first anniversary of September 11 with President and Mrs. Bush in Washington and New York. It was a somber, emotional day that started, at Mrs. Bush's request, with a church service at St.

John's, across the street from the White House. Mrs. Bush asked me to read a New Testament selection from Romans that included one of my favorite verses: "For I am convinced that neither death nor life, neither angels nor demons, neither the present nor the future, nor any powers, neither height nor depth, nor anything else in all creation, will be able to separate us from the love of God that is in Christ Jesus our Lord." (Romans 8:38–39) But as I was reading, I mistakenly transposed the words and started with *life* instead of *death*. As I rued my mistake afterward, Dan Bartlett, now the White House communications director, turned to tease me: "Typical Karen, leading with the positive spin first."

Later that day, Mrs. Bush and I talked about how all the families we saw in Pennsylvania and New York had wanted to share details and stories about the loved ones they had lost, about the joy and vibrancy they had brought to their lives. A man had come up to me at Ground Zero to commend me on my decision to move home to Texas for my son. "Nothing is more important," he said, tears gathering in his red-rimmed eyes and gradually spilling over. He had lost his only son in the World Trade Center.

"We talked every day," he told me, the

pain of his loss obviously still searing after a year.

I hugged him, and said, "God bless you," but I didn't know what else to say. I prayed for him that night, and have done so many times since.

The next day, September 12, it felt as if a weight had lifted from the city with the passing of the first year marker. Life is more normal now, but it will never be the same. Our sense of invulnerability is gone, and that changes everything, including the way we have to view threats in the world. I watched from the floor of the United Nations as the president challenged that body to face up to the dangers posed by Saddam Hussein. I thought his speech was a historic use of the power of the presidency and the moral authority of the United States of America, and I was privileged to witness it. I had said to reporters when I left Washington that I expected to spend the weekend before the State of the Union speech at Camp David, just as I always had, and I did. I traveled to Afghanistan for a meeting of the U.S. Afghan Women's Council, on which I'm now serving, and to Paris with Mrs. Bush to represent our country as we rejoined UNESCO after a nineteen-year absence.

I feel grateful, and blessed, to continue to be involved. I had thought I might have to leave it all behind when I told the president I needed to move home to Texas; I knew my boss had a tremendous responsibility to govern the country and might decide that I could not continue to play a role from afar. But he had said he wanted me to remain engaged. The skeptics had been predictably skeptical: "You can't really be valuable if you don't go to the meetings," several pundits and former Clinton White House workers said in the newspapers after I made my announcement. But I knew if the president wanted my opinions, we would make it work, and we have. I also promised the president that I would travel with him during the final couple of months of his reelection campaign, after the national convention, in the fall of 2004, just as I did in 1994, and 1998 and 2000.

"One more time; we can make it through one more time," he teased on the phone recently, as we talked of the long days ahead: the airplane up and down, the motorcade in and out, another city, another state, another rally, another speech, another rope line. My family doesn't mind as much when I travel now; they're back at home, among friends. My husband loves his job working as the assistant director of adult education at our church; my son is playing golf and baseball and thriving in school. When we visited my parents and sister in Dallas recently, they mentioned how happy Robert seemed, how grown up and self-confident. "If you ever doubt you did the right thing, just look at Robert," my sister Beverly told me on the phone afterward, but I have no doubts.

Our daughter and granddaughter live nearby; they drop in several times a week and have lunch with us after church on Sunday. We keep Lauren when Leigh wants to go out, and Leigh and Lauren stay at our house with Robert and feed the animals when we're out of town. I took Lauren, now eight, to *The Nutcracker* and shopping for back-to-school clothes, and to dinner with the women visiting from Afghanistan. I warned her they would look a little different from people she was accustomed to seeing; I explained that in Afghanistan and many Muslim countries, women cover their heads when they go out. She had heard about Afghanistan, she told me; she had read about it in *Time for Kids* at school.

"I've never met anyone from Afghanistan before," she said, and I could tell she was enthusiastic. We need to encourage our children to be eager to learn about other countries and to respect people of different faiths and cultures. I want them to grow up knowing it's important for Americans to foster ties with people throughout the world. It reminds me of the wisdom and innocence of the question asked by a little girl I read about in the newspaper in the aftermath of the attacks. Told by her mother that the hijackers had hated Americans, she asked: "Why don't we just tell them our names?" We need to make sure people throughout the world know the names of a lot more Americans.

I don't want to imply that my life back home in Texas is perfect; it's frequently not, which means it's very normal. Transitions are especially hard in my family when I return from traveling. As much as I miss my spouse and children, homecomings can be rocky. They usually start out well: we are all happy to see each other. Then, as we start to pull all the disparate pieces together again, a few gears get stuck.

"You need to take Robert a sandwich tomorrow at 12:45 before he leaves for his ball game at 1:00," my husband says.

"I can't; I have Bible study," I snap, too quickly, and too harshly, which I later regret. I'm a little annoyed, first, that he assumed just because I was home I could do it, and second, I always try to remember his Bible study on Wednesday mornings, why can't he remember I have one on Thursday at lunch?

"I can do it," he says agreeably, which makes me feel guilty. So later, I bring it up again. Revisiting topics is one of my husband's least favorite things to do.

"I can miss Bible study tomorrow if you need me to," I say.

"We've already decided that; why do you have to bring it up again?" Jerry asks. He's tired and a little cranky after spending a snow day at home, not only with our teenage son, but also with our granddaughter, whose mother had to work. Lately, the sixteen-year-old and the eight-year-old spend most of their time tormenting each other, then insist whatever is happening is all the other one's fault. Who says you have to be siblings to have sibling rivalry?

One of the most important things I did after coming home to Texas was to teach Robert to drive. It was a metaphor for what is happening in his life: he's increasingly in the driver's seat now, and his dad and I are there to help and offer advice, let him know when he's too close to the curb or on the wrong side of the center line.

I would pick him up from school, and he would climb into the car: "Want to go driving, Mom?" he would ask. After a quick snack at home, we would head out.

Robert would climb into the driver's seat, put the car in reverse and turn to me: "So, Mom, what's going on with you? Talk to the president today?"

His voice is so deep now; his independence so casual. I told my husband: "I don't think I held him enough back when he was little, back when he always wanted me to, back when his first word was *up*, as in 'Pick me up.' "

"Are you kidding?" Jerry snorts, laughing. "All you did was hold him."

Robert doesn't let me hug him anymore. Only teenage displays of affection are allowed at my house: he pokes me, or runs into me, or bumps me with his shoulder. Mostly, I'm annoying, especially when I inquire about his life, or the cut on his leg from a baseball cleat, or remind him he needs to put on sunscreen.

Like all parents, I worry that I haven't talked with him enough, haven't taught him everything he needs to know. I missed so many opportunities to do that back when he would listen, back when he dropped everything when I came home and wanted to play with me. I should have told him more on those nights when I was so tired and we would drive around the neighborhood looking at Christmas lights, hoping the car would work its magic and lull Robert to sleep. The books said you should put him in his bed and let him cry; I tried that, but I couldn't stand it. I'm sure Marie, my neighbor across the street who had reared five children, all without nighttime drives, thought I was crazy, but it was a nice way to end the day and avoid the bedtime struggle.

Now he drives himself wherever he wants to go, and sometimes goes to bed long after I'm already asleep, although I always try to wait up until he is home for the night. I've heard parents talk about the awful moment, that first time their teenager drives off in the car by himself, but that wasn't how I felt. Robert left the house about midday on his sixteenth birthday to play tennis. I sneaked over to the window to watch him leave; his friends had spent the night and were headed to their cars. I didn't want to embarrass Robert by having his mother make too big a deal of this rite of passage. He got in the car and drove off, and I prayed: "Lord, watch over him; he's really in your hands now," but I realized, of course, that he has always been in God's hands. And I felt confident. I had spent long hours driving with him. Robert is careful and responsible; he had earned my trust.

I'm home one morning and the phone rings. It's Dan Bartlett, the White House communications director, and he knows I've been out of town and returned only late the night before, so he's apologetic: "Sorry, I waited as long as I could to call you; the president has already asked twice whether you've seen the speech."

A few hours later the phone rings again: "Karen, how *are* you?" the familiar voice says, laughing because he knows that I know exactly why he's calling.

"I'm working on your speech, sir, have been since first thing this morning when Dan called me," I reply to the president.

"That's why you are who you are," President Bush replies. "Thank you; Condi had some concerns about several paragraphs; you might want to call her. As you know, this is one of those phone calls where I play like I'm calling just to hear your voice, but I'm really calling to prod you," he says, while I say, at the same time: "to set my priorities."

It always amazes me that he says thank you; it's a privilege, not an imposition, to be involved. I want to help in any way I can, and he only calls when it's important. I talk with the president or colleagues at the White House several times a week, and keep up every day through my Blackberry wireless pager, which vibrates frequently with the latest press briefings and presidential remarks.

I've done a lot of other important things at home in Texas, too: I had a dinner party for my husband's birthday, and I did the cooking. I took visitors from Afghanistan to visit a school and hospital in Austin and introduced them to my friends at a fajita dinner at my house. I joined a small group of women for a weekly Bible study and used a flashlight and a cardboard box to show the two-year-olds in my Sunday school class how God created the world. I had time for an evening Bible study called "Daily Time with God" at my church.

The point of the study was to develop a deeper, more personal relationship with God by spending time reading and reflecting on His word. I'm working on it. The method the class used was to study one verse each day — just one — not a chapter, or a book or a story, but a single verse. We were supposed to spend twenty minutes every day reading the verse, rereading it, then reflecting on it and praying about it.

The first time, I read the verse, thought about it, said a prayer and looked up: nineteen minutes to go. I've worked hard to slow down, let my mind wander, and make room for the Lord to come in and visit.

Most days at home, I dress in what Peggy Noonan memorably called "soft clothes," loose, comfortable T-shirts with shorts in the summer, and sweatpants in the winter, no hose or high heels or business clothes unless I'm traveling. I water the flowers; my dog and I go on long walks, and I watch my neighbors savor life. They may not realize that's what they are doing, but I do, as they work in the yard, chat with a neighbor or back the car out the driveway to take the kids to school.

When I feel grumpy, or out of sorts, or worst of all, sorry for myself, I walk outside to the patio, a small space on an old weathered deck. The patio furniture is one of my favorite types: big, comfortable swivel chairs with sand-colored frames and the fabric a southwestern swirl of purple, green and beige. From the deck, I can see so many amazing things: the brilliant magenta of the flowering bougainvillea that blooms for months in the hot Texas sun; the stark darkness of a soaring hawk, wings fully spread, seemingly motionless even though I know it is flying through the crystal blue sky. The Lord of Life is the creator of them all — the God of the pale and fragile petunia flowering in the pot by the pool; of the sturdy, enduring oaks that fill the backyard; the God of the peaceful, still day I see before me and the powerful, roaring surf I see every summer at the beach. I cannot be grumpy here because God has so richly blessed us with the grandeur and beauty of His creation, with the freedom to live in this country, with the family and friends that I love. And most of all, God has given us a way back to Him. The enormity of that gift is hard to comprehend: that the God of creation would humble himself to become human; that Christ loved each one of us enough to die to atone for our sins. Doesn't that change everything: how we live, how we act, what we believe? I know the answer to that question, and I know I need to remind myself of it far more often.

I find I appreciate Washington more when I visit now. One March morning, I walk down the street from my hotel toward the park I have to cross to get to the White House, then realize I can't enter it. Overnight, security fencing has been erected: rows of metal rails, linked by bands of steel, forcing even pedestrians to walk the long way around the block. I make the loop, then walk up a street lined with old houses to another fence, where a young White House guard turns away the man on the bicycle in front of me. "This sucks," the man mutters, loudly enough for the guard to hear, as he retraces his path, blocked from his usual route to work. The guard looks at me, expressionless.

"Karen Hughes," I say, not producing any official White House pass or credential. I no longer have one: I turned them all in when I left. I didn't even have a driver's license that day because I had lost it in an airport, a casualty of the new security requirement that you show a photo ID at seemingly endless checkpoints. I've been using my passport for identification, but I don't need it this time because recognition spreads across the face of the young guard.

"Sorry, ma'am," he says, stepping aside and moving the gate to let me pass, though I'm not sure why he feels he has to be sorry. He's just doing his job, protecting the president, protecting my colleagues, protecting me. I walk up to the White House appointments gate, where they know me. Before I can say anything, I hear the sound of the buzzer that releases the lock on the gate, and I push it and walk in. I hear the same buzzer at the next door, a heavy steel one, and push a little harder, then step inside the little house at the base of the asphalt driveway leading to the West Wing.

"Good morning; it's almost spring," I say to the three guards inside as one punches keys on his computer to program the white pass he hands me with the large black A for "appointment" emblazoned across the front.

"Yep. You bring this weather from Texas, Karen?" one asks, as I place my purse and briefcase on the screening machine, wave the pass across the electronic scanner, cross through the gate it unlocks and step through the magnetometer.

My husband finds all these reminders a little chilling, every time he comes, being surrounded by fences and locks and buzzers and men with guns. But I'm used to it. Even on mornings like this one, with security stricter than usual, it doesn't bother me. I crossed that bridge long ago, on the morning of September 13, when the Secret Service said the White House might be attacked and the president made it clear we weren't leaving. Besides, as Jesus said, "Which of us by worry can add one hour to the span of our lives?"

I walk past the rows of television cameras,

busier than usual this morning: several correspondents are on the air live as I walk by. I wave at the cameramen, not yelling good morning as I usually would, not wanting to interfere with the live reports.

"Getting ready for another speech?" one of the reporters yells at me, as I smile and greet the marine guard at the door of the West Wing.

"Good morning, ma'am," he says, holding the door open for me to walk in.

"Good morning, sir, thank you very much," I reply. I feel it, as I always do — the sense of privilege and honor and responsibility that comes with access to the West Wing. I head straight for the Oval Office for the morning communications meeting, nodding to the Secret Service officers who stand in the hallway outside. "Have they started yet?" I ask Ashley Estes, the president's personal secretary, who sits just outside the Oval Office door.

"Not yet," she replies. "But he's on his way back; you can go on in." I demur, mindful of the tradition that the president invites you to enter the Oval Office.

"I'll just wait until he gets back," I say, then I hear him call: "Come on in," as the president, Vice President Cheney, Chief of Staff Card and National Security Adviser

Rice walk in the other door, returning from a National Security Council meeting in the Situation Room.

"Look who's joined us; this is old person's day," the president teases, jovially noting my presence. Dan Bartlett comes in, and the president picks up the phone: "Is Karl joining us? Tell him to get in here if he's coming. Dan, what have you got?" the president asks, turning to his communications director to review the day's news and messages.

It's springtime, but Washington does not feel light. The tulip magnolia buds I can see in the Rose Garden are heavy, swollen, almost ready to open. Spring is waiting to burst forth, yet the entire city, even the blossoms, seems to be holding its breath, waiting for the president's decision on Iraq.

"The press asked me how you are," I tell the president. "I said resolute."

"Interesting you would say that," he replies. "The producer downstairs asked me and I said the same thing — determined."

"I told them you had to think this all through a long time ago. When you went to the United Nations to challenge them to back their words with actions, you had to be ready; you knew it might come to this, even though you tried to avoid it."

"Exactly," he replied.

I couldn't help but think how many crises he has had to deal with. He's had to hug mothers who've lost their sons, and wives who have lost their husbands; he has consoled the families of astronauts who died as their space shuttle hurtled across the skies of Texas. He's comforting and comfortable with people who are grieving; he makes them feel better because he shares their feelings, although I know it takes a tremendous toll on him. He's had to make the most profound decision any president can possibly make: committing our country's sons and daughters to war. He did so with a discipline and mental toughness that belied the emotional price of the responsibility for those lives.

The presidency ages its occupants, and I can see it in my friend: his hair is grayer now, and although he still has his easy smile and quick sense of humor, some of the weight of the world is also etched in the lines on his face. He never really gets a break; even during August in Texas, his mornings start with intelligence briefings, the most recent snippets of information about terrorists around the world who want to kill more Americans. And I marvel that despite it all, he never seems to view the job as a burden:

he sought it, and he seems to relish it. When a crisis comes, rather than sagging under its weight, he springs to meet it, glad that it is his team who is there to help deal with it.

I visited Washington in March of 2003 intending to stay only a few days. The president and Condi had asked me to stay close as we prepared for the war against Iraq. One night when I checked in from Texas, things seemed especially tense, and I asked the president whether he wanted me to come to Washington.

"Sure, come on," he said, but my son was on spring break, and I didn't want to travel unless it was necessary, so I pressed: "Are you sure?"

"We'll take a vote," he said, "Condi's here and Andy and Mrs. Bush; let's see, we've got four ayes and one abstention," he reported.

"Who abstained?" I asked.

"I did," the president said. "That's the way everybody's treating me." Earlier in the evening, he had called the president of Mexico to try to get a final answer on whether he would support a UN resolution to act against Iraq; President Fox hadn't committed. Several days after I arrived in Washington, as it became clear that President Bush would issue an ultimatum to

Saddam Hussein, I canceled a speech I had scheduled in Hawaii, partly to be there to help on the president's speech, partly just to be there during what I knew would be a difficult week.

President and Mrs. Bush invited me to Camp David for the weekend. As we left the lunch table on Saturday afternoon, he was headed toward a game of bowling, and a rare quiet afternoon with his family. He turned back, wanting to be hospitable as he walked out of the room: "Karen, I don't have to worry about you, do I?"

I felt bad that he even had to ask the question; now that I'm around less frequently, he may feel a little more obligated to pay attention when I am. But he shouldn't: I'm one of the few people in the world he doesn't have to entertain, or worry about, or feel as if he has to be "on" with.

"No, sir, you don't need to worry about me," I replied.

I traveled with him to the Azores for his meeting with Prime Minister Blair and President Aznar of Spain. On the way back to Washington, Mike Gerson brought the draft speech issuing an ultimatum to Saddam Hussein into the conference room and we reviewed and revised it.

The next night, almost a week after I had

arrived in Washington for a couple of days, I had to go shopping; I hadn't brought enough clothes. A woman stopped me in the mall and wanted to introduce me to her daughter. "I'm glad you're up here," she told me. "Everything's going to turn out all right, isn't it?" she asked, then laughed nervously. "I mean, I probably shouldn't be asking you that, but . . ." her voice trailed off. "I'll just feel better if you think things are going to be okay."

I tried my best to look reassuring: "Yes, I think everything's going to be fine."

People stop me frequently. Many thank me for my service, and I'm always touched because I don't feel my sacrifice was great, especially when compared to so many others: the Secret Service agents who risk their lives to guard the president, the police and firemen who protect us every day; the military personnel and intelligence officers who are on the front lines of the war against terror. Other people ask me about my decision to move home, or tell me about a similar choice they made. I've been surprised by the large number of men who stop me to talk about balancing career and family. A Secret Service agent told me he and his wife have been thinking about moving back to their hometown so their children will feel rooted there; another man told me about turning down a promotion because he didn't want to have to move to a different city at a critical time for his teenager. I tell them all what I believe: you can have a family and a career and meet your responsibilities to both; you'll have to make choices along the way, but you don't have to choose one or the other. That doesn't mean it's easy, or that I'm especially good at it.

A few months after I returned to Texas, I was at church one Sunday morning, chatting after the service. I felt someone tugging at my leg. I looked down and it was Lauren, my granddaughter.

"K-K, where have you been?" she demanded to know.

"I've been in California for a few days, traveling with the president," I told her.

"Oh," she replied. "If you love your family, how come you leave them so much?"

We've all been there, haven't we: if you love your family, why are you working so hard; why did you miss my dance recital or the big game? I can make seventeen of eighteen baseball games in the season, and the one I miss is the one my son remembers. A few years ago, I headlined a charity event at my church. The organizers called it An

Evening with Karen Hughes. My husband saw the invitation.

"*I'd* like an evening with Karen Hughes," he said.

The years with my children have taught me there is no such thing as quality time; there is only time, and if you spend enough of it, some of it turns out to be quality.

I wouldn't trade my time in Washington, but I have no desire to go back for anything more than visits. Working there confirmed for me that I don't want to be consumed by my job, or by anything else. Work is important, and sometimes we all have to work hard: income tax time for accountants, trial preparation for lawyers, campaign season for those of us involved in politics. But work is not your entire life. Work is what you do; it is not who you are. My identity is not based on any title or position or proximity to power. I may have those things for a while, but they are no more or less important than my other roles as wife, mother, friend, Bible-study partner. And who knows? While decisions made at the White House influence a lot of people, I may influence a child at church, or a young woman Afghanistan even more.

As we were leaving Washington, the minister at our church there, Dr. Craig Barnes announced that he was stepping down as the senior pastor at National Presbyterian Church to pursue a quieter, more reflective life. The last sermon I heard him give liberated me from any vestiges of guilt I felt about leaving the president and my colleagues: "God approves of the passion to live with joy," Craig said. "To live with joy is to reflect the image of God. Whatever the hand finds to do, do it with all your might, work hard, and on the seventh day, God rested, to step back and enjoy all that he had created. You are free to follow your passions knowing God can use them for his own purposes." I know Craig was talking about himself, too, but I viewed it as a final gift on my way home to Texas.

I've spent a lot of time since I've been back at a place I think is especially joyful: the beach. I've always said the beach is my soul place: I walk, think great thoughts, and am reminded by the ceaseless erasure of the surf that my musings are not nearly as important as I think they are. The sea comforts rhythmically: the tide splashes in and splashes out, tossing trash and treasure on the shore with equal abandon. Children scamper happily, dribbling sand, flinging seaweed, digging and pouring and running. Adults relax under tents and umbrellas, reading and visiting.

They've built one of those water amusement parks, with slides and tubes and various thrills at one end of my favorite beach at South Padre Island; I don't approve. I have nothing against water parks, but the beach is one place where artificial amusement is not necessary; it teems with its own life and energy. In front of me, a young boy runs, the waves chasing him; he squeals as one catches his toes, then he falls, and jumps up, wet and delighted. Another youngster sits scooping sand, slowly pouring it on top of his legs, watching, fascinated, as it drips back down to be caught up by the surf again. Almost everyone is smiling; even the teenagers jump in the waves and throw balls back and forth. One of the problems with our consumer culture is that we are so often discontented, wanting more — more entertainment, more action, more money, more things. The beach is one of the few places where we can stop and burrow our feet in the sand and let our souls rest from all that wanting.

The noise of an airplane demands my attention. I look up and see it is towing a banner: "MARILYN IVE POURED MY ♥ OUT NOTHIN LEFT LUV WES." I idly wonder: is that the end, or the beginning? I imagine what might have happened: Wes has confessed an affair, and is pleading for Marilyn's forgiveness — the banner is one last effort to melt her anger. Or he's sworn his love, and is waiting and hoping that she returns it. I could have given him some message advice: the banner is clearly some sort of appeal to Marilyn, but the words are about Wes — what he has done, how he feels. He should have made his message about her. I realize it's the same mistake Trent Lott made when he was first asked about his glowing comments about the presidential campaign of Strom Thurmond, who ran on a platform embracing segregation. He delivered a lengthy and impassioned apology, but also said, "I apologize for those that got that impression," appearing to place the blame on those who might have heard the words the wrong way, not on the fact that he said something wrong. Nonrepentant apologies don't work.

I realize that I'm being ridiculous, applying my communications strategies to an airplane banner on a beach. It reminds me that although I have more time to think now, some things about my life haven't changed much at all. I still analyze words and messages. Reading the newspaper each morning continues to be an aerobic exercise.

I read, or at least scan, three newspapers: *The Austin American Statesman*, *The Dallas Morning News*, and *The New York Times*. The *Times* especially sends my blood pressure soaring because I can see so clearly the subtext that often underlies the words of its stories.

Summarizing the president's day at a NATO summit, the *Times* reports: "Mr. Bush has also been at ease, American and foreign officials said, in one-on-one meetings." (Subtext: What a surprise that he could be "at ease" in meetings with fellow world leaders when he's a unilateralist and doesn't know much about foreign policy.) "His style will never be that of former president Bill Clinton, who could talk for hours on a breadth of subjects." (Subtext: There it is again — the old lightweight rap; President Bush will never know enough to talk for hours about anything, much less a "breadth of subjects.") The words themselves are fairly straightforward, but the attitude of conventional wisdom that clearly frames their choice boils over with bias. No doubt Bill Clinton could talk for hours; so could George W. Bush if he really wanted to. But why would he want to? President Bush gets to the point, straight and fast and direct — you know exactly where he stands. His words are clear and consistent, just like his convictions; I think it's one of the things that makes many in Europe, and his critics in America, so uncomfortable.

I'll be reading my morning newspaper, and suddenly my pulse races, and I find myself furious at the misrepresentations I see. The headline on the front page on July 14, 2003, reads: RUMSFELD SAYS IRAQ MAY NEED A LARGER FORCE. I had seen Secretary Rumsfeld's interview on television, and that wasn't my impression of his comments at all. I had to read five paragraphs down in the article to find out what Secretary Rumsfeld had really said: "It seems to me that the numbers of U.S. forces are unlikely to go up. Now, could they? You bet. If they're needed they will be there."

Secretary Rumsfeld had said the opposite of what the headline suggested: that forces were "unlikely" to increase. This happens for a couple of reasons. The status quo is not news, so the media always pushes the envelope toward change. And journalists are skeptical of official pronouncements: if Secretary Rumsfeld is acknowledging that the forces "could go up if needed," he might have a secret plan to do just that. So right there in my morning newspaper, the secretary of defense is protecting his options, and the media is highlighting a possibility he has characterized as "unlikely."

These days, when people ask me what to believe in the media, my best advice is to listen to what our leaders actually say, rather than what the reporters say about what they say. I've realized, back home in Texas, how hard that is to do. A minute-long television news report often includes only seven or eight seconds of the president's actual words; the remainder of the report consists of the correspondent characterizing his remarks.

And from my kitchen, reading my morning newspaper, I watched as the destructive power of leaks worked against our country's interests. In August of 2002, someone leaked a memorandum, from White House general counsel Al Gonzales, concluding that the president did not have to seek congressional authority to take military action in Iraq. I knew what the newspaper did not: the president had no intention of acting without a vote of Congress. We had discussed it before I left the White House: if we had to take military action, he wanted to do so with the full moral authority of the United States of

America. And although he had not yet made a final decision, he was inclined to go to the United Nations, as he later did. Yet the leak of the memo to the newspaper set off a series of stories that created the opposite impression, and got us off on the wrong foot in Europe: the cowboy from Texas is about to pull the trigger unilaterally. I couldn't stand it, so I called the president, who was on his way to chop cedar at the ranch. "You've got to make a statement soon," I told him. "These stories are creating all the wrong impressions."

"It's about time you had a good idea," he joked. "Call Condi," he ordered, and hung up. But before I could place the call, my phone was ringing. It was Condi; he had called her himself and told her to call me, as he does whenever he thinks something is important. Condi and Steve Hadley and I got on the phone and came up with a plan; the president made a statement soon after he returned to Washington in early September: "At the appropriate time, this administration will go to the Congress to seek approval for . . . necessary to deal with the threat. At the same time, I will work with our friends in the world."

Impressions become cemented so quickly in these days of all news, all the time. Once something runs for twenty-four hours on Fox or CNN or MSNBC, the impression is dried and very hard to change. That makes it difficult for our leaders. The press values speed, not thoughtfulness. Early in his presidential campaign, Governor Bush was criticized for not speaking out on U.S. action in Kosovo until the morning after President Clinton's prime-time speech; he actually wanted to listen to the president's rationale before commenting on it. A newspaper story criticized President Bush for waiting "four hours" before commenting on the power outage that affected New York City, Canada and the Midwest; he wanted to get the facts before he talked about them.

Another trend that troubles me is that the media are increasingly becoming virtual participants — instead of observers — in the political process. This is especially evident in a daily political briefing called *The Note*, sent out via e-mail by ABC News and its political unit. Directed by Mark Halperin, it frames much of the context in which America now gets its political news because most political journalists and campaign operatives read it every morning. Along with its summary of the political news of the day, *The Note* adds its own observations (called "Note Notes") and even suggestions to the candidates: "We must ask: if the environment is so important to the presidential candidates who are senators, will any of them vow to filibuster an EPA nominee they find lacking?"(June 27, 2003) No need to thank us; it's just a friendly suggestion from those observing your presidential campaign.

If I sound harsh, I realize I'm not yet in recovery from the addiction I developed during the presidential campaign: critiquing the way the media critique us. As I've said, I like many reporters, and I am the first to turn to my morning newspaper to find out what's happening in the world. But I am troubled as I witness the editorializing that creeps into the daily news, often in the media's quest to provide "context," which is shorthand for their version of how you should view events. And I don't like the way conventional wisdom in the media creates caricatures of people who make enormous sacrifices to be public servants.

It hit me when the man who delivered a table to my house in Austin recognized me and went on the attack: "I'm sorry," he said, apologizing before he even started, "but I just have to say that I think Richard Perle and Paul Wolfowitz are traitors."

I was so taken aback, I didn't respond. I'm sure this man had never met either

Richard Perle or Paul Wolfowitz; he knew them only by their media caricatures. I've only met Richard Perle a few times, but I got to know Paul Wolfowitz during our campaign. He's a thoughtful man: smart, passionate and sincere. He is conservative, and he has strong opinions, but from everything that I have seen, he offers them in what he believes is the best interest of the country.

The media caricature of Karl Rove portrays him as a grand puppet master who pulls the White House strings and taints all decisions with things political, but Karl would be the first to tell you that although he has a great deal of influence, so do others. And he isn't just political; he also has a great deal of policy knowledge and understanding. It's maddening that Republicans are viewed as right wing unless they compromise on their conservative principles, while Democrats are rarely described as left wing. And you frequently hear about the antiabortion policies of the Bush administration, although I don't recall even once hearing anyone refer to the proabortion policies of the Clinton administration.

"How is it that a nice woman like you got to be a Republican?" a woman who was obviously not a Republican asked me at one of my recent speeches. I am a Republican because I believe the Republican Party has the right understanding of the role of government and the role of the individual. Government must act for the collective good in defending our country, enforcing laws, protecting the vulnerable — government must support the conditions and climate for individuals to seize opportunities and pursue their dreams. But government that is too big crowds out individual initiative and ambition. I believe the philosophy of my political party fosters individual freedom and individual responsibility.

I remain a fan of the American political process, and continue to be impressed by most of the people in it. One of the most interesting things I've done since leaving the White House is campaign for Republican candidates around the country. I even traveled to Hawaii for Linda Lingle, who became the first Republican governor of that state in modern times. Mrs. Bush was out campaigning, too, and we talked about how we found ourselves caught up and vested in the candidates we helped as we met their spouses and families and staffs, and watched them pour so much energy into their campaigns. I realized that it's true, what then-candidate and now Congressman Chris Chocola said on that day when Mary Matalin and I campaigned for him: we share a set of beliefs, and a conviction that our values and positions on issues can make life better for people in our communities and in our country.

To people who tell me they've lost interest in politics, or they don't like any of the candidates, I say every election comes down to a choice, and perfect is not on the ballot. You may not like the candidates, but surely one of them more closely represents your views, or you think one might do a better job. You are going to end up with one of them, like it or not, so you might as well get the one you like a little better, or dislike the least.

One of the things September 11 reminded us of was that as citizens we bear certain responsibilities: we live in this great country; our freedoms are not free; and the least we can do is participate. People who give so much of their time and sacrifice their privacy to serve as our leaders deserve our gratitude and respect, and a little more slack than the press or the rest of us give them. They are human, too, and I watched as most of them gave generously of themselves, carrying out their jobs with integrity and commitment.

I hope my work at the White House and my decision to come home say several things: you can be measured by the quality of your work, not by how late the light is on at the office; you should choose your bosses carefully — not only because mine became the president, but also because your boss can either support or undermine your own priorities; you are not trapped by your circumstances — you have more freedom than you think — so don't be afraid to try something different; you have to have a foundation on which to build your choices.

St. Augustine used a beautiful phrase: *ordo amorum*, the order of the loves. The most important thing you do in life is choose your loves and order them very carefully. I reordered mine when I came home to Texas, and I've since learned that so many of the things we consider normal are actually quite extraordinary and precious: being there to make breakfast when your teenage son and his friends wake up in the morning, and they think your homemade pancakes are so much better than the frozen or toaster ones; working the concession stands at the school baseball games, sharing information and experiences with other parents. "You look familiar," parents from the visiting team will sometimes say, and the mothers on my team will laugh, "Well, in her other life, she's famous"; feeling calm and relaxed enough to want to spend an evening at dinner with our friends Steve and Janice Margolin, enjoying watching as their children Alex and Laura grow up. The women in my Bible study — Bev Moore, Christi Engomoen, Shelly Aunspaugh and Debbie Hair — think what I do is important; I think what they do is important. Some of them work outside of their homes; some of them don't — but they all spend a great deal of time caring for family and friends.

I no longer feel as cynical or negative as I once did about Washington. People there were kind, and more thoughtful than I ever expected. Despite my busy hours, we made some genuine friends — parents of some of the boys at my son's school, and my minister's brother and his wife, Ron and Nancy Fletcher. Condi Rice and Andy and Kathi Card and Don and Joyce Rumsfeld had us to their homes for parties and dinners. As I was leaving Washington, Colin Powell graciously spent time giving me advice about the speaking circuit. The spouses of our senior staff and cabinet formed a support group after September 11 to encourage each other and help at a local charity, and

Jerry enjoyed participating. My White House colleagues became dear friends and we continue to spend time together.

I left the White House with two profound and ongoing commitments: a passion to help the people of Afghanistan and a conviction that we will never win the war against terror until we teach all the world's children to respect one another's different faiths and cultures. The world does not love America — many people admire our freedom, most respect us, but that respect is too often accompanied by great resentment. We have an obligation to foster more than a world that is safe and secure; we also have an obligation to foster a world whose citizens have greater freedom and more opportunity. We believe all lives have meaning and value, including the lives of Palestinians and Israelis, and the lives of those in Iraq and Afghanistan we helped liberate. It's really the fundamental difference between us and the terrorists we fight. As President Bush said, "We value every life; they value none — not even the innocent, not even their own."

I finally got to visit Afghanistan in January of 2002 as part of a State Department delegation. As we flew from Oman to Kabul in an Air Force C-130, the crew donned bulletproof vests and helmets and went through a combat-entry checklist as we flew over the border entering Afghanistan. I felt a surge of pride in our military as I watched the pilots work with precision and efficiency; they are so well trained, and it shows. I saw firsthand the incredibly rugged mountainous terrain. When you look down with your naked eye, you see nothing but seemingly uninhabitable mountains. When you look down wearing night vision goggles, you see hundreds of fires scattered across the landscape, marking homes and camps that would take days or weeks of hiking to reach. When we landed at the airport in Kabul, we were greeted by officers from the Turkish military, and I was grateful for the international partners who are helping us secure and rebuild the country. I was surprised as we drove into the city from the airport that the few women we saw on the streets still wore burkas.

"Their problem is not burkas; their problem is survival," someone told me when I asked about it.

We saw devastation greater than I could have imagined. Most buildings have no windows; only a few even have plastic covering the holes in a place where the temperature can drop to zero at night. Only a few government buildings had heat or running water. Yet every so often, in the midst of a pile of rubble, we saw a place where someone had swept up bricks, put up a sign and was going into business.

At all the relief programs we visited, the demand far exceeded the supply. Thousands of families lined up hoping to get quilts at one location; only hundreds were available. At a bakery that employs widows, only the neediest were able to get coupons for bread. One woman who had been turned away came back as we arrived. She held open the rag she was wearing as an apron to show me something. At first, I thought she had something to trade. But the ambassador explained: "She's showing you that those few pieces of straw are all she has. She has no wood, nothing to build a fire or cook with." I could only think of the straw Mary laid in the manger for the baby Jesus, when there was no room at the inn. The woman pulled up her burka, and I saw the desperation in her face. As she looked at me, tears began flowing past the creases and wrinkles; it was as if after all the years of drought and war and killing, this failure was the last, unbearable defeat. The ambassador had warned us not to hand out money, fearing we could provoke a riot.

"Can I buy her some bread?" I asked the manager of the program. "The need is great," he said, shaking his head. They didn't want to buck the system, a system designed to make sure the neediest were helped first.

"I know," I pressed, "but just for today, could we buy bread for this woman and the people who come here? Just for today?"

"The need is great," he repeated, then told the translator he would try to do something. Undersecretary Paula Dobriansky and I dug in our wallets and gave him money. As we left the bakery, the woman was still waiting. I handed her a roll they had given me inside, praying that they would, as promised, give her some bread. I thought of what Mother Teresa had said: "We sometimes feel that what we do is just a drop in the ocean, but the ocean would be less because of that missing drop."

We saw hope in the midst of ruins at a bombed-out school where thirty girls were crowded into a room on the first floor, learning to read and write. And I realized that education for the women of Afghanistan, women who have been treated as second-class citizens for so long, will involve more than the three R's. They also must be educated that their lives have worth and value and dignity — after all, those things were stolen from them during eight long years of the Taliban rule.

We visited another literacy program, where Paula asked the young women what they hoped to do when they grew up. Most of them answered with the only job they had ever seen modeled: teacher. One of the members of our delegation was a senior editor from *Fortune* magazine, and Paula asked whether any of the students might consider becoming journalists or writers. One young woman raised her hand and said she wanted to write a book.

I approached her privately later and told her I was writing a book and would like to say something on her behalf in mine, until she could publish hers. Her answer, through the translator, was quick and un-equivocal: "Women should have the freedom to choose their husbands, go to school and go to work." She was thirteen. As I left, the translator pulled my sleeve. "She wants to tell you something else," she said. "She hopes you won't forget them; please help them live in freedom."

The inquiring faces of the children there followed me home, their eyes asking: do you really believe my life can amount to something? I'm working with Mrs. Bush on several teacher-training and education projects in Afghanistan, because we believe education is the key to helping the country develop as a stable and modern Muslim state. Afghanistan has seen the worst of the radicalization of Islam as expressed in the cruel brutality of the Taliban regime, and its people recognize that. Everywhere I went, people said two things to our group of Americans: "Thank you," and "Don't leave." I've also been working with my church on an adopt-a-school program. Why would a church in Austin, Texas, adopt schools in Afghanistan? Because the need is great; because it's in our country's interest that Afghanistan never again become a haven for terror; because our Lord said, "To whom much is given, much more is expected"; because He said that whatever we do for the least of these, we also do for Him; because the ocean would be less without the missing drops.

We all have power, just in different forums. Not all of us can be president or counselor to the president, and even those who are will only serve in those positions for a time. The real question for each of us is how we use the forums in which we are placed — as parents, as employees, as friends, as people who have an opportunity to make a difference around us.

My life for the last several years has been a long way from normal. But I've realized normal was never my destination in the first place. And a lot of what my faith teaches is not normal anyway: turn the other cheek; pray for your enemies; invite people who cannot return the favor; whoever wishes to be the greatest must be a servant; you must lose your life to find it.

I worry that Christians, myself included, give Christianity a bad name because we so often fail to model the love and humility displayed by the life of Jesus Christ. If I could debunk one myth about my faith, it would be the feeling that Christians are sanctimonious, holier than thou. Nothing could be further from Christ's message; he chastised the religious leaders of his time for putting on airs and placing themselves above other men. To the contrary, my faith instills in me a deep sense of humility and gratitude, reminding me how often I fall short and how much I need the Savior, and how thankful I am that God has done for us what we could not do for ourselves. My faith calls me to try to live a life that is a joyful response to that good news. And whenever I get overwhelmed, or it seems too hard, I remember all that I am required to do: "Act justly, love mercy, walk humbly with your God" (Micah 6:8).

Nothing about life's final destination is normal. I'm on my way to heaven — not the heaven of quiet and rules that I envisioned as a child, but a heaven of joy and delight, where God has prepared a banquet, with fellowship and a big team, all in supporting roles. You don't have to spend your life trying to get the best seat because a seat has already been prepared for you, and rank won't matter: the last will be the first, the least will be the greatest.

For years, intellectually, I knew that, for a Christian, death was a passport to a new, more complete and wonderful life with God. Yet emotionally, it seemed frightening, dark and forlorn, until the day my minister shared a beautiful story from the funeral for an elderly man who had spent much of his life in a wheelchair. During his last days, his daughter was understandably devastated. But he told her to cheer up when she felt like crying because when he got to heaven, the limbs that had limited him, that had failed to support or sustain him through life, were going to be wonderfully, miraculously, marvelously free. "When I get to heaven," he told her, "I'm learning to dance." What freedom! What a reward!

That's the promise of heaven for all of us. I'm certain I'm going to heaven, not because I am faithful, but because God is. Jesus promised, and I believe: no one can snatch me from His hand. I am confident that by the time I get there, Jesus will have nurtured in me a longing for peace, a liking for harmony, a sense of contentment that I can only dream of in this earthly life. And when I get to heaven, I'm learning to sing.

ABOUT THE AUTHOR

Karen Hughes served as counselor to the president, was one of three people who ran his presidential campaign and worked as his communications director during his six years as governor of Texas. She is an elder and longtime Sunday-school teacher in the Presbyterian church. Mrs. Hughes lives with her husband and son in Austin, Texas, where she continues to advise President Bush from her home.

The employees of Thorndike Press hope you have enjoyed this Large Print book. All our Thorndike and Wheeler Large Print titles are designed for easy reading, and all our books are made to last. Other Thorndike Press Large Print books are available at your library, through selected bookstores, or directly from us.

For information about titles, please call:

(800) 223-1244

or visit our Web site at:

www.gale.com/thorndike
www.gale.com/wheeler

To share your comments, please write:

Publisher
Thorndike Press
295 Kennedy Memorial Drive
Waterville, ME 04901